WITHDRAWN

MORAL COMBAT

MORAL COMBAT

HOW SEX DIVIDED AMERICAN CHRISTIANS AND FRACTURED AMERICAN POLITICS

R. MARIE GRIFFITH

BASIC BOOKS
NEW YORK

Basic Books
Hachette Book Group
1290 Avenue of the Americas, New York, NY 10104
www.basicbooks.com

Printed in the United States of America

First Edition: December 2017

Published by Basic Books, an imprint of Perseus Books, LLC, a subsidiary of Hachette Book Group, Inc.

The Hachette Speakers Bureau provides a wide range of authors for speaking events. To find out more, go to www.hachettespeakersbureau.com or call (866) 376-6591.

The publisher is not responsible for websites (or their content) that are not owned by the publisher.

Print book interior design by Jack Lenzo.

Library of Congress Cataloging-in-Publication Data

Names: Griffith, R. Marie (Ruth Marie), 1967- author.
Title: Moral combat : how sex divided American Christians and fractured American politics / R. Marie Griffith.
Description: New York : Basic Books, 2017. | Includes bibliographical references and index.
Identifiers: LCCN 2017037768 (print) | LCCN 2017040616 (ebook) | ISBN 9780465094769 (ebook) | ISBN 9780465094752 (hardback)
Subjects: LCSH: Christianity and politics--United States. | Sex--Political aspects--United States. | Sex--Religious aspects--Christianity. | Christians--Political activity--United States. | Protestant churches--Relations--Catholic Church. | Catholic Church--Relations--Protestant churches. | United States--Church history. |
BISAC: HISTORY / United States / 20th Century. | RELIGION / Christianity / History. | RELIGION / Sexuality & Gender Studies. | RELIGION / Religion, Politics & State.
Classification: LCC BR516 (ebook) | LCC BR516 .G75 2017 (print) | DDC 261.8/3570973--dc23

LC record available at https://lccn.loc.gov/2017037768

ISBN 978-065-09475-2 (hardback)
ISBN 978-065-09476-9 (ebook)

LSC-C

10 9 8 7 6 5 4 3 2 1

CONTENTS

For Zach, Ella, and Jasper

INTRODUCTION

When the US Supreme Court released its 5-4 decision in *Obergefell v. Hodges* finding a constitutional right to marriage for same-sex couples, the national reaction was as polarized as the court itself. Most progressives and liberals celebrated the outcome as a long overdue affirmation of equality for gay, lesbian, and bisexual people, while many conservatives condemned the decision. Some Christian traditionalists blamed the ruling on "the emotional terrorism of the left" and identified it as a dire blow to religious liberty and the nation's welfare. Religious leaders on the right admonished their flocks that, as a Family Research Council official put it, "the truths of Scripture regarding human sexuality are not malleable" and that "neither the rulings of a court nor the pressure of secular culture should sway their allegiance to clear and authoritative biblical instruction on men, women, family, and marriage." The influential Catholic lawyer Robert P. George, past chair of the National Organization for Marriage, a group opposing same-sex marriage, wrote that *Obergefell* should be regarded much as Abraham Lincoln viewed the *Dred Scott* decision in 1857: as an "anti-constitutional and illegitimate ruling in which the judiciary has attempted to usurp the authority of the people."[1]

The *Obergefell* decision, released on June 26, 2015, made same-sex marriage into settled law. But it hardly stemmed the attempts to shun, restrict, and even outlaw such marriages. Within weeks, Kim Davis, a county clerk in Kentucky and a conservative Pentecostal Christian, became a media sensation and a heroine to the grassroots right for going to jail to avoid authorizing same-sex marriage in her jurisdiction. Others sought exemption by refusing such services as wedding cakes to same-sex couples, hoping the judicial system would support their religious freedom to do so; indeed, courts will be hearing cases related to the ruling for years.

Such fiery emotions and legal wrangling have not been restricted to the issue of same-sex marriage. Shortly after the 9/11 attacks on New York and the Pentagon, a prominent fundamentalist Christian leader appeared on national television and blamed the terroristic violence on "the pagans, and the abortionists, and the feminists, and the gays and the lesbians who are actively trying to make that an alternative lifestyle . . . all of them who have tried to secularize America."[2] Another blamed a mass shooting in Aurora, Colorado, on "a sin problem" that he saw embodied in the permissibility of abortion and similar signs of an ungodly nation.[3] Still another attributed the Sandy Hook Elementary School shooting to the effect of atheism, abortion, and same-sex marriage, saying, "We have killed fifty-four million babies and the institution of marriage is right on the verge of a complete redefinition. . . . I think we have turned our back on the Scripture and on God Almighty and I think he has allowed judgment to fall upon us."[4] Over and over, America's "sexual depravity" and embrace of various types of sexual "immorality" have been held liable for horrific acts of violence that God has ostensibly refused to prevent.[5]

Why do these sexual issues provoke such fervent and enduring debate in the United States? Why have our public debates over sex and sexuality been so numerous, so ferocious, so religiously inflected, and so immune to definitive resolution? The answer is not simple, and many of the common ideas about the origins and nature of our current impasse over sexuality—the virtual civil war that has come to seem such a disheartening and permanent part of our nation's social and political fabric—are simply incorrect. Some argue that this impasse results from fissures that opened after the sexual revolution of the 1960s, but conflicts like these have a far longer history. Many see the conflict as pitting religious people against sexual freedom, and some religious people similarly see a secular crusade against religious liberty. But neither explanation really illuminates the ferocious controversies over issues ranging from birth control to same-sex marriage.[6]

To fully comprehend how we got to this divisive and seemingly intractable culture war over sexuality, we have to come to terms with a deeply historical religious preoccupation with sex and understand how it has shaped subsequent American political debates over women's rights, gender roles, and sexual mores. That preoccupation emerged out of the long history of Christianity and was made all the more powerful by entrenched notions, both overt and unspoken, that Christian morality should provide the basis for our nation's law and politics. Certainly, religious leaders outside Christianity have also been involved, sometimes deeply, in these huge debates over morality, sexual behavior, and gender roles. But for most of US history, until quite recently, Christians played a dominant role in American life; so too Christians, across the Protestant-Catholic divide and the full range of traditionalist to progressive, have predominated as those most vigorously connecting sex and politics and waging the most passionate battles in this arena. Many citizens have believed that sexual morality consists of a system of values that must be guarded and preserved for the greater social good, but whether those values focus on obedience to traditional family norms or on freedom of sexual expression and relations has grown into a source of profound division, even within American Christianity itself. Indeed, by the time the *Obergefell* decision came down, the rupture between Christian antagonists in the sex wars felt irremediable: one could plausibly argue that American Christianity had flat out split into two virtually nonoverlapping religions.

Moral Combat tells a story of the steady breakdown, since the early twentieth century, of a onetime Christian consensus about sexual morality and gender roles and of the battles over sex among self-professed Christians—and between some groups of Christians and non-Christians—that resulted. That consensus was both Christian and national, as Christians overwhelmingly dominated the nation numerically and in terms of influence for most of its history. Up through the end of the nineteenth century, whatever else Americans disagreed about—slavery, states' rights, urbanization, immigration, labor laws—most accepted, and took for granted as natural, a sexual order in which men were heads of households, wives were to submit to husbands' authority, and monogamous heterosexual marriage was the only sanctioned site for sexual relations. Those who broke the rules were punished or shunned, as when early New England courts prosecuted sodomy, adultery, and divorce; or when communities rejected groups that forswore monogamous wedlock in favor of communal celibacy (Shakers), polygamy (some Mormons), complex marriage (the Oneida community), or free love (various associations others deemed "cults").

The modern women's rights movement—above all, the push for women's right to vote—prompted a crisis for those shared assumptions. Slowly but relentlessly, the old unanimity splintered, with some Christians embracing new ideas regarding women's rights and roles and others redoubling their efforts to preserve the old sexual order. Women's increasing presence in the workforce and growing access to contraceptive technologies further sundered this consensus. Again, many Christians staunchly resisted change; others hailed it as a step on the long march to justice. Like the wider populace, American Christians—who remain profoundly influential a century after suffrage, notwithstanding the growth of religious diversity and secularization—are a great deal more divided over sex than a hundred years ago. And with each side claiming God's blessing in pursuing its moral vision, this division has helped lead to deep, thoroughgoing cleavages in our politics.

Claiming God's blessing in political debates was not new to twentieth-century America. In fact, one of our nation's most ingrained impulses, going back to some of the early colonial settlers, has been the presumption of speaking in the name of God, willing as God wills, doing as God would have us do. But as a result of the fracturing Christian consensus, the period covered here did witness a new sort of enthusiasm for such claims by both advocates of the old sexual order and sexual progressives or reformers. Just as God-talk, broadly defined, framed countless political debates over the Revolutionary War, Manifest Destiny, and slavery and abolitionism, so too would it later underlie the political rhetoric on issues of sex and gender. Feminists supporting women's right to vote *and* anti-feminists calling on women to stay home and focus on their children, white supremacists fighting for a racially pure America along with traditional gender roles *and* civil rights workers demanding justice for African Americans and the poor, pro-life activists picketing abortion clinics for the sake of the unborn *and* pro-choice marchers invoking women's health and rights: citizens on all sides of these and other bitter political fissures have claimed godly righteousness for their cause.

For those who worked to sustain the old sexual order and resisted models for sexual relationships and behavior outside traditional marriage, a driving force has been fear. That is, fear of certain kinds of changes has aroused passionate defiance, motivated acts of resistance, and galvanized political support for the anti-change side. In the warfare over sex, the fear is typically one of three kinds: fear of increasing women's freedom, especially freedom over their own bodies as well as the ways that women's sexuality might call into question their dependence on men; white Protestant fear of encroaching religious or ethnic "others," a fear that long manifested against Catholicism and Catholic power and would later manifest against African Americans, "Muslims" writ large, and more; and a widespread and easily stoked fear that America is a once great nation now pitched into grave decline, largely because of the evil activities (very often, evil *sexual* activities) of some of its own citizens. So women, nonwhites, and homosexuals and other "nonnormative" sexual actors (the transgendered, the fluid, the flagrant) have repeatedly represented something like the enemy within, shredding the sacred fabric binding together a God-blessed nation.

In an important way, then, debates around sex can be characterized broadly as a conflict between change and tradition, at least in a very specific sense: those who oppose changes in the norms governing social expectations and legal frameworks for regulating sex and gender versus those who are comfortable with at least some of those changes or who grow comfortable in time. Those who call themselves (and whom I will call) traditionalists or conservatives tend to be of the first mindset. Progressives or liberals, from the moderate middle to the edge of the spectrum, tend to be of the second and value changes perceived to be *inclusive*, that is, those that expand access to power and influence for persons once excluded, marginalized, or stigmatized for behaving outside the norm. These labels—traditionalist, conservative, progressive, and liberal—are imprecise and imperfect modifiers, to say the least, subject to caricature and lumping people together who do not always wish to be so lumped.

But Americans have employed them for a long time, and they work reasonably well to convey particular attitudes toward change and tradition when it comes to sex and gender, as I am using them here. This "two camps" model is not to suggest that there are only two singular and coherent attitudes toward sexuality—there have always been many whose position on some issues might lean conservative and on others liberal, and plenty of people have stood somewhere in the ambivalent middle of the far poles. But our political culture, rightly or wrongly, has made it difficult to break out of these either/or options, not least when it comes to sex and gender. On any given sexual issue at any given time in the history I recount, the overall clash has ultimately crystallized into two sides: those favoring, to varying degrees, change and progress versus those keen to preserve order and tradition.

Over time, these two attitudes toward sex and sexual morality became aligned with two increasingly divergent and oppositional outlooks on modern life itself. One was eager to be open to modern ideas, inclusive of eclecticism and expansive diversity, and relatively accepting of women's equality and changing roles; the competing outlook longed for traditional order, resisted many changes to the status quo, and remained consistently wary of shifting gender norms and changing attitudes toward sexual morality. Doubtless these divergent attitudes toward change and tradition have been rife in many historical times and places; at least in the US context, however, such attitudes were once less widely aligned with opinions regarding sexual morality. More and more over the course of the twentieth century, attitudes toward sex signaled attitudes toward modernity itself: openness to changing sexual norms bespoke openness to other modern cultural and social changes, whereas resistance to such norms accompanied resistance to—and fear of the effects of—many other forces of modern change. One's stance on sex, then, has increasingly over time become shorthand for an attitude toward contemporary challenges to tradition.

As the following chapters illustrate, these competing outlooks shaped and fed on each other in a sort of dialectical process over time. Progressive gains in liberalizing or legalizing certain practices—birth control, say, or sex education in public schools—served to confirm their conservative opponents' sense that modernity was sinful; in turn, conservative efforts to fight back and restore the old values confirmed progressives' sense that sexual liberation was utterly crucial to progress. In other words, the rival attitudes of the traditionalists and the progressives have been, in crucial and persistent ways, mutually constitutive of one another; and each side has galvanized supporters with narratives of nightmare scenarios sure to occur in the absence of immediate action. Politicking for causes has always worked this way, of course; rousing adherents via doomsday threats is nothing new. But we cannot understand our own debates—over LGBT rights, trans-friendly bathrooms, abortion, marriage, sex education, chastity, sexual harassment, even religious exemptions for health-care coverage of contraception—until we go back to the past and attempt to understand this specific dialectical trajectory concerning sex.[7]

AT THE HEART OF THE twentieth-century conflict over sexual morality were debates over the very meaning of sex, gender, and sexuality. At the turn of the twentieth century, the prevailing view across the religious and most of the political spectrum was that male and female were fixed categories, the differences in reproductive organs proof that these divisions were part of biological nature and/or God's created order. Inextricably bound to these natural categories were the social and cultural meanings, expectations, and public as well as domestic roles that defined and separated men's activities from women's. Hence, these roles and meanings, too, were presumed fixed and not simply proper but, indeed, normal. If male and female were divinely fixed categories, embodied in men's authority over women and fulfilled in female chastity followed by marriage and childbearing, then any sexual relationship outside of monogamous, procreative, heterosexual wedlock was—especially for women—beyond the pale.

Over time, these premises—most particularly the relation between biological sex and the social roles ascribed to men and women—were contested and increasingly reconceived. By the end of the twentieth century and into the twenty-first, growing numbers of Americans were comfortable with a relative separation between biology and culture, or a division between "sex" and "gender"; increasingly, many came to see both gender and even sex itself as fluid manifestations across a spectrum of possibilities: open to modification, creativity, and choice rather than binary or complementary classifications of male/female. And this shift inevitably accompanied new ways of thinking about sexuality. Many others, however, resisted these changes and their implications for role norms in the family and workplace, relationships such as marriage, and identities such as transgender or intersex. These critics did not necessarily want to see, for instance, gay, lesbian, or bisexual identities accepted as regular and normal variations on heterosexual ones or public restrooms welcoming transgender persons to freely follow their identity over perceived biology. The history this book recounts is the long story of growing conflict and divergence between these points of view.

Gender, sex, and sexuality have very much been political issues: in countless ways over the decades since the early 1900s, Americans have battled out their views in the ballot box, the lawyer's office, and the courtroom. How people have thought about the core definitional questions pertaining to sex and gender—natural or constructed, fixed or fluid—has had crucial ramifications for their political reasoning about a range of issues that attach to these categories. Notably, from the beginning of these debates, the concept of women's rights in elite circles clearly referred chiefly, if not exclusively, to *white* women. This history, then, is inextricably interwoven with America's racial history and the realities of intersectional identity that, for years, resulted in women of color creating their own activist organizations with only internmittent collaboration with whites.

The politics of sex took on new urgency amid the push for women's rights that accelerated in the late nineteenth century and begat sweeping new changes in the twentieth, beginning with the right to vote. The suffrage movement arose in 1848, when the first women's rights convention took place in Seneca Falls, New York. But it only became a major political force decades later, as American women increasingly chafed at their disenfranchisement and correlative lack of political influence. By the 1910s, millions of women and men were active in the movement through its two major organizations: the National American Woman Suffrage

Association (NAWSA), headed by Carrie Chapman Catt, and the National Woman's Party, led by the more radical Alice Paul. In June 1919, the US Congress passed the Nineteenth Amendment, granting women equal voting rights; it was then sent to the states for ratification. In August 1920, after decades of hard work by many thousands of Americans, women in the United States—white women, that is, shored up by racism that refused to grant rights to black women—won the legal right to vote in all state and national elections.

The suffrage victory stimulated further determination among those who, for various reasons, resisted women's equality. There had always been antagonism to women voting from some factions.[8] Many argued that granting women full citizenship would damage their reproductive organs and hence threaten the sacred role of mother to which women were born. In 1905, former US president Grover Cleveland himself had argued against women's suffrage in *Ladies' Home Journal*, insisting the vote would destroy "a natural equilibrium, so nicely adjusted to the attributes and limitations of both [men and women] that it cannot be disturbed without social confusion and peril." Cleveland here repeated and expanded upon a sentiment he had already expressed in that same periodical, that good citizens need not fear suffrage's impact upon the country but rather "its dangerous undermining effect on the characters of the wives and mothers of our land." In other words, "Women change politics less than politics change women."[9] The specter of changing women—hardening their soft edges, coarsening their character—was a frightening one, indeed.

The suffrage opposition included a great number of women too, women who believed truly terrible changes would result from female suffrage. The National Association Opposed to Women's Suffrage, formed in New York in 1911 and led by fervently traditionalist women, published a journal originally called *The Woman's Protest* that in 1918 became *The Woman Patriot*, subtitled "A National Newspaper for Home and National Defense Against Woman Suffrage, Feminism and Socialism." The group claimed a membership of 350,000 people across the United States and sought to paint suffragists as mannish sensualists who put an unfeminine love of self above love of country. They and other anti-suffragists argued that granting women the vote would not increase but in fact reduce women's influence in the political sphere, destroy home life by producing women greedy for commercial employment and aloof to family, diminish women's interest in charitable and civic activities, and, by ending many of the protections enjoyed by women, encourage men to divorce and leave penniless their wives—thus forcing women to work outside the home. Even when the suffrage amendment succeeded, a considerable number of Americans held some version of this view.[10]

The greatest hostility to suffrage came from the Jim Crow South, where conservative ideas about gender roles blended with an old states' rights suspicion of any federal political action, most especially action that might expand the franchise to black women as well as white. It had only been a few years since Kentucky-born filmmaker D. W. Griffith had adapted a novel by the Southern Baptist minister Thomas Dixon into a blockbuster film, *The Birth of a Nation*, which thundered against the concept of racial equality by conjoining it with black men's purported lust for white women (the fearsome specter of black-on-white rape permeates the film). Many white Southerners invoked similar themes as the suffrage battle raged: Virginia legislator Hugh White, for instance, argued that female suffrage and black suffrage were essentially the same issue and that both threatened white supremacy, a basic Confederate value that remained defiantly alive. Mildred Rutherford, president of the Georgia United Daughters of the Confederacy, warned her state legislature that women's suffrage "comes from the North and West and from women who do not believe in state's rights and who wish to see negro women using the ballot." South Carolina senator Benjamin "Pitchfork Ben" Tillman repeatedly argued that female suffrage would have a major impact on the nation's rate of births, deaths, infidelity, and divorce: just as women's rights had led to the downfall of the Roman Empire, so too would the affliction of suffrage "usher in another thousand years of moral blight, sexual depravity and degradation," annihilating America. The equation was clear: women's rights would trigger both rights for black people and sexual degradation, resulting in not the birth but the effective murder of a nation.

Opponents of women's political equality—defenders of the status quo in politics, religion, and society—had more to worry about than suffrage alone, both before and after the ratification of the Nineteenth Amendment. In 1920, Americans still shook in the aftermath of World War I and the vast societal shifts of recent decades, when the United States had rapidly transformed from a predominantly agricultural and rural economy to one more industrial and powered by cities. Reverberations from this change were still felt in labor strikes and battles over working conditions in mills and factories, as well as through elevated poverty and unemployment statistics. High rates of immigration frightened many urban residents, and worries grew about the spread of Communism, anarchism, and other radical philosophies in America. The so-called Red Scare of 1919–1920 witnessed the deportation of thousands of foreigners believed to be importing these seemingly corrupt beliefs into the United States, and the resultant phobia encouraged legislators to craft the Quota Act limiting immigrants to 350,000, passed in 1921, and the far stricter National Origins Act, passed in 1924. Alcohol use had been greatly curbed by the Eighteenth Amendment, which took effect in January 1920, but the illegal activities spawned by Prohibition inflated organized crime, another menace to dread. For Americans trying to make their way in the early twentieth century, these were tumultuous times.

The achievement of national suffrage for women also took place amid larger challenges to old ideals and hierarchies of race and gender. An ethos of freer sexual expression burgeoned in this era, particularly in urban areas, as an underground gay culture flourished and more women donned short "flapper" dresses, bobbed their hair, and in other ways flaunted their disdain for the Victorian morality embedded in social norms and the law. For critics, the menace of the "New Woman" now coming into her own could wreak havoc on the nation's morals, despite the obscenity statutes sustained by threats of imprisonment. Meanwhile, if an African American man was imagined, rightly or wrongly, to have had so much as a fleeting lustful thought about a white woman, prison was the least of his worries; instead, he could be lynched: publicly hanged (and often mutilated) while jeered by raucous mobs ostensibly protective of white women's honor. Conservative forces retrenched through mechanisms such as fundamentalist churches and the reorganized Ku Klux Klan, an organization for native-born white Protestants that agitated against people of color, immigrant Catholics and Jews, and others deemed threatening to white supremacy. Progressives were likelier to partake in the popular eugenics movement, which promoted many of the same race-based theories under a different guise but with the same hope of bettering a pure white race while containing the proliferation of black and brown bodies.

Efforts to buttress the old order took place on many fronts, but none were more vigorous or enduring than the endeavors that focused explicitly on reproduction, motherhood, and sex. The arguments fueling these efforts echoed the suffrage crusade, with one side demanding women's rights and their opponents casting such demands as the product of selfish ambition, debauchery, and anti–family values. The more that traditionalists fought against women's rights on these terms, the more liberal supporters worked to expand their base of support and fortify those rights, deepening the fault line that divided two increasingly antagonistic frameworks for construing women's roles and gender more broadly. As we will see, debates on social concerns ranging from birth control to same-sex marriage spring from these same seeds.

In short, the intermixing of religion, sex, and politics took on a specific sort of urgency after the failure of anti-suffrage efforts in 1920, and, for progressives no less than traditionalists, the urgency of these issues has only escalated through the decades. As the fissures deepened, the stakes seemed ever higher: by the late 1960s, a fight over sex education had become, at least for the most ardent participants, an urgent struggle for the fate and future of America. When issues like abortion and gay rights moved to the center of the nation's politics, conservatives and progressives alike increasingly viewed the stakes in terms of national destiny: whether, for conservatives, the nation would embody traditional Christian values and whether, for liberals, the traditional privilege accorded to white hetero-male authority would be dismantled or sustained. If sex and gender alone have not encompassed all the issues dividing us—and they emphatically have not—they have nonetheless been key points of conflict in our public life from the time when women got the vote. *Moral Combat* begins at that crucial historical moment and narrates what has transpired since.

TELLING SUCH A COMPLEX AND far-reaching story over a century's historical trajectory is a challenge. Some nuance is inevitably lost when a broad narrative attempts to explain critical events over a long duration, and any historian must select what to include and what to omit, hoping for coherence without oversimplification. The pages that follow highlight a series of episodes over a full century that I believe are key to understanding the conflicts and transformations in this profoundly consequential history. The saga opens amid the victory of women's suffrage in the United States, a moment that presaged the breakdown of the old Christian and national consensus on sex. The first chapter surveys the acceleration during the 1920s of the powerful movement for birth control, a cause that prompted fierce conflicts during the feverish decade of the 1920s. Subsequent chapters turn to other controversies that raged with particular heat during subsequent decades: over censorship and obscenity in the 1930s, over interracial sex and race-mixing in the 1940s, over new findings about women's extramarital activity in the 1950s, over sex education sponsored by schools in the 1960s, over abortion in the 1970s and 1980s, over sexual harassment in the 1990s, and over same-sex marriage and citizenship rights for sexual minorities in the early 2000s.

All of these battles had important protagonists who played a crucial public role, and so my discussions of the controversies highlight the central roles of particular individuals: Margaret Sanger, the feminist and birth control crusader; D. H. Lawrence, censored writer and painter; the anthropologist Ruth Benedict, whose late work ignited a congressional firestorm over interracial intimacy; the biologist and best-selling sexologist Alfred Kinsey; the physician and sex education crusader Mary Steichen Calderone and her longtime antagonist, the fundamentalist preacher-publisher Billy James Hargis; the Baptist minister Howard Moody and the Catholic feminist Frances Kissling, both activists for legal abortion; Anita Hill and Paula Jones, two former government employees whose allegations of sexual harassment made them the center of national controversy; and Gene Robinson, the first openly gay bishop in the Episcopal Church. All of these pivotal individuals and their public work enduringly shaped social attitudes toward sex, gender, and sexuality that continued to develop long after their time in the spotlight.

Moving through central portions of these characters' stories—snapshots in the longer arc of their lives that reveal their impact on changing gender norms—the following chapters entwine their struggles in a protracted moral combat.

Whether self-avowed Christians or proponents of another creed, these figures fought on behalf of what they believed was good for America and its people. All gathered fervent supporters and also faced fierce opposition from those religious believers who saw both their personal moral values and their country under threat. Dire warnings against the destruction these revolutionaries would reap echoed unremittingly over time; indeed, even when the forecasts seemed to fail, the condemnations and warnings never ceased but rather remained robust in every historical moment, a ceaseless sexual Cold War overhanging the mood of the nation. Indeed, it should go without saying that all of the specific issues animating these conflicts continued to be contested long after the decades in which I examine them: none—not one—has been settled to all citizens' satisfaction, and all persist as targets in both American religion and our fraught politics.

The persistence of stalwart activists on all sides confirms the high stakes for those wanting to conserve a particular model of the status quo that maintains an older notion of traditional order, gender hierarchy, and obedience to strict sexual limits—as high as they have been for the revolutionaries seeking something new. Those fearing change have instilled that dread in others through warnings of moral ruin and the wholesale failure of American civilization if sexual rules are relaxed, while those welcoming it have offered visions of a healthier society freed from archaic constraints. That's a charged conflict, indeed—closer in many minds, perhaps, to a *mortal* combat. This book shows how sex has been both a source of profound fear and an effective tool for fueling the most basic political clashes and power struggles of recent American history. Ultimately it reveals how the old consensus shattered and why.

CHAPTER 1

THE BATTLE OVER BIRTH CONTROL IN THE ROARING TWENTIES

T HE BIRTH CONTROL MOVEMENT, WHICH first arose in the mid-1910s among free-thinking radicals and social reformers in New York, generated fierce controversy and debate stretching over decades. The achievement of women's equal voting rights boosted the movement's momentum, and it gradually attained some measure of respectability in the 1920s. But even as support for contraceptive access spread widely during that decade, opposition increasingly mobilized to try to halt the movement. Two key developments resulted: the growth of deep, consequential divisions among Christians regarding sex—more specifically, the morality of nonprocreative sex within marriage—and the far-reaching politicization of those divisions, involving a ferocious contest over political power and the law. By the early 1930s, the Christian consensus on sex that framed the nation's morals prior to this time had cracked, and advocacy for contraception within marriage was increasingly viewed as morally acceptable and, crucially, as perfectly consonant with American liberty.

No person played a greater role initiating these developments than Margaret Sanger, the signature leader of the birth control movement. Sanger dedicated most of her adult life to the fight for women's contraceptive access and reproductive rights. Her frankness about the importance of women achieving the ability to control their childbearing, and her tireless labors to that end, earned her keen admiration as well

Birth control activist Margaret Sanger. *KEYSTONE-FRANCE/
GAMMA-KEYSTONE VIA GETTY IMAGES.*

as fervid loathing among Americans, including many notable American Christian leaders and the wider Christian citizenry, both Catholic and Protestant. During the 1920s, Roman Catholic leaders consolidated their resistance to birth control, growing more vocal and organized in their opposition to it. Meanwhile, many influential Protestant leaders, persuaded by Sanger's lobbying, relaxed the opposition that had marked the nineteenth-century Protestant stance on contraception, moderating their positions within the framework of marriage and family norms. Both sides mobilized supporters by building up doomsday scenarios, arguing that the failure of their cause would mean victory for an enemy whose ultimate goal was the wholesale degradation of womanhood. On that much—that those were the stakes, dire indeed—the rivals agreed.

Protestant Christians campaigning against perceived vice and immorality had, for decades, worked to restrict access to contraception, none more successfully than Anthony Comstock (1844–1915). In 1873, Comstock, a Civil War veteran for the Union side and a pious Protestant with strong ties to the Young Men's Christian Association (YMCA), founded the New York Society for the Suppression of Vice, a group chartered by the New York legislature. Comstock's fellow incorporators— seventeen men, many of whom had served on the YMCA's own anti-vice committee before creating this new organization—elected him secretary and chief special agent, and he remained in that role for more than forty years, until his death. Comstock's organization was soon joined by the New England Society for the Suppression of Vice (later renamed the New England Watch and Ward Society), as well as like-minded associations of crusading Protestants in cities such as St. Louis, Chicago, and San Francisco. All worked to eradicate publications deemed obscene, but Comstock led the way in his dedication to the cause.[1]

Since the early nineteenth century, information about both pregnancy prevention and termination had been available through midwives and print publications; by the 1850s, advertisements for contraceptive products appeared in newspapers, magazines, and other popular literature. The growing visibility of contraceptive devices and information made them an obvious target for Christian outrage and obscenity charges, and their prohibition became authorized in the Comstock Law passed by Congress on March 3, 1873. Officially called the Act for the Suppression of Trade in, and Circulation of, Obscene Literature and Articles of Immoral Use, the federal law stipulated imprisonment and steep fines for anyone who possessed, published, sold, or mailed any printed object, image, or instrument deemed obscene, including "any article whatever, for the prevention of conception, or for causing abortion."[2] Search-and-seizure warrants could be issued by a judge to an appropriate authority, who would take possession of such materials and destroy them. This far-reaching law raised almost no controversy at the time, and many states subsequently passed their own anti-obscenity laws, so that offenders could be prosecuted in state as well as federal courts.

The national prohibition on mailing obscene materials meant that postal workers too were now censors, and President Ulysses Grant promptly appointed Comstock to serve as a special postal agent to oversee and implement mail confiscation procedures. As early as January 1, 1874, Comstock claimed to have seized 194,000 obscene images; 134,000 pounds of obscene books; and hundreds of thousands of printing plates, contraceptive writings and devices, sex-related drugs, and more. This decades-long fight against obscenity resulted in scores of high-profile trials, book burnings, and the arrests of bookstore workers, writers, activists, actresses, and art gallery owners.

The Comstock Law, and the proliferation of similar state laws that followed, made the distribution of contraceptive information illegal and sharply curtailed the practices of midwives. After 1873, many states punished people who received information about contraception as strenuously as those who disseminated it. Fourteen states—Colorado, Indiana, Iowa, Massachusetts, Minnesota, Mississippi, Missouri, Montana, Nevada, New Jersey, New York, Pennsylvania, Washington, and Wyoming—proscribed oral instruction about birth control. Others criminalized the possession of written guidelines, some authorizing search-and-seizure procedures for suspected offenders. One state—Colorado—thought it possible to ban the transport of mere knowledge pertaining to pregnancy prevention into its borders, while another state—Connecticut—prohibited the very act of preventing conception.[3] Methods that had been well known, accessible, and increasingly reliable in the nineteenth century—condoms, vaginal sponges, and pessaries or "womb veils" (early versions of what would come to be called the diaphragm)—were now banned for large sectors of the population. While some states exempted doctors or druggists from the laws, seventeen states along with the District of Columbia barred doctors from contraceptive instruction even in their own medical offices. The success of Comstock and his allied Protestant reformers in outlawing contraception was truly vast in scope, illustrating the broad Christian consensus that existed regarding concepts of sexual vice, immorality, and the need for legal constraint.

Efforts to legalize contraceptive access gained momentum in the early twentieth century, largely through the work of radicals such as

Margaret Sanger, who eventually became the movement's major leader. Born Margaret Higgins, she was the sixth of eleven children born to an atheistic father and a pious Catholic mother of Irish descent. The family lived in Corning, New York, amid a largely Catholic community of laborers who mixed little with the affluent class. Her mother took the responsibility of seeing to it that young Margaret was baptized and confirmed in the Roman Catholic Church.[4] Her father, however, was a staunch critic of the church who valued freedom of thought—"freedom of the mind from dogma and cant," as she later put it; it was he, she wrote, who "taught me to think." After her father brought the famous freethinker Robert Ingersoll to Corning for a speech, the family was shunned and her father's livelihood greatly reduced in spite of her mother's well-known piety. In her mother's life, Margaret wrote, she saw the brutal costs that childbearing could impose on women. After bearing eleven children over twenty-two years, her mother died at fifty; her father lived into his eighties.[5]

Margaret married William Sanger in 1902, and they had three children together, living first in Westchester and then New York City. Margaret's real passion for contraceptive access emerged when, a few years after her marriage, she worked as a nurse and midwife among poor families in lower Manhattan. She later described how the cruel conditions facing women and girls horrified her. Women were forever pregnant or nursing, children were always hungry, babies died from neglect and hunger (sometimes to the relief of their haggard parents), and the cramped quarters facilitated men raping their own daughters. "The menace of another pregnancy hung like a sword over the head of every poor woman I came in contact with," she wrote. As a result of these conditions, improvised abortions were rampant, and full of perils that women were lucky to survive.[6] According to Sanger's autobiography, the destitute women spoke bitterly of how "the rich" knew tricks for preventing pregnancy, while poor women resorted frantically to remedies ranging from drinking turpentine and rolling down stairs to shoving shoe hooks or knitting needles high up into their cervices. Catholic women spoke of "Yankee tricks" among the wealthier classes and asked "what the Protestants did to keep their families down"—a sign that well-to-do women outside Catholic circles seemed to have some knowledge of controlling conception, legal or not. Sickened by this "heartbreaking" situation, in which impoverished women lived terrified lives as "beasts of burden," Margaret recalled, "my own happy love life became a reproach."7 The death of one of her patients after a second attempted abortion was the last straw. Haunted by her own ignorance and failure to ease poor women's suffering, she had found her cause.

In New York she participated actively in the Socialist Party and the labor activism of the Industrial Workers of the World, among comrades who included radicals such as Emma Goldman, ten years her senior and a strong proponent of legalizing contraception. Sanger's labor activism amplified her concern about the suffering of destitute women and children, further confirming her sense that women needed access to contraception. Not only were working women unable to control their childbearing, but the starving, shivering mothers who attempted to join strikes against their employers risked further poverty for their children. All of this suffering—so needless, in Margaret Sanger's view, if Americans could only bring themselves to act on their humanitarian ideals—was her professed motivation for launching a movement to give women access to contraceptives and to making reproductive rights her life's work.

Sanger clashed almost immediately with Comstock. In early 1913, he banned her weekly sex education column, "What Every Girl Should Know," printed in the Socialist paper the *New York Call*. (The following week, the indignant editor ran an empty box under the heading, "What Every Girl Should Know—Nothing! By Order of the Post Office Department.") In 1914, after launching her own magazine (*The Woman Rebel*) to challenge Comstock's restrictions on sexual information, Sanger was indicted for indecency and the first issue seized by the post office; she was soon arrested and charged on criminal counts that carried a possible sentence of forty-five years in prison, impelling her to flee for Europe. She remained there in exile until late 1915, when Comstock was safely in the grave. His death that September at age seventy-one had come shortly after his final trial: a dogged and ultimately successful endeavor to convict her husband William Sanger under the Criminal Code for distributing a birth control pamphlet she wrote. His *New York Times* obituary reported that up to his final year, Comstock "caused the arraignment in

State and Federal courts of 3,697 persons, of which 2,740 either pleaded guilty or were convicted."[8] Despite his death, Comstock's impact would long be felt as what Sanger termed "the dead hand" that still imprisoned contraceptive information; for although Comstock's "body has been entombed," Sanger wrote five years after his death, "the evil that he did lives after him," forcing ignorance on the people and oppressing them with his "witch hunting" crusade.[9]

Sanger refused to let that "dead hand" control her. After his death, this nurse-midwife who had been galvanized by her early public health work in the immigrant ghettoes of New York worked steadily to promote a movement for birth control, which she profoundly believed to be a just, noble, and humane cause. Over the next few years, as she recognized the need to appeal to broad factions of people in order to build strength for the movement, she grew more pragmatic in her tactics. The New York papers and national magazines like *Harper's Weekly* and *Current Opinion* published sympathetic pieces that treated contraception as a scientific issue, examining questions of eugenic improvement, public health, and women's rights.

Not all attention was sympathetic, though; her growing influence prompted the formidable Catholic leader and Catholic University of America social ethicist John A. Ryan to urge his fellow clergy to be clear, forceful, and persistent in articulating the moral law against contraception, as well as staunchly enforcing that law.[10] Ryan's ethics included support for social justice and labor rights as well as opposition to "race suicide," a term popularized some years earlier by President Theodore Roosevelt in warning Americans that the fertility rate of immigrants and ethnic minorities outpaced that of white Anglo-Saxons and that for the latter to use birth control was to risk the extinction of the white race. Ryan and other Catholic leaders, while less direct about whiteness, clearly meant to call attention to the greater hazard of reducing the population of what Ryan's fellow Jesuit M. P. Dowling called "those who are in a position to rear sturdy sons and daughters, who are best fitted to be the bulwark of the nation . . . the privileged classes."[11] In the eyes of these Catholics, Sanger was steering the nation to race suicide; indeed, she was becoming what one historian calls "a particular bête noire" to clerics because, to their minds, she encouraged women to be selfish and materialistic in refusing to bear as many children as God would send.[12] Sanger herself increasingly sensed that Catholic leaders could be a potent enemy to her cause.

Her fame growing, Sanger traveled widely to deliver lectures, and she lobbied for reform of obscenity laws. In October 1916, she opened in Brooklyn the first American clinic explicitly focused on birth control (Planned Parenthood dates its origins back to this very facility). She was again charged with distributing birth control information and devices, and although she and her lawyers made sure that court witnesses heard testimony from Brownsville mothers about the horrific conditions in which they lived and the assistance they and their infants received from Sanger's clinic, she was jailed for thirty days anyway. She worked with, though did not belong to, both of the competing birth control associations in New York, and she began publishing pamphlets (including her collected columns "What Every Girl Should Know") and the *Birth Control Review*.[13]

In 1920, the same year that women's suffrage triumphed, Sanger earned still more recognition from the publicity surrounding her latest book, a feminist manifesto titled *Woman and the New Race*. An argument for contraception as an essential instrument for women's freedom (and, incidentally, for men's full freedom and happiness as well), the book spoke directly of the need for a "new sex morality," in contrast to that of conservative religion: a morality crafted by women themselves and one that differed substantially from current values, in that "the new standard will be based upon knowledge and freedom while the old is founded upon ignorance and submission." Sanger knew that this morality threatened church doctrine, and she proclaimed it proudly: "Let it be realized that this creation of new sex ideals is a challenge to the church."[14] The book was an immediate success, selling out in hardcover and undergoing several printings before being reissued in softcover by Truth Publishing, a radical press whose list prominently featured other titles in sexology and birth control.

In 1921, Sanger worked to bring together a wide range of American and English birth control advocates for the First American Birth Control

Conference, held that November in New York. Convening such a conference was an audacious act, teetering toward the gray areas of the laws still forbidding obscenity. The conference would become the starting point for the American Birth Control League—the predecessor organization of the Planned Parenthood Federation of America—and it would enduringly transform the way Americans thought and talked about contraception. It would not be an exaggeration to say that the furor unleashed by the events of the conference, which pitted Protestants against Catholics while also dividing Protestants into opposing camps, marked the start of the culture wars over sex that would divide Americans for decades to come.

Sanger's ambitions for the conference were exceedingly high, and she privately predicted it would be a "turning point" for American attitudes toward contraception. She also knew that many would come out especially to hear her.[15] Her supporters—a number having cut their teeth in the movement for female suffrage—held equally high aspirations, convinced that birth control was the next vital step in women's emancipation from patriarchal control and the tyranny of unplanned pregnancies. Physicians, economists, ministers, and at least one rabbi would attend and speak at the conference, while Dr. Karl Reiland, Episcopal rector of the famed St. George's Church (on whose vestry the senior J. Pierpont Morgan served), was slated to preside over the final public session on birth control's morality, featuring a culminating speech by Sanger at a newly built venue in Manhattan, the Town Hall.

Sanger had amassed more than ninety women and men to serve as conference officers and committee members. It was a motley group of true believers, social climbers, and calculating hangers-on who had their own reasons for associating with Sanger's cause: a strategically assembled federation of radical feminists and wealthy socialites, prominent physicians and New York financiers, theatrical celebrities and high-powered literati, economists and clergy. Bertha Rembaugh, the formidable lawyer for the Women's Trade Union League of New York who passionately defended factory workers, young immigrant women, and prostitutes, was there alongside Louisa (Mrs. Pierre) Jay, better known for frequent attendance at high society debutante balls than for gritty political activism. Affluent members of the Whitney clan, such as Dorothy Whitney (Mrs.

Margaret Sanger with fellow birth control advocates, New York, circa 1924. *UNDERWOOD & UNDERWOOD/UNDERWOOD ARCHIVES/GETTY IMAGES.*

Willard) Straight and Mabel Whitney (the second Mrs. Dexter) Blagden, had social profiles resembling that of Mrs. Simeon Ford, wife of the owner of the Grand Union Hotel and also a committee member. But here, rather than being mere ladies of leisure, wealthy women could unite in common cause with the brilliant Dr. Alice Hamilton, the socially conscious physician and first woman appointed to the Harvard Medical School faculty, and the outspoken Mary Halton, a well-known gynecologist and feminist in Greenwich Village. Such mingling was hardly unusual: many elite women of the period had been goaded into political work by the suffrage movement, which perhaps reduced the shock of seeing society dames support this outwardly radical and seemingly illicit venture.[16] At once interested in women's rights, "racial improvement," and their own wealth and social prestige, they proved an ideal fit for Sanger's activism.

Many men stood alongside the women on the conference committee. They were liberals, at least on social issues, and willing members of an organization headed by a famously feminist woman. Their numbers included husbands of suffragists as well as Kendall Banning, an author and the managing editor of *Hearst's Magazine* and *Cosmopolitan*; Lowell Brentano, the author, playwright, and heir to the Brentano's book firm, which had published *Woman and the New Race* in hardcover; Rabbi Rudolph I. Coffee; Herbert Croly, the editor of the *New Republic*; the noted writer Theodore Dreiser; the Harvard biologist E. M. East; the Yale economist Irving Fisher; the inventor John Hays Hammond Jr.; and the physician Dr. S. Adolphus Knopf. Like the women, they supported Sanger's cause for a variety of reasons: to reduce poverty and overpopulation, improve public health, diminish psychiatric disturbances and infant mortality, and create better conditions for fair labor laws, among others. Diverse ideals united this motley group of men, no less than their female counterparts.

Sanger also made sure to include Protestant clergy, underscoring the fact that Protestants no longer spoke with one voice regarding contraception. Clerics affiliated with the conference committee were well known for their social activism: the Episcopal priest Arthur E. Whatham, for instance, had much earlier decried racial discrimination in the South and in the Episcopal Church, promoting the cause of hiring black bishops and corresponding with Booker T. Washington; Karl Reiland was "one of the Episcopal Church's most outspoken liberals," of whom it was said that he preached a gospel "burned with social zeal and a love for his fellow men."[17] Reiland would roundly call on the church to change its attitude toward birth control and "support this method of raising the level of existence," lambasting religious objections as "irrelevant."[18] As their sermons and writings then and later made clear, these clergymen believed Christian leaders should champion birth control for the health of mothers and children and for the good of marriage and the family, themes that would be treated expansively in the conference.

On the morning of November 11, the conference began, and for two long days, professionals delivered prepared lectures promoting contraception as a vital panacea for women, especially poor women whose high birth rates brought about poverty and frequently led to life-threatening abortions and even infanticide. Freedom for women was a vital plank in the conference's platform for traditional family life, linked to concerns about children's well-being: women who were free to make choices about how many children to bear would ostensibly be better, more loving mothers. Monogamous marriage was "the most important institution in any community" and the home the "backbone of the state"—the very foundation upon which the nation must be built. Happy marriages required purposeful rather than unplanned reproduction.[19] This traditionalist child- and home-centered message—a focus on the family and most especially poor families, for the sake of America's future—was an ever-present theme of the conference and the activism that surged in its wake.[20]

Yet concern for the family often mixed with other social and nationalistic aspirations, caught up in the eugenic ideas then common among the white middle and upper classes. Controlling reproduction could ensure happy marriages for all, and for many, it was also a way to reshape the population. Birth control supporters frequently articulated a hope that the movement would aid in reducing the birth rates of "foreign," "defective," and "unfit" groups so that they would not come to outnumber healthy Anglo-Saxons. Birth control was not only about female emancipation, then; it was also about controlling the racial makeup of the nation, often quite overtly. Both ideals—women's freedom and racial improvement—seemed to many American-born whites in this period to share a common basis in science, and countless numbers believed that eugenics held the key to a better future for the nation.[21]

Sanger invoked eugenics in her own first formal address to the gathering, noting that the "healthy and fit elements of the nation" carried the burden of the unfit, who were increasing at a dangerous rate. Both nationally and globally, "the masses of the unfit" had propagated to such an extent that they had to be warehoused in "palatial residences for the unfit, for the insane, for the feeble-minded—for those who should never have been born." Poverty, imbecility, delinquency, crime, and even war were some of the troubles resulting from a "weakened and deteriorated race"; the solution was to stop such misery at its source.[22] Sanger tapped into common fears, then prevalent among the white upper class, that immigrants, African Americans, and other "others" would soon subsume the entire white race in America. The future of civilization itself, then, appeared to rest on the success of birth control programs, in the United States and abroad.

But this negative eugenics program was far from the only driver of the movement; in fact, advocates were deeply conflicted about questions of coercion that surrounded birth control. Most participants at the First American Birth Control Conference were concerned that global over-population was "a menace to the peace of the world" and were enthusiastic about birth control to alleviate this problem.[23] But there was an active debate about choice and coercion. While clearly advocating methods of controlling the unfit, most participants expressed the general view that, as one put it, "we are advocating Birth Control only for those who want it." Birth control should be "an individual matter," a "choice," many professed. Sanger herself spoke fervently of motherhood being "the function of dignity and choice, rather than one of ignorance and chance." Physicians, sociologists, psychologists, and more spoke explicitly about birth control as a matter of personal preference that must be guided by sound morals as well as scientific principles.[24]

Like Sanger, many speakers expressed a deep concern for women, those who were poor no less than those who were well-to-do, who had been destroyed by the demand that they serve as baby machines; indeed, several argued strenuously that women's subjugation was a causal factor in the "unfitness" of many children who had been born unloved and were poorly cared for in infancy and childhood. Virginia C. Young, an Episcopal deaconess long committed to practical mission work among women and the poor, detailed this view in her own address, "Problem of the Delinquent Woman." She insisted she was there "to speak for those who cannot speak for themselves," for she lived and worked among streetwalkers, incarcerated prisoners, and other women treated as "flotsam and jetsam," above all "the City Negro and the City Prostitute": "all of them potential mothers, many of them already mothers, and most of them so badly-born themselves that they might often be said to have been 'damned into the world.'" Young promoted the "distinctly spiritual values underlying this movement" for birth control: devotion to a world in which all children were wanted, every citizen was loved, and each person felt equally called to "a fostering of all that is beautiful and worthy and precious for the strengthening and enriching and glorifying of human life." Until women were freed from subjugation, children who were unwanted, unloved, and unfit would continue to be born and suffer lives of misery.[25]

At last, on November 13, it was Sanger's turn to deliver her long-awaited culminating lecture at the conference. Arriving at the Town Hall that evening, the famous woman thrust her way through a boisterous crowd to the entrance door. But instead of entering triumphantly, Sanger found the doors locked against her—an attempt by Manhattan police to halt the meeting. When the doors opened to let out the crowds already gathered inside, she was whisked up by adoring and indignant fans and propelled to the stage, where she made repeated attempts to convene the meeting and address the promised lecture subject, "Birth Control: Is It Moral?" to no avail. Within minutes, Captain Thomas Donahue had physically seized her, escorted her offstage, and arrested her along with fellow activist Mary Winsor. Officers paraded the women to police headquarters while hundreds of Sanger supporters defiantly sang "My Country 'Tis of Thee" in their wake. Sanger could not have staged a more dramatic episode to publicize her cause—or, as it soon turned out, to highlight what she now perceived to be the gravest threat to American liberty and women's freedom: the Roman Catholic hierarchy.

Sanger and Winsor spent the night in jail before a court magistrate released them without charges the next morning for lack of evidence, and the police disruption of the meeting made front-page news for days.[26] The most explosive story appeared on November 15 in the *New York Times*, "Birth Control Raid Made by Police on Archbishop's Order." The first sentence put it bluntly: "The police suppression of the birth control meeting at the Town Hall Sunday night, which culminated in the arrest of two of the speakers after they had refused to leave the stage, was brought about at the instance of Archbishop Patrick J. Hayes of this Roman Catholic Archdiocese." Hayes's secretary, Monsignor Joseph P. Dineen, had been present at the meeting, and reporters put the pieces together from there: Sanger had invited the archbishop to the meeting, the archbishop's office had sent a complaint to police headquarters, and the monsignor met up with Donohue at the meeting to induce him to shut it down.[27] The legal reasoning for halting it was shaky—hence the police acted extralegally—but church leaders believed it was morally justified. The conference conveners rescheduled the meeting on birth control's morality for November 18, as Sanger worked tirelessly to stir public indignation toward the Catholic leaders' bullying tactics.

At stake in the ensuing skirmish over public discussion of sexual morality were the limits of liberty as well as religion's role as a help or hindrance to democracy. Rivals debated what sort of religion was compatible with American freedom, an issue that had long percolated in American culture. But unlike the period in which Comstock's directives loomed large, in the wake of women's suffrage many were concerned with how religion would or could accommodate women's newly gained rights. Sanger's allies and a broad swath of birth control supporters believed that such rights included the freedom to speak publicly about contraception; religion could not rightfully restrict that privilege. Sanger's ouster and arrest at the hands of those who apparently felt otherwise bestowed these issues with new urgency.

In a public statement printed in the *Times*, Sanger informed readers that Catholic leaders, including the renowned John Ryan, had spurned an invitation to debate her publicly at the conference's closing session (travel expenses defrayed), in favor of surreptitious sabotage. Sanger made sure to note that the offer still stood. She continued, "I am inviting Archbishop Hayes, or any representative he wishes to send, to the meeting next Friday night. We hope the Archbishop will attend or be represented to present the Catholic Church's side of Birth Control."[28] In advertising these invitations to conservative religious figures, Sanger suggested that she extended the privilege of public debate even to those unwilling to extend the same courtesy to her; the birth control cause, she proposed, had nothing to fear from open examination of all sides of the issue. Catholic leaders' refusal to debate Sanger publicly, while pressuring police behind the scenes to silence her, cast them as both timid and undemocratic.

The press saw it her way, and the affair quickly became a story of Catholic cowardice and patriarchal bullying, transforming Sanger's cause by adding and amplifying an anti-Catholic component to it. Subsequent reporting highlighted statements by birth control supporters that the "utter absurdity" of police attacking the meeting was "the very best that

could have happened," for the harassment motivated apathetic bystand-
ers to awaken and fight the Catholic despots.[29] Members of the conference committee stoked such sentiments by adopting a resolution that
protested "the outrageous action of the police in closing the mass meeting, especially in view of the statements that the action was taken on the
direction of the Roman Catholic hierarchy."[30] Many of the social elites
making such charges were of the sort who, until very recently, surely
would not have dreamed of discussing contraception in polite society,
whatever they thought of the Comstock laws. A dramatic shift in conventional wisdom was underway regarding the importance of Sanger's cause
and her right to promote it.

The venue of the police interference surely helped frame the debate. Finished only ten months before, the Town Hall had been built by
the League for Political Education, an affluent group of suffragists and
socialites intent to create a civic space devoted to open inquiry and discussion of assorted topics. Protestant, Catholic, and Jewish leaders had
publicly united at the laying of the cornerstone in praise of free speech,
democratic education, and what Rabbi Stephen S. Wise called "the religion of America," all embodied in the new edifice and its activities.[31]
When the Town Hall opened in January 1921, the festivities lasted a full
week. "YE SHALL KNOW THE TRUTH, AND THE TRUTH SHALL MAKE YOU
FREE," declared the plaque on the building's façade, quoting John 8:32.
Indeed, the building's patrons, religious and secular, were confident that
open inquiry would lead, inevitably, to the heights of emancipated civilization. Standing at the heart of Times Square—123 West Forty-Third
Street, between Sixth Avenue and Broadway—the structure loomed tall,
a monument to free speech more majestic than the glittering temples of
consumer capitalism surrounding it. With its suffragist provenance, the
building also stood as a proud symbol of women's freedom, at least the
freedom of those who were white, native-born, and well-situated. For
those still skeptical of Catholicism's compatibility with American ideals,
wresting Margaret Sanger off that particular stage was nothing less than
a strategy to muzzle democratic principles and stifle an emancipated
woman.

When Sanger finally delivered her lecture on November 18 at the Park Theatre, twenty policemen and an additional twenty private guards stood watch over a setting where, according to the *New York Times*, "fully 8,000 persons, men and women, struggled to get into a place that holds only 1,500."[32] The subject of Sanger's address remained, "Is Birth Control Moral?," but the event now supplied an opportunity to denounce the tactics of suppression used by church and police and to link these tightly with Catholic opposition to birth control writ large. The Episcopal priest of St. George's Church, Karl Reiland, chaired the meeting as originally planned, and he publicly announced his "emphatic protest against the outrageous and unwarranted interference" that stopped the earlier meeting. Others spoke too—notably Harold Cox, an English journalist and former member of Parliament—and highlighted the moral values behind the birth control crusade while castigating Catholic pretensions to serving as arbiters of Nature and natural law.[33]

Sanger's speech was the main event. She addressed head-on the question of morality, contrasting her approach to that of her Catholic opponents and contending that the discussion of morality belongs not merely to theologians and scientists but to "the people," and most especially those oppressed for centuries: women.[34]

> The church has ever opposed the progress of woman on the ground that her freedom would lead to immorality. We ask the church to have more confidence in women. We ask the opponents of this movement to reverse the methods of the church, which aims to keep women moral by keeping them in fear and in ignorance, and to inculcate into them a higher and truer morality based upon knowledge. And ours is the morality of knowledge. If we cannot trust woman with the knowledge of her own body, then I claim that two thousand years of Christian teaching has proved to be a failure.[35]

In this, the speech of her life, Sanger threw the Catholic hierarchy's accusations of women's selfishness back against church leaders themselves. What was truly selfish and immoral, she argued, was to keep women

down by force, rather than encourage their flourishing through knowledge. Church leaders gave few signs of being anything but power-hungry
and cruel, in her rendering. Their disruption of the Town Hall meeting—
"a disgrace to liberty-loving people, and to all traditions we hold dear in
the United States"—was thoroughly in line with their suppression of
women.[36]

Sanger plainly believed that the Catholic Church embodied a patriarchal hierarchy that used fear and intimidation to demean and de-
grade women. She thus condemned Catholicism on the two grounds that
mattered most to her promotion of birth control: the church's treatment
of women as slavish procreators and the threat of increasing race degeneracy if Catholics and nonwhites bore too many children. The right of a
child "to be desired" was also crucial; indeed, controlling conception dignified the mother-child relationship and expressed a more civilized moral
code of "greater forethought for others" and ultimately "a higher sanction
for the value of life itself."[37] Female emancipation, the rights of children,
and racial uplift were once again stitched together into a seamless whole,
this one a protest against the Catholic hierarchy and a reassessment of
what it meant to value life.

Following Sanger's performance, opponents rose to air their views.
Archbishop Hayes had not responded to her invitation to speak that
evening, but other critics were on hand, most notably Canon William
Sheafe Chase of the Garden City Episcopal Cathedral. Chase issued a
fiery condemnation of the reformers' ostensible atheism, calling them
"deficient in moral and psychological insight" and preoccupied with "outward and material progress." Their "vague humanitarianism without
God" caused them to resort to "mechanical means" for race betterment,
when they ought instead to be "educating souls in self-control."[38] For the
birth control advocates on hand, Canon Chase, known for his activism on
behalf of Prohibition and censorship, was an heir to the reviled Anthony
Comstock. Indeed, Chase represented an extension of Comstock's model
of anti-obscenity activism: he went on to fight obscenity in the movies
through his Federal Motion Picture Council, and he also worked assid-
uously to oppose the sex education materials distributed by reformers,
objecting vociferously to any mention of female sexual pleasure. Chase

exemplified the continuing skepticism among some Protestants toward the sorts of moral arguments made by Sanger, even as the tides began to shift around them.[39]

After the critics concluded, Sanger got the final word. She responded to their advocacy of sexual self-control over birth control by noting that the nation's laws robbed married women of the very right and possibility of sexual self-control, placing the decision for sex entirely within the realm of men. Those laws plainly had to change, Sanger declared, and the American woman "must have control over her own body." Men too needed the right to control procreation; this was a freedom not solely intended for women. Above all, Sanger advocated a freedom that was to be in service to marriage, not debauchery—to love and fidelity against the painful circumstances that led to adultery and marital breakdown.[40]

Sanger's final comments aimed specifically at the notion she took to be central to the Catholic position: that the sole purpose of sex was for the procreation of children. Calling that argument "perfectly absurd" because it reduced humans to the level of animals, she pled for sex as the "sacred" and "beautiful" expression of love between two people, even when they did not intend to have children. "I contend that they can go into that relationship with the same beauty and the same holiness with which they go into music or to prayer."[41] Calling sexual power that which "gives us spiritual illumination," Sanger echoed sex mystics from Alice Stockham and Ida Craddock to Edward Carpenter and D. H. Lawrence, who sought to raise sex from the gutter in which they felt Comstock and Catholics had thrown it.

In the immediate wake of the Town Hall raid, church leaders—well acquainted with Sanger's notoriety and radicalism—hardly leapt to her defense. The *Christian Century*, the weekly organ of American mainline liberal Protestantism, appears to have simply ignored the raid altogether; in 1921, the topic of birth control remained too delicate a subject for open and public discussion in the Protestant churches. That would rapidly change, however, spearheaded by the explosive revulsion for what seemed to the mainstream press to be Catholic prudery and anti-American authoritarianism. So successfully did the tide turn after Sanger's public ouster from the Town Hall that even many who had heretofore opposed her cause rallied sympathetically to her defense, marking a sea change in the news coverage of Sanger, birth control, and the Catholic hierarchy. An editorial in the *Outlook*, a widely read weekly news journal, made the point clearly, saying that while editors were "not in sympathy with Mrs. Sanger's methods" and "very doubtful about the good taste and wisdom of discussing the subject of birth control . . . in a public hall before a popular audience," the "violent" and "brutal" behavior of the police warranted protest as "a dangerous and, we think, illegal violation . . . of the fundamental right of free speech guaranteed by the United States Constitution."[42] The event tapped into old Protestant trepidations about tyrannical church control of civic issues—an issue that, in the press coverage, virtually trumped discussion of the sexual issues at hand. Freedom itself, more than chastity, appeared to be the moral value most clearly threatened in this dispute.

A blistering editorial in the *New Republic*, a periodical that had long favored legalizing birth control, made this connection even clearer, insisting that Archbishop Hayes's behind-the-scenes enlistment of the police as "puppets" for the suppression of free speech could have easily gone unexposed, had Sanger not been "so courageous a woman" or the magistrate who dismissed her case not "upright." The writer, likely *TNR* editor Herbert Croly—a friend and supporter of Sanger—pointed out that Hayes's protest was the church's clearest and most public sign yet of wholesale opposition to birth control, and that these positions (anti–free speech and anti–birth control) were deeply linked. "Birth control is obnoxious to men and women of obscurantist mind," he wrote, and the effort to deny public discussion of the issue showed the weakness of its case. Catholics opposed divorce too, after all, but American lawmakers did not think they needed to abide by "natural law," much less suppress discussion of the topic. Gleefully, this writer noted that the archbishop's failed tactics of suppression had only strengthened Sanger's cause and that, consequently, "the outlook for the birth control movement is brighter than it ever was."[43]

Hayes continued to stand at the center of the birth control movement's spotlight, exhibit A for what, to critics, was so awful about the

Catholic Church: its insistence on "compulsory maternity," its romanticization of suffering and refusal to ameliorate the miseries that followed upon "unregulated breeding," its dogged claims of the "unnaturalness" of contraception, the forced obedience to arbitrary dogma, its reliance on thought control and denial of the right of people to think for themselves, its imposition of sexual abstinence on the priesthood, and its aim of suppressing sexuality writ large among the human population.[44] Sanger's critiques circulated widely as, together, *Woman and the New Race* and *The Pivot of Civilization*—two works that elaborated these claims in detail, along with her own felt persecution at the hands of Catholic leaders—sold 567,000 copies between 1920 and 1926.[45] Catholic leaders had "worked miracles of publicity that would have been impossible to a regiment of press-agents," she later wrote; she reveled in making that point every chance she got.[46]

The First American Birth Control Conference and the Town Hall raid, as it came to be known, launched a decade of tumultuous religious conflict over contraception. Popular support for birth control grew, and many religious leaders sought to clarify, revise, or rethink their positions on contraception. Sanger's own role was never uncontroversial, and many distanced themselves from her more radical pronouncements. But there is little doubt that both her outspokenness and the very fact of having her speech stifled prompted many to reconsider their attitudes no less than it spurred Catholic critics on the other side. American church leaders knew of Sanger's loathing of their patriarchal suppression of women; indeed, their apparent involvement in the Town Hall raid suggested how dangerous Archbishop Hayes feared her to be.

Sanger persistently framed the debate as one about bedrock American values, particularly free speech and American democratic principles of equality. The Catholic Church could preach what it wanted to its own people, but turning doctrine into law was antidemocratic.[47] She berated church authorities in Rome for irresponsibly encouraging the uncontrolled breeding of poor and rich alike, resulting in enormous and interconnected social evils that weakened the nation, such as poverty, prostitution, low wages, child labor, and war. Over and over again, she built on the theme—already developed prior to the conference but immeasurably aided by the Town Hall raid—that Christian hierarchs were mulish obstacles to change who, "for the sake of an outworn dogma of submission," would shamelessly wreck the lives of women by calling on them to "breed, breed, breed" and "condemn their progeny to pain, want, disease and helplessness."[48] The full and equal citizenship of American women, only recently earned at the ballot box, was at stake.

The most important effect of the Town Hall episode, with Sanger's arrest front and center, was that it directly situated sex at the center of a widely publicized and very public debate. Sex itself was a subtext in a much vaster quarrel about the meaning of American ideals. Questions of free speech and democratic deliberation, religious authority and the power of the state, the limits of liberty and women's emancipation: all were now, more explicitly than ever before, linked to publicly disputed norms of sexuality and reproduction. Cherished sexual values were subjected to frank and open examination, if not entirely denuded of euphemism. Sanger's arrest helped her to make not just a *moral* argument for contraception but also a *political* argument for contraception—or at least for the right to talk about it. With this argument, she recast contraception advocacy from something radical into an all-American pursuit, and opposition to birth control as fundamentally anti-American.

The fracas following Town Hall accelerated a war between competing religious authorities and modes of moral advocacy, one that started in high circles of leadership but would soon permeate the pews and disperse widely into the American citizenry. Sanger linked claims about morality and about sex with claims about politics, casting those who disagreed with her about sexual matters as *both* immoral *and* un-American. By doing this so successfully, Sanger—perhaps more than any other figure before or since—drew the battle lines employed by religious and political leaders in the long national war over sex. In years to come, the emerging disagreements between Protestant and Catholic leaders evident during the Town Hall raid controversy would widen. Even as they increasingly diverged and looked on each other with disdain, if not contempt, the Catholic and Protestant views of sex shaped themselves into newly settled dogma.

CATHOLIC OFFICIALS HAD SOUGHT TO quiet Sanger's advocacy of contraception by saying such discussion was inappropriate. Paradoxically, the clergy's efforts to silence her and—when she was not silenced—their subsequent rebuttals of her position actually provoked leaders to speak more loudly about sex than ever before. This was surely an inadvertent effect of the attempt to prevent the Town Hall meeting from taking place, which aimed at ceasing public discussion altogether. After that event, clerical authorities who had worked hard to show that American Catholics were just as virtuous and patriotic as other Americans, found themselves on the defensive in this conflict, and those at the top of the US hierarchy were forced to defend church doctrine to large-scale audiences of often suspicious non-Catholics.

By the early 1920s, after several long waves of European immigration, there were approximately twenty million Catholics in America, comprising about 20 percent of the population. But while Catholic people were very much a minority, the numbers had increased by about eleven million in the past forty years, and the Roman Catholic Church was the largest single religious body in the nation.[49] To many non-Catholics, its political influence was outsized and worrisome, and many feared that Catholics ultimately wanted an American theocracy based on church doctrine. These fears were especially profound in urban areas with large Catholic populations—such as Boston, Chicago, San Francisco, and above all New York, the largest and reputedly wealthiest Catholic archdiocese in the United States at the time—where local bishops could wield tremendous political power.[50]

This was certainly the case with Archbishop Hayes in New York. As a fairly new archbishop in 1921—he had risen to the post in March 1919—Hayes was perhaps best known as one of the creators of the National Catholic War Council (NCWC), the first permanent organization of Catholic bishops throughout the country (later renamed the National Catholic Welfare Conference). In this role, Hayes was one of the four American Catholic bishops who signed the progressive "Program of Social Reconstruction," written by John Ryan. For leaders like these, birth control was the very opposite of a social justice issue: as Ryan wrote in a scathing letter to one birth control proponent who had the audacity to solicit him for money and membership in the American Birth Control League, "I had much rather give the money to an organization for the training of prize-fighters. It would aid in the development of at least *some* manly and human qualities."[51] Fighting birth control was a fight for the poor, as they saw it; and they surely resented the fact that Sanger and her allies had framed the Catholic position in such different, wholly negative terms—as an authoritarian grab for power and the wholesale repression of women's rights.

In a public statement outlining his opposition both to the conference's public forum and to birth control more generally, Archbishop Hayes spoke as "a citizen and a churchman, deeply concerned with the moral well-being of our city," and he argued that his "protest against the use of the open forum for the propaganda of birth control" was in no way sectarian but for the welfare of the larger public. Hayes declared that he spoke for nearly a million American women, not counting the "thousands of other indignant women and distressed mothers" who were shocked by the public discussion of "a subject that simple prudence and decency . . . should keep within the walls of a clinic." But like Ryan, he also showed agreement with some of the eugenic appeals of birth control, adducing evidence from those he deemed "distinguished scientists" concerned to head off "the impending deterioration of the race." Hayes cited the recent New York meeting of the International Congress of Eugenics for its emphasis, "if the race was to be better born," on such goods as monogamous marriage, "more children in the families of the well-to-do as a moral duty," and "better safeguards against the marriage of imbeciles and insane."[52] Far from refuting any of this eugenic language of a "better born" race, Hayes concluded, "Human experience confirms all this." His conclusion made a similar appeal to nativist, eugenic fears of the demise of the American (white) race, particularly the upper classes: "May Divine Providence inspire America to fix its canon against self-slaughter at the very source of human life, lest the sacred and highest end of the family— mother and child—vanish from our homes, and the stranger, alien to the American ideal, who, however, obeyed God's command to increase and multiply, enter to possess the land."[53]

Catholic teaching staunchly opposed basic assumptions of the birth control movement, and Catholic leaders at this time sought to refute what they deemed Sanger's malicious misrepresentations of their moral priorities. According to Catholic doctrine, contraception distorted God's plan for a holy Christian marriage by interfering with the sexual act between husband and wife and preventing the natural possibility of conception. That teaching was simply nonnegotiable (outside of what would later be termed the "rhythm method"). Catholic leaders also opposed the movement's advocacy of women's freedom to own and control their bodies. To traditional Catholics, women did have a moral duty to preserve and uphold traditional values; they were not supposed to create a "new sex morality" quite distinct from church teaching, as Sanger would have it.[54] Feminine submission in marriage and motherhood (or, alternately, in the chasteness of the convent) was a divine duty, not a relic of the past. Moreover, just because the clergy forbade birth control did not mean the church was imprisoning its own people by means of fear, ignorance, and a merciless doctrine of submission to authoritarian leadership. Church leaders understood the ideas they were up against in terms of the very definition of womanhood which the birth control movement threatened to upend.

While the Catholic position did not exactly harden, in this climate it gathered passionate intensity for a robust defense. Reasonably enough, Catholic leaders took full advantage of the birth controllers' anti-Catholic rhetoric for their own ends. As they worked to stoke lay Catholic indignation at Sanger's persistent ill treatment of them, they harnessed that anger for the cause of sexual morality. A 1923 article by Paulist father J. Elliot Ross, published in the popular *Catholic World*, was typical. Ross, citing Tertullian to the effect that "The blood of the martyrs is the seed of new Christians," consoled readers that "persecution is good for the Church." That apparently universal truth boded well in the present context, since, Ross noted, a "bitter campaign of vilification" against Catholics was raging. For over a year, accounts had been coming in of anti-Catholic discrimination: public schools were terminating Catholic teachers, for instance, and it seemed to some as if a wholesale Protestant boycott against Catholics were being waged. Formerly lax and lukewarm

Catholics were not only now shoring up their faith and renewing their interest in the church but growing more activist on the issue of birth control. "Persecution brings out a latent faith," Ross assured readers, "just as war brings out a latent patriotism." And not only that: the anti-Catholic campaign had drawn in many non-Catholics as well. Ross concluded on a gleeful if bloodthirsty note: "If they would only be goaded into giving us a few real martyrs, if they would actually kill a few Catholics because they were Catholics, converts would roll in like a great tidal wave."[55]

Less than two and a half years after the First American Birth Control Conference, on March 24, 1924, Archbishop Hayes rose to the rank of cardinal. The Vatican appointment seemed clearly indicative of Rome's approval of Hayes's public defense of the faith against the sort of emancipatory freethinking agenda represented by Sanger. An apparent favorite of Pope Pius XI—a writer for *Time* magazine in 1935 noted that the pope called him *caro fratello* ("dear little brother")—Hayes remained in that post for the rest of his life, mostly refraining from the sort of public confrontation he had earlier executed with Sanger.[56] But he did speak out against birth control when he deemed it necessary, as when he deduced non-Catholics were once again misrepresenting the Catholic position and delivered a sermon at St. Patrick's Cathedral emphasizing his regret and uncomfortable embarrassment at addressing this subject "to good, clean people like you." Nonetheless, the "Prophets of Decadence" were loudly preaching this "perversion" of the reproductive faculty, and therefore it was "impossible for me to remain silent."[57]

It is no small irony that what spurred Catholic leaders to speak more directly and vigorously in public about contraception than they had likely ever done before was Sanger's activism. Later observers have agreed that Sanger had greater success than church leaders in informing Catholics of their own church's position on contraception. And since it was untenable to allow her such leeway to educate their flocks, Sanger and the birth control movement forced Catholics to speak when they, like Hayes, may have wished to remain silent. That is, while Catholic leaders would say that American culture was changing (and declining) while the church remained a fortress of natural, long-promulgated law, Sanger herself in fact *impelled* the church to speak loudly about sex.

And not only loudly: later observers would note that it was largely due to Sanger's public notoriety and activism that the Catholic Church developed its stance into an inflexible position that ultimately "eviscerated nuance," as one put it: a refusal to differentiate between beliefs about natural law, human life, God's authority over sex, and the value of suffering compressed these into "a tightly woven rhetorical package," such that Catholics "lumped contraception, forced sterilization, euthanasia, and abortion into the same abhorrent category."[58] By this logic, access to contraceptives was basically equivalent to these other evils, and allowing it led to what editors at the Catholic periodical *Commonweal* warned would be "the ultimate destruction of human liberty at the hands of an absolute pagan state."[59] This equivalency position, with its dire political overtones, was a position that many outside the church increasingly found inexplicable, rigid, and antiquated. That seemingly inflexible Catholic standpoint combined with the fame that rapidly accrued to Sanger in the wake of the First American Birth Control Conference essentially transformed the feminist leader into one of the most famous and effective activists in the nation's history.[60]

In February 1926, the director and executive secretary of Sanger's American Birth Control League, Anne Kennedy, had a private meeting with Patrick J. Ward, who was employed by the National Catholic Welfare Conference. That "unlikely political encounter," as one expert called it, revealed the "widening gulf between Catholic and Protestant perspectives on marriage" less than five years after Sanger's ouster from the Town Hall stage. In an urgent memorandum to his superior, Father John Burke, concerning this meeting, Ward first dismissively listed Kennedy's reasons for favoring birth control. "Little new in her statement of the case. Advanced the usual stock arguments of economic conditions, being practical, spacing children, mothers' health, the right of people to ask and physicians to give medical information, etc., etc." Plainly, the "stock arguments" of Kennedy and Sanger carried no weight with Ward or his priestly leader.[61]

Then Ward got to the real shocker:

She holds that aside from the propagation of children, the sexual act has of itself a spiritual and uplifting (!) value which it was intended

to have by the Creator. It is an expression of supreme attachment
and the unity of two beings. It can therefore be indulged in not only
legitimately but is a help in our spiritual progress, apart altogether
from its use to bring a child into the world. For this reason science
is helping man in his spiritual progress by putting into his hands
means more hygienic and prophylactic than heretofore used. . . . I
told Mrs. Kennedy the so called spiritual value she was putting on
the sexual act was a purely emotional and sensual one. The spirituality of the act lay *solely* in the knowledge and in the disposition at
the moment of conception that a human being was being brought
into existence endowed with a soul in God's image and likeness, and
which it was God's intention should one day return to Him to enjoy
eternal bliss.[62]

The parenthetical exclamation point accented how absurd the Catholic
hierarchy found the suggestion that sex might be a wholesome act even if
conception did not occur.

But "the most important result" of this meeting, in Ward's terms,
was Kennedy's disclosure that the American Birth Control League was
"considering *Federal legislation* to allow doctors to give contraceptive advice" (emphasis in original) and, still more, to distribute and sell contraceptive devices obtained directly from manufacturers. Coming efforts to
change American laws pertaining to birth control would pose a whole
new host of challenges to a church that had been compelled to take a
more public stance on contraception, for in light of such legal challenges
Catholics found themselves entangled in national political debates on intimate sexual matters. The tides were shifting on women's roles and the
regulation of sex, thanks in no small part to Sanger, the woman once baptized Roman Catholic, and American Catholic leaders felt duty-bound to
speak out politically like never before.[63]

PROTESTANTS, TOO, WERE TRANSFORMED BY Sanger and the birth control movement, particularly as a result of the Town Hall raid. Sanger had
opened a door to church leaders in her final speech, when she asked them

Sanger has her mouth bound as a protest against not
being allowed to discuss birth control, Boston, 1929.
BETTMANN VIA GETTY IMAGES.

to "have more confidence in women." That invitation was tinged with a
taunt, of sorts—"If we cannot trust woman with the knowledge of her
own body, then I claim that two thousand years of Christian teaching has
proved to be a failure"—but she held fast in her hope that some church
leaders saw it her way and would work collaboratively with her movement.[64] That hope bore fruit—for whatever ambivalence toward contraception remained prior to the Town Hall raid, Protestant acceptance of
birth control coalesced quickly and dramatically during the 1920s.

    Fear of Catholicism was an important factor enabling Sanger's
rapid and far-reaching success among Protestants. Aided by the associations between Catholic authoritarianism and anti-Americanism, and
by widespread indignation that a celibate clergy would dare to halt even
discussion of contraception in a democratic society, Sanger exploited
anti-Catholicism to secure Protestant support. She worked diligently,

often behind the scenes, to reach out and secure greater openness on the part of Protestant leaders toward birth control—and toward sexuality more broadly. However little stock she may have put in the religious arguments about morality that occupied Protestant clergy and church committees grappling with the subject, Sanger understood the importance of securing Protestants as allies. And she continued, in this endeavor, to make the most of the strategic usefulness attached to anti-Catholicism.

One of Sanger's allies, the Anglican priest William R. Inge, dean of St. Paul's Cathedral in London, elaborated this view of the Protestant-Catholic contrast with particular disdain. In a 1923 *Atlantic Monthly* essay, revealingly titled "Catholic Church and Anglo-Saxon Mind," Inge sought to explain precisely what distinguished Protestantism from Catholicism. All sorts of racial presumptions pervaded the article (submissive Poles, Irish, and Mediterraneans versus the hard-working Nordics), but Inge's chief point was to show that the Catholic Church "has steadily developed, in accordance with the inner logic of its principles, into an autocratic, militant empire claiming universal sovereignty." The fatal flaw was indelible and permanent, as the very notion of independence, to Inge, was "absolutely irreconcilable with Catholicism." Inge went on to make typical claims about Catholics being more loyal to church teaching than to their own nation (describing the church as "a powerful solvent of state loyalty").[65] Ultimately, the Vatican was "anti-democratic," Inge noted; there was no room for any notion of progress, and the best thinkers of modern times were "banned as poisonous." In short, "the Catholic universe of truth is static." Inge's unforgiving conclusion was that Catholicism, despite its "numerous and potent . . . attractions" for masses of people, was "an imposture." Protestantism, by contrast, was "the religion of the genuinely modern culture, the civilization of experimental science and hopeful political experiments." Protestantism did not merely accept but openly welcomed the advances of "philosophy, Biblical criticism, and natural science," making it ultimately "the form of religion which is homogenous with and adapted to modern civilization." Inge spoke for many birth control supporters in condemning Catholicism as, at base, anti-American.[66]

While Protestant anti-Catholicism played a significant role in the Protestant acceptance of birth control, animus toward Catholics was not the only, or even the most important, factor. As Inge suggested, the Protestant position on birth control followed an internal modernist logic consistent with a progressive position on a number of other issues in American society, including the teaching of Darwinian evolution and the publication of literature formerly deemed obscene. Progress appeared inevitable and largely good; knowledge led to illumination and the betterment of society; independence of thought and intellectual freedom were absolutely essential to true understanding and development, and antithetical to self-appointed authorities. These were some of the positive grounds on which Protestants could base their support for birth control access as well as critique the Catholic Church. Protestants knew that the Catholic hierarchy was insistently anti-Protestant and had been since the Protestant Reformation of the sixteenth century. If American Protestants were open about voicing their own anti-Catholicism, it was within a much longer context of vocal conflict and dissent.

Among white Protestant clerics, Sanger scored a major victory in March 1925, at the Sixth International neo-Malthusian and Birth Control Conference held at the Hotel McAlpin in New York. There, after a session on the religious and ethical dimensions of birth control, a number of Protestant and Jewish clergy—the Protestants including Episcopalian, Congregational, Unitarian, and Baptist ministers—endorsed birth control, passing a resolution calling on churches to support it as "a moral and religious duty for the betterment of the human race and the establishment of the Kingdom of God among men." Rabbi Stephen Wise of the Free Synagogue gave a vigorous defense of the movement, noting that a child's life was so sacred that it should only be brought forth if society could give it "fair opportunity to find its highest service." The Reverend Dr. Charles Francis Potter, a Unitarian, called birth control "the greatest moral issue before the church today" and urgently advocated for the open distribution of technical knowledge as an antidote to immorality, insisting that even if knowledge led some into sin, the greater harm was the suffering caused by ignorance—a sign that the very definition of "immorality" was shifting. The Reverend Potter showed himself to be partisan to the eugenic side of the movement as well, insisting upon the Christian duty to stave off the births of the "unfit."[67] The topics of these and the other clergy talks varied, but the general message endorsed birth control on the grounds that it would promote monogamy, morality, peace, and health. Perhaps it was the resonance of this message that inspired Sanger to appeal to Protestants' deepest ideals for Christian life in a book she published the following year: *Happiness in Marriage* was a paean to the institution and a guide for ensuring that sex between a married couple was not solely meant for procreation but was a sacred experience.

By 1927, one of the nation's most prominent liberal Protestant clergymen, Harry Emerson Fosdick, was widely known as supporting birth control. He had first gained national renown with his 1922 sermon "Shall the Fundamentalists Win?," which criticized fundamentalist intolerance and called for a model of "Christian fellowship" defined as "intellectually hospitable, open-minded, liberty-loving, fair, tolerant."[68] Five years later, and fourteen months after his appointment as the pastor of New York's Park Avenue Baptist Church (the church of John D. Rockefeller Jr., which would shortly move to Riverside Drive), Fosdick delivered an explicitly pro-contraception sermon that received wide media coverage. Fosdick cited overpopulation as his main rationale for favoring birth control, while asserting the need for sexual self-control and ridiculing the "new freedom" of sexual expressionism that undercut monogamy.[69] Fosdick's sermon—along with a 1929 article, "Religion and Birth Control," which received wide distribution and circulation when Sanger's newly formed National Committee on Federal Legislation for Birth Control (NC-FLBC) reprinted it as a pamphlet—perfectly encapsulated the grounds on which religious leaders were willing to support the birth control cause, none more important than strengthening marriage.[70] Indeed, as one historian has noted, it was marriage itself that gave Protestant clergy an "existential opening to other-than-absolutist views on marital contraception," differentiating themselves sharply from Catholics.[71]

The NCFLBC aimed to generate a national lobbying effort to convince members of Congress to amend the federal laws that still listed contraceptive information and devices as obscene and forbade their transmittal through the postal service. Sanger knew that Protestant leaders and their denominations were a crucial constituency that needed to be lobbied, and she did so with gusto, attending countless church conventions in order to reach religious leaders directly and corresponding regularly with them by mail, as she urged them to reach out to fellow ministers within their own denominations. Although her legislative goals were not quickly met, her extensive efforts with clergy bore much fruit among religious communities.

A number of Protestant leaders interacted with Sanger behind the scenes. For instance, in April 1929, the Unitarian John Haynes Holmes, minister of the Community Church of New York, initiated a correspondence with Sanger that would last several years. It began with Holmes offering his support in the wake of a recent raid upon Sanger's clinic, "a perfectly outrageous affair" that Holmes believed was initiated by "the same old benighted forces" she had long fought.[72] Sanger thanked Holmes for his offer to help, and by September 1930 he was serving as vice chair of the eastern district of the National Committee on Federal Legislation for Birth Control. She spoke at Holmes's church on more than one occasion and wrote a short blurb to honor his twenty-fifth anniversary in the church's ministry in 1932; in between, Holmes actively supported Massachusetts senator Frederick Gillett's bill to remove significant federal restrictions on physicians' ability to distribute contraception. As their warm correspondence shows, Sanger and Holmes worked collaboratively on several fronts to persuade others of the rightness of the birth control cause.[73] Protestant denominations began taking a stand in favor of her committee's bill to repeal the Comstock law.

Sanger was gaining allies not only among white Protestants but among African Americans as well, including religious leaders. During the 1920s, coverage of Sanger's campaign in the black press was overwhelmingly positive, as black writers editorialized about the positive gains to be made from the birth control movement. In February 1923, a writer for the Baltimore-based *Afro-American*, a black-owned-and-operated newspaper, remarked approvingly on Sanger's recent visit to Baltimore and noted that the government must either permit women to obtain contraceptive knowledge or set aside funds to aid their children. Two years later, William N. Jones, in his regular column for the *Afro-American*, wrote of the progress to be wrought from the movement's promotion of "the deeper meaning of the marriage vow in future children." A few years later, the paper transcribed the entire commencement address delivered by Dr. Adam Clayton Powell of New York's Abyssinian Baptist Church to Nannie Helen Burroughs's National Training School for Women and Girls in Washington, DC, where he quoted Margaret Sanger's words in a recent address: "'Supreme happiness does not consist in seeking one's own pleasures, but in working for the good of others.'"[74]

Glowing articles in New York's major African American newspaper, the *Amsterdam News*, accompanied a lecture by Sanger at the 135th Street branch of the New York Public Library, sponsored by the North Harlem Community Forum. The coverage focused again on the divide between what Sanger termed "two classes" of American women: "those who have birth control and those who have not"—rich and poor. Enthusiasm accompanied Sanger's hope of establishing a birth control clinic in Harlem, and in October 1929, the social workers of Harlem, meeting at the New York Urban League headquarters, voted to endorse the plan after a persuasive speech by Sanger insisting that birth control "reduces both infant and maternal mortality," improves "the health of the mother," and raises "the economic condition of the entire family." When the newly established birth control clinic in Harlem held its official "house warming" in November 1930, the featured speakers included no less than the revered African American intellectual leader Dr. W. E. B. Du Bois and the Harlem Hospital surgeon Dr. Louis T. Wright, along with prominent black clergy: Shelton Hale Bishop of Harlem's St. Philip's Episcopal Church (the second-oldest black Episcopal congregation), Floarda Howard of St. Jude's Chapel (also Episcopalian), and Willard Monroe of Memorial Baptist Church. According to the *Amsterdam News*, "they all welcomed the establishment of such a center in Harlem," and their support of Sanger's work would long continue. In her column for the paper, "The Feminist Viewpoint," Thelma Berlack Boozer praised Sanger and recommended the recent "Negro number" (a special issue focused on issues facing African Americans) of the American Birth Control League's *Birth Control Review*, praising the league's position that federal law should legalize birth control. Birth control was necessary, Boozer insisted, in order to solve the nation's poverty and attendant ills.[75]

As time went on, not all coverage in the African American press was positive. In 1934, Cornelius Scott's *Atlanta Daily World* rebuked Sanger and her movement for interfering with "God's law and His plans" and lamented the selfishness of modern women who would shirk their homemaking role.[76] Another negative reaction to the movement would grow among African Americans suspicious that the birth control campaign targeted blacks and was a surreptitious method of genocide. But even when her support for negative eugenics was pronounced, she made clear that the targets were "the mental defectives, the morons and those with transmissible diseases" and not racial groups, as she told an undergraduate interviewing her for the Yale University newspaper in 1934.[77] Sanger condemned racism on numerous occasions and told Earl Conrad of the *Chicago Defender*, "The Negro's plight here is linked with that of the oppressed around the globe." With her message that birth control aided in dismantling racism by placing greater value on each human life, Sanger consistently had the support of many African American leaders, including clergy. The Reverend Martin Luther King Jr. would eventually become an ally of the birth control movement, accepting Planned Parenthood's Margaret Sanger award by proclaiming the importance of family planning to white and black Americans alike: "Together we can and should unite our strength for the wise preservation, not of races in general, but of the one race we all constitute—the human race."[78]

The Christian leaders, black and white, who supported Sanger in the 1920s counted on her defense of traditional marriage. As a sex reformer who needed to secure deep support for her cause from religious allies, Sanger adopted a pose of conventional morality in her prescriptive writing, one she did not always live out in her private life. She believed that it was necessary to speak to potentially sympathetic constituencies in terms and values with which they identified. In this case, marriage and the family were major points on which she connected with many supporters; after all, she too had married and lived the domestic life (though eventually divorced), and she too was a mother. Church leaders' attempt to reconcile support for contraception with a continued defense of traditional marriage would soon come under fire from conservative

Protestants who saw the two as incompatible. But leaders increasingly saw support for contraception as a necessary engagement with modern realities. Whatever remnants of hesitation lurked in the hearts of Protestant leaders in 1921 about the need for substantial change regarding birth control virtually evaporated in subsequent years.

BY THE END OF THIS tumultuous decade, the polarization over birth control within American Christianity had noticeably intensified. The divergence was evident in three documents on contraception issued in close proximity to each other—one Anglican (important and influential for the Episcopal Church in the United States, and broader American Christian debates as well), one Roman Catholic, and one American Protestant. Together, these revealed much about the deepening gulf among Christians and how these groups faced the dilemma of shifting societal views on sex and gender. While Anglicans made minute but discernible adjustment to conservative principles, Catholics responded with determined retrenchment against shifting values, and American Protestants with outright acceptance of, and adjustment to, modern realities. None of these positions was without controversy. The Protestant documents generated internal disagreement during the process of their creation—there were dissenting votes on both—and all three prompted substantial conflict among American religious leaders and church members. But they did indicate the broad contours of the increasingly divided landscape.

The Anglican statement emerged out of the seventh decanal Lambeth Conference—a global convening of Anglican bishops and other church leaders to discuss matters of Christian import and offer guiding principles—which took place in August 1930. The body passed a total of seventy-five resolutions apropos various doctrinal and logistical matters, declarations that were not binding (as no Lambeth resolutions could be) but carried moral weight and influenced many American Protestants both among and beyond America's Episcopal elite. A number of these focused on marriage and sexuality. Resolution 13, for instance, affirmed the sexual instinct as holy and divinely implanted in human nature and acknowledged the bonding function of sexual intercourse in marriage.

Resolution 16 condemned abortion as an abhorrent, sinful practice. Reaping nearly all the attention in the conference's wake, however, was Resolution 15, which argued that any "clearly felt moral obligation to limit or avoid parenthood" should follow a Christian method, the most obvious of which was total abstinence from sexual intercourse. Only when there was a "morally sound reason for avoiding complete abstinence" could other methods be used. The resolution roundly denounced the act of preventing conception, whatever the method, arising from "motives of selfishness, luxury, or mere convenience."[79] But it explicitly suggested that contraceptive methods other than abstinence did have an acceptable use, and in this, it went squarely against the 1920 Lambeth Conference, whose leaders had warned emphatically against artificial means of contraception no matter the circumstances. The change in Anglican teachings on contraception was not universally embraced. Nearly a quarter of the bishops present at Lambeth in 1930 rejected this particular resolution (193 voted for it, 67 against), and the resolution prompted a firestorm throughout the international Anglican communion, including the Episcopal Church in the United States.

Traditionalists criticized the Lambeth resolution as vague (what constituted "a morally sound reason" for eschewing abstinence?) and confused (why was abstinence so praised in a document commending contraception?), and they condemned the apparently sudden departure from doctrinal convention that disapproved of all unnatural barriers to conception. The most caustic critics understood the document to be opening the door to chaotic disruptions in Christian thinking about sex. The renowned poet and social critic T. S. Eliot (a convert to Anglicanism from Unitarianism) published a rebuttal that scathingly disparaged the statement's excessive reliance on the individual conscience at the expense of seeking spiritual counsel from the clergy.[80] In a thoroughgoing defense of traditional Christian sexual morality, the Welsh historian and government administrator J. Conway Davies argued against dislocating the sexual relationship from its biological function, raging that the Lambeth bishops were trying to intermix a Christian view of sex with a radically distinct notion of sex as "soul-union." The latter view, exemplified in the British writers Edward Carpenter and D. H. Lawrence (not to mention

Sanger herself), promoted sexual love as what Davies belittled as "an act of practical Mysticism." The Lambeth bishops, Davies argued, had ultimately forsaken Paul and Augustine for Carpenter and Lawrence, Sigmund Freud, and the birth controllers, succumbing to thinly evidenced psychology that attributed modern neurosis to sexual problems rather than to sin and spiritual malaise.[81]

Such acid evaluations made clear that birth control—more precisely, the pagan, mystical, romantic, and ostensibly selfish assumptions that justified its use—led inexorably to "feminine revolt," and to the destruction of family and society. In opening the door to contraception, claimed critics, the bishops amended two centuries of traditional teachings on human nature, gender, virginity, and the role of the church in society as well as individual salvation, presenting a "Reduced Christianity." Now, Davies concluded in despair, "in contrast to the great Pauline utterances on the warfare between flesh and spirit, we are given a set of side-long glances at some modern problems, concluding to a prudent and circumspect muffling of the drums."[82] No matter that the bishops had meant to strengthen marriage and the family by cracking the door open to contraception. Birth control was not a humane response to practical problems; it was a warhead annihilating the traditional meaning of sex both inside and outside marriage (since birth control information could not easily be restricted to married couples). From this perspective, the Lambeth document marked a wholesale revolution in long-established Christian thinking about crucial issues of body and soul, gender and power, and the hierarchical relation between male and female.

Four months after the release of the Lambeth documents, and with many Anglican elites still up in arms, the leadership of the Roman Catholic Church clarified its own position on birth control. Pope Pius XI elucidated the church's condemnation of contraception in the papal encyclical *Casti Connubii* (*Of Chaste Wedlock*), released on December 31, 1930. Along with its affirmation of the unchanging nature of the moral law and Catholic teaching, the encyclical directly criticized those—the Anglican bishops, that is—who adjusted their stance for rashly departing from centuries of Christian doctrine. The document also affirmed the sanctity of marriage as an indissoluble union and offered strong censure of divorce and abortion, and it charged priests to do everything possible to enforce these moral teachings among lay Catholics. *Casti Connubii* underlined the importance of women's homemaking role and summoned wives to be obedient to their husbands, holding fast to traditional gender roles and meanings of sexuality as divinely ordained. All of these teachings, the text insisted, were part of a timeless, seamless, God-ordained whole.

While the document strongly reiterated the teaching that the primary end of intercourse was procreation, it recognized "secondary ends" that were not prohibited so long as the act remained "natural"—that is, open to the possibility of procreation. Such secondary ends included marital love, a theme that Catholics were not accustomed to hearing much about from official Catholic teaching. *Casti Connubii* also appeared to acknowledge (if somewhat obscurely and not certainly) the acceptability, so long as one did not reject parenthood outright, of intentionally avoiding intercourse during the fertile days of the wife's menstrual cycle, presumably a licit way to forestall pregnancy through timed abstinence (what would come to be called the "rhythm method"). Nonetheless, this was an encyclical that bolstered existing church doctrine and sought to ensure that Catholics did not go the way of the Lambeth innovators. The Vatican statement was a sharp rebuke to Anglican leaders who had broached the possibility of "Christian" methods of contraception other than abstinence—and a dire warning to any others who might be tempted to follow.

Four more months passed before the third significant religious document emerged, this one from American Protestant leaders. The US press had given extensive coverage to both the Lambeth document and *Casti Connubii*; both were closely studied by leaders of the Protestant denominations affiliated with the Federal Council of the Churches of Christ in America (FCC), a body that claimed to represent between twenty-one and twenty-two million Protestant church members in the United States. After years of political wrangling over birth control and extensive efforts by Sanger's office to lobby church officials, it was time for Protestants to decide where they stood.

Shortly after Lambeth sanctioned birth control in limited circumstances, the FCC formed a Committee on Marriage and the Home for the purpose of rethinking its own position. Universalists, Unitarians, and Reform Jews had already clarified their support for contraception; from one angle, then, the choice facing the Protestant representatives was between standing with the traditionalist Catholic hierarchy and the Anglicans or with those religionists who had already adopted a more liberal view.[83] Views were mixed, to say the least: the House of Bishops in the Protestant Episcopal Church had spoken out against birth control in 1925, but some clergy were shifting their views on the subject, as were leaders in other denominations. Chaired by the Reverend Howard C. Robbins, the former dean of the Cathedral of St. John the Divine, and comprising a total of seventeen men and eleven women as signatories, the FCC committee issued a statement in April 1931 that received wide attention, including a report on the front page of the *New York Times*. The report showed a majority of committee members accepting birth control within marriage as "valid and moral" and as insisting that "this undoubtedly represents the prevailing Protestant point of view"; a small minority (three out of twenty-eight) claimed that the morality of contraception remained in doubt and that Christians ought to "uphold the standard of abstinence as the ideal" without recommending artificial methods.

Those committee members who endorsed the moral validity of "the careful and restrained use of contraceptives by married people" reasoned that such use allowed for the appropriate spacing of children and control of family size, protected mothers and children from undue travails and poverty, and acknowledged the inherent goodness of intercourse as an expression of a married couple's spiritual union and love. Admitting the possibility of an increase in such evils as adultery as a result of contraceptive knowledge, the signatories further urged church, society, and parents to educate and instill morals into the nation's youth, so that this new knowledge would be used for good rather than for ill. The dissenters, including the committee chair and two of its female members (Mrs. Orrin R. Judd, a Baptist and the president of the Council of Women for Home Missions, and Emma Bailey Spear, a Presbyterian and president of the board of the Young Women's Christian Association), accepted the goodness of sex in marriage but held fast to abstinence as the only moral method of preventing conception.[84]

But the FCC committee's disagreements were far less consequential than the points on which it agreed. The FCC committee took pains to explicate the two amazing "mysteries" that were at stake when it came to marital sex and contraception. The first and more obvious, in the context of the period's discussions of birth control, was the creation, with God, of new and precious human life and the resulting experience of parenthood. And if it sounded traditionalist to describe the mother role as the highest realization of womanhood, the statement as plainly called the father role the supreme fulfillment of manhood. The egalitarian note struck by the equation of fatherhood and motherhood continued in the second mystery, which was the divine meaning of sex between married partners as the "supreme expression of their affection and comradeship" and a "manifestation of divine concern" for their joy—literally, a gift from God to reward their faithfulness. Committee members wanted it to be understood that, despite their disagreement on the single issue of artificial contraceptive methods, there was overall agreement that sex in marriage was good and holy quite apart from its procreative potential. Keeping desire within bounds was essential, the statement warned, in order to maintain this holiness and avoid "sex indulgence," just as one would avoid excess in other appetites. But the statement's bold emphasis on the sacred goodness of marital intercourse—stated in plain language, without qualification—was a significant development in American Protestant discussions of sex.[85]

Praise for the FCC report was soon forthcoming. The prominent Congregationalist minister Russell J. Clinchy's defense of it appeared in the *Washington Daily News* (alongside an opposing piece by the Catholic priest Francis J. Hurney) and again in a prominent Congregationalist journal. Calling the report "a wise, balanced and scientific study of the physical, mental and spiritual factors of birth control," the progressive Clinchy praised the authors for "commend[ing] the judicious, scientific and ethical use of methods of contraception for medical, eugenic and moral purposes." He struck a robustly feminist note in emphasizing the health and well-being of the mother, insisting that a woman's "prime function" was "not as a breeder of children" but as a "spiritual personality," a "daughter of God" who should not be coerced into motherhood. The notion of a woman's God-given right to control her own reproductive life could hardly acquire a more forceful defense. Clinchy also defended contraception on the grounds of children's rights to be cared for before other children are conceived, and on its support for the happiness and lasting love of the married couple. Excessive sexual continence was "both undesirable and impossible" to couples who truly loved each other. Scientific birth control was, therefore, valid for reasons spanning a range of virtues. Clinchy imagined his audience as a like-minded group of "moral optimists" who would agree that most people would use this new technology for good, rather than for ill, and that contraception was an instrument of progress that could usher in a happier, healthier world. For those, like Catholics, who believed that this new control over reproduction was "of the devil" and had only carnal implications, "it will be the opening of the gates of death." But for those who believed this new power was "of God," it would bring a new era of life and love. Clinchy articulated, as well as any Protestant, the hopeful future to be sought through the liberation of married sexual love via birth control.[86]

The FCC report attracted reproach as well. *Commonweal* excoriated it in an editorial. Analyzing the report for an ethics course during his fellowship year at Union Theological Seminary, the young German theologian Dietrich Bonhoeffer wrote sourly in his notes about the American Protestant turn toward the ethical, "since the dogmatic is no longer understood by Protestants," the birth control report being one more example of the American indifference to true theology.[87] The American document sparked tremendous controversy among Protestant detractors, so much so that members of the FCC spent two years fighting over it before finally laying it aside without endorsement.

The report had a massive influence nonetheless, suggesting why Sanger had worked so hard to shape it. It was both a bellwether of change and a spur to public discussion, and it was crucially shaped by Sanger's intensive work with FCC clergy. Without acknowledging her own role in its creation (which could have been deadly to some clergy whose constituents were skeptical of Sanger), she roundly praised its emphasis on birth control as a perfectly moral way to promote women's health and family happiness, and she maintained, as a newspaper headline put it shortly afterward, "It's What I'd Have Written Myself."

Protestants of this period who were increasingly accepting of birth control typically held what one historian has described as "a curious mixture of liberal and conservative views on contraception." The "liberal" elements in Protestant acceptance of birth control included a positive view toward science and medical opinion (much of which was on contraception's side), a focus on the laity and interest in ordinary people's experience, an interest in privacy, an emphasis on individual rights (including the rights of women and children), a romantic sense of sexuality that interpreted human sexual intercourse as a spiritual experience, and an optimism that rightly educated people would mostly choose to be moral. The "conservative" elements that blended with these ideas were, chiefly, a concern with marriage between one man and one woman as the bedrock of civilization, a profound concern for social order and stability (hence the appeal of eugenics), a positive view of the self-control necessary to all human social relations, and an interest in holding on to important aspects of tradition even as times were changing.[88] That mix was essential for persuading a wide range of Christians that contraceptive advocacy was contrary neither to their faith nor to fundamental American values.

Sanger's cooperation with clergy continued after the report was issued, and the FCC found itself in need of her help. Amid the controversy over the report, a high-ranking FCC administrator, Worth M. Tippy, wrote a worried letter to Sanger noting that the birth control statement had "aroused more opposition within the Protestant churches than we had expected" and that some churches were dissociating themselves altogether from the FCC. Tippy asked her for names of wealthy birth control supporters from whom he could appeal for money, adding, "I assume that you would not want your name used in any such appeals." Sanger scribbled a note on the letter that she would "help in every way *gladly*," and her formal response affirmed that she was "grieved" by this opposition, would eagerly send names to help the FCC, and had "no objection whatsoever to your using my name in any way possible if it will be of help to you." She continued, "I admire so tremendously the courage the Federal Council has had in taking up this subject that I want to help in every way possible to strengthen your hand and I know that there are hundreds of others who feel the same way." Tippy regularly came back to Sanger with specific monetary amounts he needed and begged for her further assistance, which she regularly gave, including contributions from her own funds.[89] The money she helped raise even paid for the hiring of a new administrator, L. Foster Wood, whose work appeared to focus entirely on educating churches for birth control. Sanger periodically reached out to supporters, such as the wealthy banker and philanthropist George Blumenthal, to help pay Wood's salary and the budget for his work.[90] Keeping careful track of donor names and contributions—and making clear that she expected her investment to reap real results in terms of support for the birth control movement—Sanger helped the FCC financially in this way for a number of years to come, helping it to survive the loss of support from conservative Protestants.

Hence the Federal Council of Churches continued on a steady course in a progressive direction on birth control and sex more generally, despite the growing complaints of some conservative members. In 1932, its Committee on Marriage and the Home compiled and published what it titled *A Bibliography on Young People's Relationships, Marriage and Family Life*, a twenty-three-page annotated list of recommended books in this area. While most titles focused on subjects such as parenting, instilling religious values in children, health, and "mental hygiene," a good number of the sources had something to do with sex: for instance, *Parents and Sex Education*, by science writer and educator B. C. Gruenberg; *The Sexual Side of Marriage*, by physician M. J. Exner; and *The Sex Life of Youth*, by Grace Loucks Elliott and Harry Bone. Another typical title was *Young People's Relationships*, a pamphlet manual for church leaders of young people ages sixteen to nineteen, penned by Benjamin S. Winchester for the FCC's Conference on Preparation for Marriage and Homemaking.[91]

Winchester's pamphlet played a small but telling role in the growing opposition of the conservative Protestant camp to the changes that were afoot in mainline Protestantism in the wake of the twin movements for women's rights and birth control access. A fundamentalist weekly, the *Sunday School Times*, became a frequent critic of the FCC while under the editorship of Charles Gallaudet Trumbull, who nineteen years earlier had written a heroic biography of Anthony Comstock. In August 1932, an uncredited writer for the paper lambasted Winchester's publication as "vile" for discussing such topics as dancing, "petting," and the possible naturalness of "the sex impulse"; the writer also approvingly cited a Southern Presbyterian missive associating the FCC with "sex filth" and a Northern Presbyterian dissenter reacting with disgust to the FCC because of "the horrible birth-control scandal of last year." While the fundamentalists echoed the Catholics in opposing contraception, they were also critical of Catholicism: in the same issue, for instance, a writer denounced "the sensuous charm of the great cathedrals of Roman Catholicism, enslaving mortal souls by pagan rites rendered alluringly beautiful" and the "cheap and tawdry idolatry of this great apostate church."[92] Catholic-fundamentalist rapprochement around sexual issues was far in the future, but the birth control issue intensified both Catholic and fundamentalist Protestant opposition to the FCC and the mainline Protestants it represented.

Despite persisting disagreements between liberal and conservative Protestants regarding birth control, there were signs of widespread approval among the public in the years following the Lambeth and FCC Committee reports. After taking a poll in 1938, *Ladies' Home Journal* reported that 79 percent of American women approved of contraception.[93] By 1940, polling by George Gallup consistently showed that between 70 and 80 percent of all Americans favored "the distribution of birth-control information to married persons by government health clinics."[94] As birth control gained in acceptance among Protestants and lay Catholics alike, culminating ultimately with the Supreme Court's overturning remaining bans on birth control access for married couples in *Griswold v. Connecticut* (1965), other issues took its place as key points of contention. But the ire of conservative critics over birth control and sex more generally would not be easily assuaged.

THE PERIOD FOLLOWING 1920 AND the passage of the Nineteenth Amendment witnessed conflicts and controversies of many kinds. Especially for conceptions of women's rights and sexual freedom, the 1920s was a period of discord and decisive change. Sanger's campaign for frank discussion of and legal access to birth control marked a pivotal moment in the history of American debates about sexuality and morals, and the acrimonious religious and political realignments of the period secured her deeply bifurcated reputation. Catholics, along with traditionalist Protestants, continued to denounce and view her in demonic terms. Liberal Protestants persisted in a mutually profitable relationship with Sanger, as they sought to distance themselves from Catholic authoritarianism—gradually adopting Sanger's language supporting women's right to control their own bodies and to experience sexual pleasure not bound to procreation.

Certainly the political, religious, and philosophical divisions among these disparate parties were deep, and they traded bitter accusations. But all cared passionately about the betterment of the human race and the improvement of American society. All believed that both the nation and the world would benefit from increased propagation of particular types of human beings, and from decreased breeding among others. And all sought to persuade others of the rightness of their own position—by distorting or silencing the other side, if necessary—and to shore up that stance by every legal means available.[95]

At stake, ultimately, in the religious war over birth control were competing moral visions about human liberty, autonomy, and freedom: rival convictions about the very definition of humanity and the proper place of choice, duty, and pleasure in human life. Catholic leaders loathed Sanger because they believed she sought to destroy the ties of love and fealty between mother and child, husband and wife, church and person. Sanger detested the Catholic hierarchy, in turn, because she believed it sought to control not only the thought and behavior of faithful Catholics but also the people, laws, and culture of the United States (indeed, of the whole world). Each position attracted adherents beyond the immediate constituencies of Sanger and Catholic leaders, as both parties made broad appeals to morality and referenced the human family, the needs of children, the goodness of parenting future generations, and the awesomeness of life itself. Both factions deeply believed in the rectitude of their cause, and there were vast and irreconcilable differences between their moral visions. The sharpest differences were matters of gender and power—a fact seen plainly by Sanger no less than by traditionalists such as Archbishop Hayes. The conflict over birth control was, in this sense, part of a much larger cultural debate in this period about female autonomy, one intensified by the successful suffrage campaign. As voters, women had now secured rights unknown to their foremothers; the larger impact on the nation of women's citizenship was an unknown and, to many, truly terrifying prospect.

But the birth control debate also revealed similar divisions regarding the authority of science, the limits of free speech, and the shape of modernity itself. Indeed, the debate about gender in the 1920s was deeply interwoven with an equally significant dispute about the role of religion amid modernity and about the status of scientific knowledge in relation to religion. While some political progressives saw religion as an essentially conservative if not downright oppressive force—an institution that sought unrestricted privilege and self-propagation in service to its rich, powerful, mostly male leaders—others viewed religion as a potentially progressive and vital institution, caring for the poor in a heartless world by agitating for a living wage over and against the capitalistic exploitations of the period. Just as progressives were leery toward anything that looked like a fundamentalist or Catholic attempt to suppress science or subjugate women, conservatives were suspicious about the free exchange of sexual knowledge and anxious to advance their version of traditional morality for the sake of church and nation. These forces—gender, science, knowledge, free speech, and modernity—collided in the furor over birth control in the 1920s, which changed forever the American conversation about religion and sex.

CHAPTER 2

CENSORSHIP OF LITERATURE AND POPULAR ENTERTAINMENTS

THE BIRTH CONTROL CONFLICT THAT burgeoned in the 1920s intensified dissent in both religious and political realms over the exchange and distribution of sexual knowledge. Broad disagreements about the meaning of obscenity lingered into the next decade, only to erupt over materials quite distinct from contraceptive information. And the fault lines deepened: just as liberal Protestants had shifted to a more open position on birth control during the 1920s, the 1930s witnessed their gradual but steady retreat from censorship-minded public scrutiny of entertainment. This period witnessed the visible emergence of religiously rooted defenses of free expression, however cautious—as well as new disagreements among religious people regarding what should be considered obscene and whether government or religious authorities were in the best position to regulate obscenity. Mainline Protestants who might once have endorsed official or unofficial censorship became more skeptical of state efforts to censor art and literature, even as some religious people were growing more tolerant of the spiritualization of sex that had colored the FCC statement on home and marriage. Many of their fellow Christians demurred, however, and grew more adamant about the need to protect virtuous citizens from the ill effects of sexually suggestive ideas and graphic depictions of passion.

The 1930s witnessed a new openness regarding sex in literature, accompanied by the proliferation of forms of popular entertainment often

Writer and artist D. H. Lawrence. *BETTMANN VIA GETTY IMAGES.*

seen as provocative and trafficking in obscenity. These prompted new efforts at censorship by religious people, as local citizens and church people across the nation joined efforts to stamp out erotic matter that might boost immorality among youth. But this era of censorship was notable for several new developments: Catholics supplanted Protestants as the most visible and vocal advocates of censorship in the United States, some liberal Protestants became more openly skeptical of censorship, and censorship created opportunities for collaboration, or at least alignment of interests, between Catholics and traditionalist Protestants.

A dispute over one particular novel illustrated the swiftly changing fate of censorship in this period and signaled a new era in which censorship was more controversial than it had been under Comstock. On November 25, 1929, a Massachusetts district court convicted a local Cambridge bookseller, John DeLacey, and his store clerk for selling obscene literature in the form of *Lady Chatterley's Lover*, D. H. Lawrence's sexually explicit novel about an adulterous love affair. DeLacey's Dunster House Bookshop in Harvard Square was a favorite of college professors, cultured locals, and erudite readers who lived in or visited the area. Still, the shop had not stocked Lawrence's book; DeLacey had only acquired it at the insistence of a customer who turned out to be John Tait Slaymaker, an agent of the anti-vice group known as the New England Watch and Ward Society. Despite the whiff of entrapment, money had exchanged hands in the procurement of an obscene book; local laws mandated a guilty verdict. Judge Arthur P. Stone issued an eight-hundred-dollar fine and a severe sentence to DeLacey—four months' imprisonment in the House of Correction—along with a two-hundred-dollar fine and two-week sentence to the clerk.[1]

Edged with the titillating forbiddenness long associated with Lawrence, the author of some twenty prior volumes that included the previously censored *Sons and Lovers* and *Women in Love*, the story was ripe to make headlines in major newspapers across the country. Slaymaker, using only part of his name to avoid recognition and persisting even after DeLacey noted that he did not carry the work in his shop "because of its nature," had demanded that the bookseller order the novel for him from a third party. Newspapers splashily exhibited the spectacle of a bookish college supplier selling smut to an anti-vice crusader posing as a scholar, one who must have felt grimly triumphant as he returned to Watch and Ward headquarters bearing—finally!—his prize. The Middlesex County district attorney, Robert T. Bushnell, condemned the deceptive tactics of the Watch and Ward Society, whose crusading in Boston dated back to 1878. Remarkably, although he was the prosecutor handling the case and would have been the right person to denounce DeLacey, Bushnell warned instead that to "induce and procure the commission of a crime," as agent Slaymaker did here, was to engage in "criminal conspiracy."[2] Nonetheless, the law demanded that he prosecute DeLacey, and he did.

The court ultimately revoked DeLacey's jail sentence altogether, lest the "brazen piece of effrontery" committed by Slaymaker vindicate the solicitation of a crime. Although censorship of *Lady Chatterley's Lover* endured, the stunt at Dunster House Bookshop damaged the anti-vice cause's credibility and reaped extensive public criticism. After Bushnell's denunciations of the Watch and Ward Society's methods, three members of the society resigned, and the board of directors initiated an impartial investigation to see if any "illegal, improper, or unethical" methods were employed in the Dunster House Bookshop case. Vigilante justice, which in the view of the Watch and Ward Society's many supporters served the cause well, proved deeply embarrassing to other Cantabrigians, who found its methods unseemly and disliked the national spotlight such belligerent acts shone upon their fair city.[3] Ripening beneath these disagreements over tactics, though, was a more fundamental dispute about whether it was appropriate to target literature for censorship in the first place.

The Dunster House Bookshop made Boston "the butt of national ridicule"—"I am sick and tired of having Boston and Massachusetts represented as backwoods sections populated by yokels," said District Attorney Bushnell after DeLacey was prosecuted. It also deeply damaged the standing of the Watch and Ward. Whether out of conviction or desperation, in 1930 the society invited the Roman Catholic leader of Boston, William Henry Cardinal O'Connell, to serve as an honorary vice president of the organization. The attempt by a Protestant organization to collaborate publicly with a Catholic leader known to warn his own flocks against consorting with Protestants was surprising, to say the least, although the society had cooperated with Catholic law enforcement officials in the past. The cardinal, well aware of the stain on the Watch and Ward's reputation, declined.[4]

Catholic leaders and some conservative Protestants began to shift their efforts beyond strict censorship laws to internal ecclesiastical modes of controlling the literary consumption of their flocks. The secretary of the Massachusetts Bible Society did join a campaign for reforming the state's obscenity laws, but the leadership of Boston's Catholic diocese conceded that censorship laws typically provoked "a resentful counterattack waged with the weapons of ridicule and satire which largely nullify the good of the prohibition" and that "civil law is not a cure-all adapted to remedy this evil." Shifts in tactics by no means signaled a change in values, but this famous trial foreshadowed later modifications in efforts to uphold decency. By the end of the 1930s, the Massachusetts Civil

Liberties Committee reported that Boston's Watch and Ward Society had wholly ceased its efforts at prosecuting obscene books and had "completely withdrawn from the field."[5]

The Dunster House Bookshop case augured new fault lines regarding censorship and the religious control of literature containing sexual content. The deep conflicts that were developing in Anglo-American religious thinking about sex intensified those fault lines, and these conflicts were on vivid display in the wider religious debate over *Lady Chatterley's Lover*. As censorship lost credibility in many prominent circles, conservative critics continued to blast works and writers they deemed blasphemous. Analyzing Lawrence's intentions for that novel along with its critical reception during the 1930s provides a way to link the political and religious conflicts that worked together to deepen the fracture in American Christian thinking about sex.

While popular audiences would later think of Lawrence as little more than an author of titillating smut, he was celebrated by many nonconformists and literature critics in his own day, even as censors and traditionalist Christians viewed him with disgust. Denunciations of Lawrence, including scorn for his literary talent, were always deeply inflected with moral pronouncements about his subject matter and his determination to write about sex in the frankest language imaginable, defiantly using words many considered vulgar. Such words appeared in his last novel, *Lady Chatterley's Lover*, which roused the most polarized reactions and was the subject of the fiercest controversies. The religious debates regarding that novel and Lawrence more generally reveal the deeper conflicts in Anglo-American religious thinking about sex that would roil obscenity debates for years to come.

DAVID HERBERT LAWRENCE (1885–1930) WAS born to a miner father and former schoolteacher mother in a coal-mining town in Nottinghamshire, England, the fourth of five children. A sickly child who was an avid reader and painter, he was part of a conventional family, and his upbringing was traditional and rigorously religious. His mother made sure that he and his siblings regularly attended Sunday school and services at

Eastwood's Congregational Chapel, known for its stern morality.[6] As an adult, Lawrence would criticize the prudery of Reformed Protestantism, yet he ardently praised other facets of the tradition, notably its music. Lawrence began writing poetry and fiction while working as a school-teacher in London, publishing his first novel, *The White Peacock*, in 1910.

In 1912, at the age of twenty-six, Lawrence fell in love with Frieda Weekley, the wife of one of his former college professors. She left her husband and children for him, and they married and remained together for the rest of Lawrence's life. Frieda was avant-garde in her views about sex and marriage; she had had several lovers during her first marriage, including the psychoanalyst Otto Gross, a follower of Sigmund Freud who had published notable work on sexuality. Already a devoted fan of Nietzsche, Frieda drank in Freud's ideas as reinterpreted through Gross, focusing on one in particular: "the act of sexual love was a sacrament and if the sacrament were freely given and taken the ills of society would disappear."[7] Frieda carried this view with her into her relationship with Lawrence and also continued to have numerous extramarital liaisons while with him; this understanding of the sacramentality of sex would emerge repeatedly in Lawrence's writing. Lawrence cherished the roman-tic themes of sexual passion, raw physicality, and the wondrous beauty of human bodies in his writing, as well as his life, and for him, they had everything to do with true religion: sex itself was potentially a sacred experience.

It was during his early married years that Lawrence's literary work first encountered controversy, when his 1915 novel *The Rainbow* was la-beled obscene. It contained scenes of lesbianism, nakedness, and exu-berant sex, all depicted in graphic detail. After receiving a complaint, a London court ordered the publisher, Methuen and Company, to hand over all unsold copies of the book; the publisher then demanded that Lawrence return his advance of three hundred pounds. Lawrence's New York agent confirmed that with its explicit scenes the book could not be published in the United States.[8] *Women in Love*, a subsequent novel first written in 1913 and thoroughly revised in 1917, was rejected by several publishers for fear of a similar reaction before eventually find-ing acceptance—and courting much controversy among those desiring purity in print. Even friends and former disciples sometimes turned against Lawrence, as when one described *Women in Love* as "sub-human and bestial." There were other criticisms of Lawrence's work: he often wrote from personal experience, and associates who recognized themselves as characters in a Lawrence story sometimes threatened libel suits. Still others found his writing far too earnest, stilted, pompous, and preachy to be taken seriously.[9]

But to Lawrence, the most dangerous critics were the censors, and he refused to concede any ground. His work was in no way smut, he argued, for it focused not on the dirtiness but the very holiness of sex. "Let us hesitate no longer to announce that the sensual passions and mysteries are equally sacred with the spiritual mysteries and passions," Lawrence urged in the foreword to *Women in Love*. "Who would deny it any more? The only thing unbearable is the degradation, the prostitution of the living mysteries in us." Lawrence was here writing directly against the American censors who were complaining of his "Eroticism," a charge that greatly puzzled him. "Which Eros? Eros of the jaunty 'amours,' or Eros of the sacred mysteries? And if the latter, why accuse, why not respect, even venerate?" But the trouble seemed to be not that Lawrence wrote of the spiritualization of sex, but that he wrote of sex at all. That subject landed his works in the lap of the law, over and over again.[10]

In 1925, living in Italy, Lawrence wrote his last significant novel and the one that would become the most infamous of all, *Lady Chatterley's Lover*. He also painted a number of oils and watercolors featuring naked bodies (many of them depictions of himself and several of Frieda), phallic imagery, and love and eroticism as sacred themes. Both on the page and on canvas, he conveyed very similar messages about sex, love, and life that centered on liberation from social norms and full surrender to the wise god of experience. His erotically charged painting *Contadini* (1928), a sensuous depiction of a naked Italian peasant man, was representative of both his work and its reception: Lawrence was photographed painting it, he mentioned it in several letters to friends, and a later biography pointed out that the figure's "dark head and nude torso link him to Mellors," Lady Chatterley's fictional lover.[11] When a London art gallery exhibited a good number of these paintings in 1929, reportedly attracting some twelve thousand spectators, critics complained of lasciviousness and indecency, until Scotland Yard detectives seized thirteen of the "filthy productions" for obscenity. Lawrence could only take what a free speech activist called "a poet's revenge," publishing a derisive rhythmic poem depicting the "lily-white" officers fainting "in virgin outrage" upon beholding one of Lawrence's nudes. The "hypocrisy and poltroonery" of these "craven, cowardly" officials, he wrote to the gallery owner, were contemptible.[12]

Struggling with tuberculosis and profoundly frustrated with the relentless censorship of his writings and his paintings, Lawrence entered a sanatorium in Vence, France, in early 1930—even as, across the Atlantic Ocean, John DeLacey awaited his final fate in the Dunster House Bookshop case. On March 2, the very day after his medical discharge, Lawrence died. Photographs accompanying the obituaries showed a worn-looking man who appeared far older than his forty-four years. His admirers would argue that Lawrence died brokenhearted though unwavering, a man who never tried to hide his loathing and contempt for those "grey Puritans" and prudish Victorians who pursued his work with salacious abandon in order to ban it for the ostensible sake of purity. The Dunster House Bookshop case was noteworthy enough to be mentioned in an appreciative *New York Times* obituary appearing two days after Lawrence died.[13]

GRASPING THE FORCES ARRAYED AGAINST Lawrence requires understanding the history of literary censorship in Europe and America. Legal restrictions on obscene literature long embodied a Christian consensus regarding sexuality and sexual morality, reflecting the belief that to read about sexual sin was profoundly dangerous. Leaders of the Catholic Church kept a list of publications they deemed objectionable for sexual or heretical content, called the *Index Librorum Prohibitorum*. An early list of prohibited works appeared in the ninth century, and the first modern edition appeared in 1559. Later editions grew longer and longer, as more books appeared that church leaders found offensive, either for potentially inciting lust or for challenging church doctrine.

In France and England, anti-vice laws in the nineteenth century had generated obscenity statutes that were both more specific and more expansive than their antecedents. Between 1821 and 1892, government officials in France prosecuted twenty-six literary works, from Gustave Flaubert's *Madame Bovary* and Charles Baudelaire's *Les Fleurs du mal* to Marguerite Eymery's *Monsieur Vénus* and erotic poetry by Paul Verlaine and Guy de Maupassant. In England, authors and artists fought battles of their own with officials and citizens seeking propriety and the preservation of national character. The Obscene Publications Act of 1857 gave courts the power to seize and destroy materials deemed obscene; sale of such corrupting materials was a criminal offense, and offenders were regularly punished for over a century. British officials famously condemned Radclyffe Hall's 1928 lesbian novel *The Well of Loneliness*, one judge at trial noting, "These unnatural offences between women which are the subject of this book involve acts which between men would be a criminal offence, and involve acts of the most horrible, unnatural and disgusting obscenity."[14]

In America literary censorship arrived on the *Mayflower*, with Plymouth's governor, William Bradford, inflicting punishment in 1628 on a rebellious colonist found to have "composed sundry rhymes and verses, some tending to lasciviousness."[15] The first literary censorship trial in the United States took place in Massachusetts in 1821, over the printing of John Cleland's 1749 erotic novel, *Memoirs of a Woman of Pleasure*—more popularly known as *Fanny Hill*—a case that went all the way to the US Supreme Court. Officials fought against writers such as Walt Whitman and Herman Melville because of the ideas expressed in their writings, and sometimes because of their behavior as well. And we have already seen the ways in which American censors such as Comstock and the array of vice societies that burgeoned and flourished during the Progressive Era pursued not only novelists but also freethinking activists like Margaret Sanger, whom they saw as jeopardizing virtue and the status quo.

The religious underpinnings of literary censorship were personified in Comstock, for years the king of the nation's Christian censors. He argued that lewd writing would breed lust, which "defiles the body, debauches the imagination, corrupts the mind, deadens the will, destroys the memory, sears the conscience, hardens the heart, and damns the soul." Obscene literature had enormous power, overwhelming and overtaking even the best of people. Ordinary readers of such material, he warned, inexorably became "rakes and libertines," polluting their families, abandoning their children, and desecrating their homes. But Comstock reserved his greatest ire for those "so-called 'liberals' of this land" who fought the censors and turned "monsters" and "devil-men" into martyrs for free speech. This "mawkish sympathy for criminals" left no room for the true victims: "the youth cursed for life, the wife widowed, the child orphaned, the family disgraced, pauperized, and destroyed." To Comstock and those who shared his way of thinking, obscenity ruthlessly ensnared all who touch it, wreaked familial disorder, and devastated the broader social world; the vile sin had to be eliminated at its very source.[16]

During this period, tensions were growing between modernist literature and traditions of literary censorship. James Branch Cabell's *Jurgen* endured charges of being an "obscene" book upon its 1919 publication, as John S. Sumner, the head of the New York Society for the Suppression of Vice since Anthony Comstock's 1915 death, attacked its sexual content and prosecuted its publisher and editor. In 1920, editors of a well-known American avant-garde periodical, *The Little Review*, were hit with obscenity charges for printing work by James Joyce—excerpts from what would eventually become *Ulysses*. Likewise, Theodore Dreiser's novels *Sister Carrie* (1900), *The Genius* (1915), and *An American Tragedy* (1925) also enraged the censors for their supposedly immoral content. In a letter to a university student writing his master's thesis on literary censorship, Dreiser wrote starkly, "Any writer, artist, painter or sculptor, or thinker of any breadth of mind who wants to present reality is now being ignored or misrepresented by a kept Press." In that environment, it took "real courage" to write truthfully of sex.[17]

Those who supported censorship viewed the enforcement of purity and decency as a crucial way of maintaining order, or of restoring it during a time of change. Awash in societal changes brought about by immigration, urbanization, modernization, and feminism, as well as the economic uncertainties wrought by the stock market crash of 1929, Americans might well seek stability in traditional social norms and reassurance that younger generations would uphold them. The minds of youth, still in formation, needed protection from corrupt literature intended to arouse sensation and encourage debauchery, lest they be overtaken by lust and cease to be functioning citizens contributing to a well-ordered society. The flesh could overtake the spirit, a warning that ran deep in the Christian tradition starting with the apostle Paul's own inner warfare; stringent disciplinary regimens had long been advocated as barriers to temptation. Perhaps this was a low view of human nature, rendering persons helplessly impressionable and even imprisonable by the power of print, but literature could also uplift, and the wholesome variety might well abet virtue. Even as many early-twentieth-century writers and readers were chafing against longstanding rules of propriety in literature, then, others held to them as pillars of moral constancy and social control. Little wonder, in such a milieu, that the literary censorship of sex became a battleground.[18]

The controversy over Joyce's writing that began in 1920 did not end quickly. Joyce's work was the subject of trials in the United States that stretched to 1934, when a federal appeals court upheld lower court judge John M. Woolsey's earlier decision allowing for publication. It was a euphoric moment already, as Prohibition—the one against alcohol sales—had just been rescinded in December 1933; that, along with the pro-*Ulysses* decision, could seem to augur a more lenient age. In his foreword to the first legally published edition of *Ulysses*, the civil liberties lawyer Morris Ernst wrote jubilantly about the victory over the "prudery-ridden" censors who "have fought to emasculate literature . . . , have sought to reduce the reading matter of adults to the level of adolescents and subnormal persons, and have nurtured evasions and sanctimonies." The outcome for *Ulysses*, Ernst continued, was "a turning point" and "a body-blow for the censors." Writers could eschew euphemisms and "describe basic human functions without fear of the law."[19] But regardless of the *Ulysses* decision, literary censorship continued, with books like Henry Miller's *Tropic of Cancer* and John Steinbeck's *The Grapes of Wrath* attacked for supposed indecency countless times over many decades, and the government's ban on *Lady Chatterley's Lover* in effect until 1959.

MOST AMERICANS, OF COURSE, DID not have access to Lawrence's infamous love story in its early days, and the vast majority in the 1930s likely accepted the notion that it was a dirty, immoral book. Debates over popular entertainment hit more people directly, and attempts to censor various products marketed for popular amusement garnered significant disagreement. Motion pictures, long a target of Christian censors like New York's Canon William Chase and the Woman's Christian Temperance Union (WCTU), came in for years of more highly regulated scrutiny, for instance. Hollywood already had a reputation for debauchery, partly because of the publicity given to the romances and sexual escapades of its movie stars, and a series of scandals that shocked audiences and attracted reproach to the film industry drove industry representatives in 1921 to hire a moral overseer who would ensure decency in motion pictures. They selected Will Hays, a Presbyterian elder and postmaster general of the United States, and made him president of the Motion Picture Producers and Distributors of America (MPPDA), which they established in 1922. Industry leaders were trying to avoid censorship and increase mass audiences, and they hoped that the MPPDA would stem the rising protests against sensationalism and ostensibly lewd content in films.

One of Hays's first actions was to invite two thousand representatives of influential religious, educational, and civic organizations to a conference in New York, offering them a voice in evaluating film content and advising industry representatives. He forged a Committee on Public Relations to serve as a liaison between the MPPDA and the public, informing the Hays office of its objections to any films and promoting approved films to the public so that filmmakers would be incentivized to make more. Religious groups were part of that committee from the outset, including the National Catholic Welfare Conference and several other Catholic organizations, the Central Conference of American Rabbis along with other Jewish groups, and the FCC as well as other Protestant associations. Hays's office worked steadily with Hollywood producers, eventually producing a list known as the "Don'ts and Be Carefuls"—situations and topics that films should avoid altogether or treat with special care, most having to do with sex.

Hollywood moguls Louis B. Mayer, Cecil B. DeMille, and Fred Niblo, with Catholic clerics, 1929. *JOHN KOBAL FOUNDATION/GETTY IMAGES.*

Some Christian censors were not immediately mollified by the work of Hays and the MPPDA. For instance, the Woman's Christian Temperance Union, which had focused attention on the dangers of motion pictures as early as 1906, shortly after the five-cent theaters opened, continued to target movies into the 1930s, on the grounds that their power over children and youth was formidable and that viewers could become "addicted" to film no less than to alcohol. Seeing Hays's office as ineffectual, a group of churchmen, women's groups, and business leaders calling itself the Federal Motion Picture Council sought government regulation of the movie industry. In 1930, the WCTU responded to a new wave of so-called sex pictures by leading a host of Christian organizations— churches, missionary societies, women's clubs, and more—in pressuring Congress to enact a strong censorship law and save the nation from the movies' dangers.[20] Such legislation was exactly what the MPPDA had repeatedly attempted to forestall.

The Catholic publisher of the film industry's leading trade paper, the *Motion Picture Herald*, was thinking deeply during this time about how to promote movies that offered virtuous entertainment to families and that reflected, or at least did not undermine, the values of the Catholic Church. Like Hays, Michael Quigley disliked the idea of movies being subject to federal oversight, but he believed a suitable instrument could be created from a code of decency whose rules were clearly articulated and would be compulsory for all filmmakers—a more formalized tool than the "Don'ts and Be Carefuls." He worked on devising such a code with a couple of Catholic priests, including one who was also a playwright and dramatist, and he consulted with Hays along with members of the industry. The document was decidedly Christian in orientation, its details leaving "no room to doubt," as one observer put it, "that the agenda was primarily concerned with sins of the flesh."[21] Adopted in 1930 as the Motion Picture Production Code, this system of self-regulation was intended to preempt federal censorship by producing salubrious movies for mass entertainment. Implemented correctly, the code itself would regulate the content and distribution of all Hollywood films concerning issues such as profanity, crime, and sexuality. The Hays office did not emphasize the Catholic origins of the code; it was better, in that climate, to describe it merely as reflective of broadly American moral values.

The code's section on sex was considerably longer than those treating murder, religion, and other topics, and it began by insisting, "The sanctity of the institution of marriage and the home shall be upheld. Pictures shall not infer that low forms of sex relationship are the accepted or common thing." Specific instructions covered such subjects as adultery ("sometimes necessary plot material, must not be explicitly treated or justified, or presented attractively"), passionate love scenes ("should not be introduced except where they are definitely essential to the plot . . . passion should be treated in such manner as not to stimulate the lower and baser emotions"), rape ("never the proper subject for comedy"), and interracial sex ("sex relationship between the white and black races is forbidden").[22] Other sections regulated the showing of bedrooms, dances, vulgarity, and more. By accepting the code, motion picture producers hoped to persuade critics that they could successfully regulate themselves on sexual and other moral content.

But apprehension about the sincerity of studios' dedication to clean entertainment continued to grow, particularly as the Depression depressed movie ticket sales and racked up enormous losses that Hollywood filmmakers determined could only be reversed by more exciting, racy movies. Between 1930 and 1934, films were more sexually explicit than they had ever been, and the Hays Code was largely ignored. Henry James Forman's best-selling book, *Our Movie Made Children*, published in 1933, alarmed American audiences by describing the moral damage wreaked on children by these decadent films, a message taken up and spread by Christian writers in numerous periodicals and other vehicles that blamed Hollywood for the sexual promiscuity of American youth. That same year, the president of the National Council of Catholic Women warned that Hollywood was creating films that were "a menace to the physical, mental and moral welfare of the nation."[23] In this climate, many felt that external pressure on the studios would be needed to hold the line on wholesome film.

Protestants were apprehensive too: even those who were gradually liberalizing, though uncomfortable with the tactics of anti-vice societies, wanted wholesome amusements and knew some regulation was necessary. In late 1931, for instance, the *Christian Century* pontificated against an editorial in the *Nation* that excoriated censorship of literature and film alike. Against the *Nation*'s advocacy of "permitting grown-ups to decide for themselves what books they shall buy, what plays they shall see, and even what pictures of undressed females they shall look upon," *Century* editors contemptuously scorned "the glib rationalizing of liberals of this kind—found in large numbers in the Manhattan sector." While agreeing that citizens should be "freed from capricious and tyrannical state control," it was obvious to the writers that there was a need for "some community control over the commercial activities of the individual," lest the United States become a nation of "smut." The occasional overreach by censoring authorities was simply "the price that the community must occasionally pay" for decency.[24]

In 1934, US Catholic bishops established the Legion of Decency as a mechanism for mobilizing the faithful and other concerned Americans to work for decency in movies, urging adherents to stay away from films deemed dangerous to their moral well-being. Within a few months of its founding, Catholic leaders declared that over two million Americans had signed the Legion's pledge.[25] Advocating consumer boycotts rather than federal legislation, the Legion soon eclipsed the efforts of the WCTU, which acknowledged the Catholic organization's good results, noted the cooperation of Protestant organizations in its efforts, but continued to push for federal legislation. The film industry, sensing that self-regulation under the Legion was highly preferable to a federal law, began more intently to work on self-censorship.

That year, a prominent Catholic and public relations officer in the Hays office named Joseph Breen was appointed head of the Production Code Administration, serving as the chief enforcer of the Hays Code. Under Breen's direction, officials worked to cut suggestive lines from scripts and change plotlines when they were deemed too immoral. After the censors read the script for the film *Casablanca*, for instance, filmmakers made adjustments to lessen the suggestion of adulterous sex in the affair between Rick and Ilsa, though it remained strongly implied. A few years later, because of the censors, the strong sexuality of *A Streetcar Named Desire* was toned down, and a full four minutes of scenes were deleted before its release. The censors also banned a French film version of *Lady Chatterley's Lover* (*L'Amant de lady Chatterley*).[26]

Catholic concern about the cinema's influence was so high, in fact, that in 1936 Pope Pius XI issued an encyclical letter on the topic, *Vigilanti Cura*, that praised the Legion of Decency while condemning the "lamentable progress—*magni passus extra viam*—of the motion picture art and industry in the portrayal of sin and vice." Vatican leaders had already twice addressed delegations of the International Motion Picture Congress, the second held in Rome earlier in 1936. But the subject was of "such paramount importance" and the hazards of "pernicious and deadly" effects on morality so grave that the leadership deemed it necessary to address it in this encyclical. The document reproached film industry leaders for not carrying out their pledge to safeguard "the moral welfare of

Film censor Joseph Breen of the Hays office inspects
the garb of two actresses to ensure their harem
costumes are fit for the moviegoing public.
BETTMANN VIA GETTY IMAGES.

the patrons of the cinema." It exhorted bishops across the world to press
Catholics in the motion picture industry to work for virtuous entertainment, as part of the larger program of Catholic Action (the organized
effort mobilizing lay Catholics for church work as well as broad social reform and spiritual improvement). Bishops were also to obtain an annual
pledge from members of their dioceses similar to the one developed by
the Legion of Decency, promising to abstain from motion pictures "offensive to truth and to Christian morality." Moreover, the pope's encyclical called for a bishop-led national office in every country to review all
films and categorize them as "permitted to all," "permitted with reserva-
tions," and "harmful or positively bad." Such a system, though expensive,
would protect the morality of Catholics and non-Catholics alike and help
ensure that films in all nations would promote "the highest ideals and the
truest standards of life."[27]

Popular pulp magazines also received attention from concerned citizens, especially Catholics—who were, after all, long accustomed to literary bans because of the Vatican's *Index Librorum Prohibitorum*. Convinced that the lewd stories printed in such magazines were a "moral poison" and part of a "widespread . . . campaign to destroy the morals of both youth and adults," Catholic bishops in 1938 founded the National Organization for Decent Literature (NODL), which was headed by John F. Noll, bishop of Fort Wayne, Indiana, and a committee of other Catholic leaders. Concerned that popular romance, true confession, and crime and detective magazines glamorized premarital and extramarital sex, divorce, and criminality, the NODL enlisted local Catholics across the country to help eliminate such publications from stores and communities and make them inaccessible to Catholics and non-Catholics alike. NODL supporters took a pledge to abstain from reading such literature and, still more, to refuse doing business with stores that sold it. Local NODL members visited drugstores, newsstands, and other shops to urge sellers to get rid of these materials for good; if urging didn't work, the threat of a boycott just might. In some areas, compliant storekeepers could display NODL certificates of approval to assure customers of their respectability.[28]

As these organizations found success in their efforts to suppress sexual content not only for believing Catholics but for the whole of American audiences, resistance arose. As early as 1936, the *Nation* editorial board warned readers of the insidious Catholic influence over the motion picture industry, noting that the Hays Code had been written by the Catholic hierarchy and that Breen had now been given "dictatorial powers" to demand revisions in movie scripts even before production began. According to the editors, the MPPDA and the Legion of Decency were in cahoots, and the Catholic Church was all but running Hollywood. Given that seventy million Americans attended the cinema each week, while there were only around twenty million Catholics in the nation, non-Catholic moviegoers surely had the right to decide "whether they wish to have their films censored in advance by the Catholic church."[29]

The syndicated columnist Drew Pearson later gave the same treatment to NODL, denouncing the Catholic "zealots" who "have become unofficial censors of American magazines" with far too much public power. Pearson was especially incensed at the influence NODL had on US postmaster general Frank Walker, a Catholic. Similar complaints echoed in the liberal Protestant magazine the *Christian Century*, where articles condemned Catholic censorship efforts as encroachments on civil authority and American liberty. An article titled "Vigilante Censorship Is Spreading" denounced the church's "cultural Ku Kluxism," "terroristic censorship," and "cultural storm troopers," while the magazine's editor, Charles Clayton Morrison, called the church hierarchy "the counterpart (or should I say, the prototype?) of the fascist or nazist or communist 'party' with the dictator at its head." Edmund Wilson, criticizing Catholics' role in suppressing his *Memoirs of Hecate County* and their more general "efforts to interfere with free speech and free press," likened the church to the Stalinist comintern. The visibility of Catholics as censors prompted liberal Protestants to retreat from advocating moral monitoring of popular entertainments. It was a protracted sequel to the war over free speech and Catholic power that played out in the birth control controversy of the 1920s.[30]

Just as liberal Protestants had loosened their stand on birth control during the previous decade, in the 1930s they shifted away from supporting censorship of mass entertainment. Their aversion to the methods of both the Legion of Decency on film and the NODL on literature evinced a shift in liberal Protestant sensibilities whereby, as one historian puts it, "moral criticism of public entertainment went from being a duty of the middle-class to evidence of its outmoded prudishness."[31] As Catholic leaders in essence took over the role of public moralists, those same Protestants who had as late as 1931 scorned the "glib rationalizing" of the anti-censors more or less joined their cause.

With Protestant-Catholic tensions so rife in the nation, it was early for conservative Protestants and Catholics to collaborate significantly on issues of mutual concern. But censorship was one area where they could and occasionally did. One contemporary writer, R. L. Duffus, intrigued by the "patchwork of incongruities" that had come to characterize contemporary Boston, placed censorship cases such as the Dunster House Bookshop incident at the center of his perceptive analysis of the emergent religious realignments that were rapidly transforming the "little old Boston" of the Boston Brahmins, those cultured descendants of the commonwealth's founders. Once a largely Protestant city, Boston's majority was now Irish Catholic. Differences of both opinion and temperament divided these English and Irish settlers, Duffus noted, but "in respect to their opinions about domestic morals the two stocks and the two religions are not far apart." Likening Cardinal O'Connell and A. Z. Conrad—Boston's Catholic archbishop and the long-serving pastor of the Park Street Congregational Church just off Boston Common—Duffus noted that their different theologies did not prevent concurring attitudes toward "questionable" literature. Catholic and conservative Protestant cooperation was nowhere better evidenced, according to Duffus, than in the New England Watch and Ward Society, a "perfect example of the catholicity—with a small 'c'—of Boston's Puritanism." Although Protestant in origin and administrative leadership, it was an important vehicle where "Catholic and Protestant joined hands" in unity against immoral books. Catholics and conservative Protestants had discovered their agreement about "modern influence[s]" that, to their minds, imperiled the traditional family; their collaborations were just beginning.[32]

In the wake of the Dunster House Bookshop case, the religious politics of censorship shifted away from federal law toward attempts by religious authorities to oversee and regulate the bounds of propriety. Traditionalist Protestants and Catholics alike took steps to impose order over popular literature and mass entertainments, and the efforts of groups like the Legion and NODL, like those of Watch and Ward, generated critique from those who did not fully share their worldview or their sense of what was appropriate to read or see on the movie screen. The ideas about religion and sex that D. H. Lawrence conveyed in his novels reaped divided reactions even when the books were out of court and the national spotlight, serving as a bellwether of much that was to come.

LAWRENCE WAS A PARAGON OF unconventional, nonconformist thinking, and his writing represented a threat to the nation's Christian consensus on sex. It was not simply that he advocated for a wholly different morality than that of Christian chastity, traditional marriage, and the family; the larger threat lay in the fact that he presented his own vision of love and sex as a genuinely religious one, a compelling and authentic alternative to traditional Christianity. His work, influenced by radical thinkers such as the sexually daring writer Edward Carpenter, pioneered a fusion of sexual candor and religious ecstasy that would help shape how future sexual revolutionaries, including some Christians, thought about sex and sexual morality. While that wider impact was not yet evident in the 1930s, the substance of his writing, most especially *Lady Chatterley's Lover*, helps explain how he drove a wedge into the Christian agreement about sexual virtue.

"I am a passionately religious man," wrote the twenty-nine-year-old Lawrence in 1914, "and my novels must be written from the depth of my religious experience."[33] Whatever Lawrence may have meant by the word—and critics have long wrestled with his intention—neither he nor his works were "religious" in any conventional, institutional sense. The author was a seeker of physical and spiritual vitality, a lover of spontaneity and inward feeling as well as fleshly embodiment, a romantic who opposed the aridity of the rational intellect to dream of sacred creativity. He wrote elsewhere of poetry as "religious in its movement," of "the essential feeling in all art" as religious, and of cosmic reverence as driving all of life.[34] As a later observer would note, in order to achieve his own religious quest and escape from "dead beliefs and ideas," Lawrence had to "break free of any religious life-experience that was regimented by legalistic and moralistic religious tradition."[35] A "passionately religious man" he was, by his own definition, but even so, his brand of religiousness was sure to alienate if not incense those committed to a more traditional piety.

In an eloquent and highly personal essay published in 1928, "Hymns in a Man's Life," Lawrence wrote tenderly of the Protestant hymns he learned as a child, acknowledging that "they mean to me almost more than the finest poetry, and they have for me a more permanent value, somehow or other." However "banal" they might be in structure and substance, he urged readers to imagine the wonder they had excited in him as a child and that remained with him still. Indeed, Lawrence meditated, such wonder was surely "the most precious element in life," one that alone could stave off the boredom and deadness of modern civilization, the "sense of wonder" was "the religious element inherent in all life, even in a flea," "our sixth sense," "the *natural* religious sense." Science, too, wrote Lawrence, partook in this selfsame wonder and was in this sense "as religious as any religion," at least until it became stuffily didactic ("as dead and boring as dogmatic religion").[36]

As a onetime devout Protestant, Lawrence remained throughout his life consumed by the Bible, Jesus, and the theme of holy love, but his was no ordinary religiosity. In one critic's wry words, Lawrence aimed to "keep the poetry of the hymnal" as well as "desecrate the church."[37] In condemning its rigid prudery, however, he meant to call attention to the deeper joy and purity he felt the institution had destroyed, in its Protestant and Catholic forms alike. As he wrote in an essay posthumously published in England and not published in the United States until 1953, "A Propos of *Lady Chatterley's Lover*," the Catholic Church was not inherently anti-sexual, since it had made marriage "a sacrament based on the sexual communion, for the purpose of procreation," such that the "act of procreation is still charged with all the sensual mystery and importance of the old past." If the church taught differently now, it was the pope and the priests who had distorted its true message. Lawrence rejected what he believed to be the dry, cracked disembodiment of the Protestantism of his time in favor of a rich sacramentalism that had a mystical reverence for physicality and sexual union at its center.[38]

Interwoven throughout Lawrence's hot-blooded religiosity, then, was a keen sense of the vitality, the basic *sacredness*, of sex. In his essay "Making Love to Music," Lawrence wrote that "sex is so large and all-embracing that the religious passion itself is largely sexual."[39] In another essay, he denounced the hypocrisy that forced men and women to renounce their own sexuality in service to some distorted morality. Writing of the accusations levied against his so-called lurid and obscene novels, Lawrence retorted that he was "one of the least lurid mortals," for he absolutely detested "cheap and promiscuous sex . . . heartless sex." Rather than cheapening sex, Lawrence saw himself as writing against the artificiality of modern life, above all against contemporary forms of prudery that brought only coldness and misery into human relations. Sexuality, which enacted the "natural flow" of sympathy between creatures, was central to Lawrence's highest religious ideal.[40]

Lady's Chatterley's Lover deliberately and unremittingly represented such ideas. The novel is a love story between unlikely lovers: the aristocratic Connie Chatterley and her estate's gamekeeper, Oliver Mellors, both unhappily married to other people. Their relationship centers on their sexual passion and compatibility, suggesting the mutual sympathy and dynamism they find in one another and the restoration of their religious awe after years of dismal numbness. Connie's unpleasant husband, Clifford Chatterley, is an example of the absolute deadness of most men of his class, a man the novel early on describes as having a cold heart, paralyzed and impotent from his time in the war, "chirpy" and "watchful" with a "slight vacancy" about him, a "blank of insentience." Connie, on the other hand, is "a ruddy, country-looking girl with soft brown hair and sturdy body and slow movements full of unused energy," sensual in every respect. When, walking in the wood, Connie and Clifford happen on Mellors and she sees him for the first time, she feels him as "a swift menace . . . like a sudden rush of a threat out of nowhere." Gun slung over his shoulder, the "almost handsome" servant stares "straight into Connie's eyes with a perfectly fearless, impersonal look, as if he wanted to see what she was like"; she spies in his eyes "a look of suffering and detachment, yet a certain warmth" and sees him as "curiously full of vitality." Their eyes meet, and it is "as if he wakened up"; subsequently, once Connie returns to her daily life with the dull Clifford, she is filled with "an inward dread, an emptiness, an indifference to everything." The chapter ends with Connie going through her days "drearily, wearily," stuck on the "empty treadmill" of habit. "Nothingness!" she inwardly despairs. "To accept the great nothingness of life seemed to be the one end of living. All the many busy and important little things that make up the grand sum-total of nothingness!"[41]

Mellors lives close to the earth and is more comfortable around the animals he tends than people. Indeed, he seems animalistic himself, in Lawrence's descriptions, living by instinct and closer to nature than civilization. When Connie later chances on him bathing outdoors and first sees his beautiful naked back, sculpted by years of outdoor physical labor, it is "a visionary experience" that "hit[s] her in the middle of her body."

She saw the clumsy breeches slipping away over the pure, delicate white loins, the bones showing a little, and the sense of aloneness, of a creature purely alone, overwhelmed her. Perfect, white solitary nudity of a creature that lives alone, and inwardly alone. And beyond that, a certain beauty of a pure creature. Not the stuff of beauty, not even the body of beauty, but a certain lambency, the warm white flame of a single life revealing itself in contours that one might touch: a body!

Before long, Connie and Mellors have sexual intercourse, which "lift[s] a great cloud from her, and give[s] her peace." After the first time Connie and the gamekeeper "come-off together," her sexless husband Clifford detects "something new in her, something to him quite incomprehensible." Indeed, much has changed: "the flux of new awakening," "the new bath of life," "the voiceless song of adoration." The sex itself is her newfound salvation: "Connie would not take her bath this evening. The sense of his flesh touching her, the very stickiness upon her, was dear to her, and in a sense, holy."[42]

Some time later, after a rapturous night in which "the reckless, shameless sensuality shook her to her foundations, stripped her to the very last, and made a different woman of her"—the "sharper, more terrible . . . thrills" of anal sex—Connie compares her experience with Mellors to that of Abélard and Héloïse as well as the Greek gods, the electric sensation "burning the soul to tinder": "The refinements of passion, the extravagances of sensuality! And necessary, forever necessary, to burn out false shames and smelt out the heaviest ore of the body into purity. With the fire of sheer sensuality." While Connie had before imagined that a woman would die of humiliation at such sexual abandon into "the last and deepest recess of organic shame," instead she experienced blissful wonderment and dissolution of all embarrassment and fear; "naked and unashamed," she was stripped to "the real bed-rock of her nature." It was a triumph: "So! That was how it was! That was life! That was how oneself really was! There was nothing left to disguise or be ashamed of. She shared her ultimate nakedness with a man, another being." Poets and purportedly civilized people were "liars" for trying to persuade people they wanted sentiment, when "what one supremely wanted was this piercing, consuming, rather awful sensuality. To find a man who dared do it, without shame or sin or final misgiving!" Refinement and coarseness merge through this consuming, purifying union of lady and gamekeeper—both joyous, and she finally alive to "the very heart of the jungle of herself" after years of walking death.[43]

By novel's end, Connie is pregnant with their child, and both are seeking divorces from their livid spouses so that they may be permanently wed to each other. Theirs was what Lawrence called "a deeper morality" than obliging people's ordinary "little needs": the morality of seeking out the full achievement of the rhythm of life and death, the "vivid and nourishing relation to the cosmos and the universe." This rhythm emerged tangibly in love: When Connie asks what Mellors believes in, he pauses before responding, "I believe in being warm-hearted. I believe especially in being warm-hearted in love, in fucking with a warm heart. I believe if men could fuck with warm hearts, and the women take it warm-heartedly, everything would come all right. It's all this cold-hearted fucking that is death and idiocy." Later, after Connie tells Mellors that what distinguishes him from other men is "the courage of your own tenderness, . . . like when you put your hand on my tail and say I've got a pretty tail," he bluntly boils down his own quality of tenderness to its perfect essence: "cunt-awareness," or the courage to touch another embodied, passionate soul. "Sex is really only touch, the closest of all touch. And it's touch we're afraid of." The final sentence of the whole book comes from a letter Mellors sends to Connie, a droll farewell from his penis to her vagina: "John Thomas says good-night to lady Jane, a little droopingly, but with a hopeful heart—." However contrived, turgid, sexist, or absurd any of this may sound, the novel's worship of ecstatic physical union could not be more obvious.[44]

Lawrence was not entirely alone in writing of sex this way, but his popularity made him a sort of spiritual tribune for a new sexual morality. In his own repeated clarifications of his aims in writing *Lady Chatterley's Lover*, Lawrence said that he sought to write of the beauty, holiness, and cleanliness of sex, over against pornography (which he elsewhere defined as "the attempt to insult sex, to do dirt on it"). He was delighted to see the "real revolution" in sexuality wrought by the young, whom he praised for "rescuing their young nudity from the stuffy, pornographical hole-and-corner underworld of their elders, and . . . refus[ing] to sneak about the sexual relation."[45] Defending *Lady Chatterley's Lover* against the censors, Lawrence explained, "And this is the real point of this book. I want men and women to be able to think sex, fully, completely, honestly and cleanly."[46] Restoring the "deeper . . . greater morality" of humankind required returning to "vivid and nourishing relation to the cosmos and the universe." The solution Lawrence offered was not Christian—he believed it was older than Christianity, Plato, or Buddhism—for "the Christian religion lost, in Protestantism finally, the togetherness with the universe, the togetherness of the body, the sex, the emotions, the passions, with the earth and sun and stars." But "sex is the great unifier," and "in its big, slower vibration it is the warmth of heart which makes people happy together, in togetherness."[47] Lawrence's eclectic religious interests took in far more than Christianity, but there was no doubt that he perceived sexuality in profoundly sacred terms.

Many of Lawrence's detractors deemed him abnormally obsessed with sex and offered armchair psychological diagnoses explaining his fixation. He was "a sex-crucified man," one wrote in typical fashion—a casualty of warped cravings for whom sex was "a means of escape that will give him neither refuge nor rest, a perpetual thorn in the spirit, a reminder of his own insufficiency and weakness and lack of courage." A tortured man whose art was merely self-justifying autobiography: such was the ignominy heaped on Lawrence long after his death.[48]

The censorship of *Lady Chatterley's Lover* supposedly centered on its steamy depictions of adulterous sex. But take another look at the full context of that sexual activity. The traditional marriage between the aristocratic and sedentary Clifford and bored but dutiful Connie is one of hierarchy and the subordination of a submissive wife to her sexless but demanding husband; against that arrangement, Connie chooses to be with a common man of a much lower class, one who disbelieves in such hierarchies and who is muscular, carnal, and erotically thrilling. Mellors speaks crudely yet treats her as an equal and speaks openly about viewing her sexual fulfillment as important as his own. Connie rejects aristocratic roles and norms of propriety in favor of a simpler, more modest life with an unrefined man who seems wholly indifferent to social conventions, disdainful of manufactured measures of social class, and untroubled by sexual equality. Hers is an unambiguous rejection of civilized society with its hierarchies and upward ambitions, in favor of the rough-and-tumble world of intimate passion she fashioned with Mellors in the forest. It is this world, characterized by freedom and personal abandon, that Lawrence promises will nourish and sustain Connie and Mellors over time, in contrast to the cramped, angry, and stifling realm of conventional wedlock.

For traditional audiences, the scandal of the book was not merely sex or an unfaithful tryst. The greater outrage was the wholesale repudiation of traditional marriage, gendered order, and elite male power. The book described more than secret infidelity, the kind that might just tear apart a marriage; it bespoke the annihilation of cherished social norms, if not Christian civilization itself.

LAWRENCE'S RELIGIOUS VISION OF SEX was controversial. However much he battled the censors and sought to explain the far distance between his writings and obscene pornography, he could not overcome their hostility. Those most vexed by Lawrence—admiring his literary gifts while detesting the content of his work—included a set of conservative Christian literary critics. The most prickly (and most influential) of these was Thomas Stearns Eliot (1888–1965), the Missouri-born writer and St. Louis native who moved to England in early adulthood and eventually became a British subject. In England, Eliot converted from the liberal Unitarianism of his upbringing to a conservative strain of Anglicanism, describing his conservative predilections in 1929 as "classicist in literature, royalist in politics, and anglo-catholic in religion."[49] The Anglo-Catholic Eliot, orthodox in his Christian devotion, loathed the unorthodox Lawrence and at times seemed intent on grinding his literary reputation to dust.

T. S. Eliot did have occasional words of measured praise for Lawrence; an early reference from 1917 has Eliot describing him as "a poet of quite peculiar genius and peculiar faults."[50] But the attacks far outweighed admiration. In 1927, Eliot published his first critique of Lawrence for *La Nouvelle Revue Française*, a French journal about English novels. Eliot argued that Lawrence's "splendid and extremely ill-written novels—each one hurled from the press before we have finished reading the last" had but one subject in mind. He described Lawrence as "a demoniac, a natural and unsophisticated demoniac with a gospel," arguing darkly that Lawrence's characters lacked "all the amenities, refinements and graces which many centuries have built up in order to make love-making tolerable." When those characters "make love—or perform Mr. Lawrence's equivalent for love-making—and they do nothing else," they essentially moved backward through evolutionary time, passing backward the ape and fish to "some hideous coition of protoplasm." Eliot shuddered at the "progressive degeneration in humanity" exhibited in the novels, lamenting, "This is not *my* world, either as it is, or as I should wish it to be" (emphasis in original).[51] It was rather a world in which Eliot found, or at least claimed to find, sex quite intolerable. Eliot's acerbic portrait diminished Lawrence not simply to the level of brutes but to the most primitive stage of living cells.

Lawrence returned the invective, identifying Eliot as the very type of dry, lifeless corpse he found so abhorrent among civilized people. He may also have gotten back at Eliot in a slyer way. Some literary critics pointed out that Lady Chatterley's dour husband, Clifford, seemed closely modeled in his ideas and language on Eliot, and that some of his speeches insisting on ordered emotions and belittling passion and the body struck themes from Eliot's own writing.[52] Further, Clifford had become a writer after his disabling injury in the war (an injury that left him impotent), and his writings, in Lawrence's words, contained "no touch, no actual contact": "It was as if the whole thing took place on an artificial earth," yet Clifford was "morbidly sensitive" in wanting the approval of all. Chatterley/Eliot was a pathetic, needy, and crabbed person, all malice and superficiality, of little substance.[53] He was just the sort of traditionalist Christian who would despise Lawrence's work and deem it demoniacal.

Indeed, Eliot exemplified a particular Christian way of thinking about religion and sex that Lawrence spurned, representing an attitude toward passion that would have been at home with the Christian censors.

After Lawrence's death, he wrote that Lawrence had "failed completely" at creating genuine art, for he merely reveled in his own sensations without turning them to greater ends. Lawrence was "a very sick soul," and Eliot vilified Lawrence's "offensive" use of Christian faith for "non-Christian or anti-Christian" ends, attributing this tendency to the decadent lure of a "shadowy Protestant underworld" that picked and chose its religious symbols at will and was far outside the bounds of orthodox Christianity. Lawrence mistook human love to be the highest good, rather than the love of God; he pined for a degree of human intimacy that was impossible between living persons, particularly for one who did not realize that "the love of two human beings is only made perfect in the love of God." Political reform, social justice, racial equality—all were ultimately as egotistic and as inadequate for genuine human connection and meaning as sex, in Eliot's view.[54]

Eliot repeated and embellished these critiques in his 1934 book on the moral failings of modern literature, *After Strange Gods: A Primer of Modern Heresy*, in which he described Lawrence as a "great genius" sickened by "a distinct sexual morbidity." Denouncing "the deplorable religious upbringing which gave Lawrence his lust for intellectual independence," Eliot scoffed, "like most people who do not know what orthodoxy is, he hated it." He damned Lawrence's lack of "tradition" and analyzed him as having had "no guidance except the Inner Light, the most untrustworthy and deceitful guide that ever offered itself to wandering humanity." Having adopted what Eliot plainly deemed a "spirituality" that was flighty, self-righteous, and unmoored, Lawrence exhibited a "spiritually sick" vision, a "social obsession" with upending the proprieties of social class. Lawrence's characters displayed "the absence of any moral or social sense," betraying "no respect for, nor even awareness of, moral obligations" or conscience. They epitomized the worst instincts of humanity: the very model of modern heresy, the destruction of the moral universe.[55] The renunciation of traditional marriage signaled a wholesale rejection of civilized manners and obedience to the dictates of society.

Eliot was not alone in his contempt of Lawrence's spiritual earnestness toward sex, his dismissal of civilized conventions, and his determination to renounce modesty and bring sexual matters out into the light.

Not long after Lawrence's death, Ruth Frisbie Moore, a conservative literary critic, wrote disparagingly of his frank language—calling "spades spades"—and "outrageous grossness," a quality of the "spade cult" who claimed Lawrence as "its major prophet": "Lawrence himself treated [*Lady Chatterley's Lover*] as an inspired utterance, and the more radical critics approached it in a religious spirit, according it the reverent treatment a true Fundamentalist offers to Jonah and Genesis." Lawrence and his "disciples" displayed "perfect moral certitude" in their assessments, a snobbery about their explicitness that was dogmatic, self-righteous, and "cock-sure"—altogether pious to the point of ludicrous condescension. "For those of us with a devout upbringing," she wrote, "there is a decidedly musty odor about some of Lawrence's statements." His defenders were "veritable Impuritan Fathers," making "obeisance to his gods" in endless praise for his work as "rhapsodic," "flamingly intense," "rapturous," "ecstatic," and more. Harold Gardiner, the long-time literary editor of the Jesuit magazine *America* and a widely influential Catholic critic, lamented "the minute detailing of sexual aberrations" in the novel and noted that it was like other restricted books that do not merely depict sin but in fact "*teach* immorality." Lawrence, in the view of such antimodern critics, had mistaken health for sickness, honesty for vulgar desecration. By making depravity seem alluring, his writings posed an urgent danger to the culture.[56]

Whereas Lawrence saw it as both possible and essential to reconcile religion and sexual candor, Eliot and many other conservative Christians believed that the sort of sexual openness embodied in Lawrence threatened the very essence of Christianity. Even if it was a "serious quest for an alternative spiritual tradition" spurred by many of the same impulses that nurtured Christian faith—alienation from rational scientism and the worship of money—it was "will-worship of the ego," another Anglican writer put it.[57] A young Thomas Merton, who would become one of the major American Catholic writers of the twentieth century, pronounced Lawrence "a complete pagan" whose "gospel culminated in the proclamation of himself as a Messiah, as one who had come to save the world from intellectualism and give back to men the joyful 'mindlessness' of the Hopi snake dance." A "very flourishing cult of Lawrence the

Messiah" existed, in the view of these critics, and its antidote could not come soon enough.[58] From the traditionalist Christian point of view, the possibility of a rich and powerful alternative to Christianity coming to fruition was dire, as it would dethrone the powers of church authority in favor of something earthier and disorderly, the rejection of self-sacrifice and church authority alike. Eliot and his cohort could not abide Lawrence's antinomian challenge.

Female sexual awakening, an important theme in Lawrence's writings, was also a threat to a conservative Christian worldview that continued to uphold traditional gender norms as well as a hierarchy that remained closed to the idea of women's equality within the church and the broader society. The notion that women did not merely tolerate sex for the higher good of childbearing but that, once awakened, they realized they needed sex—such an idea certainly did not trouble all Christians, but in the ordered world of the conservatives it was hazardous. The specter of the sexually liberated female, ominously embodied in Margaret Sanger, also saturated Lawrence's work: however cogently later feminists would critique those portrayals for reifying gender hierarchy and female objectification, they were nonetheless subversive to the Christian worldview of the period. Lawrence's frank acknowledgment and graphic depictions of female appetites was shocking in the 1930s. The threat to Christianity posed by writers such as Lawrence appeared twofold: the problem of a seemingly decadent, pagan religion was but the flip side of the hazard posed by a positive view of sexuality and the honoring of sexual pleasure for women.

Eliot and many other Christian writers detested Lawrence's fiction for its anti-church anarchism and its renunciation of tradition, marriage, and social customs, and their perspective reflected the public Christian consensus still ascendant in the 1930s. Soon enough, however, liberal Protestants and even some Catholics reread Lawrence and undertook to defend him, sometimes even resurrecting part of his vision of sexuality for illumination and Christian appropriation. These reassessments appeared in the 1940s and into the 1950s (and beyond). Brother George Every, a British Anglican scholar and poet, wrote several times about Lawrence and showed increasing admiration for the ways in which his

work illuminated "the limitations of the liberal, democratic, and scientific outlook" and exemplified a critique of "modern scientific and sociological thinking" that made some sense—even though, from Every's
Christian worldview (and certainly Eliot's and Merton's), his solutions
were antithetical to Christian truth.[59] Citing Every's writings, an Anglican priest argued in 1951 that some "amends" were necessary to counter
"the abuse that has been hurled" at Lawrence "by so many Christians."[60]
The renowned Nathan Scott, a literary scholar and ordained Episcopal
priest who helped found the academic field of "literature and theology,"
gave ample attention to Lawrence and reassessed the linkage between religion and sexuality that had so profoundly offended Eliot, by resituating
Lawrence within a particular mystical stream of tragedy in the European
Romantic tradition; Lawrence, Scott pleaded, understood and deeply felt
the "anguish" of humanity's *ontological solitude* and utilized sex to il-
lumine both humans' alienation from one another and divine union or
completion.[61] This kind of openness to Lawrence's writing signaled the
new sorts of religious thinking about sex that were beginning to emerge.

By the summer of 1959, when a federal district court overturned the
postmaster general's refusal to transmit the infamous *Lady Chatterley's
Lover* through the mails and thus freed it from US censorship, Lawrence
was winning praise as a religious visionary. As derision of Lawrence gave
way to various degrees of admiration, even a theologian at Concordia
Seminary, a school of the very conservative Lutheran Church–Missouri
Synod, could write, "Pastors involved in marital counseling and theologians involved in the doctrine of creation will be stimulated by Lawrence's
holistic principle to search the Biblical Word anew." Influential Christian
thinkers were treating Lawrence's work as a font of creativity for Christian theologizing and praised his deep understanding of the meaning of
Christian love and sexuality: if not quite a Christian himself, Lawrence
could now be seen, in the words of one critic, as "almost a Christian."[62]
Perhaps the culmination of this new thinking came some time later, in
the 1960s, as when Horton Davies, a Welsh historian of Christianity
and ordained Congregationalist minister who taught at Princeton University, wrote a piece on Lawrence that began somewhat theatrically, "Is
David Herbert Lawrence also among the prophets? Is this adopted son

of Sigmund Freud also among the saints?" Davies's article focused entirely on Lawrence's writings about sexuality, love, and the body, and his
responses to these questions was an unambiguous yes.[63] For traditional
Christians, Lawrence had gone from being a despised anti-Christian
pagan to a prophet and a saint.

The Dunster House Bookshop case and successive shifts in Protestant and Catholic modes of censorship and control of literature and
film are important for revealing new fault lines in American religious
attitudes toward sex and the sexual content of popular entertainments.
The religious debates about *Lady Chatterley's Lover*, popular movies, and
pulp magazines showed growing disagreements over how best to protect
the morals of the nation—especially American youth—and maintain
social order. The censors had perceived *Lady Chatterley's Lover* to be a
menace, believing that Lawrence's sexually wild religiosity threatened to
upend the gender hierarchy and conservative religious norms of the time
and jeopardize the stability of the nation itself. Similar worry greeted
other suggestive materials, even as the strategy shifted away from censorship laws to active religious involvement in the control and distribution
of film and literature. Ultimately, the concerns articulated about sexual
content were deeply tied up with worries about modernity, challenges to
traditional church authority, and anxiety that feminism would upend the
godly male order of the created world.

Conservative Protestants and Catholics remained suspicious of one
another throughout the 1930s and beyond. But they were united in believing that sexually risqué materials should be rigorously monitored and
kept out of the hands of youth. Decades later, in one of those ironies of
history, it was a Catholic—Justice William Brennan, devoutly religious
and no fan of graphic sexuality, and the only Catholic then on the Supreme Court—who wrote the majority opinions in the 1964 cases that
overturned America's strictest twentieth-century obscenity laws, dramatically transformed the very meaning of "obscenity," and sharply restricted
the bounds of censorship.[64] Among other lessons, it was a reminder that
Protestants weren't the only Christian group splitting ranks over sex.

CHAPTER 3

SEGREGATION AND RACE MIXING IN THE EARLY CIVIL RIGHTS ERA

MUCH OF THE DEBATE OVER censorship in the 1930s centered on content deemed overtly sexual or depicting extramarital relationships. Most regulations did not aim to suppress portrayals of adult relationships that might fall outside of general conventions: love affairs between Catholics and Protestants, for instance, were not regulated by the censors or production codes, even if many people in both religious groups disapproved of them. Only one kind of consensual adult relationship between a man and a woman not married to other people was forbidden by the Motion Picture Production Code: intimate relationships "between the white and black races." The taboo on interracial intimacy in movies prevailed because the very idea of love and marriage across the color line was offensive to white Americans at this time. For years, there was no topic more forbidden, no issue more explosive, than interracial sex.

Race, of course, has always been one of the most contentious issues in American life. The African slave trade that began in the 1620s led to almost two hundred and fifty years of legally sanctioned white enslavement of black people, horrifically brutal in every respect and predicated on assumptions of black inferiority and white supremacy. Officially, slavery ceased with the end of the Civil War in 1865, but what followed were decades of conflict over the conditions by which white and African American people could coexist and interact in the United States. By the

1940s, when World War II proved to be a moment of decisive change in the nation, calls for full equality were gaining traction, even as resistance by whites remained strong; some of the most heated political debates of the time concerned race. And nothing stoked greater fury or fear than the idea of interracial intimacy, love, and sex.

The taboo white Americans placed on intimacy with African Americans long predated the 1940s, but it gathered particular momentum during that decade. Apprehensions over gender, purity, and the future of civilization that had roiled the debates over birth control and censorship found potent manifestation in the fear that this taboo might be eased or even eradicated. White Christians in the World War II–era South maintained their slaveholding ancestors' belief that God created separate black and white races and that He intended them to stay that way for the sake of white purity; framed by assumptions permeating white Southern culture, their reading of the Bible made such a worldview appear starkly obvious, and they pressed this view on each other and their children. The very thought of sex between a black man and a white woman infuriated white Southerners who wished to maintain both gender and racial hierarchy; this had been true for decades, and the prospect was a key argument used to shore up segregation, not to mention a recurrent rationale for lynchings and other murders of black men. But challenges to segregationist Jim Crow laws in the South lately seemed to be coming fast and furious, mainly from a federal government that most white residents thought had no right to interfere with Southern tradition. As desegregation increased, both by force and by choice, the pious aversion toward racial intermixing, marriage, and reproduction in some quarters only grew more belligerent and explosive.

In the mid-1940s, amid the horrors of World War II and the fascist reign of Adolf Hitler in Germany, this issue blew up in both houses of Congress. The outburst stemmed from a 1943 collaboration between two anthropologists at Columbia University, Ruth Benedict and Gene Weltfish, who coauthored a short pamphlet they titled *The Races of Mankind*. In 1944, distribution of the months-old pamphlet abruptly halted when it was deemed subversive by critics suggesting that the two anthropologist authors were likely Communists out to undermine the United States.

Anthropologist Ruth Benedict (undated).
BETTMANN VIA GETTY IMAGES.

Unwittingly or not, the authors had struck a nerve deep in the heart of Christian Dixie, threatening the architecture of racial separation and white supremacy that forbade sex across the color line. Anti-Communist sentiments were strong, and the McCarthy hearings were just around the corner; the repugnance for interracial sex that was so fierce among religious white Southerners helped speed along this new era of fear.

HOSTILITY TOWARD SEX ACROSS RACIAL lines—and especially toward sex between white women and black men—long rested on a specifically religious basis or rationale. Rooted in the history of slavery and emancipation, the taboo against interracial love was deeply entangled with ideas about God's racially ordered plan. Whether they owned slaves or not, white Americans who supported the slave system had no difficulty believing that the biblical references to slavery meant that the enslavement of Africans was just and that slavery was divinely sanctioned, in the eighteenth and nineteenth centuries no less than biblical times. Further, many white churchmen both in and beyond the South creatively inferred from the book of Genesis that God had cursed Noah's son Ham and his generations of offspring with black skin, consignment to bondage, and general subjugation to whites. In short, white Americans found support in the Bible not only for slavery specifically but also for racial inequality and segregation more generally: sex across the color line was thus a religious violation of God's law.[1]

The word "miscegenation," meaning the mixture of two or more races, first appeared in 1864, but laws prohibiting sex and marriage between the races in America went back to the 1660s, when colonial governments forbade interracial sex to bolster racial hierarchies, keep the so-called white race pure, and guard against the putative sexual depravity of black people. Stereotypes of Africans as more sexual and aggressive than whites had come over the ocean with the English settlers, who believed such people were "lewd, lascivious and wanton people" and were keen to mate across the color line.[2] By 1705, the Virginia Assembly was resorting to six months' imprisonment and a large fine for any white person caught fornicating across the color line, and ministers who performed interracial marriages were also fined.[3] Such statutes eventually pervaded all of the Southern colonies and, later, states: at least forty-one states enacted anti-miscegenation laws at one time.

Of course, these laws rarely applied in practice to white men; both before and after emancipation, black women were vulnerable to multiple forms of sexual coercion. Enslaved black women habitually suffered the humiliation of rape by their white masters, so much so that rising numbers of mixed-race babies motivated colonial governments to pass laws declaring the children of enslaved women to hold slave status as well. Slave masters could literally increase their own wealth by raping and impregnating their female slaves, even as white women giving birth to a so-called mulatto or mixed-race infant were severely punished. The legal apparatus developed to prohibit all sexual activity between white women and black men was wholly absent for black women, who were, without penalty, subjected to forcible sex, whipping, physical restraints, and public nudity.

Such practices were obviously about white control over black labor, but they were also, as one historian starkly puts it, about "feeding the sexual appetites of the powerful and about the degradation of those made to feel powerless."[4] Mixed-race children could still shock those not from the elite South: a Vermont native visiting Monticello in the early nineteenth century wrote to his father about Thomas Jefferson's interracial household and his slave, Sally Hemings: "The story of black Sal is no farce—That he cohabits with her and has a number of children by her is a sacred truth—and the worst of it is he keeps the same children slaves—an unnatural crime which is very common in these parts."[5] The right of white men to manhandle black women, rape them, impregnate them, and keep those offspring as slaves was rarely questioned, adding cruel absurdity to laws forbidding interracial marriage between freely consenting partners. These ravages of the American slavery system would live on in the later sexual violence inflicted by white Ku Klux Klansmen and gangs on black women perceived to be a threat (or whose husbands were perceived as such).

Far from being a negligible factor or an afterthought, religion was foundational in the anti-miscegenationist worldview. White disgust toward miscegenation rested on—and was reinforced by—Christian theology and racialized readings of the Bible. God had created separate and distinctive races, the argument went, and He expected them to stay that way. Whites had long associated blackness with contamination and impurity and built ample religious justification for this link from the Bible, generating what later commentators have called a "theology of segregationism."[6] This theology sometimes addressed sex specifically. Christians had long believed that the fall of Adam and Eve in the Garden of Eden came about through sexual sin; the serpent that lusted after Eve and tempted her into eating the forbidden apple was presumed to be male. Some pro-slavery writers before the Civil War characterized the serpent not just as male but specifically as a pre-Adamite black man, the Louisianan Samuel Cartwright going so far as to call the serpent a "negro gardener."[7] Tennessee clergyman Buckner Payne accepted this view, along with the corollary that as a creature created before Adam, the black figure was subhuman and had no soul. In 1867 Payne wrote, "A man can not commit so great an offense against his race, against his country, against his God, in any other way, as to give his daughter in marriage to a negro—a *beast*—or to take one of their females for his wife." Those who disagreed weren't simply wrong but evil: "The states or people that favor this equality and amalgamation of the white and black races, *God will exterminate*" (emphasis in original).[8] Cartwright similarly argued that "the hybrids" created through race mixing "were so exceedingly wicked" that they impelled God to destroy the world in the great flood. Miscegenation seemed to be the root of all corruption, the vilest of sins.[9]

If Christian theology could so thoroughly support slavery, racism, and opposition to interracial sex specifically, it could also validate the Southern cause in the Civil War. In 1863, delegates to meetings of the pro-slavery Southern Baptist Convention—a breakaway denomination formed eighteen years before, when northern Baptists underscored their opposition to slavery—pronounced the Civil War "just and necessary" and praised God's "divine hand in the guidance and protection of our beloved country." The North's opposition to Southern ways was, noted the Virginia Baptists, "alike subversive of the teachings of Christianity and the genius of constitutional liberty and order." Their own faith lay in the "sweet assurance that our cause is a righteous one." Pro-slavery congregations throughout the South deemed the Southern war effort a religious calling of sorts, a sacred duty in upholding God's laws for the races.[10]

Even after the South's defeat, white Christian clergy often led the way in teaching their flocks that they were nevertheless an honorable people with every right to rule over blacks, and that they were waging God's war against the evil, atheistic North. It was a theology, in other words, that upheld racial inequality as divinely established: "We do not believe that 'all men are created equal' . . . nor that they will ever become equal in this world," averred a Southern Baptist minister in 1883.[11] Gender hierarchy was fundamental to this interpretation of Christianity; so was racial hierarchy. With the end of slavery, old legal boundaries between white and black had been erased; for whites concerned to preserve their dominance in the status quo, blacks and whites needed to be thoroughly separated, and black people needed continual reminders of their limitations and their place in society—reminders that were aggressively enforced.

Slavery's destruction did not change the core belief in black inferiority held by so many whites—Northerners as well as Southerners—committed to white supremacy. In the South, most policies of Reconstruction failed as white Southerners managed to re-create structural hierarchies of racial dominance and subordination, all while they read their Bibles, prayed, attended church, and considered themselves true keepers of the Christian faith. Trading pro-slavery for pro-segregation theology, many white Americans were adamant in their belief that they were a people chosen by God who were in every way superior to African Americans. They must therefore remain separate and not intermix. Legislatures and courts enacted this theology into law, and not only in the South: two years after the Civil War ended, the Pennsylvania Supreme Court upheld the legality of segregated railway cars, affirming that "the natural law which forbids [interracial marriage] and that social amalgamation which leads to a corruption of races, is as clearly divine as that which imparted to [the races] different natures." State supreme courts in Indiana, Alabama, and Virginia also invoked God's divine law to uphold bans on intermarriage and to reinforce in human law the "theology of separate races."[12] By assumption, custom, and eventually law, the presence of even so little as "one drop" of nonwhite blood in a person's family history could exclude him or her from laying claim to whiteness.

Scientists and other scholars working in the latter decades of the nineteenth century took for granted this Christian view of the divine origin of racial separation and the evils of race mixing. Under the pseudonym "Caucasian," the author of *Anthropology for the People: A Refutation of the Theory of the Adamic Origin of All Races* (1891) wrote, "From this theory, that God made the yellow and the black races inferior, physically, mentally and morally, we infer that he designed them for a subordinate and dependent position." There was no question that God demanded the preservation of "blood purity," for which He implanted "the instinctive mutual and universal repulsiveness of races" so that the very idea of "political and social equality" would be "repugnant." Lest there be any doubt, Caucasian warned that miscegenation "is not only an enormous sin against God, but a degrading bestiality which can result only in unmitigated evil and final destruction." He echoed Payne and Cartwright in declaring that the biblical flood recounted in the book of Exodus resulted from mixing between white and nonwhite races, creating a situation so corrupt that God destroyed the world and began again.[13]

Other white Christian writers echoed similar claims into the twentieth century. Charles Carroll's *The Negro a Beast* (1900) and *The Tempter
of Eve* (1902) argued vociferously that miscegenation was the worst of all
sins. The Congregationalist minister and social scientist H. Paul Douglass, a vocal opponent of racial bigotry, bewailed the vast influence of
The Negro a Beast in the South, noting that door-to-door sales of the
book had helped it become "the Scripture of tens of thousands of poor
whites, and its doctrine is maintained with an appalling stubbornness
and persistence."[14] Published by the American Book and Bible House
in St. Louis, the book was nearly four hundred pages of scriptural exegesis and liberal quoting from other Southern Christian writers, and it
included numerous illustrations of caricatured black people and ethe-
realized whites. One, showing a wedding between a black man and a
white woman, was titled "The Beast and the Virgin" with this caption:
"Can you find a white preacher who would unite in holy wedlock, a burly
negro to a white lady? Ah! parents, you would rather see your daughter
burned, and her ashes scattered to the winds of heaven."[15] Certainly, less
dramatic versions of this taboo were far more widespread throughout
the country; after all, the Motion Picture Code had, as one of its general
principles, forbidden movie depictions of relationships between the races.
But "Professor" Carroll, as the publisher called him, advanced "biblical,
scientific, and common sense arguments" to make a dramatic Christian
case against racial mixing.

During and after the Reconstruction era, white violence against
black men accused of sexual crimes rose dramatically. Officials, Ku Klux
Klansmen, and other white vigilantes patrolled neighborhoods and attacked both men and women who were believed to be having sex across
the color line. Fear of black people's increasing political power blended
with anti-miscegenation ideology, so that white Southerners translated
black calls for economic opportunity and political equality into black
men's purported sexual desire for white women. This "threat to white
womanhood," one historian writes, upheld "a powerful alibi for denying
black people the basic rights of citizenship." The Democratic Party's very
coalescence across the class lines that divided whites was grounded in
their successful fearmongering about interracial sex, which took on new

THE BEAST AND THE VIRGIN.
Can you find a white preacher who would unite
in holy wedlock, a burly negro to a white lady? Ah!
parents, you would rather see your daughter
burned, and her ashes scattered to the winds of -
heaven.

Illustration decrying the horrors of interracial marriage,
from Charles Carroll, *The Negro a Beast* (1900).

urgency as "social equality" took on the insinuation of coerced sexual intercourse between black men and white women.[16]

Democrats in the postwar South consistently asserted that African Americans would inevitably seek not only sex with white women but
interracial marriage itself, and that the mixed-race progeny of such marriages would augur devastation of the pure white race. Blacks resisted
this narrative: as the African American minister Henry McNeal Turner
wrote in 1866, the notion that black men wanted white women was a

"foolish dream" of "Southern fanatics": "What do we want with their daughters and sisters? We have as much beauty as they. . . . All we ask of the white man is to let our ladies alone, and they need not fear us."[17] But the anti-miscegenation narrative was brutally effective in maintaining white power over newly emancipated African Americans. The ostensible sexual immorality of African Americans was a persistent rationale used during Reconstruction by white leaders who opposed full rights for freed blacks and their descendants. Whole categories of black Christians— ministers, lay people, and entire church assemblies—were painted with accusations of licentiousness, the repetition of which charge helped sustain and feed whites' beliefs in their own superiority and the unfitness of blacks for citizenship.

Shadowing this creed in the South, incidentally, was the reality that many communities continued to tolerate the concubinage relations between white men (particularly those of high status) and black women who might well bear their children, receive financial support, and serve as a second family. The journalist Ray Stannard Baker's *Following the Color Line* (1908) documented the commonness of these families throughout the South, while noting that "the better class of Southern people" were starting to attack these conditions along with other cross-racial encounters, starting with the clergy. When a Methodist pastor in Alabama railed against the fact that Montgomery had "four hundred Negro women supported by white men" and "thirty-two Negro dives operated for white patronage," the local paper reported the statistics and railed against such vices.[18] The anti-miscegenation taboo and the specter of rape also veiled the murky fear that white women might conceivably desire to be with black men if they could. W. E. B. Du Bois noted in 1913 that whites acknowledged but one racial problem, put most frantically as, "Do you want your sister to marry a Nigger?" As he observed, however, the ban on interracial marriage must be destroyed, "not because we are anxious to marry white men's sisters, but because we are determined that white men shall let our sisters alone."[19]

White Americans violently maintained the prohibition on miscegenation well into the twentieth century, most notably through the lynching of African American men and women. According to one study, of the thousands of African Americans who were lynched in the Southern states between 1877 and 1950, more than half were accused of murder or rape.[20] The chief justification for lynching itself was its ostensible use as a deterrent to black rapists. Writing to the *Nation* in 1916, a white Northerner transplanted to the South spoke for many when he noted how "troublesome and insolent" Southern blacks were to whites and connected this to sexual brazenness before advocating lynching for rapists: "It may be bad to lynch, but is it not far worse for a demonized fiend, swelling with bestial lust, to lay his cursed hands on a pure, defenceless woman to satisfy his animal nature? Mr. Editor, you have never had a sister, a wife, or a child outraged by a beast who has all the privileges of respectable men."[21] As the study showed, white vigilante mobs killed black men even if there was no evidence or identification by the alleged victim. The Southern definition of black-on-white "rape" was expansive, as white laws and institutions refused the possibility that any white woman would willingly have anything to do with with a black man.[22]

Undergirded by white Christian visions of purity and sometimes ritualized by the invocational prayers of white ministers, large numbers of these lynchings were what one historian calls "spectacle lynchings," with hundreds or even thousands of spectators present—some with cameras to document the occasion—in what was essentially a religious rite of purification. Prayer services sometimes preceded such lynchings. Many white churches, in fact, were patently indifferent to them, for lynch mobs often included their own parishioners. While some ministers condemned lynching and occasionally took action to prevent it or admonish participants, the expulsion of church members who had participated in lynch mobs could and did result in the defection of other members and criticism from the press.[23] Many Southern white Christians believed the Bible supported the practice, some citing Phineas's divinely ordered killing of an adulterous Israelite consorting with a woman of another race (he killed her too), recounted in the book of Numbers. The 1899 lynching of Sam Hose in Newman, Georgia—Hose was accused of murdering a white farmer and raping his wife—took place on a Sunday, "just after church let out." His torturers cut off his ears, castrated him, and burned him slowly—with "absolute order and decorum," one paper absurdly reported, until he died.

One older man was quoted screaming, "God bless every man that had a hand in this" and "thank God for vengeance," even as men quite indecorously rushed to cut off fingers, grab pieces of bone and skull, or otherwise acquire a fragment of Hose's dead body as a souvenir.[24]

Anti-lynching campaigns invariably faced accusations of abetting sexual violence, as when Tennessee representative Finis J. Garrett argued in late 1921 that an anti-lynching bill should be retitled, "A bill to encourage rape." His Mississippi colleague John E. Rankin agreed, arguing the following month that the bill "will cost the lives of innocent white women and children throughout the South, if not throughout the entire country." Rankin continued, "The shadow of the Negro criminal constantly hangs ... like the sword of Damocles over the head of every white woman in the South, and no one knows just when or where it is going to fall."[25] No fear better maintained Jim Crow segregation than that of rape across the color line.

Legal segregation met few successful challenges through the end of the 1920s. But opposition was growing, and attacks on segregation expanded in the 1930s, eventually with some support from Franklin D. Roosevelt's administration. Legal thinkers like Howard University School of Law's Charles Hamilton Houston believed that segregated education, especially, was at the core of racial inequality in America and thus the key area to challenge. The National Association for the Advancement of Colored People (NAACP), founded in 1909, had long fought against racism and racist violence; under the leadership of Walter White, who became secretary in 1931, the organization commenced a steady campaign against the disfranchisement of black Southern voters and against segregation laws, especially their impact on unequal education for black students. The NAACP also aided the successful campaign to defeat the Supreme Court nomination of North Carolina judge John J. Parker—who had made comments opposing black suffrage—and spearheaded a major anti-lynching campaign in hopes of passing a federal law against lynching.

In the same decade, President Roosevelt—prodded on civil rights by his outspokenly liberal wife, Eleanor—appointed Mary McLeod Bethune, an African American Republican who became a Democrat because of Roosevelt's policies, to serve as one of his African American policy advisors, a group of African Americans sometimes referred to as the president's "Black Cabinet." Both as the founder of the National Council of Negro Women in 1935 and as the Roosevelt-appointed director of the Division of Negro Affairs of the National Youth Administration in 1936, Bethune worked tirelessly for early civil rights reforms and for "the integration of all [America's] people regardless of race, creed, or national origin." When, in 1938, the Supreme Court ruled that states providing a school to white students had to provide a school to black students too, segregation received its first major challenge since "separate but equal" was upheld in *Plessy v. Ferguson.* The following year, federal officials reacted when the Daughters of the American Revolution refused to allow Marian Anderson, the great African American contralto, to sing at its segregated concert hall in Washington; instead, thanks to the efforts of First Lady Eleanor Roosevelt and Interior Secretary Harold Ickes, Anderson sang outdoors at the Lincoln Memorial to an audience of seventy-five thousand people, black and white alike, and was introduced by Ickes, who proclaimed, "In this great auditorium under the sky, all of us are free. . . . Genius, like justice, is blind. . . . Genius draws no color line!"[26]

Many white Americans, particularly white Christian Southerners, were outraged by these efforts toward racial integration, and many worked vigorously to uphold white supremacy in law and in daily life. White Southern parents committed to this ideology continued to indoctrinate their children; as one historian writes, with extralegal methods of violence becoming intolerable, "white supremacists were forced to shift the process of socialization away from the public sphere and into the home."[27] Parents of this mindset did all they could to prevent their white children from mixing with black children, continuing to teach sons and daughters that they were superior to people of other races. White supremacists with more power to resist civil rights did so in the arenas they could, whether in housing discrimination, resistance to school integration, or political and legal work. Lynching, though in decline, remained the resort of choice for vigilantes.

The evils of interracial sex, and the specter of rape, remained a potent rationalization in this effort, the overriding basis for maintaining any means necessary to keep the races apart and control African American men by fear. In 1938, Senator Theodore Bilbo of Mississippi—a licensed Baptist preacher and an open white supremacist who was a proud member of the Ku Klux Klan—invoked this rationale when filibustering an anti-lynching bill before the Senate in apocalyptic terms:

> If you succeed in the passage of this bill, you will open the flood-gates of hell in the South. Raping, mobbing, lynching, race riots, and crime will be increased a thousandfold; and upon your garments and the garments of those who are responsible for the passage of the measure will be the blood of the raped and outraged daughters of Dixie, as well as the blood of the perpetrators of these crimes that the red-blooded Anglo-Saxon white southern men will not tolerate.

To outlaw lynching was to abet black rapists, Bilbo argued. Of all the crimes white Southerners could fathom, none was more worthy of swift reprisal, torture, and death than sex across the color line, an act that, even in the late 1930s, could only be fathomed as rape.[28] In response and as part of an effort to counter the deep South's belligerent hold on lynching and other racist practices, in 1939 Roosevelt's attorney general, Frank Murphy, created the Civil Rights Section of the Justice Department to work with the NAACP and prosecute perpetrators; the division took seven years to win its first lynching conviction.

As the 1930s turned into the 1940s, African Americans were making strides in educational and economic mobility, and segregation laws faced further challenges. In 1941, under pressure from the March on Washington Movement, Roosevelt banned racial discrimination in defense industries that contracted with the government and created the Fair Employment Practice Committee (FEPC) to enforce this mandate. In 1942, the NAACP opened its Washington Bureau, Marian Anderson sang in a fully integrated Constitution Hall, and a group of students at the University of Chicago founded the Congress of Racial Equality (CORE), which the next year organized the first restaurant sit-in, a strategy that would long be used by civil rights leaders to challenge segregation of commercial and public spaces. The civil rights movement for black equality would continue to grow and meet successes in many areas for years to come.

But Southern white Christians who were committed to Jim Crow segregation continued to resist. Many Southern Baptists focused renewed attention on evangelism and missionary work within the black community as a means of "improving" race relations and deflecting African American interest in the civil rights movement. In 1942, the denomination's Home Mission Board hired a black man—its first African American administrative staff member—to serve as a liaison between the white Southern Baptist constituency and the African Americans in the National Baptist Convention. Denying him an office because of its pro-segregation policy, the board editorialized the following year that such mission activity "makes it possible for Southern Baptists to cross all racial lines in preaching the Gospel without raising the question of racial or social relationships." That same year, the Florida Baptist Convention's Social Service and Temperance Committee, also working on interracial missions, assured white Baptists that "a happy relation between the races does not mean an amalgamation."[29]

Religion was no mere postscript to the anti-miscegenationist worldview that was part and parcel of American racism eight decades after slavery was outlawed; with the Bible its keystone, Christianity was deployed for disgust toward racial mixing. Numerous Southern ministers and lay people alike maintained that racial separation was divinely ordained by God and proven by Scripture: obliterating racial distinctions, contaminating white blood, and creating a so-called mongrel race violated God's plan for humanity. Integration and intermarriage—which went together, the one advancing the other—fostered amalgamation, thereby demolishing the people God had picked to rule the nation and the world.

It was precisely this sort of racism that Ruth Benedict devoted much of her career to combatting. She was appalled by the racial animus so acutely visible in the United States during her lifetime, and she wanted to help eradicate it. Her perspective was rooted in an understanding of

human culture that prompted her to be equally skeptical of sexual hierarchies and universal morals. Her background and training made her an
ideal campaigner to call out anti-miscegenationist ideology and elucidate
it for broad public audiences.

She certainly understood the powerful appeal of religious faith. Born
Ruth Fulton in New York in 1887, her childhood was steeped in the Baptist
tradition, though her version of Christianity was somewhat different from
that of the Southern segregationists. Her religious upbringing was conven-
tionally strict, and she embraced the religious world of her devout mother
and grandparents. As a child, she was a regular attendee at Sunday School
and worship services, including midweek prayer meetings, missionary programs, and other church events, and she was devoted to her Bible and to
the figure of Christ himself. Ruth's childhood church followed Baptist tradition in concluding each Sunday morning service with an invitation to
the unsaved to make their public profession of faith and seek baptism. She
made her own public profession at the age of eleven and eagerly anticipated
her baptism in her diary, writing happily, "Jesus will wash away my sins."
She had a fondness for the stories of missionary women her mother read to
her, and at that age she sometimes imagined herself becoming a missionary
to heathen peoples herself. Instead, the adult Benedict grew skeptical of
many of her early religious beliefs, and her engagement with other cultures
would lead her to see religion as a product of human culture, deeply meaningful to its adherents but not of divine origin.

Ruth received a scholarship to Vassar, where she matriculated
in 1905. The question of female suffrage pervaded the women's college
during her years there, as did smoking—both symbols of women's emancipation. At Vassar, she became enamored with the writings of Walter
Pater, Charlotte Perkins Gilman, John Burroughs, Walt Whitman,
and Friedrich Nietzsche. After graduating in 1909, Ruth spent a year
abroad traveling in Europe and learning a great deal about foreign cultures, customs, and outlooks on her own home country. She then did a
stint as a social worker in Buffalo, working with poor families—many of
them immigrants—but, feeling helpless to bring real help to those living
in poverty, she quit to take a teaching position in Los Angeles. But this
work too felt empty in comparison to the vibrant intellectual life she'd

had at Vassar. During this period, she read Olive Schreiner's *Woman and Labour*, a manifesto that argued for full economic freedom, social independence, and meaningful work for women as the means that would "for the first time fully enfranchise" true sexual love between women and men and bring about "a higher appreciation of the sacredness of all sex relations." The work influenced her greatly, as a call to a feminism that would unify the sexes and overcoming the conflicts caused by old Victorian ideals coming up against new social realities.[30] She married Stanley Benedict, a chemist, in 1914 and became Ruth Fulton Benedict. Though happy at first, she was also restless in their suburban town and, still more, intellectually starved. She worked on a writing project devoted to strong historical women—Mary Wollstonecraft, Margaret Fuller, and Schreiner—even as the marriage soured, with Stanley resisting her demands for equality within the marriage.

When she was thirty-one, Benedict went back to school, studying educational philosophy with John Dewey at Columbia University before taking a class in 1919 on sex and sex roles across different societies, taught by the feminist sociologist-turned-anthropologist Elsie Clews Parsons at the New School for Social Research. In a paper she wrote for that course, Benedict argued that women ought to be free to have sex exactly as they chose and with whomever they wished, marriage notwithstanding. That she also believed fervently in passionate love between two people was clear there as well as in her journal entries; no fan of casual sex was Benedict, but she was indignant at the societal and legal rules that made it difficult to liberate oneself from "the perpetual lock and key of marriage," especially one that was loveless.[31] Her interest in anthropology deepened as she discovered how it offered a way to explore such intimate matters in depth. Turning her sights to doctoral work, she received admission at Columbia, then a vibrant center of new thinking in anthropology, and obtained a PhD in anthropology under Franz Boas in 1923. After a long search for a permanent job, in 1931 and at the age of forty-four (and separated from her husband), Benedict received an appointment as an assistant professor at Columbia.

Benedict and Boas had common intellectual interests and a shared commitment to social justice. Boas, a German-born Jew who had immigrated to the United States a few years before joining the Columbia faculty in 1896, was the foremost anthropologist of his day. He famously promoted the concept of culture, teaching that environment was a far more important influence on human behavior than biology and race. As an organic set of learned beliefs, customs, and morals, cultures were not closed or static systems, immobile over time; rather, they were fluid, dynamic, and ever-changing. Cultures varied widely across the globe, not because some ethnic groups were more intelligent or physically stronger but because local histories and circumstances varied, leading to seemingly boundless variations on human beliefs and behaviors. Boas and his students were the modernists of their field, questioning principles that others believed to be absolute givens and acknowledging unlimited variety. They critiqued universal truths and theories that promoted a fixed model of human progress toward enlightenment, liberation, and beneficence; the horrors of their own age showed the folly of that model. Instead, they stressed the messiness and fascinating complexity of cultural development in all of its variety, seeing the makeup of societies as the product of chance rather than of intentional design. So-called primitive peoples received a measure of respect as complex social builders who may well be more sophisticated in their ordered webs than supposedly more evolved civilizations. Human development was anarchic, in the most enthralling way.[32]

Benedict shared this way of thinking about human cultures, and she set out her views in *Patterns of Culture*, published in 1934. The work sought to persuade the American public that "primitive" cultures were in no way inferior to supposedly more sophisticated civilizations. She focused on three different cultures: the Pueblos (particularly the Zuni) of the American Southwest, the Dobuans of Melanesia, and the Kwakiutl Indians of the Northwest Coast. She argued that every culture had its more and less intelligent people, its more and less physically robust populations—genes and hereditary traits varied within cultural groups as much as, if not more than, beyond them. But environmental and historical factors were far more important in determining a person's makeup than were any inherent natural traits such as skin color. Rules such as those pertaining to sexual behavior were shaped by cultural patterns rather than dictated by divine law, and so, she extrapolated, there was little to fear from the loosening of those rules among younger generations in contemporary America: "The minor changes that occasion so much denunciation today, such as the increase of divorce, the growing secularization in our cities, the prevalence of the petting party, and many more, could be taken up quite readily into a slightly different pattern of culture," she noted. They would soon come to seem "traditional" and "would be given the same richness of content, the same importance and value, that the older patterns had in other generations." Rather than despise such differences across cultures, "wisdom consists in a greatly increased tolerance toward their divergencies."[33]

The interest and tolerance that Benedict directed toward "divergencies" stretched over many subjects, including sexual behavior. "The whole question of sex and sex differences has been a passion with me throughout my life," Benedict wrote in a 1936 letter to her close friend Margaret Mead, and that appeal certainly came out in her work.[34] In fact, Benedict regularly sounded an appreciative note when comparing other cultures' attitudes toward sex with those of mainstream Americans, which she not so subtly critiqued. The Zuni might look as "Puritanical" as our own repressive culture, but the Zuni people had "no sense of sin," carried no "guilt complexes," and did not frown upon sex as "a series of temptations to be resisted with painful efforts of the will." They disapproved of chastity and delighted in sex, conveying on the whole a much healthier attitude toward it than did most Americans. Where Americans moralized and tsk-tsked, the Zuni way of commending a good man was to say, "Everybody likes him. He is always having affairs with women." For the sexually healthy culture, Benedict concluded, "sex is an incident in the happy life," rather than a source of shame.[35] Benedict's call for cross-cultural understanding was plainly tied up with a tolerant attitude toward sexual diversity and a skepticism toward religious ideas like sin that produced guilt and shame.

While Benedict was hardly the first to make this cross-cultural argument, *Patterns of Culture* put the idea and its implications into clear, digestible prose. The book became an influential tool for conveying this theory of culture's influence, over and against models of biological determinism: it was widely reviewed, and it transformed how many Americans understood both their own culture and others. Social scientists as well as many members of the wider public embraced this paradigm shift toward understanding the power of culture to shape moral codes, and they understood the implication that America's own moral codes were no less rooted in culture than those of the Pueblos and the Dobuans. All value systems had developed out of a rich repertoire of possibilities and choices, and none could be considered objectively right or wrong. Readers came to accept, if not appreciate, Benedict's message: persons could remain wedded to their own value systems, but it was arrogant to presume one's system to be divine truth and blithely moralize against others' values, whether having to do with sex or other ethical matters Benedict drew out in the book. When, a few years after its initial publication, the book came out as a twenty-five-cent paperback, it was a best seller. As one observer later noted, Benedict's ideas "truly became 'common coin' in the American psyche."[36]

In 1939, as Benedict worked to popularize theories of human culture, Boas inaugurated a campaign to improve the way that American schools and teachers taught students the concept of race. That year, Boas had conducted a study, funded by the American Jewish Committee, which found that 20 percent of school textbooks were presenting eugenic ideas about the immutability of race, and superior and inferior races, that scientists had rejected decades before. Boas's study repeatedly found texts in geography, history, biology, civics, and other subjects that promoted the white race's superiority, with statements like, "Civilization has been developed and history has been made chiefly by the white race."[37] White supremacist assumptions permeated popular culture and much else besides, but Boas hoped these findings would stoke outrage in American readers aware that the German government was forcing that nation's schools to teach false Nazi theories of racial superiority. Surely such doctrines had no place in American taxpayer-funded public schools. Indeed, they were profoundly detrimental to the vital role of education in strengthening American democracy.

Determined to change how schools thought about race, Boas publicized his findings as widely as he could. He produced a pamphlet titled *Can You Name Them?*, asking readers to see if they could identify the nationalities of the men featured on the pamphlet's cover based on physical appearances alone; of course, he intended the answer to be no, as the pamphlet focused on disproving popular misconceptions about racial characteristics and the "false dogma" of racial traits that had been used "to justify political domination" and "led to merciless persecution of minorities."[38] Boas mailed the pamphlet to major newspapers across the country, including African American papers such as the *Chicago Defender*, and many ran stories covering his efforts. With other like-minded anthropologists, he also worked through various media—public speeches, pamphlets, exhibits, and radio programs, for instance—to teach teachers how to think more accurately about race. They were open regarding their goal of undermining "racism," a recent term that they defined as "the attempt of individuals of one group to dominate another group based on false racial theories."[39] Teaching students about the role of culture as a force shaping human diversity would undermine false racial theories, lessening the prejudiced assumptions many people held about people who were physically unlike themselves.

Through Boas, Benedict grew convinced that public schools were a crucial place to intervene against racism. She joined the Commission on Intercultural Education of the Progressive Education Association, which aimed to help teachers and school administrators create programs to instill tolerance across ethnic groups. She worked to improve the curricula of intercultural education, a model created by well-meaning educators but one she felt was superficial in its handling of the real plight faced by groups such as Jews and African Americans. In 1940, she published *Race: Science and Politics*, a book she hoped would, like *Patterns of Culture*, reach a wide audience and help readers understand how scientists like her and Boas thought about race—and the implications for reducing racism. Benedict also wrote a resource guide for secondary school teachers called *Race and Cultural Relations: America's Answer to the Myth of a Master Race*, telling readers, "No subject you study in school today is more fraught with consequences than this subject of race."[40] Benedict did not merely support equality of access and opportunity for all Americans, regardless of race; her anti-racism was part of a larger critique of the standing social order, one she shared with many other anthropologists, who argued that much more needed to change and that resources ought to be more equally distributed. It is not difficult to see why some to her political right were beginning to wonder if she were a Communist.

At that time, anthropological thinking about race was thoroughly in opposition to the ideas that still held sway at the time, especially in the South—ideas whose exponents wished to guard at all costs. And one of the chief grounds on which they made their case was sex.

It was as a result of these efforts to popularize the new anthropological thinking about race that Ruth Benedict found herself in 1944 at the center of a public controversy over the pamphlet she cowrote with her fellow Columbia anthropologist Gene Weltfish, also a former student and then colleague of Boas. They had written *The Races of Mankind* at the request of two organizations: the United Service Organizations (USO), a nongovernment association created to support and raise the morale of military officers and their families, and the Public Affairs Committee of the US Office of War Information, a distributor of information and propaganda relating to America's role in the war. USO officials intended to distribute the pamphlet to armed services personnel, hoping to encourage them as they fought the Japanese alongside nonwhite allies in the Philippines and Solomon Islands; the pamphlet would also work to counter Nazi theories of a "super race" and perhaps reduce racial prejudice in the soldiers' own ranks.

The pamphlet was a short document whose basic message was that racial differences are only skin deep and that economic and educational factors—not race—explain cultural and social disparities between different groups. It cited a range of scientific, social, and educational research to prove that there were no "superior" and "inferior" races among humans. Distinctions that are purely physiological, such as skin color and hair texture, do not map onto intelligence or morality, the two wrote; all peoples are much the same in those areas, until one takes into account social, cultural, economic, and other factors that bring difference of opportunity into being. Indeed, intelligence tests performed on US soldiers during World War I showed higher scores for African Americans living in the North than white men from the South, readers learned. While there were, indeed, "races," these meant little in light of the fact that "all the peoples of the earth are a single family and have a common origin." The biblical story that recounted Adam and Eve as the biological parents of the entire human race "told centuries ago the same truth that science has shown today": that all are brothers, and their very bodies represented "the record of their brotherhood."[41]

Popular misconceptions to the contrary, in fact, the races that did exist were not really "pure" at all. Humans in earlier historical eras had regularly bred across cultural and ethnic lines—which meant, the authors explained, there was neither an unadulterated white race nor a pure black race. "Race mixture" had been produced "since before history began." Moreover, "no one has been able to show that this is necessarily bad." Different cultures might make such mixing "a social evil," and in such a culture, "sensible people will avoid contributing to it by grieving if their children make such alliances. We must live in the world as it is." Yet there were "no immutable laws of nature" that rendered race mixing injurious.[42] German Nazis who believed in the purity and superiority of blue-eyed Aryans as a race had it all wrong—but then, so too did American whites who believed their own race was pure and superior to the black race. The further implication was clear: if races were not pure, nor even meaningful categories of differentiation, there was no inherent reason beyond societal disapproval that people could not love, marry, and reproduce across racial lines.

Easy to read and sold for ten cents, the tract was considered "a masterpiece of popularization of scientific knowledge," according to its editor and the secretary of the Public Affairs Committee.[43] Its enthusiastic promoters hoped it would be a tool to overcome race prejudice and its attendant ills, and its initial reception seemed promising. Like earlier interventions by Boas and Benedict, the pamphlet received an enthusiastic response among educators. When it appeared in print in October 1943, the New York City Board of Education recommended it to teachers for use in their continuing drive for tolerance, while the Detroit public school administration delivered the pamphlet and an accompanying educational poster series to every school in the district. The success of the pamphlet, along with the version produced for children, *In Henry's Backyard*, was

Cover of *The Races of Mankind* (1943),
a pamphlet that drew great ire from
white Southern leaders incensed at
its premise of racial equality and the
acceptability of race mixing.

impressive enough that the American Council on Education tapped
Benedict to study "the treatment accorded religious and racial matters
in basic teaching materials used in our public schools and colleges." The
National Conference of Christians and Jews funded the study.[44]

But the public reception concealed trouble brewing behind the
scenes. Even before publication, the pamphlet attracted apprehension in
the USO, the organization that had set out to sponsor it. The USO president, Chester Barnard, wrote a five-page, single-spaced letter rejecting
the prepublication manuscript on the ground that its distribution would
be a "political effort" subject to interpretation as subversive. "The doctrine of equality of race runs directly counter not only to social practice in
large sections of the country, but also to definite legal [proscriptions]. . . .

Distribution of such material on a large scale by an organization such as the USO will inevitably be regarded as an effort to change governmental policy." The chair of the Public Affairs Committee responded that while the USO could choose what literature to distribute, Barnard's rationale would "restrict the educational policy of any organization to limitations imposed by the most ignorant, the least trained, and the noisiest part of the public it seeks to serve."[45]

The Public Affairs Committee persisted in publishing the pamphlet, submitting it to various USO member agencies despite Barnard's concern. The initial run of thirty thousand copies in October 1943 proved not enough; second and third printings produced more pamphlets. The orders were staggering: the Army and Navy Division of the YMCA immediately ordered seventy thousand copies, the Rosenwald Fund ordered eleven thousand, and the US Army ordered fifty-five thousand copies for its orientation courses.

And then, suddenly, the pamphlet became the center of a public storm that would reach all the way to both chambers of Congress. In January, USO president Barnard ordered an end to its distribution by USO units to the armed forces, considering it "too controversial" for servicemen. Critics denounced this decision; as one writer mocked, "Perhaps Mr. Barnard and his board consider racial truths too heady a wine for the men who are ready to fight and die for the Four Freedoms and the Atlantic Charter." Another noted, "if you happen to believe that the earth is flat you will find every book on geography 'controversial.' . . . I fear that epithet is used by people who don't like to have the facts presented." Infuriated by the seeming cowardice on display in Barnard's decision, scientists and other public figures protested the USO's action, while other orders for the pamphlet poured in: the National CIO War Relief Committee announced its intent to mail copies of the pamphlet to all servicemen in the United States and, it hoped, overseas, as "one of the best answers to Hitler's Aryan creed."[46] A fourth printing of the pamphlet produced a hundred fifty thousand copies in January, and a fifth added a hundred thousand more pamphlets two months later.[47]

Further furor erupted after a member of Congress (possibly Representative Bob Sikes of Florida) publicly announced that the US Army

had procured fifty-five thousand copies for the purpose of training officer candidates, stirring up Southern white segregationists. Outrage filled
the editorial pages of Southern newspapers. The *News-Tribune* in Rome,
Georgia, editorialized, "If the Government has any surplus energy, it
should be put into winning the war with the Axis, not into the crusade
for social equality." The *Telegraph* in Macon, Georgia, went still further:
"If our representatives in Congress have any respect for themselves and
their constituents they will utterly destroy the crawling vermin who are
responsible for things like this."[48]

Southern segregationists had caught more than a whiff of racial
equality, integration, and racial amalgamation from the book, sensing a
subversive intimate subtext that, while only indirectly stated, was clearly
present. In March, US representative Andrew J. May of Kentucky and a
few other Southern congressmen led the House Military Affairs Committee to pressure the US Army into halting its planned distribution of
The Races of Mankind. Since that congressional committee controlled the
army budget, the army had little choice but to comply, and it eventually
destroyed its entire cache of pamphlets. The chief reason given by May
for his opposition was the tract's use of data that showed Northern blacks
scoring higher on intelligence tests than Southern whites. In April, a
House military subcommittee led by Representative Carl T. Durham of
North Carolina assailed the pamphlet again, complaining that even if
it were true that people of all races were brothers, "even brothers in the
same family are not necessarily equal mentally, physically, socially, politically, or morally." Indeed, the pamphlet's problems extended "all the way
from half-truths through innuendos to downright inaccuracies."[49]

In the category of "innuendo" Durham and his allies surely included
the pamphlet's detailed discussion of "racial mixture" and the long history of peoples traveling, meeting others, and breeding with persons
across races. As the authors wrote, "Thousands of Negro slaves have been
brought into Europe at various times. Where are they now? People have
come and gone in Europe for centuries. Wherever they went, some of
them settled down and left children. Small groups were absorbed into
the total population. Always the different races moved about and inter-
married." For this reason, and against everything German leaders were

then saying about the so-called Aryans, "no European is a pure anything." A "pure" race did not exist. Americans, too, were mixed and descended from all kinds of ancestors—"Cro-Magnons, Slavs, Mongols, Africans, Celts, Saxons, and Teutons." And while further mixing of the races could "be made a social evil," the authors wrote, "as far as we know, there are no immutable laws of Nature that make racial intermixture harmful."[50]

Dixie statesmen would not stand for such a thing. Representative Joseph Bryson made an impassioned case for white supremacy against "the intermingling of the races" on the House floor, condemning the "long-haired men and short-haired women" who did not recognize the "innate intellectual superiority of whites over Negroes" and who persisted in "agitating for the amalgamation of the races." Clearly, these agitators were subversive radicals and likely sexual deviants, as their rebellious hairstyles indicated (another favorite descriptor often invoked by critics was "starry-eyed"). In fact, Bryson insisted, against the clear trend toward culturalism in anthropology, "Archaeologists and evolutionists are quite unanimous on the subject of white supremacy."[51]

Race mixing remained a profoundly disturbing idea to many white people, including these white Southerners, in the 1940s. White Southerners' conviction, in one scholar's words, that "the South was the last repository of the 'pure' white race" and their "pathological fear of miscegenation" ran ever higher as fear of Communism heightened during and after the war. White Southerners were profoundly aware that the Communist Party of the United States (CPUSA) held no opposition to interracial sex, and charges that the pamphlets' authors were Communists were soon to come.[52] Indeed, the FBI reported "with unease" that *The Races of Mankind* had made the rounds in the Communist Party headquarters in New York.[53]

Congressional leaders in both the Senate and the House were still fulminating about the pamphlet in May, when it emerged pointedly as a subtext in the heated debate over H.R. 7, a bill that would outlaw the requirement of poll taxes as requirements for the right to vote. Senator John Little McClellan of Arkansas warned his fellow legislators that to outlaw the poll tax was to start down a slippery slope of sexual chaos into intermarriage. He protested, "We do not discriminate concerning marriage

in the South; we simply do not let the whites and Negroes intermarry."
The Southern Baptist senator Bilbo made this issue the very centerpiece
of his own vigorous argument against H.R. 7, several times referring to
the anti–poll tax measure as an effort to "rape the Constitution." Noting
that the Communist Party of the United States had, "in the first place,"
called for "the abolition of all laws which prohibit the intermarriage of
the races," Bilbo railed directly against "the statements of Dr. Benedict
and Dr. Willfish [sic] in their book entitled 'The Races of Mankind'":
"There has never been a more disgusting conglomeration of scientific and
physical facts than is to be found in this book. The whole scheme looks
to the consummation of the plank in the platform of the Communist
Party calling for the repeal of all laws forbidding the intermarriage of
the races."[54] Bilbo's tirade made the connection clear: the advocacy of intermarriage and sex across the color line was linked to Communism, an
ideology seen to be both anti-American and anti-Christian.

Like Bilbo, Representative Malcolm Tarver of Georgia drew a similar link between the sin of intermarriage and the scourge of Communism. He was next to lambaste *The Races of Mankind* in a lengthy speech
aiming to strike funding for the Fair Employment Practice Committee
from the war appropriations bill. Convinced that the FEPC was itself a
Communist-inspired plot to force black and white mixing, Tarver argued
it was engaged not in the war effort but in "an effort to foist certain ideas
of social, not economic, equality, which have long been entertained in this
country, upon the white people of the country who feel a certain pride in
their race, and justly so, and who, while they are willing and anxious that
the Negro shall have his economic rights, are not willing, and will never
submit, to his being forced upon them as a social equal and bedfellow."
It was "God Almighty" himself who had created the white race superior
to the black race, and "while these facts have been controverted in the
communistically prepared publication The Races of Mankind, which was
prepared for circulation among our armed forces and which has been severely condemned by a subcommittee of the Military Affairs Committee,
they cannot be successfully challenged by men and women of intelligence
who are, in good faith, endeavoring to state facts."[55]

Mississippi's Bilbo continued to raise the twin specters of intermarriage and racial "amalgamation" every chance he could, blaming anthropologists from Columbia's Boas to William Leo Hansberry of Howard University. Still inveighing against the FEPC in June, Bilbo informed Senate colleagues that, "Back in the heart of every Negro in America who is behind movements of this kind is the dream of social equality and intermarriage between whites and blacks"; and why shouldn't they so dream, when, "Dr. Frank Boas, the great anthropologist of Columbia University, boasts of the fact that the intermarriage and the mingling of the two bloods would bring about a better race." (Indeed, Boas had long suggested that racial hatred would be combated, over time, by "intermixture.") In a speech to the Mississippi legislature that he insisted on preserving for posterity in the congressional record, Bilbo warned, "We have only to look about us and to read what time has recorded about race relations to realize that there are only two permanent solutions to the race problem—separation or amalgamation. If this first—a physical separation of the races—is not chosen, then the results will inevitably be the latter—amalgamation, a mixing of the blood and the destruction of both races." Propounding falsely "negrophilistic" Christian gospels of universal brotherhood would lead to the embrace of miscegenation and "plunge the Southland into hopeless depths of hybridization," a degraded, "mongrelized" condition that "neither wealth, nor culture, nor science, nor art, nor morality, nor religion itself" could cure. Civilization itself would collapse if sex and marriage were permitted across the color line.[56]

Bilbo's own racial views received considerable support from Southern white church leaders, ministers and lay people alike, who were affiliated with local segregationist Citizens' Councils. One of his favorites, Archibald Stimson Coody IV, was an influential Sunday School teacher at the First Christian Church in Jackson, Mississippi, and what one scholar dubs a "folk segregationist theologian." An open member of the Ku Klux Klan, Coody tapped into the resentment increasingly felt by many lay people toward the racially moderate position taken by some ministers and church bodies, and he insisted that white Southern Christians were under attack by an international conspiracy—whose methods

Mississippi senator Theodore Bilbo delivering
a typically flamboyant speech in 1946.
KEYSTONE/HULTON ARCHIVE/GETTY IMAGES.

included "mongrelization," immigration, and taxation—made up of Communists, federal government officials, the NAACP, the National Council of Churches, and the United Nations. In 1944 he published a pamphlet titled *The Race Question* that strenuously defended the lynching of black rapists, noting that African Americans were far likelier to commit rape because of "atavistic sadism, or sadistic atavism," an "irresistible oestrus," and wholesale lack of "will power and character." Not only was white men's "summary execution" of such a vile wretch "natural and instinctive," it was a noble exercise of every man's "right to kill in defense of his person his home and his family." Essential to the "safety of the white woman" was "the prompt extermination of every beast that commits any overt act against her sanctity." Coody even described four lynchings in detail, some of them performed as hangings and one the burning of a live man chained to an iron stake in the town's public square. "And that was the end of that," he bluntly concluded. "Was it any worse than burning a witch?"[57]

Bilbo utilized Coody as a speechwriter and advisor, and he was among the many dyed-in-the-wool Mississippians who wrote Coody with praise for *The Race Question*. He ordered extra copies to distribute to Senate colleagues and wrote coolly, "I believe if we will continue to propagandize the American people with the slogan of a physical separation of the races as the only solution of the race trouble that when all this 'hell breaks loose' we can get some real cooperation on the part of the public leaders of both North and South to a resettlement of the negro in Africa. It may be that we will have to kill half of them before the other half will be willing to seek a new country in Africa." Through the national platform he occupied in the US Senate, Bilbo was able to transmit and popularize Coody's brutal ideas to an audience far beyond Mississippi.[58]

During this time, Walter White, still heading the NAACP, spoke of his travels to visit with US soldiers in Great Britain, northern Africa, Italy, and the Middle East, and he denounced the racism that "a highly aggressive and vocal minority" of soldiers from the American South had carried with them into their overseas duty. The impact on their ability to fight successfully for freedom had been greatly compromised by their attempts to instill segregation overseas. But White reserved his greatest contempt for "what is going on here at home" to fuel that racism. "The news we have received abroad during the past 4 months has been almost universally depressing. It has been of certain Members of Congress pouring forth hate-filled tirades against the Commander in Chief of our Nation, and against racial and religious minorities, as vicious and intemperate in content and tone as any sent out by Goebbels from Berlin." He singled out Bilbo for his "blatant boasts of filibusters against the anti-poll tax bill," and he decried the congressional bloc that made it so difficult for American soldiers, "both white and Negro," to get "objective information" on racial issues, placing blame directly on Andrew May's successful halt of army distribution of "a factual, nonpropaganda pamphlet on The Races of Mankind, written by two of America's most distinguished anthropologists, Profs. Ruth Benedict and Gene Weltfish."[59]

Bilbo saw nothing but anti-Christian, anti-American propaganda in what Benedict and her fellow anthropologists were teaching about the races, and he continued his attacks, outraged that the culturalists appeared to be winning. He repeatedly called out Boas, whom he constantly reminded readers was a "German Jew" who had poisoned the minds of all his students, including Lillian Smith (author of *Strange Fruit*, the best-selling novel about interracial love that Bilbo called "one of the dirtiest pieces of literature that has ever been printed and circulated"). "Miscegenation and mongrelization and hybridization" were the entwined themes that "old Dr. Boas taught in Columbia University," Bilbo railed yet again in 1945. Racial mixing, "whether one likes their odor or not," was the anthropologist's dogma, all in hopes of fueling sexual intercourse that was against God and nature. "He taught it to his students, and that damnable doctrine and poison has been scattered all over the United States through Columbia University and his teaching. Today he has students posing as teachers of ethnology and anthropology and trying to teach the American people that there is no difference between the white race and the black race, that they are the same, and had the same common origin." Anyone who believed such things deserved to be "liquidated, deported, or put out of business in some way," warned Bilbo—only violence could halt such a vile crime as interracial union.[60]

This nasty rhetoric against the pamphlet and its authors was a staple of the pro-segregationist literature of the time. Soldier Ira Calvin's *The Lost White Race* (1945), republished under the title *Only Blondes Are Angels* by Ira Calvin White, censured "that pamphlet *The Races of Mankind*" and promised that it would forever be a blot on Franklin Roosevelt's presidential administration. "If you are a decent person you will need a clothes pin on your nose while you study it, for it stinks." White women's virtue was clearly at stake. Calvin penned the poem "Pretty Pink Skin, Blue Eyes and Blond Hair" ("Out here in the far South Pacific / I have learned something quite terrific; / Your lovely skin is what I adore / And is just what I am fighting for") and wrote that "all sane white men consider any union of a white woman with a Negro as immoral, and dog-level prostitution, no matter what kind of marriage rites may have been performed beforehand." Calvin railed against sex across the color line in godly terms:

just as "God made the tiger the enemy of the lamb," He made "the colored man the certain destroyer of the white man." This was "not the fault of the white man," who was, in fact, an innocent recipient of this arrangement: "Why God made white women beautiful like His own angels, and gave white men eyes with which to recognize this fact, and then created other women not lovely to white men's eyes, is a matter we need not take up here." The very notion of white women mating with nonwhite men was too disgusting to contemplate. "White men haven't protected and preserved the delicate whiteness of their women's skins these thousands of years to wind up by handing them over to the colored races to despoil. They will die first!" And in this regard, Calvin assured, "rebellion against destruction is obedience to God."[61] Religion, racism, and anti-Communist politics entwined here as in the ideology of Bilbo, and the weight of this concoction rested on the taboo against interracial sex.

These writings continued to build off one another and were repackaged again and again. Benedict's name and work reappeared once more in Bilbo's final 330-page segregationist sermon, *Take Your Choice: Separation or Mongrelization*, self-published in 1947, shortly before his death. There he wrote that the "underlying purpose" of *The Races of Mankind* was "to further the program of amalgamation in this country." Proclaiming the commingling of white and black blood in marriage an "unpardonable sin against race" and insisting with full religious fervor that "nothing is more sacred than racial integrity," Bilbo devoted a full chapter to denouncing Boas and his students for their "evil, disastrous, and racial suicidal preachments" and "insane and corrupt doctrines of miscegenation, amalgamation, intermarriage, and mongrelization" that were destroying America. In his aim to produce "a Nation of mulattoes and mongrels," Boas cared not that this "new brown race of Americans" would still carry "the odoriferous African aroma which forever remains with a human being no matter how small an amount of Negro blood flows in his veins." Gathering Boas, Benedict, and Weltfish into a group that also included G. A. Borgese, a University of Chicago professor and author of the article "A Bedroom Approach to Racism," Bilbo insisted that educators like these were filling the young minds of their students with "damnable doctrines of destruction." A white person so willing to be "a disgrace to his own race" by advocating the death of racial purity and of "white man's culture and civilization" must be completely "ostracize[d] from white society."[62]

After Bilbo's death in August 1947, a fellow Southern Baptist from South Carolina, the young Strom Thurmond, would be the most outspoken segregationist to take up Bilbo's mantle in the Senate. Likewise offended by anything that threatened to reduce the stigma of race mixing and intermarriage, in 1948 Thurmond—then the governor of South Carolina—ran for president on the third party ticket of the Dixiecrats, or the States' Rights Democratic Party, which was a split-off from the national Democrats. Denouncing President Harry Truman's civil rights proposals, he regularly told audiences that the separation of the races was necessary for "the protection of the racial integrity and purity of the white and Negro races alike" and thundered to supporters, "I want to tell you, ladies and gentlemen, that there's not enough troops in the army to force the southern people to break down segregation and admit the nigger race into our theaters, into our swimming pools, into our homes, and into our churches"—a theme repeated throughout his long career. Fifty-five years after that presidential campaign, a seventy-eight-year-old woman named Essie Mae Washington-Williams came out publicly as Thurmond's daughter, the product of a union between twenty-two-year-old Thurmond and a fifteen-year-old black servant in his parents' home.[63] The prolonged white segregationist paradox lived on: repulsion toward one sort of cross-racial sex—between black men and white women—and fascination when the gender/race roles were reversed.

THE 1940S RACIAL CONFLICTS OVER segregations and miscegenation left a sustained legacy, as religious arguments for and against race mixing endured long after Benedict and Bilbo. Sex remained a profoundly divisive instrument in American Christianity and the nation's larger political milieu, now sharpened by intensifying disagreements about race. To some liberals, conservative sexual morality would come to seem profoundly if not permanently tainted by racism, corrupted by the hate that appeared to fuel segregationist theology and the hypocritical disgust for open love across the color line. To Christian conservatives, anti-racist activism appeared hopelessly mired in an anthropological "culture" paradigm of cross-culture relativity that encouraged sexual decadence and amorality; from that angle, the fight for racial equality was bound up with a newly unleashed moral laxness and a hedonistic sensibility careless of social order. Whether caricaturish or factual, such divergent interpretations of the sexual politics of racial attitudes fueled a deepening rupture within American Christianity that simmered only just below the surface of broader party politics before breaking through a few years later.

Anti-miscegenationist and anti-Communist views became deeply entwined in the controversy over *The Races of Mankind*. The governmental attacks on Boas, Benedict, and Weltfish in wartime were just the beginning of a years-long crackdown on many scholars in anthropology and other disciplines for their alleged Communist sympathies and subversive activities undermining the nation. In the minds of anti-Communist crusaders, the threat represented by proponents of racial equality, in particular, was vast. In the early 1950s, Senator Joseph McCarthy, elected to the US Senate in 1946, summoned a wide range of artists, filmmakers, activists, and scholars before his Permanent Subcommittee on Investigations (part of the Senate Committee on Governmental Operations), the group aiming to root out Communist ideologies. Benedict was dead by then, but Weltfish was one of those called in 1953.[64] The specter of interracial sex and miscegenation was one of the factors that brought her to the committee's attention.

Only weeks after the Supreme Court in May 1954 handed down its anti-segregation decision in *Brown v. Board of Education*, White Citizens' Councils arose to fight integration as well as mechanisms such as voter registration drives targeting potential African American voters. Citizens' Councils widely distributed pamphlets like *A Christian View on Segregation* by Reverend G. T. Gillespie, a white minister in the Southern Presbyterian Church and the long-time president of Belhaven College in Mississippi. Gillespie blamed anti-segregation agitation on "negroes of mixed blood" along with "sources outside the negro race, and outside of America"—above all, Soviet Communism, which aimed to instigate a world revolution and "the complete amalgamation of all races." Besides quoting segregationist statements from Thomas Jefferson, Abraham

Lincoln, and Booker T. Washington, the pamphlet cited numerous biblical examples as data pointing to God's establishment of segregation, including the earth-destroying flood God sent to punish the "promiscuous intermarriage" of the different races descended from Adam and Eve; the prohibitions given to Moses not to crossbreed diverse strains of cattle, plant mixed seeds, or mix wool and linen in clothes; the warnings of Moses and Ezra to the Israelite Jews not to intermarry with pagans; and the order by Jesus to his twelve disciples to go "only to the lost sheep of the house of Israel" in their first gospel mission.[65]

Soon thereafter, a young Baptist minister named Jerry Falwell tapped into Southern associations of civil rights and Communism. Preaching against school integration to his congregation in Lynchburg, Virginia, Falwell said, "Russia has made our racial problems her top ammunition in her propaganda scheme of proving the fallacies of capitalism to the world. . . . If Chief Justice Warren and his associates had known God's Word and had desired to do the Lord's will, I am quite confident that the 1954 decision would never have been made."[66] The White Citizens' Council of Montgomery, Alabama, agreed, attacking a children's book titled *The Rabbits' Wedding* in which the male rabbit had black fur, the female white. Author and illustrator Garth Williams noted at the time that the book had "no political significance," adding drily, "I was completely unaware that animals with white fur, such as white polar bears and white dogs and white rabbits, were considered blood relations of white human beings."[67] The independent Baptist fundamentalist John R. Rice, editor of the widely influential periodical *The Sword of the Lord*, wrote that Jim Crow laws were preferable to "unrestrained intermarriage of the races."[68]

W. A. Criswell, pastor of the world's largest Southern Baptist church (in Dallas) and one of the most influential Baptist leaders of the twentieth century, spoke out against desegregation to a joint session of the South Carolina state legislature, begging: "Don't force me by law, by statute, by Supreme Court decisions, . . . to cross over in those intimate things where I don't want to go. Let me build my life. Let me have my church. Let me have my school. Let me have my friends. Let me have my home. Let me have my family." The Georgia Baptist minister T. C.

Hardman wrote to the *Christian Index*: "To enforce social equality, as would result from mixed schools, would mean miscegenation and this brings about amalgamation, degeneration and approach to the level of the lower of the race."[69] As yet another white Southern minister put it, "To meet the requirements of being God's chosen for a purpose, racial purity is essential."[70]

These fundamentalists continued to rail against the twin specters of amalgamation and intermarriage as the chief evils to be avoided, often declaring that the real agenda of the NAACP was not merely desegregation but fostering intermarriage between blacks and whites. In the words of the fundamentalist Southern Baptist minister James F. Burke, "the amalgamation of races is part of the spirit of anti-christ. The Word of God is the surest and only infallible source of our facts of ethnology, and when man sets aside the plain teachings of this blessed book and disregards the boundary lines God Himself has drawn, man assumes a prerogative that belongs to God alone."[71] Many followed the example of Falwell, who founded Lynchburg Christian Academy, a private school that excluded African Americans and other nonwhites and exclusively served white children—literally, a segregation academy to keep the races apart and prevent sex across the color line so as to protect the purity of whiteness.

The South Carolinian Bob Jones went so far as to refuse African Americans admittance to his Christian college, Bob Jones University, until the Internal Revenue Service threatened its tax-exempt status in 1971—and then prohibited interracial dating by BJU students for nearly thirty more years. Pastor Noel Smith, who edited the Baptist Bible Fellowship's *Baptist Bible Tribune*, repeatedly invoked the threat of intermarriage as the natural—and most fearsome—outcome of the civil rights movement, writing crudely in 1961, "To make intermarriage between Whites and Negroes as commonplace as black tomcats squalling in back alleys is the supreme goal of this integration campaign."[72] The trial judge writing to sustain Virginia's anti-miscegenation law in *Loving v. Virginia* (1967) invoked the so-called fact that God had intentionally placed different races on different continents as clear proof that God "did not intend for the races to mix."[73] But the US Supreme Court, unbound by traditionalist white Christian antipathy for sex across the color line, did not agree and struck down the statute, opening the way for interracial love to flourish in legal marriage in Virginia and throughout the nation.

The events surrounding *The Races of Mankind* in the 1940s laid the foundation for these later conflicts. White segregationists, conservative in their Christian theology, grew ever more convinced that liberals were culturally relative, sexually amoral, racially subversive, and likely sympathizers with Communism. Their liberal counterparts increasingly saw racism and conservative sexual mores bound up in the same tight package of rigid adherence to a tradition of white male power upheld by fear. Sex and love across the color line threatened the racial hierarchies dear to many Southern whites. Those hierarchies were, in the minds of those devoted to them, the will of God and the ballast of a great American nation, even as others saw them as relics of a brutal racist past. Birth control and racy entertainments had already shocked the American Christian consensus of the early twentieth century. Interracial sex too, it seemed, could destroy the world.

CHAPTER 4

THE KINSEY REVOLUTION AND CHALLENGES TO FEMALE CHASTITY

A FTER WORLD WAR II ENDED in 1945, the United States faced new political challenges. Tensions quickly mounted with the Soviet Union and led to the Cold War, a hostile standoff between the two global superpowers that lasted nearly a half century. The threat of possible nuclear disaster hung heavy over Americans and especially so in the near aftermath of the 1945 bombings of Hiroshima and Nagasaki. Rates of religious membership, church and synagogue attendance, and religious institution building markedly increased in the immediate postwar era, as Americans sought a measure of peace and reassurance amid the political uncertainties of the time.

The national anxiety of this postwar period fortified a tendency to hold fast to familiar social and cultural norms, including traditional assumptions about sex roles, gender, and the family. Beginning in 1946, a spike in the nation's birth rate occurred that would come to be known as the baby boom ("boomers" are those born between 1946 and 1965). Families who could afford it, and who weren't prevented from doing so by the widespread redlining against ethnic minorities, moved their families into the suburbs, where they hoped to find safety in secure enclaves. The chosen lifestyle of most white Americans was purposefully traditional, and the values upholding it were part of the broad Christian consensus that continued to hold regarding marriage, casting sex as appropriate only

Biologist-turned-sexologist Alfred Kinsey. *BETTMANN VIA GETTY IMAGES.*

within monogamous, heterosexual wedlock. Those flaunting or violating such norms—such as bohemians, unmarried girls who got pregnant, and divorced women—could pay a heavy social price, and some—like gay people—were treated as criminals.

Crevices were continuing to form beneath the surface, and forces not yet visible in 1945 would shortly burst onto the scene, causing them to heave and expand. One of the most explosive episodes occurred thanks to two major studies on American sexual behavior nicknamed "the Kinsey reports," a study of men published in 1948 and a report on women that came out in 1953. Both volumes were exhaustive in their coverage and boldly explicit in their descriptions of ordinary people's sex habits, the upshot of each study being that Americans in private were far more sexually adventurous than their decorous public norms permitted. The books were publishing sensations that reaped divided reactions. American Christians were especially split in their responses: on the one side stood conservative Protestants and Catholics, on the other liberal Protestants, and especially younger generations of Christians. Even more important than these divided reactions was the fact that the reports induced figures across this religious spectrum to opine, for the first time, very publicly about sex. The reports thus spurred two sorts of upheavals: a revolution in religious thinking among some church people about how to think about normal sexual behavior and a sharp rise in open discussion and debate about sex, which pushed both liberal and conservative Christians into publicly staking out divergent stances on sexual morality.[1]

The taxonomic reports that electrified the nation had as the chief author Alfred C. Kinsey, an entomologist-turned-sexologist who did not shy away from provoking any audience. The two major volumes he supervised, *Sexual Behavior in the Human Male* (1948) and *Sexual Behavior in the Human Female* (1953), were the publishing sensations of their day and roused zealous if discordant responses, as did their author. To admirers, Kinsey was a pioneering scientific researcher in an age of moral hypocrisy, a tireless investigator of human desire and intimate behavior whose contributions to human history ranked with those of Karl Marx, Charles Darwin, and Adam Smith. To critics, he was a dissolute pseudo-intellectual bent on shredding the moral fabric of the nation by wrecking the family. Towering scientist and liberating revolutionary to some, lascivious fraud, religious threat, and likely Communist to others: Kinsey stood with Senator Joseph McCarthy as one of the most divisive personages of the 1950s.[2]

One of the most important legacies of the Kinsey reports was the revolution they inspired in religious thinking about sexuality. While he has often been credited, or blamed, for the so-called sexual revolution of the countercultural 1960s and the youth who based their (im)morals on "sex, drugs, and rock 'n' roll," his impact was just as significant, if not greater, on religious leaders inspired to rethink Christian moral and ethical norms about sex. A virtual revolution in religious thinking about sexuality occurred in the wake of his reports, thanks in part to his dogged commitment to working with religious leaders where he could.

FROM THE START, KINSEY'S ACADEMIC work on sexual matters encountered mixed reactions from religious figures. In 1938, when he was forty-four years old, Kinsey began teaching a course on marriage at Indiana

University that included frank information on the biological aspects of sex as well as lectures from other faculty members relating to economics, law, religion, sociology, and psychology. He also began conducting interviews with students and colleagues that he termed "sex histories." That fall, a member of the campus religious council sought to assure skeptics that the marriage course emphasized "the positive aspect" of sexual behavior, namely "the everlasting beauty of the sacrament of marriage." The course soon became infamous for its explicit discussions and graphic illustrations of sexual practices, however; within two years, indignant members of the local ministerial association petitioned the Indiana University administration to do something about the course, and the pressure forced Kinsey to stop teaching it. Undeterred, he focused his energies on interviewing as many men and women as possible to collect their sex histories, detailed accounts that sought to document the full range of their sexual feelings and behavior from earliest memory to the present. By 1939, Kinsey's standardized questionnaire for these sex histories contained two hundred and fifty questions.

Among those whose sex histories Kinsey wished to learn about in detail were religious people. A nonbeliever himself, Kinsey had grown up in a devout Methodist home but had rejected the faith in adulthood and was critical of the role played by both Jewish and Christian sexual codes in fueling shame and guilt among the religious. He had a strong interest in understanding how religion affected sexual behavior, and he tirelessly pursued interviews from an array of religious sources, including clergy, for his planned books on the sexual behavior of ordinary people. A typical letter posted in September 1944 thanked Leonard Anderson, an Episcopal priest and director of Chicago's first home for dependent African American boys, for giving his own sex history and also getting those of "all the boys who were in the house." In another letter from early 1945, Kinsey wrote to E. Fay Campbell of the Board of Christian Education of the Presbyterian Church (USA), describing the parameters of his research and politely requesting Campbell's own sex history, as well as introductions to other church people for additional histories. "If our sample is to cover the whole range of society," pleaded Kinsey, "it must include a goodly representation from persons who are active in religious groups." That request was apparently less successful, for though Campbell wrote back to thank Kinsey for his "interesting letter," he ignored the request for sex histories and broader contacts.[3] Kinsey persisted, however, eventually amassing a rich trove of interview data from diverse religious sources.

On January 5, 1948, Kinsey's *Sexual Behavior in the Human Male*, based on his interview data, was published by Philadelphia's W. B. Saunders Company, a staid and relatively unknown publisher of medical texts. Nevertheless, the volume had been well publicized and heavily marketed in advance, and reviews preceded its official publication date in major venues such as *Newsweek*, *Harper's*, the *New Yorker*, and the *New York Times*. These early appraisals were quite positive, as were most other assessments in the secular press. Some religious commentators rushed to condemn the book before it was even published, however. An editorial in the Jesuit publication *America* lambasted the book's advance publicity as "pandering to prurience."

> The sound conclusions of genuine science are part of God's truth and as such are never to be disowned, flinched from, hushed up. But there is a vast difference between the recognition and use of scientific truth by those who have a legitimate interest in it and its helter-skelter popularization among those who have no ground for interest save curiosity. As well might one popularize for the masses a strictly scientific treatise on the compounding of poisons.

With the "poisons" analogy, the magazine suggested its deeper concern with the book's effect on American youth: its potential to contaminate and debase the innocent.[4]

One of the features of Kinsey's analysis that would attract attention was his commentary on religion. In the first volume, his discussion of religion was consistent with the book as a whole, which aimed for a tone of detached objectivity, of pure reportage on the facts as he and his research team had found them. The topic of religion received brief mention from time to time and lengthier analysis in chapter 13, "Religious Background and Sexual Outlet." Here Kinsey established his chief historical claims:

There is nothing in the English-American social structure which has
had more influence upon present-day patterns of sexual behavior
than the religious backgrounds of that culture. . . . This is no place to
work out the details of the historic development, but it is important
at this point to realize that these present-day codes are quite ancient,
that they are the product of still older religious systems, and that
throughout their history they have been the bases for the law which
has formally expressed society's interest in controlling human sexual
behavior.

Kinsey was interested in the effects of religion on the more devout members of the major religious groups he studied (Protestant, Catholic, and
Jewish). He concluded that religiously inactive males of all faiths were far
more likely to masturbate and pursue sexual pleasure outside marriage
than were their devout counterparts. But he was still more interested
in how these older religious teachings continued to influence contemporary sexual habits even among the nonreligious. In Kinsey's view, few
recognized the enduring influence of Jewish and Christian concepts of
sexuality on modern notions of right versus wrong and natural versus unnatural. To uphold such categorical distinctions was perforce to "stoutly
defend the church's system of natural law."[5]

If religious leaders were relieved to hear that regular worshipers
mostly heeded their teachings on sexual discipline, few showed it; immediate reactions from Catholic authorities were exceedingly critical of
Kinsey's book. Shortly after its publication, Chicago's Loyola University issued to the media a "News Release on the Kinsey Report," comprising a condensed version of a speech made by a Catholic physician in
Loyola's School of Medicine, Herbert A. Ratner. The speech criticized
Kinsey's research for conflating two distinct concepts: that of the "aver-
age" and that of the "normal," complaining that Kinsey's approach would
entice readers to imagine sinful behaviors as normal and good simply
because of their alleged frequency. Other Catholic commentators condemned Kinsey's Darwinian biologism (which they perceived to reduce
human affections and behavior to amoral instincts) and ostensible ethical relativism while raising further questions about the study's sample

and statistical conclusions.[6] Such critiques did not initially appear to influence parishioners, however: George Gallup's mid-February poll of Americans across the country found that "both Protestants and Catholics in the population express approval of the Kinsey study, although Protestants are more in favor than Catholics are." According to Gallup, Protestants approved of the study as a "good thing" at a rate of 57 percent, compared with 10 percent who thought it a "bad thing" (the rest had no opinion or mixed responses); meanwhile, despite a dearth of positive statements about the volume from Catholic leaders, lay Catholics who expressed an opinion approved of it at a rate of 49 percent to 19 percent.[7]

As *Sexual Behavior in the Human Male* climbed best-seller lists, other publishers rushed to hop on the lucrative Kinsey bandwagon with a series of commentaries and discussions of the famous volume. Most were collections of articles by academic experts, and all of them included contributions from religious thinkers. One of the earliest, Albert Deutsch's *Sex Habits of American Men*, was released by Prentice-Hall in May and featured comments from Protestant, Catholic, and Jewish clergymen, along with psychiatrists, psychologists, anthropologists, and other specialists. The Catholic writer Charles G. Wilber sharply criticized Kinsey's suggestions about Catholicism (including the roughly 50 percent of "allegedly devout Catholics" reported to be petting to orgasm) and expanded on some of the critiques made by Ratner, protesting that the report's authors "treat man purely as a zoological specimen" rather than as "a free agent who has duties and rights, and whose acts have social and moral implications." Against the implication that the nation's sex laws ought to be rethought, Wilber sharply retorted, "the *mores* of some of the people in the northeastern states should be changed to conform to the natural law."[8]

However, the essays by Jewish and Protestant leaders were more measured, suggesting the range of religious reactions that greeted the Kinsey report. Rabbi Louis I. Newman, a colleague of Stephen Wise and prominent Zionist as well as an advocate for Reform Jewish education, served as the book's authority on Judaism. He responded favorably to the Kinsey volume and quoted what he believed to be the finding with the most important implications for religion: "The differences between religiously devout persons and religiously inactive persons of the same faith are much greater than the differences between two equally devout groups of different faiths." That meant, wrote Newman hopefully, that "religious groups, whatever their particular symbolism and imagery, and despite their theological warfare, do influence the conduct of their members. Perhaps if a common denominator can be found for the instruction by religionists, not defying, but utilizing aright, the research of such works as the Kinsey-Pomeroy-Martin survey, we can build a more serene and effective social order today." For Newman, *Sexual Behavior in the Human Male* made the case for interreligious cooperation to ensure the best instruction in sexual morality for strengthening marriage, increasing individual and family happiness, and working for the "collective betterment" of society.[9]

The Protestant contribution was penned by the Reverend Seward Hiltner, the executive secretary of the Department of Pastoral Services at the Federal Council of the Churches of Christ in America (soon to become part of the National Council of Churches). Hiltner, who would later serve on the faculties of the University of Chicago divinity school (1950–1961) and Princeton Theological Seminary (1961–1980), would prove an important figure in altering mainline Protestant attitudes regarding sexual morality, and his open-mindedness was already evident in the 1948 essay. Hiltner voiced his agreement with certain values expressed in the report, such as diminishing hypocrisy and looking for ways to address suffering caused by rigid intolerance of some sexual behaviors, but disagreed with other principles he saw embedded in it, such as the presumption that human beings were wholly like other animals in their sexual appetites. Sharing Rabbi Newman's commitment to flexible engagement with Kinsey's text, Hiltner was adamant that the volume should be heeded by church leaders, who had a choice to make about how better to instill their tradition's sexual teachings. "We can try to be moralistic, or we can try to teach people to be ethical," he noted. Clergy could pontificate, or they could help their people decide things for themselves. "In the one case we become policemen and propagandists. In the other, we are educators and shepherds." All too often, warned Hiltner, Christianity had offered poor justification for its moral teachings while etherealizing sex beyond earthly recognition. Kinsey's view offered a crucial, fleshly corrective to such vagueness. Without appealing for changes in the church's traditional teachings on sexual morality, Hiltner called for a less prescriptive approach in guiding the faithful to observe them.[10]

A mostly favorable review of *Sex Habits of American Men* that appeared in the *New York Times* in mid-May criticized the three clergymen's articles as the weakest in the volume. "It is not surprising that this should be true," wrote the liberal reviewer, Bruce Bliven. After all, "it would hardly be reasonable to ask any clergyman at this time to discuss in a completely dispassionate way a study so violently out of accord with many of the assumptions of organized religion." That brusque dismissal by Bliven, the editor of the *New Republic* and a foe of religious fundamentalism no less than of Communism, lumped Hiltner and Newman's tempered liberal responses into the same mold of conservative indignation exemplified by Wilber, despite the fact that Hiltner and Newman offered a pointed contrast and defended Kinsey against knee-jerk moralizing. What Bliven failed to see was a distinct parting of the ways among religious groups on the subject of sex.[11]

The responses to Kinsey did not simply divide along neat Protestant-Catholic lines, however. A week after Bliven's review, the celebrated Protestant theologian Reinhold Niebuhr published his own response to the Kinsey report in his magazine, *Christianity and Crisis*. Niebuhr granted that Catholicism and Protestantism, in their traditionally "morbid and prurient attitude toward sex," had both failed to realize "the ideal of relating sexual life sacramentally to the whole of personality and to the whole of a loyal community of persons in the family partnership." Such criticisms echoed, or perhaps even went further than, Kinsey's own descriptions of religion's effects on Western sexual morality. But Niebuhr recoiled at the solution he believed Kinsey, whom he equated with "modern secularism," offered. In a quotable line that many would repeat in their own critiques of Kinseyan scientism, he concluded, "The modern naturalism which seeks to solve the problems of man's sexual life by treating him as an animal, only slightly more complex than other brutes, represents a therapy which implies a disease in our culture as grievous or more grievous than the sickness it pretends to cure."[12] Censure from this redoubtable theologian carried significant weight and influence among church leaders and lay members. *Time* magazine reported Niebuhr's critique, opining that the revered thinker spoke for "many another churchman" in finding Kinsey's attitude toward sex even worse "than the sad state of U.S. morals it indicated."[13] But although Niebuhr's condemnation of Kinsey loomed large, there was no shortage of more positive responses, most of it from younger liberals.

Some of the most vocal praise from religious leaders appeared not in the nation's newspapers but instead in Kinsey's mailbox. The Reverend Wesley J. Buck, a young Lutheran minister in Council Bluffs, Iowa, wrote an appreciative letter to Kinsey in which he also requested a job on his research staff.[14] Another admiring letter arrived from the Reverend Ward Avery from Bloomingdale, Indiana. The handwritten missive quoted the Bible on homosexuality and concluded that "God has ordained some men to be 'that way' for the purpose of glorifying Him, because they have been endowed with great spiritual capacity." Although Kinsey's staff often marked letters promulgating strong religious views with a red sticker meaning "Crank," this time Kinsey was intrigued, and he urged Avery to come to the university to give his own sex history.[15] Another missive arrived in September from a Methodist minister in Baltimore who claimed to have just completed his fourth reading of *Sexual Behavior in the Human Male* and who lauded the book's broad relevance for the church: "You and your associates deserve the highest praise for such a study as you have given to the world, with all of the facts contained. May God give us, as parents, educators, social workers, judges, ministers and others working with people, sense enough to be guided by the result of the Report, in order that we might deal with them as wise persons and not the fools we have been."[16] Such fan mail from ministers likely brought some relief and satisfaction to Kinsey, offering a reminder that opinions on the ground and at the grassroots level were more eclectic and diverse, and less uniformly skeptical, than those of denominational leaders. Not surprisingly, Kinsey was a keen correspondent with religious persons sympathetic to his research.

Initially, many religious leaders maintained a wary public stance toward Kinsey, doubtless influenced by the early caustic appraisals by

Catholic and a range of Protestant leaders like Niebuhr. But with time, the fissures evident in the divergent reactions of the Catholic Wilber and the Protestant Hiltner began to deepen, as mainline Protestant leaders grew more comfortable in articulating what they saw as the useful aspects of *Sexual Behavior in the Human Male*. A sharpened Catholic reaction made national news in mid-September, when the National Council of Catholic Women passed a resolution deploring Kinsey's volume as "an insult to the American people" and "a disservice to the nation which can only lead to immorality."[17] In contrast, the prominent mainline Protestant magazine the *Christian Century* printed an article by the liberal pastor and psychologist Roy Burkhart, warning that it would be unwise for church leaders to reject or resent these findings and calling for a "constructive attitude" toward them that would help inculcate "a wholesome attitude toward sex and love and marriage." Already nationally known as an advocate for birth control and marriage counseling, Burkhart argued that the church had "an unusual opportunity" to enter into the field of sex, "since it is the only agency that gives guidance to the individual from birth until he is born fully into the life of the Spirit."[18] Since the earlier battle over contraception, Protestant church leaders had not stopped distancing themselves from what they deemed the extremism of Catholic dogma when it came to matters of sex. A tempered Protestant response to Kinsey's work fit into that context, further deepening the divide between competing Christian worldviews.[19]

Burkhart's practical experience with married couples presumably enabled him to see the practical applications of Kinsey's work, in contrast to the abstractions offered by the more theological Niebuhr. Kinsey was distinctly aware of the varied points of view held by religious thinkers and public leaders, and he was heartened by the growing positive responses from many liberal Protestants who were actively engaged in pastoral care, chaplaincy work, and other practical professions. For instance, Kinsey commended the Episcopal clergyman Otis R. Rice—a chaplain at St. Luke's Hospital in Manhattan and instructor at New York's General Theological Seminary who would shortly become an executive in the Federal Council of Churches—for an article elaborating the pastoral utility of Kinsey's volume. In the American Social Hygiene Association's

1948 book *Problems of Sexual Behavior*, Rice distanced himself from the emotional reactions of both the "pessimistic moralists" in the church, who were filled with doom and gloom about the nation's plunging morals, and the naïve Pollyannas who so readily dismissed Kinsey's work as nonsense. Plainly, Rice noted, the pastoral counselor "has encountered sexual behavior again and again in the course of his normal ministry"; the chief value of the Kinsey report was, therefore, to remind the church of the need to rethink its basic moral tenets, as well as the need to deal more openly and directly with human sexuality as a part of helping persons attain maturity. In the wake of Kinsey's study, Rice argued, "We shall need to re-examine . . . the principles of our moral theology. We shall need to re-examine our own pastoral opportunities, our homiletical opportunities. We shall need, perhaps most of all, to examine ourselves."[20]

Kinsey's unsolicited letter to Rice was filled with gratitude and approval for Rice's balanced point of view, as he wrote that it was "encouraging to know that there are clergymen who do publicly approve of our work" and also "encouraging to know that the Church does have leaders who can be as level-headed as you are in considering the problems involved." Kinsey praised the positive effects Rice's article was likely to have on broader public opinion, remarking that he was "glad that an article like yours will help persuade the public that at least some segment of the religious leaders is ready to face fact."[21] As the correspondence continued, Rice seems to have given his own sex history to Kinsey, or at least showed a willingness to establish further contacts with religious leaders. "I quite comprehend," wrote Kinsey (as he did to many other clerical correspondents), "that it takes a considerable amount of thought for one of your station to cooperate and to give a history. In consequence, I am doubly appreciative of your help in our work with clerical groups. We shall be delighted to follow through whenever any of these possible contacts work out."[22] Like many forms of human generosity, Kinsey's was partly calculating, a means to entice friendly correspondents to join the data sample or at least to gain their tacit approval. While Kinsey was earnest in wanting support for its own sake, in an atmosphere of conservative Christian antagonism, Kinsey also surely felt triumphant in obtaining clergy sex histories.

In the months and years following the publication of *Sexual Behavior in the Human Male*, Christian leaders increasingly took issue with one another's reactions to Kinsey. The Reverend Joseph Barth, minister of the First Unitarian Church of Miami, preached a fervent sermon that sided with Kinsey against his conservative critics. Contrasting Kinsey to "conventional Christians," Barth noted that whereas Kinsey was interested in the everyday realities of human sexual behavior, the "traditional" priest or minister is "very interested in human sexuality, as he would be interested in a snake in his living room—to watch it, and to catch it and to kill it." As evidence, Barth cited the recent declaration by Catholic University of America's Monsignor Maurice Sheehy that the volume was "the most anti-religious book of our time," a description that, Barth protested, absurdly marked Kinsey's volume as more sinister than even Adolf Hitler's *Mein Kampf*. Barth admonished, "It is easy to see that from where that Christian priest sits, sexuality is the great human sin, and fascism is a lesser evil by far." The minister went on to contend that the biblical Jesus had upended this hypocritical hierarchy of sin and that Kinsey himself exhibited "more of maturely religious value in fact and attitude . . . than most of the criticism I have ever heard in this field from the lips or pens of conventional Christians." Besides its sheer wealth of facts, Kinsey's report bore witness to empathy's power over judgmental bigotry: "If that isn't, in action, the attitude of love which Christians talk so much about but so seldom practice, then I don't know what the word means."[23]

In the face of such criticisms, Christians on the theological right, both Protestant and Catholic, dug in. Catholic priests took special offense at Kinsey's declaration of the abnormality of celibacy. As Sheehy complained to one journalist, "Dr. Kinsey's report gives the impression that if one has not some hidden or overt means of sexual expression he is beyond the pale of normalcy."[24] But conservative clergy mostly chose to center their critiques on matters of broad concern. The mere fact that the report broached such unpleasant or even odious topics as homosexuality, pedophilia, bestiality, and all manner of extramarital sex meant it was not "scientific" but plainly lascivious, they argued, and hence indefensible by any civilized standard.

Although Kinsey complained of such "emotional and illogical" reactions in his correspondence with religious leaders he deemed friendlier, he did not wholly trust the goodwill of any of the religious leaders of his time and certainly not of those leaders who seemed to him to cling to outmoded theories and superstitions.[25] Yet he persisted in seeking out supportive religious leaders, and he found them in growing numbers. In June 1951 he wrote a hopeful letter to Karl Morgan Block, the Episcopal bishop of California who presided over lofty Grace Cathedral, to remind him of a pleasant meeting the two of them once had and to request an appointment during Kinsey's upcoming visit to San Francisco. A July thank-you letter shows that such a meeting did occur, laying the groundwork for Block to introduce Kinsey to other Bay Area religious leaders. Some months later, Block wrote to thank Kinsey for "the magnificent service you offered our clergy at the conference on Pastoral Counseling in the matter of sex, held in the Cathedral House April 8, 1952." Block praised the "insights and help" Kinsey gave to this group, remarking, "I can wish for nothing better for our clergy of all communions than to have the privilege of such an informal conference as was ours. Every priest and pastor will have a far more useful ministry if he obtains scientific knowledge of the sex life from one so unusually gifted and highly qualified." A pleased Kinsey noted that the meeting "renews my faith in the belief that I have always had, that there are many groups in the church who are interested in utilizing what help science may give to an understanding of human problems."[26] Although many conservative Christians disagreed, Block plainly believed that the church had much to gain from the era's most famous crusader for sexual candor. That proposition shortly grew even more contested with the publication of Kinsey's explosive new volume two years later.

RELIGIOUS APPRAISALS OF KINSEY'S WORK grew immeasurably more contentious with the publication of his *Sexual Behavior in the Human Female* in September 1953. An acrimonious telegram sent to Kinsey on the day after the book's release (and likely reacting primarily to advance media coverage) gives a clear account of how the volume was perceived in some conservative Christian quarters. John Chapple, the Catholic editor of the Ashland, Wisconsin, *Daily Press*, wrote:

> I consider your report on sexual behavior in the human female the most direct and devastating attack upon Christian civilization during the present century with the single exception of the Lenin Revolution in Russia in 1917, of which it is a tremendously effective corollary.
>
> I hope the American people recognize this report for what it is, a direct frontal attack upon Christian civilization and a dirty, beastly attack upon American womanhood. A disintegrating force let loose out of a Pandora's box of evil which only after exhaustive efforts can be effectively neutralized....
>
> As for you, Dr. Kinsey, I as one American editor consider you as one of the most loathsome wretches ever produced in human form, or else an individual utterly bewitched by the forces of evil and darkness.[27]

Although criticism from Catholic quarters was hardly surprising, this fuming missive was particularly vivid in its accusations that Kinsey was well-nigh demonic and that his report on female sexuality was no less than an assault on "Christian civilization."

Other Catholics reacted with similar venom and velocity. The Indiana Provincial Council of Catholic Women demanded information from Indiana University president Herman G. Wells about Kinsey's teaching and general influence at the school.

> If you, Dr. Wells, do not recognize how dangerous it is to popularize incendiary suggestions like these, we tremble at what may happen to our sons and daughters entrusted to the care of Indiana University.... In recent years we have seen in Nazi Germany what can happen to men when the traditional idea of moral law is questioned and then scoffed at. Dr. Kinsey questions the worth of Christian morality; he comes close to scoffing at it. Does he represent your thought, Dr. Wells? Does he represent the thought of Indiana University?

Wells's response ignored the Nazi parallel but assured these Catholic women that "Dr. Kinsey's research project is entirely divorced from the University's teaching function." Furthermore, Wells astutely countered the group's religious argument with one of his own, defending Kinsey's research and "the right of the scientist to investigate every aspect of life in the belief that knowledge, rather than ignorance, will assist mankind in the slow and painful development toward a more perfect society. To deny this right and this objective would seem to deny the belief in a divine order as it pertains to man and the universe."[28] Wells's contention could not have been clearer: scientific knowledge was a necessary element of moral progress, and to suppress the one was to stifle the other and undermine genuine religion.

Wells's response, however shrewdly it sought to turn religion to scientific ends, surely missed the point for Catholic and Protestant conservatives who attacked the female book much more furiously than they had the male volume. Two distinctive attributes of the second volume—neither of which was addressed by Wells but repeatedly emphasized by Kinsey's critics—intensified the censure. First, the book paid closer attention to religion than the 1948 volume had, seizing every opportunity to blame and ridicule traditionalist religion for its sexual prudery. *Sexual Behavior in the Human Female* did not argue against God or theism in general, but it had plenty to say about antiquated superstitions and tyrannical religious institutions. Devoted adherents could surely perceive Kinsey's contempt for their worldview, and they also sensed his glee in concluding that the "attempt in Judeo-Christian cultures to impose pre-marital chastity upon both males and females" was a visible failure, with nearly 50 percent of his sample having had coitus prior to marriage. It was surely also shocking to see in Table 92 that, of devout religious women who had premarital sex, 62 percent of Protestants and 50 percent of Catholics felt "no regret" afterward.[29] Nonetheless, Kinsey did find that, just as was true among men, religiously devout women were more obedient to religious moral codes than were nondevout women, a point of potential encouragement for Christian leaders, who could thereby affirm religion's effectiveness in instructing their most devout believers. Conservatives, however, rarely underscored these positive implications.

More offensive than the statistics pertaining to religiosity were Kinsey's blunt assessments of what he considered to be religion's negative attitudes toward human sexuality in general. Kinsey concluded (again, more pointedly than in the male volume) that those attitudes stemmed from irrational fear, which he associated with conservative Christians and Jews. Kinsey laced his discussions of "Hebrew" and Christian codes with terms such as "impediments," "restrictions," "obligations," "absolutist philosophies," and others suggestive of rule-bound legalism. Throughout the volume, Kinsey placed the blame for the "shame, remorse, despair, desperation, and attempted suicide" of women who transgressed particular moral codes on the religions that developed the codes, not on some purported "intrinsic wrongness or abnormality of the sexual act itself." Eastern religions fared much better in Kinsey's worldview, as did "primitive groups." Both were examples of the "many religious groups which have extolled the beauty and sacred nature of all sexual activity, and have incorporated sexual symbolism and sexual ceremonies into their worship." Such sex-positive religious folk as those who wrote "the ancient Sanskrit love books" offered hopeful inspiration: "The temple worship in ancient Athens and in certain Roman and Hindu cults, and religious ceremonies among primitive groups in many parts of the world, recognized the morality of both marital and non-marital sexual activities."[30]

These appraisals of religion exasperated religious conservatives, who despised the elevation of promiscuity as something "sacred" and who detected insufferable smugness pervading what was, to them, the outlandish charge that strict mores either wreaked horrific psychological damage or abetted wanton depravity. But far more sinister and worrisome than Kinsey's rendering of religion was the second attribute that decisively distinguished this book from its predecessor: its graphic focus on the sexual activity of women and girls. The volume's fastidious attention to the regularity of female masturbation, petting, premarital intercourse, same-sex activity, and other practices besides marital coitus in the supine missionary position, was the chief subject of conservative religious rage toward the book and largely accounts for the sheer ferocity of the reaction to the *Female* volume. After all, the male volume had already proclaimed that men experienced about half their orgasms in situations that most

Americans reputedly still reckoned sinful, unlawful, or otherwise objectionable. But when Kinsey claimed to find that much the same was true for women, his work threatened to upend the gendered sexual roles and expectations that, for religious conservatives, comprised the very foundation of a godly civilization. In short, gender figured deeply in the explosive reactions among religious conservatives to Kinsey's publications.

The female volume included statistics on premarital sexual activity in contemporary women's lives that made mainstream social norms look archaic and those who professed them positively two-faced. *Fifty* percent of women were having sexual intercourse before marriage? This number seemed outrageously high to religious critics, but still higher was the number who, claimed Kinsey with deadpan certainty, had been virgins in name only when they donned the wedding veil—plenty active, sexually, drawing the line only at actual intercourse. Kinsey declared that of the females in his sample born around 1890 to 1900 (members of a professedly more "sexually restrained" generation), some 80 percent described some sort of petting in their histories—sexual caressing that stopped short of intercourse—while about 90 percent of the entire sample and nearly 100 percent of those who had married had petted prior to marriage. Kinsey noted that many persons anxious about the "moral bankruptcy" of youth viewed petting as "the product of an effete and morally degenerate, over-industrialized and over-educated, urban culture." But far from being a harbinger of the collapse of American civilization, petting was the product of "ancient mammalian origins"; it was not simply harmless but downright beneficial in preparing young women for sex in marriage. Kinsey made sure that religious leaders heard these points loud and clear, insisting, "It is petting rather than the home, classroom or religious instruction, lectures or books, classes in biology, sociology, or philosophy, or actual coitus, that provides most females with their first real understanding of a heterosexual experience." Kinsey also claimed that female masturbation rates were quite high, even among the religiously devout: "In some of the most devout groups, as few as 41 per cent had ultimately masturbated," he wrote—a startling statistic for conservative Christians that did not suggest "few" at all.[31]

As for the girls who had intercourse before marriage, Kinsey assured readers that no harm was done to them: 69 percent of those who were still unmarried at the time of their interview asserted they had "no regret" about their premarital sexual experiences, while a whopping 77 percent of the married women, Kinsey wrote, "looking back from the vantage point of their more mature experience, saw no reason to regret their pre-marital coitus." Citing a variety of experts who claimed that premarital sex was naturally harmful and guilt-inducing for women, Kinsey acridly retorted that religion itself was the cause of such harm, not the sex itself. (He made a similar argument linking authoritarian religion with lesbianism, warning, "Our case histories show that this disapproval of heterosexual coitus and of nearly every other type of heterosexual activity before marriage is often an important factor in the development of homosexual activity.") Whether by petting, masturbation, or other forms of sexual behavior, women who had experienced orgasm early in life were, Kinsey insisted, much better adjusted sexually in their married lives; moreover, such premarital orgasms among women were already common. In all, Kinsey wrote matter-of-factly, "about two-thirds (64 per cent) of the married females in our sample had experienced sexual orgasm prior to their marriage."[32]

The overall pattern that emerged from the report was of vast and diverse sexual activity among girls and women, married and unmarried, in the United States. But the female volume did not claim that this situation had always been true; rather, the current scene was the product of important historical changes. The volume's foreword, written by officials in the National Research Council, the entity through which the Rockefeller Foundation funded Kinsey's work, attributed the "exceedingly rapid and revolutionary change in sex attitudes and practices" over the past half century to three factors: "woman's progressive sexual and economic emancipation," the "all-pervasive influence of Freud's views and discoveries," and the "exposure during the World Wars of millions of American youth to cultures and peoples whose sex codes and practices differ greatly from those in which they had been reared." But of these factors—feminism, Freud, and foreigners—the first provoked the most explosive response by religious critics excoriating the female report, making plain that, for them, women's emancipation represented a singularly dire threat.[33]

Sexual Behavior in the Human Female prompted an outpouring of articles in religious publications as well as pulpit and radio sermons, more than a few of which were reprinted for widespread distribution. These reflected the growing polarization in religious reactions to Kinsey's work, from irate condemnations by Catholics, Baptists, and some Methodists to admiring paeans by Unitarians along with many mainline Protestants such as Presbyterians and Episcopalians. Critics on the right repeatedly warned that Kinsey's report on women threatened to trigger the collapse of American civilization. At the First Methodist Church in Albuquerque, the Reverend William D. Wyatt raised the possibility of Kinsey's connection to Communism and urged his congregants to recognize the report as "unsubstantiated, unscientific propaganda" that aimed for "moral anarchy." First, Wyatt argued, Kinsey's results were false: they were based only on interviews with women "willing to discuss sex matters with a stranger"—women, therefore, who held "liberal views on morals." "Normal American women," he insisted, "would refuse the request for such an interview"; he quoted other self-styled experts to bolster his view that those women were abnormal in either their licentiousness or their neurotic fabrications of "sensational affairs." But worse than being false, Wyatt argued, the report was deeply dangerous, in that Kinsey had spurned "the morality of the Bible and the Ten Commandments, which has built our civilization." If its data were not seen as phony factoids amassed to "junk our morality," Wyatt warned, husbands would soon suspect their own wives of infidelity, and greater infidelity would indeed occur, since "we, like sheep, want to be like others, and are prone to yield to high-pressure propaganda." Loose women placed the institution of marriage in peril, and American civilization hung in the balance.[34]

John S. Wimbish, the pastor of New York's prominent Calvary Baptist Church, agreed with Wyatt, aiming a few more insults at the nearly six thousand women "who were lewd enough to be thus cross-examined" for Kinsey's study. The volume "constitutes an attack on our American way of life more overwhelming than that of Pearl Harbor," and Wimbish warned those who took it closely to heart that apocalyptic destruction would be its consequence:

> As our civilization totters on the brink of chaos, we need to remember that God destroyed the antediluvians with the flood because of immorality. God destroyed the cities of the plain with fire and brimstone because of immorality, and what was wrong in the days of Noah and the days of Sodom and Gomorrah is still wrong today. May God have mercy on our nation when religion is frowned upon and Kinsey is idolized![35]

The evangelical crusader Dr. Torrey M. Johnson concurred, preaching, "If Kinsey prevails there will be no future for the United States." Johnson's answer to the evils spawned by Kinsey was a "Holy Ghost revival" that would confirm the conception of the American home put forward by the Founding Fathers while satisfying a palpable fantasy of revenge. "When that day comes, the problems of America will be solved and the Kinseys and the Communists together with all other enemies of God and America—borers from without and within—will finally be driven to their holes never to return."[36]

Most prominently, the internationally known evangelist Billy Graham delivered a dramatic radio sermon on "The Bible and Dr. Kinsey," a message broadcast over the ABC network and soon published for even wider distribution in the expanding networks of evangelical Christianity. Graham castigated Kinsey for the graphic details throughout *Sexual Behavior in the Human Female* and warned, "It is impossible to estimate the damage this book will do to the already deteriorating morals of America." Graham singled out the statistics on female marital infidelity as particularly shocking, and he emphasized the "lopsided and unscientific" nature of the report's claim that "seven out of ten women who had premarital affairs had no regrets." Those women, Graham assured his audience, were not among the "millions of born-again Christian women in this country who put the highest price on virtue, decency and modesty." Those women were debased and callous in their sinful deeds, and their overrepresentation by Kinsey was an immoral misuse of science and "an indictment

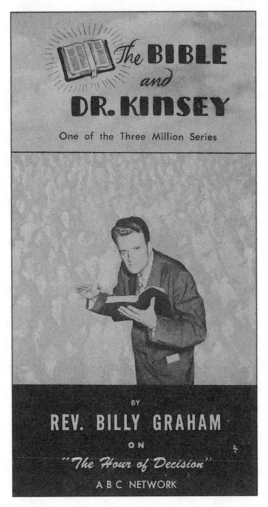

Cover of Billy Graham, *The Bible and Dr.
Kinsey* (1953), the evangelist's ardent sermon
against Kinsey and the changing times.

against American womanhood." "Thank God," Graham averred, this was
not the full story; for, as yet, "we have millions of women who still know
how to blush—women who believe that virtue is the greatest attribute of
womanhood."[37]

Over these sermons hovered the specter of bawdy, degenerate
women, treacherous in their refusal to submit obediently to the morality
of church and home. Their flouting of authority and seeming eagerness

for sexual emancipation aligned them in the traditionalist mind not only with free lovers of earlier generations but also with feminism, long an enemy to those who insisted on a divinely ordained male clergy and patriarchal family structure. Echoing older arguments against women's legal and political rights, these conservative ministers stoked fear in their parishioners: if women were allowed to run wild in their sexual behavior, American civilization would crumble to dust, and Communism along with the devil himself would rise victorious—the evil, illegitimate off-spring of female promiscuity.

In this religious worldview, the perversion of women was not the sole villain, it was conjoined with liberalism, and many of Kinsey's critics associated the report's female interviewees with the promotion of liberal morals and liberal religion more generally. Torrey Johnson put it bluntly:

> Sow to the wind and reap the whirl-wind! This is the devastating harvest resulting from the seeds of infidelity sown by liberal preach-ers and theologians. It has played into the unscrupulous hands of such people as those who prepared the Kinsey reports. The preacher who does not believe the Genesis account of the creation of the world and of the creation of man and of the fall of man and of the need of regeneration is in exactly the same category with Kinsey.[38]

Here was a newly virulent assault on liberal ministers: the charge that, by straying from traditional Christianity and undermining the authority of the Bible, they effectively caused the nation's catastrophic revolution in sexual morality. This reading of the female report served to deepen still more the religious gulf between conservatives and liberals.

Perhaps conservatives exaggerated a bit, but they were right to sug-gest that religious liberals appeared more sanguine about Kinsey's find-ings, some sympathizing with the people behind the statistics. Mainline Protestant ministers typically reacted less sensationally than conserva-tives to the female report and refrained from imbuing it with apocalyptic undertones. Lawrence K. Whitfield, the pastor of Community Method-ist Church in Millbrae, California, preached a sermon that acknowledged as valid the concerns held by many conservative Christians but called his congregation to a more hopeful perspective. "I think the time will yet come," preached Whitfield, "when we who are so deeply concerned with the 'rightness and wrongness' of men's conduct will feel indebted to Professor Kinsey and his associates for that which they have done." The prevalence of sexual misconduct outside of marriage and unhappiness within its bonds was not new, he noted, but Kinsey's blunt descriptions should help Christians realize the "imperativeness of rethinking our whole philosophy of sex relations" for the needs of the day.[39] The mainline Protestant response was hardly univocal or universally positive, however. The president of Indiana University recalled a "vicious" sermon by an influential Presbyterian pastor in Indianapolis whose church included many important alumni, calling it a "bitter broadside" that dealt a "cruel blow" at the local level.[40]

Of greater national import was a set of articles penned by Reinhold Niebuhr, still a towering figure in American public life and part of an older generation that resisted moral flexibility within mainline Protestantism. In "Sex and Religion in the Kinsey Report," published in *Christianity and Crisis* in 1953, Niebuhr railed against Kinsey's conclusions about female sexual behavior in even stronger terms than he used in his critique of the first report, decrying "the absurd hedonism which informs Kinsey's thought" and his "moral anarchism." At the same time, many young church leaders with national reach, such as Richard Lentz and Seward Hiltner, both of the National Council of the Churches of Christ (NCCC, the successor to the Federal Council of Churches), defended the usefulness of the latest report to religious leaders and emphasized the need to take it seriously. Once again, Hiltner, invited to respond to Niebuhr's scathing critique in a subsequent issue of *Christianity and Crisis*, developed a middle-ground position against Niebuhr's intemperance, one that deemed Kinsey's findings worthy of Christian reflection. Niebuhr retaliated against Hiltner with burning contempt, concluding, "An ignorant approach to a complex issue cannot be creative. It prevents rather than encourages a consideration of the real issues."[41] This squabble between Niebuhr and Hiltner, seventeen years his junior, was indicative of a generational divide within mainline churches concerning how to interpret the shifting sexual realities around them.

Amid this cacophonic reaction, Kinsey sought out strategically useful religious allies wherever he could. He penned a warm note to his trusted California colleague Bishop Block in which he expressed hope that Block had read the female volume. "If not, we should take pleasure in sending you a copy. I have had several of your Episcopal clergymen write approvingly of our research and many of them express increasing disturbance over the way in which our severe sex laws are damaging the prospects of too many of our youth." Block responded enthusiastically, assuring Kinsey that he had been reading his latest "excellent study" chapter by chapter each evening and that he hoped to have Kinsey once again address the local clergy—notably specified as "the non-Catholic clergy"—upon his next visit.[42]

No such bonds of affection existed between Kinsey and his enemies on the right, whom he mostly ignored or left to Indiana University president Wells to handle. He was pressed to respond at least once, however, when the evangelist E. J. Daniels, a Southern Baptist radio minister and director of the Christ for the World ministry in Orlando, Florida, wrote to ask permission to quote extensively from Kinsey's two major reports in his own critique of them, published in 1954 as *I Accuse Kinsey!* When Daniels submitted the quotations he wished to use, Kinsey responded explosively, pointing out Daniels had selected quotations that would wholly distort the claims and intention of Kinsey's volume. Kinsey warned Daniels that "the publishers and their attorneys are specifically concerned with the legitimate use of the material from their books." Kinsey's fury toward fundamentalist critics such as Daniels would remain potent for the remaining two years of his life.[43]

Kinsey continued to receive support from religious allies, however, including Hiltner, who wrote about the Kinsey reports more thoroughly and thoughtfully than any other Protestant leader of his time. Kinsey responded appreciatively to Hiltner's critique of Niebuhr's position, but the researcher sounded demoralized: "Certainly your discussion points up the fact that there is considerable difference of opinion within the church, and if you had to face the extreme Evangelical groups that are doing writing about us, you would agree, I think, that it is difficult for you or anyone else to speak for the whole protestant church or for any single

Cover of E. J. Daniels, *I Accuse Kinsey!* (1954),
which sought to prove that Kinsey's female report
was "unscientific, unreliable, and dangerous."

denomination."[44] Still, Kinsey appears to have been tireless in his efforts
to shore up the liberal religious response, and he publicly expressed his
belief that church leaders were beginning to rethink traditional teachings
about sexuality.

In early 1954, he traveled to New York and spoke to the Executive
Council of the NCCC, where Otis Rice was now executive director, and
also to the New York Academy of Medicine. He assured his audiences
that there had been a "'peculiar reversal' of opinion regarding his volumes
on sexual behavior," with most of his support now coming from church
leaders and his critics from psychiatric sources. Rice, a steady Protestant

backer who likely issued the invitation to Kinsey to speak to the NCCC, wrote afterward to express his "great joy" at the success of Kinsey's visit and to praise him for his ongoing research: "Your work and your point of view have helped us immeasurably in initiating a re-thinking of our constituent churches and our own Department of many of the problems relating to sex."[45] Rice's words exemplified the hopefulness of many liberal Protestant leaders and their sense that important, progressive changes relating to sex could and would happen within the churches.

The last major correspondence between Kinsey and a sympathetic religious leader began in the fall of 1954, when Kinsey wrote to the Church of England Moral Welfare Council to request their sex education booklets and other materials pertaining to sexuality. The Anglican cleric Derrick Sherwin Bailey responded with enthusiasm. Bailey was the author of *The Mystery of Love and Marriage* (1952) and was researching a study of homosexuality in the western Christian tradition; he asked to cite Kinsey's work in this regard, to which Kinsey agreed. In the summer of 1956, despite his failing health, Kinsey wrote again to Bailey, thanking him for sending "your latest report of your church committee on sex laws." While he noted his disagreement with Bailey's "analyses of the scientific data on many points involved in this report," he indicated his broader approval of Bailey's "commendable" attitude: "It is most excellent to have church groups, like yours and the English Roman Catholic group, help make it clear what distinction should be made between sin and crime. We shall be very glad to keep in touch with you and serve you if our data are of use at any time." Bailey wrote back enthusiastically on August 8 to ask for clarification of Kinsey's criticisms, which Kinsey surely would have been glad to give. Sadly for Bailey, Kinsey died on August 25, before having a chance to respond to Bailey's letter.[46]

IN THE EIGHT YEARS THAT followed the publication of *Sexual Behavior in the Human Male*, Kinsey was savvy in cultivating liberal Protestant leaders. Though he made no pretense of sharing their theological convictions, and undoubtedly found these leaders quaint in their adherence to a tradition he had rejected years before, he regularly lauded their broad-minded perspectives. Perhaps he traded flattery for endorsements that could possibly ward off more conservative foes.⁴⁷ But Kinsey engaged with an array of Protestant liberals who supported his work to greater or lesser degrees, and through private letters, interviews, and discussion meetings, he formed relationships that led to long-term cooperation even when they disputed some of his conclusions about human sexuality. Contrary to the common image of Kinsey as someone opposed to religion as a static, eternal source of human sexual oppression, he was in his last years in fact increasingly aware of religious variations and schools of theological interpretation that were open to—and, indeed, deeply influenced by— pioneering research in a range of both scientific and humanistic fields, including his own. Genuine respect for the allies he acquired among inquiring, moderate leaders was mixed with his keen recognition of their instrumental value to his continued research.

Whatever Kinsey's motives, however, his measured friendliness to liberal religionists had a transformative effect on these correspondents and on religious thought about sexuality within American Protestantism in the years following his death. The relationships Kinsey formed advanced and fortified new religious conversations about sexual ethics that his books themselves had helped initiate. Religious leaders influenced by Kinsey launched new conversations along a broad spectrum of issues pertaining to sex, marriage, and family life; and here, no less than in nonreligious quarters, subjects that were once taboo increasingly received frank and open consideration in the wake of Kinsey's reports.

Any so-called sexual revolution that occurred in Kinsey's wake, then, was not merely secular in substance or secularizing in its effects on American culture. There was another transformation underway, one less caught up in the "sex, drugs, and rock 'n' roll" ethos of the hippie culture than in the sober rethinking of moral and ethical norms about sex. The revolution in religious thinking about sexuality was no less profound than the revolution in less religious settings, and it too owed an enormous debt to Kinsey's inspiration.

Consider, for instance, Derrick Sherwin Bailey, the Anglican cleric who was among the last persons to correspond with Kinsey. Bailey had already, in 1952, written on "a theology of sex" in *The Mystery of Love and*

Marriage, in which he argued for a wholesale reorientation in Christian views of sex and presented an imaginative explication of the sacred marital union of partners into "one flesh." In 1955, after corresponding with Kinsey, Bailey published *Homosexuality and the Western Christian Tradition*, which cited Kinsey's research several times. This book received attention in the United States as well as Bailey's native England, where it influenced the famous Wolfenden Report of 1957, which recommended the decriminalization of consensual homosexual activity. It thus paved the way for the passage, a decade later, of the Sexual Offences Act, which legalized in England and Wales certain private sexual acts between consenting adult men. Bailey's interest in rethinking Christian teachings on sexuality clearly predated his correspondence with Kinsey, but he took pleasure and encouragement from Kinsey's serious critical engagement with his writing.

In 1959, Bailey published his most extensive study of sexuality, *Sexual Relation in Christian Thought*, a book twice as long as his previous treatments. This learned volume went back to Paul's teachings on sex in the New Testament (including crucial context on Judaism and the Greco-Roman world) and analyzed the patristic fathers, the medieval church, the Reformation (including early Anglicanism), and Christianity in the modern era. The study was particularly noteworthy for the degree to which Bailey agreed with Kinsey's assessment that traditional Christian doctrine was lamentably hostile toward sex. He insisted on rereading the creation stories in Genesis to derive "a more accurate exegesis" of the meaning of sexuality in the Christian tradition. As the New Testament scholar Robert M. Grant wrote in his review of the book, "Bailey's very useful work turns out to be an example of apologetic for a modern Christian view of sex." Bailey, in fact, would continue to be cited for his innovative research on homosexuality well into the twenty-first century.[48]

The liberal Protestant professor and pastor Seward Hiltner, another frequent Kinsey correspondent, would continue writing about sexuality for the rest of his scholarly career; just as importantly, he trained several generations of seminarians to think broadly about sex and sexuality in ways that would have seemed impossible before Kinsey. Hiltner occasionally expressed disappointment that religious leaders had mostly ignored his own publications on sexuality, all of which aimed in some way, as he later reflected, to get church people "to take scientific findings [about sex] into account, to update pastoral and ethical principles about sex, but to bring basic theological perspectives to bear on the subject without apology." Both of his early books in this area—*Sex Ethics and the Kinsey Reports* (1953) and *Sex and the Christian Life* (1957)—sold well in the public marketplace, he noted, yet "were largely ignored by ministers and other church leaders I had hoped to reach."[49] But through his vast mentorship of ministerial students at the University of Chicago and Princeton Theological Seminary over a span of thirty years, not to mention his work as a leader in the emergent and burgeoning fields of pastoral psychology, pastoral theology, and pastoral counseling, Hiltner played an important role in legitimizing sexuality as a crucial subject of ministerial discussion and education until his retirement in 1980.

Many prominent liberal religious leaders with whom Kinsey had not directly corresponded also joined in the public discussion in the decade following his death, marking the new shift toward openness among mainline Protestants. In 1961, the Canadian and National (USA) Councils of Churches convened the First North American Conference on Church and Family at Green Lake, Wisconsin. Over five hundred delegates came to the conference, representing thirty-three denominations and fifty-seven states and provinces. For five days running, participants presented sex research from a wide range of specialties and took part in response panels of church leaders, lengthy discussion groups, and a number of special events devoted to issues relating to sex and sex education. Sylvanus Milne Duvall, a Congregationalist minister and cochair of the conference, outlined the week's goals of addressing two major questions: the sex standards that Christians should forcefully uphold—with attention to "birth control, abortion, and homosexuality, as well as 'normal' heterosexual conduct"—and the Christian position regarding "the permanence and stability of family life," that is, whether changing conditions had made the traditional family "obsolete" or rendered permanence and stability more urgent than ever as "a crucially vital social and religious essential."[50] The proceedings were subsequently published as *Foundations for Christian Family Policy*, edited by Elizabeth Steel Genné and

William Henry Genné, liberal Protestants who were at the forefront of rethinking these questions and who also cowrote a popular book for a wide audience, titled *Christians and the Crisis in Sex Morality* (1962).

Much of Kinsey's urgent, broad-minded spirit suffused both books, as clergy "pleaded," in the Gennés' words, "for more understanding of both facts and the spirit of our gospel in place of the all-too-prevalent moralistic, legalistic prejudgments that characterize many church members." Sex researchers who had been influenced by Kinsey gave frank and thorough presentations at the Green Lake conference. Wardell Pomeroy, who, with Kinsey, coauthored both the male and female volumes and also became the director of field research at the Institute for Sex Research upon Kinsey's death, gave a frank talk on masturbation that was reprinted and cited in all subsequent publications from the event. (The Gennés, lamenting the shame heaped by church leaders on generations of Christian youth who may have succumbed to this temptation, concluded, "The church has a special responsibility to help people handle guilt feelings that may have been engendered."[51]) Pomeroy praised the increasingly "free and enthusiastic exchange" between experts and ministers and later wrote, "Returning to Bloomington from Green Lake, I could only think how much Kinsey would have enjoyed the conference."[52]

Other sex experts included at the Green Lake conference were Lester Kirkendall, a sexuality educator and later a cofounder of the Sex Information and Education Council of the United States (SIECUS); Evelyn Hooker, a psychologist influenced by Kinsey's research on male homosexuality and whose own work led ultimately to homosexuality being dropped from the American Psychiatric Association's *Diagnostic and Statistical Manual of Mental Disorders*; Ruth Proskauer Smith, an abortion rights and family planning advocate; and Mary Steichen Calderone, medical director of the Planned Parenthood Federation (and later the executive director of SIECUS), who had carried on a warm and lengthy correspondence with Kinsey during his lifetime. Working closely with these experts and other thinker-activists, Christian leaders at the conference voted to adopt a statement affirming the church as "a redemptive fellowship—friendly, nonjudgmental, forgiving, accepting." The church, continued the statement, "must be compassionate, supportive, and empathic.

It must re-examine the quality of its own interpersonal relationships. It must seek out and be ready to accept all people into fellowship, whatever they have done." Along with an appeal to "strengthen homes and families" in both religious faith and sexual teachings, the statement called the church to "re-evaluate attitudes toward marriage and sex, in light of biblical theology and scientific findings" and to "develop a positive Christian ethic on sexual behavior which will be relevant to our culture."[53] Many of the signatories to the statement subsequently committed significant time and energy to writing and speaking about the need for new and creative religious thinking about sexual ethics.

Change was in the air for liberal Protestants, and many other leaders weighed in over the next several years. For instance, Harvey Cox, the liberal Baptist theologian who would earn international fame with his 1965 book *The Secular City*, squared up against Reinhold Niebuhr on sexual issues in *Christianity and Crisis*, for an article that was then reprinted for popular consumption in *Redbook*. Citing Kinsey, Cox noted that American society was mired in hypocrisy that most refused to face, the "cant and flimflam of its sexual folkways." Cox diverged from Kinsey, though, in calling for a "de-mythologized . . . sexual ethic," one that would "reject . . . any Kinseyan inference that what is being done should determine what ought to be done" while refusing, in turn, to "pander to the cheap attempt to oversimplify the issue" of premarital intercourse. Cox admitted that his solution risked sounding like "evasion," but he argued emphatically that his nuanced approach could help Christians "outgrow our ridiculous obsession with sex, of which our fixation on chastity and virginity is just the other side of the coin."[54]

Shifts were also gradually taking place in liberal religious thinking about homosexuality, long treated as a condition of sin or sickness. W. Norman Pittenger, a theologian and Episcopal clergyman who taught for thirty-three years at New York's General Theological Seminary, authored his first book on sexuality in 1954, when Kinsey was still alive, titled *The Christian View of Sexual Behavior: A Reaction to the Kinsey Report*, and went on to author many more. His early response to Kinsey's studies was relatively conservative—he echoed others' critiques of the scientist's biologism, dedicated *The Christian View of Sexual Behavior* to "all those who in Christian marriage have been made one flesh," and wrote extensively about sexual sin. Nevertheless, he would later argue for full acceptance by the church of same-sex relationships.[55] In books such as *Time for Consent: A Christian's Approach to Homosexuality* (1967), *Making Sexuality Human* (1970), *Love and Control in Sexuality* (1974), and *Gay Lifestyles* (1977), Pittenger disavowed much of his earlier writing on sexuality as being "altogether too conventional" and made a robust case for applying identical ethical standards to homosexual and heterosexual erotic behavior.[56] His stance was unambiguous: "I am frank to say that I cannot see how the desire of the homosexual for bodily manifestation of his sexual drive is wrong, in and of itself; nor can I see why, once this has been put under human controls, it is wrong for him to act upon it."[57] By the time of his death at age ninety-one in 1997, Pittenger had spent decades supporting various components of the LGBT rights movement, including the Episcopal Church's LGBT organization, Integrity.[58]

Countless other religious liberals joined in that process of rethinking sexual ethics from Jewish and Christian points of view beginning in the 1950s. These efforts bore fruit in traditional organizations such as the Young Women's Christian Association and United Church Women, which plunged into the task of addressing hitherto forbidden sexual topics. In addition, a number of Protestant denominations redoubled their efforts to produce straightforward sex education curricula for children and teens.[59] New alliances also emerged, including a host of groups devoted to the religious and civil rights of gays and lesbians and an explicitly pro-choice network of Protestant and Jewish clergy that referred women to safe abortion providers well before *Roe v. Wade* decriminalized the procedure. Insofar as they continued to advocate committed monogamous relationships, as most religious liberals did, their perspectives hardly seem radical today; by twenty-first-century standards, indeed, they may appear traditional and conservative. But many religious liberals were, in a palpable sense, revolutionary, bearing witness to a new openness and creativity in sexual ethics spurred in no small part by the provocative work and engaged collaboration of Alfred Kinsey.

Certainly, their efforts seemed revolutionary to traditionalist Protestants and Catholics. By no means were all Christians on board with this liberalization; to the contrary, many conservatives viewed it in near apocalyptic terms. As the Cold War continued to cast its long shadow of potential destruction over the nation, the peril of gender roles and sexual norms in turmoil struck many as deeply undermining to American morale, not to mention the moral formation of youth. The cultural influence of liberals was bad enough, but efforts to change the law were profoundly unsettling and would soon meet staunch resistance.

If Kinsey's reports thrust a new glare on differences among American Christians that were growing ever more stark, it was a glare that hardly dimmed in subsequent years. The next major controversy grew out of the new openness to talking publicly about sex propelled by Kinsey but went much further and deeper in its impact, at both the national and local levels. Nothing was more controversial, it turned out, than how to teach children about sex.

CHAPTER 5

SEX EDUCATION IN THE SIXTIES AND THE SURGING RELIGIOUS RIGHT

T HE DECADE AND A HALF following Kinsey's report on women was a time of rapid changes in American attitudes regarding sex and gender. The trends uncovered by Kinsey only intensified, as the broader public culture grew more tolerant of explicit sexual themes and imagery. Hugh Hefner's *Playboy* magazine debuted in the same year as Kinsey's female report; at the same time, Hollywood films were becoming more overt in their treatment of sex. The publication of several sexually frank novels made waves, including—finally—the unexpurgated *Lady Chatterley's Lover*. By 1960, the year the first birth control pill was approved by the Food and Drug Administration and sold as Enovid, many college students were openly questioning the strict sexual standards and taboos of their parents, including disapproval of premarital sex. Helen Gurley Brown's racy best seller *Sex and the Single Girl* came out in 1962, exuberantly advocating women's sexual freedom before and outside marriage, and Betty Friedan's groundbreaking manifesto about unfulfilled homemakers and "the problem that has no name," *The Feminine Mystique*, was published the following year. Like the changes preceding them, both works signaled fresh challenges to the standing ideals of femininity and female virtue, embodied in premarital virginity and compliant marital domesticity.[1]

Meanwhile, liberal Protestant activism on behalf of gay rights (including repeal of sodomy statutes) received increasing attention in both

Sex educator Mary Steichen Calderone in her New York office.
CECIL BEATON/CONDÉ NAST VIA GETTY IMAGES.

the religious and the secular press. The Supreme Court's 1964 ruling in *Jacobellis v. Ohio* served to loosen obscenity laws, and in the same year the American Medical Association voted for the first time to recommend that physicians routinely distribute birth control information to their patients. In terms of sex, the United States looked very different in 1964 than it had a decade earlier.

This tidal shift, as many felt it to be at the time, received wide notice in the media, and countless magazine articles appeared that sought to explain to worried audiences what was happening. A *Newsweek* cover story in 1964 focused on the "Morals Revolution on the U.S. Campus" and explained that "the key to the new morality" was the understanding that "a boy and girl who have established what the campus calls a 'meaningful relationship' have the moral right to sleep together."[2] For many, especially American parents, this was shocking stuff.

One important result of the anxiety generated by these changes was a concerted effort to implement wholesome sex education. As educators and professionals across many fields sought ways to address the social problems they perceived to be erupting because of shifting sexual standards, many agreed that schools must play an important role in that effort. Sex education programs proliferated during the mid-1960s, a wave as potent as it was divisive. Attitudes toward them hinged on whether observers believed that school-imparted information would be a help or a hindrance to traditional morality. Although some parents were suspicious of such programs, growing numbers of educational experts believed they were essential to stemming the social evils made possible by changing morals.

One of the most important organizations in the development of sex education programs was the Sex [later Sexuality] Information and Education Council of the United States (SIECUS), founded in 1964 and led for the next eighteen years by Mary Steichen Calderone. Under Calderone's leadership, SIECUS made enormous inroads in school systems across the country, efforts for which it was both applauded and excoriated. SIECUS was a particular bête noir for conservative Christians who did not believe sex education programs like those produced by SIECUS should be in the public schools. Calderone's chief adversary in this battle was Billy James Hargis, an intrepid anti-Communist crusader and influential evangelist. The battle between Calderone and Hargis, and the struggle over sex education more broadly, played out in countless local clashes in school districts across the nation. Examining these dynamics helps us see the complicated forces in play at this moment: the alliances among scientists, reformers, and religious progressives that pushed for sexual liberalization, and the backlash from religious conservatives, who increasingly fueled right-wing politics with campaigns against sexual immorality and liberality. The conflict played a formative role in the early shaping of the modern Christian right.

Reactions for and against sex education echoed and intensified the acrimonious feuds fueled by the birth control movement, attempts to control erotic themes in film and literature, and public reports of extramarital sexual behavior in earlier decades. The controversy gave rise in the 1960s and 1970s to fresh waves of resentment toward a seemingly liberalizing culture that made increasing room for sexual behavior deemed unorthodox by conservative Christians. Whatever Christian consensus remained about the immorality of premarital sex was beginning to crumble in this period, and schools were expedient targets of rage. Fear that the United States was falling into corruption and anarchy was potent in the 1960s, and nothing better personified that risk than the sex education of the nation's children.

ORGANIZED PROGRAMS SEEKING TO EDUCATE young people about sex emerged from the same Progressive Era milieu that nurtured so many other reforms, including birth control. The American Social Hygiene Association (ASHA), founded in 1914, campaigned for sex education as a way of nurturing healthier populations: youth would know how to protect themselves from venereal disease, especially. The ASHA also argued that sex education would produce more wholesome citizens, by helping to overturn the gender and sexual stereotypes that fueled prostitution and unhappiness in marriage. There had been far too much tacit acceptance of male immorality, its supporters believed, and simple decency dictated that men and women alike should be held to the same standards of sexual behavior. Thus early proponents of sex education often linked a program of hygiene to the quest for women's full equality.

As contraception became more widely available in the 1930s and afterward, leaders and educators from a wide range of fields had to rethink sex ed programs. Social workers like Emily Hartshorne Mudd, who founded a birth control clinic in Philadelphia, were distressed to witness "case after case of marital unhappiness and maladjustment, based often on ignorance, fear and rejection of the whole sexual side of life," problems frequently revealed when women sought contraceptive guidance.[3] Mudd would become a pioneer in marriage counseling, where she had a long and distinguished career. Others focused on the sex education of youth, aiming to prevent marital troubles from occurring in the first place. Sex education during these middle decades continued to be aimed essentially at building and sustaining strong marriages.

Thus many such programs, though they may have appeared daring in their relative willingness to discuss private matters, had a distinctly conservative, moralistic flavor. An example from the San Diego city school system during World War II illustrates the desire to contain and exert control over the frightening changes afoot amid the flood of military personnel into the city. Through "biology, English, home economics, science, social studies, and hygiene (health) classes," the San Diego curriculum highlighted themes including the "disastrous results that interfere with happiness when an individual 'bucks' social conventions. Difficulties commonly involved when marriage is made between differing races, religions and nationalities. Individual's responsibility to the next generation. Role of both sexes in family life. Family harmony." Although there was some limited discussion of "petting" and actual sex acts, the program's deeper concern of shoring up fragile families and uncertain moral standards was unmistakably clear.[4]

Through the 1950s, what was often termed "family life education" continued to be seen as a remedy for all manner of ills, from masturbation to divorce, sexual maladjustment to crime, and marriages across barriers of social difference. Fear that juvenile delinquency was on the rise—stoked by the Kinsey reports and exemplified in headlines like *Newsweek*'s "The Kids Grow Worse"—was as palpable as fear of the atomic bomb. Adolescent sexual activity was believed to be increasing and wreaking havoc on morality. Sex ed curricula often sought to curb such illicit behavior by provoking similar fears in students. For instance, dramatic venereal disease films featured, as one former student remembered, "babies born with crusted eyes as a result of gonorrhea; both males and females in the tertiary stage of syphilis; drooling and walking with that strange gait that comes from tertiary syphilis; brain damage; open, running sores; and on and on."[5] Convincing adolescents to conform to wholesome American standards of sexual conduct took effort.

Children and child rearing approached the status of a social obsession during this period, and the stakes for mothers were especially high. "No matter how brilliant she is intellectually or how important a career she may have," advised experts in a 1952 issue of *Parents Magazine*, "she doesn't feel completely fulfilled until she has had at least one child."[6] Bound up in what the sociologist Kingsley Davis termed "the cult of marital happiness" and reinforced by a visible postwar baby boom overhung by threat of nuclear catastrophe, education in family life remained a product of the social hygiene mentality. Topics remained scrupulously mundane: "balancing a checkbook, applying for a job, learning to date, planning a wedding, finding a hobby," even "jewelry and furniture shopping."[7] Sex was an urgent subtext, but only rarely a topic of direct instruction.

But as the 1950s became the 1960s, moral standards seemed to be rapidly disintegrating. Family life education appeared a miserable failure, and rising numbers of Americans agreed that new programs needed to be developed. Views differed, as they always had, on what should be taught in such programs and how. Should programs aim at persuading young people never to have sex before marriage or simply address sex more forthrightly in its full biological and social context? There was no lack of opinion on this subject, as calls grew for schools to do a better job of instructing students in sexual behavior.

Mary Steichen Calderone was foremost among the people who answered these calls. Calderone had grown up in a sophisticated, elite world. Her mother, Clara Smith, had left her rural home in the Ozarks of southwestern Missouri, and her childhood world of Confederate pride and camp meeting conversions, to study music in Paris. There Clara met the artist Edward Steichen, who was already making a name for himself and would become an internationally renowned photographer; they married in New York's Trinity Church in 1903, both shedding their religious backgrounds (hers evangelical Protestant, his staunch Catholic) to adopt a Quaker affiliation. Mary was born nine months after their wedding, and two years later the family returned to Paris, where Steichen felt his artistic ventures would flourish more than in the United States. Baby Kate, Mary's sister, arrived two years after that. In 1908, Edward Steichen's younger sister, Lilian, married a socialist journalist with a strong interest in human rights and social reform named Carl Sandburg, who would find renown as a writer nicknamed the "poet of the people."[8]

From earliest childhood, then, Mary lived among diverse thinkers, writers, and artists. After graduating from the elite Brearley School in Manhattan, she studied at Vassar College, married and had children before divorcing, and decided to enter medical school at the age of thirty.

She earned her medical degree at the University of Rochester in 1939 and a master's degree at the Columbia University School of Public Health in 1942. She married a fellow physician, Frank Calderone, in 1941 and had two more children with him. Focused on public health, she worked as a physician in suburban New York schools for more than ten years. Her labors in the public health field were key to the development of her medical interest in human sexuality, and especially in the importance of contraceptive access and information as well as the prevention of sexually transmitted diseases.

During the 1950s, Calderone returned to her early religious roots by becoming active in the Quaker community (also known as the Religious Society of Friends), an affiliation that she considered very much a part of the larger Christian tradition. She was officially accepted as a member, or "received by request," into the Westbury (New York) Monthly Meeting of the Society of Friends.[9] Thereafter, she frequently stated her commitment to Quaker principles, which would shape her ongoing life's work, including her focus on sex. In a Quaker pamphlet she later wrote, Calderone noted, "One hardly thinks of Friends, men or women, as revolutionaries and, in truth, their outer demeanor, comportment and life style have tended to be quiet and conservative. But on major social issues—slavery, peace, alternative service during war, religious ecumenicism, racial equality—on such issues Quaker concern and conscience come on strong. Quaker voices are usually heard loud and clear 'speaking truth to power.'"[10]

In 1953, a few years before she renewed her affiliation with the Quakers, Calderone joined the staff of the Planned Parenthood Federation of America (PPFA), the organization founded by Margaret Sanger in 1938 as the American Birth Control League. True to the strong spirit of its founding mother, PPFA remained focused on birth control, and from the very start Calderone's work for the organization centered on controversial issues relating to sex and gender. An early assignment from the organization's executive director, William Vogt, was to create some kind of signature event to showcase in a fresh way Planned Parenthood itself and the need for contraceptive services. She came back to Vogt with the idea of a conference on abortion, specifically illegally procured abortions as a major public health problem that deserved attention (and one that could be mitigated by better access to birth control). Throughout the United States at this time, abortion was a crime in all circumstances except to save the life of the mother (and, in six states, to save the life of the fetus).Vogt assented and put Calderone in charge of the conference, held in 1955; she later edited the conference proceedings into a book, *Abortion in the United States*, which was published in 1958.[11] While there was no way to get trustworthy statistics of an illegal and heavily punished activity such as abortion, the conference's statistics committee estimated the frequency of illegal abortion in the United States to be "as low as 200,000 and as high as 1,200,000 per year." Many of the procedures resulted in injury and even death at the hands of the "crude abortionists" to whom desperate women often resorted, at great personal and social expense.[12]

Calderone authored her own work too, showing particular concern for the sexual problems of women as well as the obviously unequal health dangers and consequences faced by women who procured illegal abortions, often because they did not have adequate information on how to prevent pregnancy. A journal article she wrote in 1960 was called "Illegal Abortion as a Public Health Problem," and she used a strongly worded editorial in the same journal later that year to critique male physicians for their poor understanding of women's psychosexual problems.[13] In the same year, Calderone published her first full book (with help from science writers Phyllis Goldman and Robert Goldman), *Release from Sexual Tensions*, a book about sex and love that was focused especially on solving problems in marriage. Despite the curious title, which suggested nothing so much as a masturbation manual, the "tensions" invoked were interpersonal, not physiological; her interests in educating readers about these matters could almost have aligned her squarely with the family life education programs of the time.

Calderone's interest in better sex education was apparent in her work from the beginning. During her eleven years at PPFA, Calderone became a noted speaker and writer on birth control, which was still a controversial if not shameful subject in the early years of her time there. As women's health care was increasingly a prominent theme in her work, she was keenly interested in helping women gain knowledge of, and access to, contraception. She played a crucial role in persuading the American

Medical Association that doctors ought to distribute contraceptive information and offer contraceptive access to all patients who needed it, and a proposal eventually passed to affirm that family planning is "more than a matter of responsible parenthood; it is a matter of responsible medical practice."[14] That statement, she later (rightly) recalled, "really did come from my efforts, first to get them to set up the committee to develop the statement, and then to work on the committee."[15]

In 1961, Calderone participated as an invited guest and the official delegate of Planned Parenthood at the historic Green Lake conference, where she gave a plenary address focused on the need for responsible family planning and the inculcation of "a sense of responsibility about the use of sex."[16] As it was for many of the attendees, the Green Lake conference was important for Calderone. To the Reverend William Genné, director of the Family Life Department of the National Council of Churches, she wrote afterward, "Needless to say, it was a memorable experience— probably the high point for me in my eight years" at Planned Parenthood. She told one of the conference's cochairs that the event was "probably the most enriching experience I have ever had. Nothing will ever be quite the same for me again."[17] Calderone was now attuned to the exciting new work on sexuality coming out of the churches, and over the next two or three years many of the professionals who had gathered at Green Lake would continue to debate, in Calderone's words, "what are we going to do about this sex mess—the attitudes in society are very bad."[18] Although some experts insisted that education about sex should remain under the auspices of marriage counseling or family life education, others agreed with Calderone that it needed a new approach.

Eventually, Calderone came up with the idea of a voluntary health organization that would focus on sex education and "put sexuality into the field of health rather than the field of morals."[19] So it was that in the year she turned sixty, 1964, Calderone left Planned Parenthood and, with four others who had been at Green Lake—William Genné, sexuality educator Lester Kirkendall, Quaker sociologist Clark Vincent, and public health educator Wallace C. Fulton—cofounded the Sex Information and Education Council of the United States, a nonprofit organization seeking to bring scientifically based sexuality education wherever it was needed.

The SIECUS statement of purpose described its aim as "to establish man's sexuality as a health entity." This effort would be accomplished in three main ways: identifying the "special characteristics" of sexuality that were distinct from (though of course related to) human reproduction; dignifying sexuality through an open, scientific, research-minded approach; and assembling information for professionals and for people throughout society, so that all might be better equipped to act responsibly and healthfully in their sexual behavior and experience sex "as a creative and re-creative force."[20] Heading SIECUS for eighteen years, Calderone lectured frequently around the country and also published several books on sex for a range of audiences. She became nationally known for her work promoting sex education programs for use in public schools, including the widely used publication *Guidelines for Sexuality Education: Kindergarten Through Twelfth Grade*. Her hope, shared by the wider SIECUS staff and board members, was to make comprehensive sex education the norm across the nation. While SIECUS and Calderone had a broad mission when it came to educating people about sex, they became particularly infamous for promoting sex ed in schools.

Calderone believed that Americans received misinformation about sex starting in infancy, from parents, religion, and any number of other social influences; her goal was to replace these half-truths and distortions with a mix of scientific and social teaching. But far worse than misinformation, in her view, were the harmful attitudes toward sex that children picked up from prudish influences both within and beyond the home. Even when parents, teachers, or religious leaders believed themselves not to be providing any sexual education whatsoever, they too frequently influenced boys and girls alike in damaging ways. As a SIECUS publication proclaimed, "avoidance, repression, rejection, suppression, embarrassment, and shock are negative forms of sex education." A positive attitude toward sex and sexuality was crucial to the mental, emotional, and physical health of these children as they grew into maturity.[21]

As the nation's foremost nationally recognized proponent of sex education, Mary Steichen Calderone played a critical role in the cultural and religious conflagrations over sex in the United States during the second half of the twentieth century. A staunch Quaker and pacifist, and a person of emphatically conventional mores in her private life, Calderone never sought to stoke the fires of warfare, even cultural warfare. But she was a woman who dared to advocate publicly in favor of greater sexual candor and in-depth education for all Americans, and her successful efforts landed her squarely in the firing line of those who likened candor to immorality and deemed "education" coded speech for corruption.

Although very much a revolutionary in her long labors on behalf of birth control access and sex education, Calderone was a conservative insofar as she proclaimed publicly that sexual freedom was ultimately for the purpose of strengthening stable families and permanent relationships, which would thereby sustain society. In the *Manual of Contraceptive Practice* she edited under the auspices of PPFA in 1964, she made this point clear: "The role of sex is basic to the marital relationship that in itself is the fundamental building block of our society as it is presently constituted," while contraception should be regarded "as the servant of marriage, never as an end in itself." In a 1966 speech delivered at a high school in Hartford, Connecticut, she lamented that many youth now treated sexual experience as a right rather than a privilege earned through maturity and asked, "Why are we afraid to say, 'You are just plain too young?'" The journalist Mary Breasted, who interviewed Calderone at a peak moment in the controversy over sex education in 1969, argued that she advocated sex education as "basically a form of moral indoctrination," and claimed that the work of SIECUS was essentially "an attempt to bolster conventional morality by rendering it more tolerable." To *Playboy* magazine in 1970, even as she noted that she could and would not "stop society from evolving" nor "force other people to adhere to my personal beliefs," Calderone openly confessed "my really profound belief that sex belongs primarily in marriage." Because "casual sex" was simply sex for pleasure, with no regard for any relationship between the partners, she averred, "I'm not looking forward happily to a widespread acceptance of casual sex."[22]

Calderone looked on heterosexual relationships as the foundation of society, and she saw SIECUS as working to strengthen "effective, strong, permanent relationships—which usually translates into having or being part of a family." At the same time, in discussing a wide range of sexual expressions that included bisexuality and homosexuality, she noted, "I can't find it in my heart to reject anyone because of their sexual behavior. . . . There is really no manifestation of sexuality that should put us off, that should make us look down on somebody. If that's where they are, we have to accept them there." Calderone wrestled with the question of whether sexual nonconformity outside marriage would threaten familial and social stability or not. But she was tolerant and very trusting of the young people she met at her lectures, who inspired her with optimism and the courage to honor views beyond her own ingrained conventionality.[23] Her goal, at heart, was thoroughgoing honesty about bodily desires and the consequences of acting heedlessly and obliviously on them. Calderone sought to overcome prudishness and the ignorance that was its inevitable result, and in true Quaker fashion, she also sought to eradicate hypocrisy in all its forms.

SIECUS emerged directly out of Calderone's own religious sensibility. "Being a Quaker," she wrote, "lays on one the responsibility for engaging in a continuing internal process of finding out what one really believes in, and relentlessly tracking down one's bigotries, prejudices, inconsistencies, blindnesses, and refusals to recognize truth and accept it as such." At the time she formed SIECUS, with the Green Lake conference still emanating its influence, "the conviction came to me that *responsible parenthood* is but a small segment of something much larger—*responsible sexuality*—which itself is but a segment of the all-encompassing concept of *total responsibility in all human relationships*" (emphasis in original). The resulting organization had a "spirit of ecumenical professionalism" and included clergy advisors who were Jewish and Catholic as well as Protestant, representing "all shades from right to left—although not the extremes of either." In another context, Calderone approvingly quoted social ethicist and Episcopal priest Gibson Winter's statement, "The recovery of sexuality is part of our salvation—an aspect of wholeness." Traditional religion had often erred in teaching children that sex was dirty rather than "sacred and beautiful." Calderone continued by saying that part of the work of sexual educators was to draw out "*what is already there within [the child] that is good*" (emphasis in original). This itself was a religious mission, she insisted: "This belief in the implicitness of the child's goodness parallels the Quaker recognition of that of God in every man. Whether one be Christian, Jew, theist or nontheist, black or white, we cannot exist, or survive, in the absence of the profound belief that to be human is to be good. And because human beings were created sexual, then to be sexual must—or should—also be good."[24]

The Supreme Court's June 1965 decision in *Griswold v. Connecticut* offered a nexus of principles that Calderone could heartily approve. Striking down a Connecticut law that prohibited any person from using medical or other means to prevent pregnancy, the justices sided with Planned Parenthood League of Connecticut executive director Estelle Griswold and Yale School of Medicine physician Dr. C. Lee Buxton (who was the Planned Parenthood chapter's medical director), ruling in favor of a "right to privacy" for married couples and greater leeway for health providers to provide patients with birth control. For the physician Calderone, the decision correctly placed contraceptive decisions in the hands of ordinary people, who still needed to seek wise guidance from trusted authorities rather than succumb to the "sexual chaos" of the times. In an extended visit to Washington University in St. Louis just months after the *Griswold* decision, she spoke to students as the university's first "physician in residence" while again stressing her Quaker identity. "We are for the first time in history at a point where man can separate his sexual life from his reproductive life," she warned before making a Cold War analogy: "Sexual responsibility is a social responsibility. . . . Like atomic energy, sex is a potent force we must learn to use constructively or we can destroy ourselves." Once more, the credentialed professional provided the example to her audience of the sort of expert from whom such vital lessons should come.[25]

As school leaders across the country during the mid-1960s grew increasingly convinced of the need for robust programs of sex education, SIECUS was there to assist. And because SIECUS at this early stage embodied its leaders' fairly conservative outlook, the organization's materials were palatable to a wide range of educators. Calderone and her colleagues wrote passionately about social problems like venereal disease among teens, rising divorce rates, and alarming statistics about teen pregnancies; they plausibly cast sex education as "preventative medicine."[26]

Sex education programs created by SIECUS and other organizations burgeoned during the mid-1960s, as panicked parents and educators sought to remedy the sexual problems they witnessed around them. Experts estimated that nearly 50 percent of American school systems had adopted some type of sex education program by 1968.

California was especially ripe territory for the sex education movement. Governor Edmund Brown was keen to develop a curriculum in family life education to curb out-of-wedlock pregnancy, divorce, and other problems pertaining to sexuality and marriage. When the Sacramento County school board decided to act in 1968–1969, it called on SIECUS staff, including Calderone, to develop its K-12 Family Life and Sex Education program. Districts in Oakland, Palo Alto, and San Mateo County worked to create their own programs, which were much blunter about sexual details than the family life education programs of prior decades. Like Calderone and SIECUS itself, the new programs sought not to be preachy while still favoring relatively conventional sexual standards and attempting to contain youthful behavior. Teachers presented eye-raising statistics about venereal disease and stories of the sad consequences of teen pregnancy. This was the kind of sex education most parents wanted, a program that could shore up traditional morality. Both the programs that SIECUS helped set up in the mid-1960s and others that developed concurrently shared this ethos.[27]

The embrace of sex education at the local level, as in these California districts, quickly prompted a severe backlash and provoked numerous battles. As the work of SIECUS became influential and widely known, opposition to the organization and to Calderone personally grew especially fierce. Critics were dismayed by the proliferation of sex ed programs on the ground, and many came to see her as the chief adversary in this fight. The most significant opposition came from two groups that collaborated often during the 1960s: the John Birch Society, founded as an anti-Communist conservative advocacy organization in 1958, and the Christian Crusade of Billy James Hargis, himself a Bircher. Both bodies were influential in this conflict, but the particular focus on sex education by some key staffers at the Christian Crusade gave it the greater impact. Assisting sex education opponents in scores of local school battles nationwide, Hargis's institution proved a formidable challenge to Calderone's own crusade for sexual truth.

Billy James Hargis began to make his mark on the world in October 1948, when, as a twenty-three-year-old pastor in the town of Sapulpa, Oklahoma, with little postsecondary education, he started a slim newsletter. With the unassuming title *Christian Echoes* and only a tiny circulation, the paper might easily have gone the way of countless other such publications put out by ambitious small-town preachers in that era. But Hargis's tremendous self-confidence was matched by the luck of being in the right place at the right time, with a timely idea and fearsome rhetoric to match. His newsletter became the glossy, broadly distributed *Christian Crusade*, and Hargis founded an interdenominational organization by the same name in 1950. Through the magazine's wide print circulation and Hargis's success in harnessing radio and TV to deliver his message, he grew into one of the most influential evangelists and conservative crusaders of the 1950s and 1960s.[28]

Hargis saw Communism everywhere. A report in the *Nation* by an attendee at the Christian Crusade's five-day Anti-Communist Leadership School in 1962 noted that, in Hargis's mind, "all citizens who, in their political beliefs, range from slightly left of conservative doctrines to communism are Communists"; moreover, "there are only two political groups remaining—those who stand with us, and all others." The reporter, Thomas Uzzell, expressed his fear at Hargis's adept leadership among scores of fundamentalists present: "The man is an engine of energy, is something of a genius as an organizer, and has mastered the art of moving crowds who want to be freed of the burden of thinking."[29]

Hargis believed that God had chosen him, as he said in 1965, "to launch a mass movement of resistance to the trend in American life to world government, apostate religion, and appeasement with satanic 'isms' such as communism." As a young pastor in the 1940s—he was ordained to the ministry when he was seventeen, in his hometown of Texarkana, Texas—he had acted "like Moses" in initially running away from the truths of the Communist takeover of America and its churches. Once he accepted God's call, however, he never looked back. "I am the first to admit I am not qualified" for this enormous task, Hargis later said, "but no logician or materialist can ever convince me that I am not in God's Will. It has been proven again and again. . . . God needed a man to tell the truth to an ignorant and apathetic church."[30]

After a very brief theological education (two and a half months at Ozark Bible College in Bentonville, Arkansas) and a succession of pastorates, he ditched local church ministry in favor of a career as a radio broadcaster and itinerant evangelist, founding the Christian Crusade in 1950 as a print and radio outlet. During the 1950s he collaborated with Carl T. McIntire, another formidable fundamentalist with a radio empire and enormous influence. Between 1953 and 1957, they worked together on a project of the International Council of Christian Churches (ICCC)—a fundamentalist organization that opposed the more liberal World Council of Churches—to send "Bible balloons" into Soviet countries. As his radio and newspaper presence increased, Hargis moved to Tulsa, expanded into television, and started writing a newspaper column that was syndicated in papers across the country. At the start of 1962, two hundred radio stations and at least a dozen television stations aired Hargis in forty-six states. By 1964, his daily radio ministry had exploded to four hundred stations across the country, while subscriptions to his magazine were reportedly up to a hundred thirty thousand.[31] Through his relentless denunciations in *Christian Crusade* magazine and his ubiquitous radio broadcasts, his multiple books and national conferences, his speaking engagements, and his record albums of sermons and songs, Hargis had become an extraordinarily effective communicator, iterating forceful messages about the wickedness of liberal politics and liberal religion to Christians throughout the country.

By 1964, Hargis was one of the most influential conservative evangelists in America, and a figure of fear and fascination among liberals.[32] It was at precisely this time that sex burst into Hargis's writing. He had spent recent years decrying the Supreme Court's 1962 decision declaring prayer in public schools unconstitutional, alleging that John F. Kennedy's assassination by Lee Harvey Oswald had been a Communist plot, and campaigning for the nomination of the ultra-conservative Barry

Evangelist, anti-Communist crusader, and
SIECUS opponent Billy James Hargis. *GEORGE
CROUTER/*THE DENVER POST *VIA GETTY IMAGES.*

Goldwater. Now there was another target. Sex was new territory for
Hargis to tackle, and it had become highly relevant in the wake of both
the emerging feminist movement and increasing liberal sympathy for
what was then termed the "homophile" movement (the early gay rights
movement). Such flagrant rejections of traditionalist gender norms and
modes of patriarchal authority were ideal weapons for stoking conservative outrage. As usual, Hargis's timing was perfect.

The first sign of Hargis's new focus was an item in *Christian Crusade* magazine. The February–March 1964 issue included an item titled,
"What to Do About Pornography." It opened on a note of alarm: "A 'natural' outgrowth of the ultra-liberal, 'free-thinker' viewpoint, which has
finally struggled into acceptance throughout the Nation, is the horrifying
increase in the *public, legal* distribution of pornographic, smut literature,

pictures, films, etc., *in every city in the country*" (emphasis in original). The head of Tulsa's chapter of Youth for Christ was quoted in asserting that a billion dollars per year were now being spent on such materials in the United States alone—all because of the Communist-friendly liberals. The article continued, "That international Communism has long subsidized pornography in this and other countries will come as no surprise to our readers, for it fits ideally into their plans for the moral decay of non-Communist countries." In response, readers should not merely wring their hands but boycott all local stores that sold any such materials. Pornography was "A BATTLEGROUND UPON WHICH EVERY AMERICAN CAN GET INTO ACTION TODAY" (emphasis in original). The message that evil lurked at one's trusted grocery and drug stores fit well with Hargis's warnings about a "far left" enemy within.[33]

Fulminations about America's sexual degeneracy grew more and more prominent as a theme in the Christian Crusade for the next several years. Hargis crafted alarmist literature focused on sex, with the help of two men: David Noebel, his executive assistant and a *Christian Crusade* writer for many years, and Gordon V. Drake, who joined Christian Crusade in 1968 as the head of its Department of Education.[34] The books each wrote during this period give a flavor of the themes that went with this emphasis on sex: Hargis's published titles included *Communist America—Must It Be?* (1960), *The Facts About Communism and Our Churches* (1962), and *The Far Left* (1964). Noebel published *Communism, Hypnotism, and the Beatles* (1965), which he later expanded and repackaged as *The Beatles: A Study in Drugs, Sex, and Revolution* (1969). Drake wrote *Blackboard Power: NEA Threat to America* (1968) and *Is the School House the Proper Place to Teach Raw Sex?* (1968), and it was these last two that heralded the campaign against SIECUS and Mary Steichen Calderone.

Like most Christian Crusade literature, both of Drake's books aimed to be exposés. *Blackboard Power* charged one of the two major national teachers' unions—the National Education Association (NEA)—with degrading American youth by promoting Communism, popular music, African American literature, and sex education. Drake's account aimed to incite both racial and sexual panic, charging the NEA with promoting both dangerous African American writers and an anti-religious glorification of sex. The book's title, an obvious play on the Black Power movement, was illustrated by the menacing, frontal fist that was that movement's symbol—only this fist was distinctly white, set against a black background and marked by text in bright red. Whites could be as threatening toward the nation's morals as blacks, the image implied, particularly when they were masquerading as civic-minded public school teachers. Don't be fooled, Drake warned, for these men and women were as power hungry and violent as their radical black nationalist counterparts.

One of Drake's major concerns in the book was to alarm readers about the radicalism of African American authors from W. E. B. Du Bois and Langston Hughes to Richard Wright, Ralph Ellison, Dick Gregory, and Alain Locke. Drake quoted the conservative Texas columnist Earl Lively in referring to James Baldwin as "a purveyor of perverted pornographic smut." But he also had a great deal to say about the NEA and sex education, slamming figures such as Mary Steichen Calderone, Lester Kirkendall, *Sexology* magazine editor and sex education writer Isadore Rubin, and the Reverend William Genné, and above all challenging SIECUS as promoting a "secular humanism" that was "pro-MAN and anti-GOD" and that would destroy the morals of American youth by separating instruction in human reproduction from education in "the higher ideals of marriage." These "sexécutives," as Drake heatedly called them, were not only anti-Christian but also anti-American; their purpose was not to reduce rates of venereal disease and teen pregnancy but merely "to glorify sex, and ensnare students into sexual promiscuity." Cutting, decontextualizing, and reassembling their words for his own purposes, Drake darkly concluded that the young were now easily "prostituted for the 'new morality' now that the Bible and religious moral concepts have been *banned* in the schools."[35]

Drake chose to excerpt allegations regarding sex education from *Blackboard Power* in the July 1968 issue of *Christian Crusade* magazine. The piece concluded by urging readers to "get organized!"[36] Realizing this topic had struck a chord, Drake's articles for *Christian Crusade* increasingly focused on the moral crisis in American culture. He warned parents that both educational and religious leaders were secretly hosting activities in which children and teens would touch each other's bodies in order to get over their repressions, encouraging "sexual play in bedding down with new-found friends." This "sneak attack on American morals" was occurring in schools, colleges, and churches across the country by means of "sensitivity training" as well as sex education. These techniques comprised a whole educational system that was "not some academic procedure; it is, rather, an insidious teaching method which aims to destroy the morality of America's children and of young and old adults alike and then to destroy America if given the chance."[37]

Drake expanded his earlier analysis of sex education from *Blackboard Power* into a separate pamphlet, *Is the School House the Proper Place to Teach Raw Sex?* This manifesto had an enormous impact in community battles over sex education that took place across the country. Drake insisted yet again that Mary Calderone "has a burning mission: To alert and convert the youth of America to a new sexuality. She pursues children and youth for her cause as ardently as the missionary of old pursued souls." Drake contended that Calderone's method was "telling young people about their right to enjoy premarital intercourse—if they so desire." Calderone's "revolutionary gospel" aimed to get rid of God and traditional morality in one fell swoop, teaching American youth "a new sex morality independent of church and state." Drake took especial umbrage at Calderone's promotion of talking "nonjudgmentally" with youth, insisting that "nonjudgmentally simply means that SIECUS does not want teachers to inject into their discussions with children the restraints of old-fashioned morality."[38]

Despite the fact that this pamphlet, no less than *Blackboard Power*, was laden with false accusations and his "evidence" was thick with words taken wholly out of context, Drake's book quickly became a vital weapon for fighting sex education by "plugging SIECUS directly into the hot current of right-wing paranoia." Drake painted a dire picture of mind control and insisted, "The public school is intruding into a private family and church responsibility as it frightens and coerces parents to accept the teaching of sex in their schools." Calderone and her cronies were purportedly teaching children as young as three years old everything there was possibly to know about sex, their pedagogy utilizing images of animals and humans having sexual intercourse. Besides written materials, SIE-CUS teaching aids also included "unbelievably clever models which even include multi-colored plastic human figures with interchangeable male and female sex organs—instant transvestism." This "erotic stimulation" had untold ill effects on the nation's most vulnerable population, Drake maintained. Drake accused Calderone of promoting an "animalistic viewpoint of sex which is shocking," the same charge that Kinsey's detractors had aimed at him twenty years earlier. Worst of all, Calderone and SIECUS were hell-bent on destroying the credibility and authority of home and family. Sex educators wished to eliminate "any inhibitions or moral and religious taboos," thereby driving "a wedge between the family, church and school" and bolstering educators' authority above traditional family values. "If this is accomplished," Drake continued, and the new morality accepted, "our children will become easy targets for Marxism and other amoral, nihilistic philosophies—as well as V.D.!" By wrecking the ties between parents and children, church and flock, the sex educators had found the greatest weapon imaginable for destroying America—clearly the liberals' dearest goal.[39]

Drake took pains to allege that the sex educators themselves were closely allied with some of the most debauched sexologists and sex perverts in the nation, from pornographers and prostitutes to predatory homosexuals who smacked their lips at the thought of enticing young children into their snares. Readers should not be fooled by sex ed advocates' professional degrees, medical credentials, or pretensions to the Christian ministry, he warned: sex educators and sexologists representing "every shade of muddy gray morality" were in league with "ministers colored atheistic pink," campy psychiatrists, and "ruthless publishers of pornography." All were part of "interlocking directorates" and national organizations that "provide havens for these degenerates." The goal of seducing children into devoting their lives to narcissistic pleasure seeking was inextricably linked to plans for Communist takeover of the nation: Communists would stoke children's erotic desires and then urge them to slough their parents' moral teachings in favor of erotic fulfillment.[40]

Liberal ministers, so trusted by naïve parents and children, were central to that plot, in Drake's telling. Indeed, several liberal clergy sat

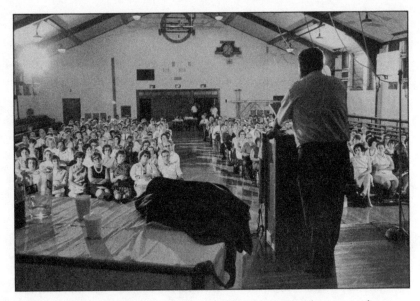

Gordon Drake speaking at a Christian Crusade meeting that opposed sex
education in the public schools, 1969. *MICHAEL MAUNEY/THE LIFE IMAGES
COLLECTION/GETTY IMAGES.*

on the SIECUS board, and Drake made sure to name them—not only
the Protestant William Genné but also the two Catholic priests, Fathers
John Thomas and George Hagmaier. Finally, noted Drake, "To complete
the religious cluster of SIECUS sexologists, the Jews have offered the
services of Rabbi Jeshaia Schnitzer of Montclair, New Jersey."[41] Drake's
listeners needed little reminder of the accusations of Communist influence that had long been leveled at the liberal clergy.

In early 1969, Drake joined forces with Noebel to present two-day
seminars on "Family, Schools and Morality" in Fort Lauderdale, Tampa,
Atlanta, Birmingham, Baltimore, Washington, DC, and Louisville.
Noebel's talks were titled, "Rhythmic-Hypnotic Music for Elementary
School Children," "Dangers of Rock 'n' Roll," and "Communist Sub-
version of American Folk Music." Drake complemented these with his
own: "Agents of Change—The Target Is You," "Sensitivity Training in
the Schools—The Hidden Threat," "The Octopus of Education Control," and, for the electrifying finale, "Raw Sex in the Classroom." The
seminars aimed to rouse parents into pressuring local schools to uphold

Christian morality and American patriotism by avoiding sex education in the classrooms.[42] So successful were these talks that by March each was touring outside the south: Noebel in Minnesota, Iowa, Nebraska, and Kansas, and Drake in Pennsylvania and New Jersey—his first stop on this anti-sex education tour being Princeton University in March 1969. The national press began paying closer attention to the sex education controversy.[43]

The Crusade's dire warnings about sex education, and Drake's books in particular, helped to foment a wave of controversies over sex ed in local communities beginning in the spring of 1968. One of the most notable occurred in Anaheim, California, a town whose public schools had incorporated a sex education program since 1965 but that was also home to a number of organizations that opposed sex ed.[44] By 1968, the school district had implemented a thorough family life and sex education program for grades seven through twelve, and it was in that year that questions about the program arose at a late August school board meeting. At a special session in October, opponents of the program presented a slide show and taped messages that took specific claims and even whole passages out of Drake's *Raw Sex* pamphlet, many of them denouncing SIECUS. The presenter sought to prove that Anaheim's program was the product of this organization run by "so-called experts with a long Ph.D. degree behind them that doesn't necessarily signify that they're qualified to drive a jeep across the street."[45]

The Anaheim battle was fierce and raged for months. Sex ed opponents were led by citizens who also fought gun control legislation and worried about interracial dating at desegregated schools, as they anguished over the morality of their children.[46] In April 1969 the California State Board of Education passed a resolution that banned the use of "SIECUS materials" in the schools. Since SIECUS did not actually produce curricula for schools—it provided information, data, consultations, and other resources for school systems and other organizations that wished to put their own sex education programs together—this technically did not much matter, but everyone understood its meaning.[47] That same year, the California legislature repealed an earlier state law in support of sex education, and the state's board of education adopted a report drafted by

Christian conservatives that warned, "A moral crisis is sweeping the land," and presented a program of moral lessons based in part on the Bible.[48]

The Christian Crusade was involved in the Anaheim controversy from the start. For the first two weeks of October 1968, Drake and Hargis worked in California to launch a statewide organization opposing sex education, California Families United. Both men were honored at a dinner at Knott's Berry Farm on October 18, which happened to be the very day after the special session with slide show had taken place. They met with the activists who would later put pressure on the California State Board of Education. Even when they were not physically present, they remained influential, since, throughout this period, local activists continued to lift talking points out of Drake's pamphlet in their activist efforts to get sex education out of their schools.[49]

Anaheim was far from the only such local fight. With something close to 50 percent of US public school districts embroiled in conflict over sex education, the influence of writers like Drake and Hargis was vast. They visited many other towns during this period and sought similar action to what had happened in Anaheim by encouraging the formation of new opposition groups and advising sex ed opponents on the best strategy for triumphing over the opposition. Drake joined a group of Tulsa parents in a lawsuit against the school board there, which had instituted a sex education program.[50]

Aware of his own growing influence, Drake published yet another tract on sex education with Christian Crusade in 1969, titled *SIECUS— Corrupter of Youth*. Although his name did not appear on the cover, a number of internal references make clear that Drake was the author. The book repeated many of the charges he'd already committed to print but embellished them still further and added a number of salacious details. Describing Calderone's recommendation of Kirkendall's book *Premarital Intercourse and Interpersonal Relationships*, for instance, Drake could not stop himself from relating to readers that the book included one case that "described how a prostitute used her mouth to cause an ejaculation of a young student."[51] Drake was prone to repeat highly exaggerated statistics and tall tales, as when he claimed that California public school children had been shown "a vagina the size of a blackboard," or that a teacher in

Flint, Michigan, had stripped in front of her students, or that a Phoenix twelve-year-old experimented sexually on his four-year-old sister after receiving sex education at school. In any case, with Calderone and SIECUS refusing to "dignify" Drake by responding to his outlandish charges in a public debate, Drake had little incentive to refrain from such exaggerations.[52]

The Christian Crusade campaign against SIECUS and Calderone inspired some flamboyant hate mail. Once its campaign against her was in full force and for years after its peak, Calderone received numerous letters like the following:

> Dear Mrs. Calderone: There has got to be a special place in hell for a reptile of a woman like—indeed, scrofulous, vile, wicked example of degenerate human being that you are. . . . Yes You Madam du Farge are at least partially responsible for the moral degradation of much of America's youth . . . with your nihilistic, ungodly, theories, which have destroyed countless youths in our country. . . . They should not callit [sic] Venereal Herpes, but Calderone Herpes in honor of its degrading and reptilian author. You will indeed be JUDGED![53]

Outraged postal correspondence had been a routine fact of life for sex reformers for years, of course; the vicious invective directed at Calderone, however, was sharply escalated from the letters directed at earlier figures like Sanger and Kinsey.

Another letter addressed itself to "MARY STEINKEN CALDERONE, MISTRESS OF THE DEVIL; MISFIT PROSTITUTE OF HELL"—the titles jabbing derisively at Calderone's MD and MPH academic degrees. The writer assured Calderone that Hades would be a place "WHERE YOU WILL HAVE MOLTEN STEEL POURED INTO YOU FROM TWO DIRECTIONS . . . & WHERE YOUR DIET WILL BE PUSS, EXCRETIONS, ROACHES, MAGGOTS & SPIDERS." Others wrote in less pictographic style but with equivalent loathing. "You people are the kind who would not be mourned in the least should you be found with millstones around your necks and at the bottom of the sea," blustered another writer. Letters this malevolent, penned by men and women alike, routinely ended up in the "Crank" files.[54] Calderone had become a perpetual target not only of the Christian Crusade organization but of its enthusiastic audiences around the country.

As opposition to sex education spread, many groups besides Christian Crusade took up the issue. Organizations ranging from the John Birch Society—which founded the Movement to Restore Decency (MOTOREDE) committee—to the Ku Klux Klan acted alongside the numerous local and national groups formed specifically to fight sex education. Gary Allen, billed as "one of the nation's top authorities on civil turmoil and the New Left," published "Sex Study: Problems, Propaganda, and Pornography" in a 1969 issue of *American Opinion*, the magazine of the John Birch Society. Allen repeated many of Drake's claims about the dire links between sex education and Communism and added more of his own, lambasting "comrades" Kirkendall, Calderone, Rubin, and Genné for being anti-patriotic haters of America. Excoriating the religious credentials of Genné in particular, Allen wrote, "In addition to his consultation in pornography at *Sexology*, the files of the House Committee on Un-American Activities record that Genné has affiliated himself with such Communist Fronts as the Stockholm Peace Petition, the World Peace Appeal, the National Committee to Repeal the McCarran Act, the Committee for Peaceful Alternatives to the Atlantic Pact, *etc*." Anyone affiliated with SIECUS was, in short, pro-Communist. In Allen's telling, SIECUS educators urged parents "to simply surrender your children to the indoctrination and 'skills' provided in the schools by Comrade Rubin and the Leftist pornographers of SIECUS."[55]

After treating John Birchers to more examples of the preposterous attempts by SIECUS to control their children, Allen hammered home his point: "Everywhere one turns with these people the reins lead back to the Far Left. Why? Clearly because it is in the interest of the Communists to promote programs like SIECUS for destroying American sexual morality, and enervating the moral fiber of our nation's youth." Communists, he reminded a readership for whom this was already gospel, had always known the strategic value of preaching permissiveness, corrupting youth, and ensuring that young people were more devoted to sex than to religion. "Historically, the destruction of morality has often been used as a technique to ready a country for Communist revolution," and readers must arm themselves with this knowledge of "What's Really Happening" with SIECUS in American life today.[56]

The links between Communism and sex education imagined by right-wing commentators received even more graphic treatment in a pamphlet distributed by the Greenwood, Indiana, chapter of the Ku Klux Klan, *It's Time to Save Our Schools.* It blamed Communists and Marxist-inspired liberals for "forced integration, illegal bussing, narcotics, homicides, assaults, violence, suicides, rapes, burglaries, drunkenness, sex education, and interracial dating." "Under the misrule of these totalitarian Leftists," the schools had become "jungles, graduating children who have never properly learned to read, write, add or subtract, or even conduct themselves in an orderly manner—but will be thoroughly schooled in sex." Teachers were frauds and charlatans, "mind benders" who imposed secret psychological tests on students that "parents cannot be allowed to see." Besides the evils of integration and the rise of interracial dating—too obvious to require lengthy commentary—the pamphlet devoted most of its space to the perversions that sex education was imposing on American children. The document warned parents that teachers were being hired who themselves oozed sexual prowess, and many advocated demonstrating sexual intercourse in class. "Sound fantastic? Remember that *today's liberal sex fantasies are tomorrow's liberal dictated school rules.*" Children and teens were learning obscene words, seeing pornography, caressing and fondling each other as part of the educational process—and in racially mixed classrooms, no less. Parents who objected would be subjected to "'mental health' concentration camps." All of this was at the behest of SIECUS, whose leaders "*have known Communist affiliations.*"[57]

By 1970, when Hargis published his own salvo in this war, *Sex Revolution in the United States,* the battle against SIECUS and Calderone had become the centerpiece of Hargis's Christian Crusade. As Hargis wrote (emphasis in original):

I do *not* feel that the greatest victory that Christian Crusade has achieved in fighting the SIECUS variety of sex education in the

> public schools has been to *expose* SIECUS, Dr. Mary Calderone
> and Dr. Lester Kirkendall; but, *instead, it has been the fact that it has*
> *united parents across the country in a protest movement against the ab-*
> *dication of parental responsibility and the authority of the home, and*
> *has alerted them to the necessity of strengthening their family ties and*
> *improving the home, with an emphasis on teaching and moral indoctri-*
> *nation, according to the family philosophy or religious concepts.*

Hargis could "point with pride" to the fact that "hundreds of thousands
of American parents" had been inspired to fight against the evils of sex
education. The victory was that increasing numbers of parents were finally "acting like Christian parents should," while more and more young
people were learning to behave. Hargis thanked God for "the Mary Cal-
derones and Lester Kirkendalls" who, through their "intemperate statements and candid remarks" about lessening the authority of parents and
of biblical authority, had helped to "illustrate how far America has gone
toward moral anarchy."[58] Sex would remain at the core of the Christian
Crusade's focus thereafter, and the backlash galvanized by Billy James
Hargis and his partners would reverberate for years to come, as similar
groups fused religion and conservative politics that were centered on a
range of issues relating to sex and gender norms.

NOTWITHSTANDING THEIR CONSPIRATORIAL CLAIMS, SIECUS's critics
were right to note that the group helped to forge a remarkable alliance
between the forces of science and liberal religion. Calderone's model for
sex education was a medical one, but she was eager to seek allies among
any religious groups willing to acknowledge the expertise of physicians
who took their cue from scientific findings. Calderone had a number of
liberal Protestant collaborators who were dedicated in their labors with
SIECUS. The group's second president was David R. Mace, a former minister, Methodist-turned-Quaker, and sociologist who pioneered marriage
counseling in Britain and the United States. Reverend Genné of the National Council of Churches served as secretary of SIECUS; William Graham Cole, a former minister and college chaplain who was then president

of the Presbyterian-affiliated Lake Forest College, served on the board of directors. By the fall of 1965, Rabbi Bernard Kligfeld of Temple Emanu-El in Long Beach, New York, had also joined the board. These clerical leaders provided important religious legitimacy for a board that consisted largely of physicians, psychiatrists, educators, counseling experts, and scholarly experts in family relations. If those entrusted with the spiritual guidance of their flocks ever worried that their authority was being supplanted by medical professionals in the realm of sex education, they did so quietly. All seemed delighted and grateful to cultivate these cross-professional collaborations on a matter of such singular social importance.[59]

The efforts of Calderone and SIECUS to forge alliances with religious leaders bore fruit in an "Interfaith Statement on Sex Education" that was publicly released on June 8, 1968. The document carried the official imprimatur of three significant US religious bodies: the National Council of Churches, the Synagogue Council of America, and—notably—the United States Catholic Conference. However bold its aims, the document struck a conservative tone, insisting on the godly nature of human sexuality and the need for spiritual and moral instruction deriving from "our Judeo-Christian heritage." Sex education was primarily a task for parents, the statement assured, but "supplementary assistance from church or synagogue" and also from schools was sometimes necessary and desirable. A lengthy set of strict guidelines laid out precisely how school educators should teach this subject: sex education "must respect the cultural, familial and religious backgrounds and beliefs" of all students, "with understanding, tolerance and acceptance of difference"; yet the document assumed an ethical framework of "moral values and beliefs about what is right and wrong that are held in common by the major religions on the one hand and generally accepted legal, social, psychological, medical and other values held in common by service professions and society generally." Calderone had succeeded in bringing Protestant, Catholic, and Jewish leaders together in a show of unity on a matter of sexual morality. The attacks of Hargis and his allies were just one of many factors ensuring that this public unity would be short-lived, but the interfaith document showed that a unified path forward seemed briefly like a real option.[60]

The attacks from right-wing religious activists weighed heavily on Calderone, who was adamant in rejecting the notion that SIECUS was imposing sex education on a nation that did not want it. "My personal belief is that a society gets what it wants. If society doesn't want sex education for children, then no one should impose it on society," she told a *Playboy* interviewer in 1970. "That's why we've never adopted an aggressive program of disseminating sex education in the schools. . . . SIECUS has simply responded and will continue to respond to requests for information." To her conservative religious and political critics who saw her as destroying the morals of America's youth, she turned the tables to place the blame on *them*, noting that "if the attitudes of adults about sex and sexuality were other than they are, the kids wouldn't be in so much trouble" or have "the hang-ups, the difficulties, the ignorance" caused by a confusing "excess of eroticism on the one hand and an excess of repression on the other." Those whom she called "reactionaries" were themselves damaged, frustrated people—"frigid wives and husbands grimly suppressing their sexual urges because they've been taught that they're sinful," then, in turn, repressing others. Those who sought to quash sexual curiosity and knowledge were themselves responsible for both the bewilderment and the ensuing waywardness of America's youth. Sex education, in contrast, would facilitate social stability and the responsible growth of young people into well-adjusted parents and citizens.[61]

Even as the right-wing attacks on sex ed and SIECUS were increasing in pitch, Calderone was growing less wedded to the sexual conservatism she had exemplified just a few years earlier. She concurred with the fourfold set of ethical values put forward in a 1970s SIECUS volume as "the core values in a democratic society" that offered a broad framework for sexual decision making: "respect for truth as a definable moral value and faith in the free play of critical intelligence; respect for the basic worth, equality, and dignity of each individual; recognition of the need of cooperative effort for the common good; and recognition of the right of self-determination of each individual." Together, these values called on each person to be accountable for his or her own sexual behavior and its effects on others while also enthusiastically affirming individual freedom of choice. There were limits to what individuals should do sexually—nothing was permitted that was exploitative, violating, or cruel—but so long as a person's actions did not violate the webs of "social obligation and welfare," they were likely acceptable. These values, she and her fellow SIECUS staff members believed, "coincide with some of the major values in the Judeo-Christian tradition: that every person is to be respected regardless of color or race; that life is better than death, love is better than hate, growth is better than deterioration; and that freedom for individual persons is a goal to strive for." Ultimately, in a nation that had grown "pluralistic" in its sexual values, the sex educator's role was to "create a genuine open forum" rather than preaching his or her own specific opinions or imposing a false consensus on alternative views.[62]

She also apparently grew more comfortable with the notion of sex as a spiritual act than she had been in the early 1960s. Despite being a physician and a scientist, in a 1973 lecture to a Quaker audience, Calderone affirmed, "The mystery of sex continues to be greater than our capacity to comprehend it." Those who claimed to have "the only pipeline to sacred truth" on such matters possessed, to Calderone's mind, a hubris no Friend could abide. At the height of her work with SIECUS, then, Calderone embraced a sort of bridge across the older liberal divide: between, on the one hand, those who sought to demystify sex and treat it as one more physiological process that should be altogether removed from the realm of the emotions and, on the other, those who sought to elevate the mystical and emotional and sheer pleasurable dimensions of sex as a way of celebrating its unique role in human life. In her 1974 introduction to the SIECUS publication *Sexuality and Human Values*, Calderone made clear she stood for both: "Right here is where I find it easiest to shift my focus from the understanding of eroticism as a scientist to the celebration of it as a religious person. Perhaps this is because of my Quaker persuasion. In any case, I find that I simply cannot convince myself that the erotic aspect of human life is not as truly integral to 'that of God in every person' as is, for instance, the intellectual, the cognitive."[63] How could something so natural and also so good, so sacred, and so joyous be a force for evil and division in the world?

Like progressive sex reformers before her, Calderone knew that myriad traditionalist Christians roundly despised what she stood for—broad access to family planning information and treatment; still more, open and knowledgeable discussion of sexuality throughout American society—but she also knew that they were not all unhinged "cranks." Unlike Sanger or Kinsey, this revolutionary made direct overtures not only to those she expected to be allies but also to many of her professional opponents every chance she could, believing that her powers of persuasion, the evidence of science, and her good-faith acknowledgment of other people's religious views could melt fear and open enemies' eyes to acceptance of sexual realism and the need for better sex education. She committed her efforts with especial fervor to American Catholic leaders, believing them to be key to her efforts' success. She assured a host of priestly leaders of their mutual goal in bolstering, as she typically phrased it, "the stability of the family under the stresses of modern life."[64]

Calderone had long before given up on the John Birchers and fundamentalists, but she thought she had a better chance working with Catholics—a confidence she retained for much of the duration of her career. Even during her years as the medical director of Planned Parenthood, Calderone had done her utmost to reach out to Catholics. By all visible measures, she did so in a spirit of deep interest and generosity, believing that if she exposed her own humanity to Catholic women and men, they would do likewise. To Catholic correspondents, she would write things such as, "I deeply respect the belief of the Catholic church and understand the principles on which it is based. I would never do anything to try and influence a Catholic in any way."[65] Words of outreach and an earnest effort to understand and empathize with Catholics characterized her correspondence, even as she sought to inform Catholics that she had the right to advocate contraception for those who wanted it. She emphasized the common ground that existed between the Catholic position and her own, writing to one Catholic journalist, "Actually you know the Catholic and the non-Catholic position is not so far apart. Our basic desire is the same: stable, happy monogamous families. The understanding shown by the Vatican in several statements of the need of parents in some instances and conditions of stress to space their children simply echoes our own feelings of concern for mothers and fathers all over the world."[66]

The effort to reach out to Catholics went deep for Calderone, and she spent enormous amounts of time writing to Catholic leaders, defending herself as a "highly moral" person who deserved a hearing from Catholics. "I have written to you at such length," she pleaded in this same letter, "hoping that these sober thoughts could be passed on by you to other thoughtful Catholics."[67] She knew that not all Catholics were the "thoughtful" kind, as she thought of them, yet Calderone remained charitable toward Catholics and hopeful about reaching them. Her 1960 book, *Release from Sexual Tensions*, adopted the same high-minded tone and plainly sought to draw Catholic readers no less than others. Indeed, on the very first page of the first chapter—and again on the book's final, concluding page—Calderone nostalgically recalled a "kind old priest" she met in France as a child and who gave her a "wonderfully true" lesson about cherishing each age of one's life. The book gave frank counsel to couples about the ordinary difficulties, sexual and otherwise, to be faced in marriage, and its list of suggested reading included *The Catholic Marriage Manual*, by George A. Kelly. Calderone also commended the church's Pre-Cana and Cana conferences (for engaged and married couples) as well as the rhythm method (though urging this to be "practiced with extreme care under the guidance of a knowledgeable physician" and extolling safer contraceptive methods for those whose religion allowed them). Sounding like the liberal Quaker she was, she wrote hopefully that those who followed their religion could see that compassion was more important than creed, and that the "main purpose of religion" was "to express God's love, not your hate."[68]

Whatever optimism she conveyed in her public speech and writings, Calderone was both intelligent and experienced enough to know that Roman Catholic leaders had no plans to shift their thinking on birth control or on sexual education, and she strove to connect with them in order to melt what she considered their recalcitrance. Her address to the conference at Green Lake had exempted "thoughtful Catholic leaders" from her condemnation of Catholic intransigence, even as she piled up real-life examples of Catholic transgressions: the Protestant woman with cervical cancer landing at a Catholic hospital, "only to receive a tongue-lashing from the sisters for the source of her referral"; the employee of a Planned Parenthood clinic who was "denounced by her income tax auditor, for the source of her income"; the army wife denied contraception at the local army hospital "because the chief obstetrician was a Catholic"; nursing textbooks declaring Planned Parenthood "a vice"; and "the new young Protestant doctors, trying to get established in a community, who are denied staff privileges in a Catholic hospital unless they sign a statement saying that neither they *nor their wives* will have anything to do with the Planned Parenthood Center" (emphasis in original). Indignantly, she emphasized, "surely these actions are unworthy of a great Christian faith."[69] Calderone's dislike of Catholic activism was plenty apparent, her avowed "respect" notwithstanding, and she repeatedly implied that Catholic lay people were victims of the church hierarchy.

Still, with her persistent outreach to Catholic leaders, Calderone was able to develop a reputation for a spirit of heartfelt openness and generosity to Catholics that was matched by few of her peers. When, in January 1964, the celebrated science and health reporter Earl Ubell wrote a detailed article about SIECUS's recent founding for the *New York Herald Tribune*, he signaled the significance of the inclusion of "Catholics on Board" in his first section heading. "Even more significant" than Calderone's recruitment of distinguished sex researchers and educators to the board, Ubell wrote, was "the inclusion on the board of directors of two men, who while participating as individuals, are of the Roman Catholic faith." These two were the Jesuit John L. Thomas, a sociologist at the Catholic institution St. Louis University, and the Paulist George Hagmaier, associate director of the Paulist Institute for Religious Research in New York. Ubell also wryly noted the "inadvertent ironic twist" provided by the fact that Calderone spent the previous decade at Planned Parenthood working on contraceptive education, "an idea anathema to Catholics."[70]

In underscoring the importance of SIECUS's goal—"to establish man's sexuality as a health entity," he noted that "Father Thomas said it best" and quoted Thomas's recent public comments that his interest in SIECUS stemmed from his conviction that "a serious reappraisal of contemporary sexual patterns is long overdue." Indeed, the Jesuit scholar agreed with Calderone in noting, "We have discarded past conceptions of sex without bothering to replace them, so that current attitudes and practices have developed haphazardly, with little concern for the profound significance of human sexuality considered in terms either of personal fulfillment and happiness [or] the requirements of a technically advanced society."[71] As Ubell noted, SIECUS's original board also included Dr. John Rock, the Roman Catholic doctor who helped develop the birth control pill, with the hope (not realized) that it was "natural" enough to become an accepted means of birth control to the Catholic hierarchy.

As we saw earlier, Calderone was inspired to leave Planned Parenthood and found SIECUS largely through her contacts with liberal religious leaders, mostly Protestants, but as Ubell rightly highlighted, she made sure to include respected Catholic authorities there as well. Calderone cherished the Catholic presence on the SIECUS board, and those she recruited certainly sounded progressive in their writing. Collegial relationships with Thomas and Hagmaier, in particular, were important to her, both personally and professionally. Both men served for several years on the SIECUS board despite the controversy their participation sometimes generated. She later told an interviewer that Father Thomas was "a beautiful man," giving the example of "a very beautiful little piece" he wrote for SIECUS in 1965 about sexuality as "a major aspect of personality" rather than a series of "isolated acts," which "really was new thinking."[72]

Thomas, who held a PhD in sociology from the University of Chicago and whose own work focused on marriage and the family, could and did speak expansively about sex. Ordained to the priesthood in Florissant, Missouri, in 1939, he had a career that flourished in a postwar context where issues pertaining to sexual morality, the family, and general "values" were at the center of American Jesuit intellectual life; indeed, his prolific writings helped to put them there. Along with many scholarly articles, he wrote numerous books and essays for Catholic readers as well as the broader public, including an accessible and widely read sociological study, *The American Catholic Family*, and *Marriage and Rhythm*, described by one historian as an "admirably pastoral" (i.e., empathic) book on the rhythm method for Catholic couples. He was known, in fact, for what a Jesuit historian would later call "the persistence he brought to the task of reconciling the defense of traditional values with a social scientist's recognition of the economic and demographic transformations undermining the bastion of these values." While Thomas's chief goal appears to have been the reinforcement of traditional Catholic family norms (including gender roles) amid a rapidly changing society, his conservatism did not aim toward hopes of gaining political power or making Catholic morals "the law of the land" but rather toward the preservation of Catholic morale and identity in a potentially hostile world. Like his famous Jesuit contemporary John Courtney Murray, Thomas's concern was, in one researcher's words, "the fate of Catholicism in a pluralist setting."[73]

In the 1965 essay cited by Calderone, Thomas wrote about human sexuality as a "connected whole" to which people should react with "healthy openness." More surprisingly, at least in the context of other Catholic writings about sex, was Thomas's affirmation that sex roles were "culturally defined" and "radically conditioned by . . . the social environment within which the individual develops." From childhood, "boys and girls in a given society" were "trained" to behave in certain "culturally defined" ways that would "later determine their relative social positions, accepted areas of action and permitted aspirational goals as members of an adult community." Thomas's social scientific training was evident in these words, which could easily have been penned by Ruth Benedict.[74]

But Thomas was neither a cultural relativist nor a social constructionist on gender. To the Catholic readership of *Commonweal* magazine, he wrote critically of "our day of Margaret Sanger and India Edwards" (Edwards was a prominent Democratic official who strongly advocated for women's greater involvement in US politics). American society's view of appropriate gender roles was rapidly changing, and, "with each change, women further invade the traditional male bailiwick," with no common framework for evaluating "these female incursions." Woman's domestic duties—"her core-function in the home"—had been devalued by "our permissive society," and the divinely ordained dual role of wife and mother needed to regain the prestige it deserved. In a 1968 interview conducted after he had left St. Louis for the Cambridge (Massachusetts)

Center for Social Studies, Thomas noted that in defining human sexuality his "basic starting point, of course," was "full acceptance" of God's gendered order in creating male and female, "and it is ultimately on the basis of, or in terms of, this complementary relationship that we determine the meaning of human sexuality." As a Catholic scholar later summarized, for Thomas, "changes in expectations and family practices could be accommodated insofar as they did not usurp habits of gender stratification."[75]

Calderone agreed with much of this rather traditional way of viewing sexuality, though she did not promote (or live) any notion of female submission to her husband's headship—a notion Thomas took for granted. But the differences between their points of view were acute. As a Jesuit deeply committed to what he termed the "time-and-space-ignoring solidarity" of Catholicism, Thomas believed in the interdependence of Catholic precepts and in Catholic ideology as "an organic body of religious truth" based on "a universal, unchanging, and timeless consensus in basic doctrines among all the faithful of every age and condition." Holding this view, Thomas strongly upheld the Catholic Church's opposition to birth control, blaming the "social acceptance and widespread use" of birth control for American women's confusion about their domestic roles and the devaluation of motherhood. Elsewhere Thomas laid out the church's view even more broadly, writing that the Christian worldview that maintained humanity's "essential qualitative difference from other higher forms of animal life," necessitated the rejection of birth control.[76]

Indeed, Thomas's point could be extended well beyond birth control to matters pertaining to sexuality more generally, as he wrote that disagreements about the "licitness" of particular acts "must logically be based on differences concerning basic moral principles, and since these are based on our concept of the nature, origin, and destiny of man, any worthwhile discussion of disagreements must ultimately center on this point." When, much later in 1982, he reflected on the many radical changes in belief and behavior he saw around him, including among Catholics—greater openness to premarital and extramarital sex, high rates of abortion, broad acceptance of contraception—he despaired. "Most Americans evidently have learned to accept the normalcy of the morally pathological." This was not merely a problem about sex or even the snuffing out of fetal life; far worse, it held catastrophic implications pertaining to obedience. That is, "the widespread tacit acceptance of sexual freedom as a right," concomitant with the elevation of the autonomous self above and against the broader social order, was "the most erosive challenge currently confronting the Church in the Western world." This impulse, which "appears as a significant element in the various youth, minority, and women's movements of recent years" was gravely undermining "the Church's entire traditional teaching regarding impulse control, responsibility, and fidelity to binding commitments." By this time in the early 1980s, he and Calderone had long ceased their working relationship through SIECUS, a tie that simply could not be sustained across the vast gulf of their differing viewpoints.[77]

Calderone's other close Catholic associate, George Hagmaier, held views that appear to have been somewhat closer to her own. Ordained to the priesthood by the Paulist order in 1951, just shy of his twenty-eighth birthday, Hagmaier later grew interested in studies of religion and psychiatry and earned a doctorate in education from Columbia University before working for the Paulist Institute for Religious Research and, starting in the mid-1960s, teaching at the Catholic University of America. In his highly regarded 1959 book, *Counselling the Catholic* (cowritten with the Jesuit Robert W. Gleason), Hagmaier highlighted the crucial role that sex education played in one's subsequent life. "A very important aspect of self-acceptance involves the kind of sex education, or lack of it, which the growing child is given," he wrote. Sex education not only was about biological reproduction but "includes the concepts a child has of masculinity or femininity, his growing capacity to give and to receive affection, and the kind of relationship he has to his own father and mother." Families were critical to the development of these concepts, as "Pope Pius XII made it very plain that it is a grave duty of parents to instruct their children by revealing gradually, simply, and truthfully each fact and detail which the child has the capacity to assimilate."[78] With these points, nearly any Catholic could agree. What was more remarkable, and closer to Calderone's own views, was Hagmaier's close attention to the communication of "healthy attitudes toward sex," not mere information, and his insistence that parents were often all too "Victorian, Puritan, or Jansenist" in their inhibited prudishness when tenderly broaching the subject. "Children of such parents come to regard sex with uneasiness and misgivings, and are soon afraid to ask further about it."[79]

Hagmaier expressed pride in his work with SIECUS, which he performed while working extensively in various areas of religious education: conducting mental health workshops for community organizations, interfaith clergy groups, and religious communities, for example, and revising seminary curricula in pastoral counseling. He was fully supportive of the idea that schools should develop sex education programs, a position that not all priests shared. In a report to his superior, Hagmaier wrote of his recent election to the position of executive secretary at SIECUS, noting that as one of only five executive officers who oversaw the organization's policies and operations, "I feel I have significant influence in the formulation of important goals. I have tried to take into account the many ways in which an essentially secular concern is given Christian and religious dimensions. I feel this is another of those unique opportunities that have found Paulists involved in the beginnings of important movements." He could be a positive Christian influence on SIECUS, Hagmaier maintained. "In a way the [Paulist] Community has lent me to Siecus recently for a good part of my working hours, and I feel it has been a most happy collaboration."[80] Not all Catholics agreed. One Paulist historian later noted that his association with Calderone, "the controversial sexologist," and his involvement with SIECUS "upset many conservative American Catholics." But in the wake of the Second Vatican Council and the Catholic Church's apparent "new openness to the world" in the mid-1960s, both Hagmaier and Calderone believed this to be important, necessary work.[81]

With that same heady, ecumenical spirit filling the air, Catholics began reaching out to Calderone, just as she had for some time been reaching out to them; indeed, her intentional collaboration with Catholic leaders at last promised some useful dividends. In May 1966, through Hagmaier, she was able to attend an important colloquium on women's sexuality at Louvain University in Belgium that was called by Leo Joseph Cardinal Suenens, a major leader in the Second Vatican Council who strongly advocated the spirit of renewal and open-mindedness to change that was summed up as *aggiornamento*. According to the colloquium report Calderone later wrote (apparently to other SIECUS administrators), some sixty participants attended the event, hailing from France, Italy, West Germany, Austria, Holland, Great Britain, Ireland, and the United States, as well as Belgium. The group assembled was a mix of physicians, nurses, lawyers, clergy (chiefly pastoral counselors), and academics of various sorts. Despite the fact that the meeting focused on women's sexuality, Calderone was the lone woman in the US delegation. Fortunately, a Belgian female professional at the event soon made, in Calderone's words, "a spirited suggestion that if we were to discuss the sexuality of women, we should begin to think in terms that had reality to the women themselves, rather than in concept and terms derived by men only." Calderone leapt at that remark in agreement and furthered the discussion. Hoping for a broader discussion of sexuality from her interlocutors, she shifted her own remarks to marriage stability—a topic of common concern for both her and the Catholic leaders heading the event.[82]

The rest of the US delegation to the Louvain University Colloquium on the Sexuality of Woman consisted of Hagmaier, who was then teaching marriage and the family at Catholic University; Louis Dupré of Georgetown University; Elmer Gelinas of St. Mary's College in California; Thomas Hayes, a biophysicist at Berkeley; John Noonan of Notre Dame, whose book on contraception and natural law had been published the previous year; Bernard Pisani, an obstetrician at St. Vincent's Hospital in New York; and Reuben Hill, a well-known sociologist at the University of Minnesota who worked in the areas of marriage and family life and who also served as a program officer in population studies at the Ford Foundation. (As Calderone noted in her postconference report, Hill was also a Mormon and to her knowledge the only other non-Catholic present at the gathering.) At this same event, Calderone was approached by Canon Charles Moeller, undersecretary to the Congregation for the Doctrine of the Faith (the Roman Catholic office responsible for transmitting and defending church doctrine), who spoke with her at length and asked her to send books published in the United States that "would seem to have the most relevance to all of the complicated matters under discussion, particularly as they relate to sex and marriage." When she remarked that some of this material might prove challenging to the church, he replied, "'Yes, but it is essential that our theology be based on the most accurate scientific knowledge.'"[83] Calderone was deeply impressed that these Catholic leaders wanted to grapple with real science, unbound by the pabulum and wishful thinking that she worried were the tools of local Catholic leaders.

As we saw earlier, Calderone's work with SIECUS played a significant role in gaining the imprimatur of the US Catholic Conference in the June 1968 "Interfaith Statement on Sex Education," published jointly with the National Council of Churches and the Synagogue Council of America. A month after the document's release, however, her hopes for further cooperation with Catholics were dashed. Pope Paul VI issued the papal encyclical *Humanae Vitae*, which condemned all forms of contraception in no uncertain terms and linked birth control to abortion and to sexuality issues much more broadly.[84] As the encyclical stated, these were not new teachings but strong reiterations of points that had been made for some decades in other official (and unofficial) documents. The response of Catholics in the United States was largely tepid, as angry disbelief cooled to indifference. A month after *Humanae Vitae* was publicly released, a Gallup survey found that only 28 percent of American Catholics who had heard of the encyclical agreed with it; even among the more devout Catholics, fewer than half supported it. As historians have shown, Catholics continued to use contraceptives, their defiance marking a "trend toward nonconformity with Church teaching" that "continued unabated."[85] But more public work, like collaboration with an increasingly controversial organization, had to cease—it was now too fraught for Catholic leaders to participate actively in SIECUS.

Of her many accomplishments, Calderone was particularly proud of her outreach to Catholics. She singled out a speech she gave about "how Planned Parenthood can cooperate with Roman Catholics" as one that "gave me great satisfaction." As she recalled, her point there had been to work *with* rather than against Catholics, honoring the rhythm method and teaching Catholic women to use it as scientifically as possible: "Don't try to subvert her faith to other methods. Instead, make the rhythm method a part of the services offered by Planned Parenthood."[86] Her openness paid off, for "as a result of that speech" to Planned Parenthood about Catholics, the theology department at the University of Notre Dame invited her to deliver a lecture in its annual Marriage Institute— the purpose of which was "to illucidate the meaning of love and sexualogy [sic] in marriage." That Calderone was the author of "the most comprehensive medical textbook" on contraception was duly noted in the advertising of her lecture, one of four that would together earn attendees a certificate "fulfilling the Church's required pre-Nuptial instruction." According to the postlecture write-up in the student newspaper, her talk on "Sex and Sexuality" stressed societal conditioning and the current need to "re-evaluate assigned sexual roles" and was delivered to "an overflow crowd." Notre Dame theologians had selected Calderone to fill a requirement of the Catholic Church for marriage preparation![87] And yet Catholics were forbidden from partaking of her broader program for individuals to exert control over their sexual reproduction. Calderone had made inroads of politeness, but the breach between worldviews was wider than ever.

As CALDERONE CONTINUED TO ENDURE attacks on her and on SIECUS by the John Birch Society and fundamentalists like Drake and Hargis, she grew wearier and angrier but no less determined to fight for access to sex education that would be accessible to all people. Once in a while, she responded in a tone that matched that of her opponents, as when she snapped at a reporter that the right-wing groups and "ignorant parents" who opposed SIECUS were "sexual illiterates."[88] More often, she struck a disconsolate note when discussing fundamentalist religion.

In a presentation at the International Congress of Sexology in Montréal, Québec, she reminded her listeners that the chief enemies of sex education had long been church leaders, who remained powerful obstacles in this field. "Historically, the prime contender for control of the sexuality of a person by an outside agency is, and continues to be, religion." A deep suspicion of pleasure and privacy was at the root of religion's repressive force, in her view: an "almost paranoid fear that exists, not only of sexual pleasure itself but also of the recognition of one's body as a valid source of that pleasure." Rather than noting, as she often had before, the many liberal Protestant and Catholic leaders who were working for change in this regard, she cited several studies to demonstrate that lay people were simply circumventing their leaders on matters ranging from masturbation and birth control to a wide array of sexual practices outside of marriage. Calling for "a coalition of strengths" to bring professionals together in service to a "universal approach to realistic sexual knowledge for *all* ages and socioeconomic groups" (emphasis in original), Calderone noted that religion "can be especially helpful in such a coalition," but only if religious leaders were willing to agree with this statement: "That sexuality itself is morally neutral, but that how we learn or are taught to use it throughout life has heavy moral implications." "Such moral implications," she insisted, "should—and indeed must—transcend differences in religious dogma." Working together in this way would turn what were internal sexual battlegrounds into "private peacegrounds."[89]

As Calderone knew, however, her words were hardly religiously neutral. The fight over sex education had contributed enormously to the hardening of opposing views toward sex: the very idea that "sexuality itself is morally neutral" was the core notion that so angered her critics. Liberal religious allies could align with Calderone, yes, but their opponents were also coalescing to gird their loins for battle on the other side.

Weary though she was, Calderone was determined to continue her work. Every chance she could, she pointed out to audiences and readers that the Christian Crusade and the John Birch Society were willing to "use totally unchristian methods," such as outright lying, to achieve "a political end: control of public education."[90] In a journal aimed at Protestant pastors, she wrote that she was "one of the few persons singled out for the most ruthless attempts at character assassination. I do not know those who hate me, but I know their words. I do not hate them, but have only compassion for them because they know hate. They refuse to know my words, yet they hate me and have no charity for me. How can this be?"[91] At this point in her life—Calderone was sixty-six—she was more than ready to call it sexism. "The personal attacks focused on me, a woman, have almost all been made by men," she wrote. She knew she did not embody the Christian Crusade's idea of appropriate Christian womanhood—the malicious crank letters that flooded her mailbox made that point with venom—and hence they wished to deny her the "personhood" that women in the United States, with the help of liberal religion, had at long last attained.[92] Despite persistent opposition, however, the work of SIECUS and Calderone, in particular, moved sex education from the margins to the center of the American educational system, with nearly all public school systems offering some form of sex education to students.[93]

Billy James Hargis's own crusade against sex ed and other forms of sexual immorality crashed to a halt when *Time* magazine published its 1976 account of his sexual improprieties with both male and female students at his American Christian College in Tulsa. Although a friendly local reporter subsequently published a sympathetic piece that gave Hargis's side of the story, the damage was done, and Hargis became an untouchable in the conservative Christian community. Writing the autobiographical *My Great Mistake* nine years later, he blamed turncoat employees of Christian Crusade—Noebel, above all—for falsely betraying him (he called the *Time* story "pure trash"). Though he admitted he had grown extremely arrogant in his ministry, and repeatedly described himself in vague terms as the chief of sinners, Hargis insisted that the sexual charges were untrue, admitting only to having allowed an excessive "familiarity" to grow between himself and the young people at the college and fiercely denying the taint of homosexuality. The sex scandal, in Hargis's account, had been invented so that his traitorous associates could take over his hard-earned ministry. His bitterness toward all his onetime Christian friends who deserted him in the wake of the scandal remained raw. "I have found that some Christians are the most unforgiving people in the world," he wrote. "They want to believe the worst of anybody. . . . They love to gossip. They will believe gossip before they will believe anything good about a man." In a mantra he repeated on television interviews and again in print, Hargis lamented, "Christians are the only army in the world that kill their wounded . . . and leave their leaders on the field to die."[94]

The struggle over sex education was a war, all right: a battle over the moral frameworks in which sexual knowledge would be embedded and over who had the right to determine just what those frameworks would be. The religious progressives in this story were beginning to think of morality much more in terms of relationship than purity, and many were starting to imagine that sex in situations outside of heterosexual marriage might be acceptable even within a Christian context. The conservative Christians who opposed them were not contesting the need for factual knowledge of sexuality—a denial of sex that, to their minds, was more the goal of celibacy-favoring Catholics—but, rather, insisting that the facts be embedded in a whole constellation of specific moral values, centered on chastity and their ideal model for domestic relations. Education about sex was critical to the maintenance of this model, but that education needed to be contained, regulated, and sanctioned by Christian wisdom.

This was not simply a conflict over knowledge, then. More directly, it was a battle for the authority to define the boundaries of Christianity and to set the terms for gendered order within marriage, the family, and American society at large. Equating sexual freedom with child endangerment, and confident that only they could prevent the nation's destruction, Christian Crusade leaders promoted themselves as America's valiant saviors and encouraged their followers to see themselves as a remnant of virtuous Christian citizens in a hopelessly decadent world. Hargis and Drake's accusations against SIECUS enabled the Christian Crusade to grow and expand in influence well beyond its early anti-Communist days. Tirades against sex education proved a brilliant political strategy in the nascent forging of a new Christian right, even as they helped to bring together religious and secular progressives in hopeful alliances against it.

Those who fought against sex education, moreover, had great success in displacing this progressive religious alliance from power. If the progressives seemed to be winning at first—triumphing over an older traditionalism as the mid-1960s caused attitudes toward sex to change, and getting moderate sex ed programs accepted all over the country—they were soundly knocked back on their heels by the attack stoked by people like Hargis. The liberal confidence regarding gradual progress toward greater enlightenment that emerged from Green Lake was, by the 1970s, replaced by the world-weary outlook that an embattled Calderone had by then adopted: a perspective that saw a long struggle ahead against people like Hargis. As the new Christian right began taking shape to serve as the righteous guardian of moral issues on all matters relating to sex and gender, their liberal Christian counterparts had to prepare and strengthen themselves for the conflicts yet to come.

CHAPTER 6

THE ABORTION WAR BEFORE
AND AFTER *ROE V. WADE*

In August 1972, the Gallup Organization reported, "Two out of three Americans think abortion should be a matter for decision solely between a woman and her physician." A "record high" of 64 percent of Americans supported "full liberalization of abortion laws," including a majority of ordinary Catholics surveyed (56 percent). Three in ten respondents (32 percent) disagreed, although two-thirds of that group "would make an exception in the case of a woman whose mental health is in danger." More Republicans (68 percent) and independents (67 percent) than Democrats (59 percent) agreed with the statement that decisions regarding abortion should be made only by a woman and her physician—a statistic that highlighted the prominence in the Democratic Party of Catholics, many of whom remained unenthusiastic about abortion rights.[1] But both political parties contained strong support for the expansion of safe and legal abortion services to American women.

On January 22, 1973, the Supreme Court handed down its 7–2 ruling in *Roe v. Wade*, declaring that women had a constitutional right to abortion throughout the first two trimesters of pregnancy prior to fetal viability. Responses to the ruling from religious and secular citizens came swiftly and quickly arrayed themselves into a moral pattern. Two camps emerged that were particularly visible. One was made up predominantly of Catholics who were joined by conservative Protestants in associations such as Billy James Hargis's new organization, Americans Against Abortion. This camp called itself "pro-life" and emphasized the sacredness of the fetus within the womb, and it insisted that legislative efforts must be made to overturn *Roe* and end what they condemned as abortion on demand. The Catholic Church itself, in fact, spent $4 million in 1973 alone to lobby members of Congress for restrictions on abortion.[2] To pro-life advocates, the Supreme Court's decision had sanctioned the murder of innocents. The other side was essentially secular in orientation but included a broad swath of Protestants and Jews as well as many liberal Catholic lay people. This camp called itself "pro-choice," a name that aimed to signify the preeminence of women's autonomy and personal moral decision making when it came to terminating an unwanted or medically adverse pregnancy. To pro-choice advocates, the court's decision guaranteed women the basic right to determine when and whether to bear children.

Evangelical Christians were not major players in the pro-life movement at this time, and many supported abortion's legalization. A symposium sponsored by *Christianity Today* a few years earlier had shown most to agree that "family welfare" issues could justify abortion. Southern Baptist leaders, who held very conservative positions on sexuality and who would eventually become staunch opponents of abortion, initially seemed to be squarely in the pro-choice camp: the Southern Baptist Convention had recently passed a resolution calling on members to work for abortion's legalization under such capacious conditions as "rape, incest, clear evidence of fetal deformity, and carefully ascertained evidence of the likelihood of damage to the emotional, mental, and physical health of the mother." Ninety percent of Texas Baptists surveyed in 1969 had felt their state's abortion law should be loosened. After the *Roe* ruling was announced, one of the denomination's most prominent leaders, W. A. Criswell, praised the court's decision and publicly stated his belief that abortion was not murder and that "what is best for the mother and for the future should be allowed."[3] Many Southern Baptist and other evangelical leaders would change their minds in a few years, but the main activists on the pro-life side at the time of *Roe* were Catholics.[4]

Media coverage of pro-life and pro-choice activist groups often framed both sides as angry and righteous, and certainly many fit the mold, employing fiery rhetoric that demonized their opponents and presented them as dangerous, hypocritical, and, above all, immoral if not downright evil. Many pro-lifers referred to the pro-choice camp as "pro-abortion," a term pro-choicers insisted was deliberately misleading; pro-choice advocates countered with the dismissive term "anti-choice," maintaining that abortion foes were keen to prevent women from making moral choices about reproduction. Regular attempts were made by well-meaning peacemakers to bring representatives of the two sides together, in hopes of finding ground and fostering collaboration on ways to reduce rates of unwanted pregnancies and abortions alike, but these usually foundered when the parties got tripped up by divergent moral attitudes toward matters such as contraceptive access. Before long, it was growing apparent that the politics surrounding abortion had become a zero-sum game and that both sides saw near apocalyptic consequences to going down in defeat.

Instead of rapidly accelerating the trend toward support of abortion that had been visible in the 1972 Gallup poll, the Supreme Court's *Roe* decision prompted a ferocious conflict between the 64 percent who had been for "full liberalization" and the 32 percent who had opposed it. The familiar narrative of what came after *Roe* describes how evangelical leaders seized on the abortion issue to mobilize conservative Protestants as voters, new alliances emerged between evangelicals and conservative Catholics, and abortion became a wedge issue dividing conservative religious Republican voters from secular feminists and liberal Democrats. That story is true, as far as it goes, but it neglects the fact that religious people were divided on abortion, and that many of the pro-choice feminists were part of Christian communities and still committed to them to greater or lesser degrees. Both before and after *Roe*, prominent Christian voices, from men and from women, made a moral case for abortion rights. By making their own pro-choice case on explicitly religious grounds, they prevented the pro-life camp from commanding the only Christian stance on this profoundly fraught issue. As each side built up its case, they worked to shred the arguments of the other—deepening the divide over abortion within American Christianity far more acutely than most would have dreamed before *Roe*.

Two progressive Christians stand out for having been born, bred, and steeped in churches and cultures on the other side before undergoing

Reverend Howard Moody speaking in New York.
*JOHN ORRIS/*THE NEW YORK TIMES *VIA REDUX PICTURES.*

a kind of conversion in their religious and political perspectives. Both, moreover, were also deeply invested in theological and moral reasoning about abortion: their support for abortion rights came not from secular politics but from religious convictions. Howard R. Moody, the son of "devout hard-shell Southern Baptists," as he described them, was immersing himself in sexuality issues at the same time that another Texas-born minister, Billy James Hargis, was turning to sex in the pages of *Christian Crusade*. Moody had a starkly different outlook on sex, by 1964 condemning the conservative Christian outrage over pornography and its simultaneous apathy toward far more important matters of human

Frances Kissling, president of Catholics
for a Free Choice, in her office with
CFFC poster and literature, 1985.
*CYNTHIA JOHNSON/THE LIFE IMAGES
COLLECTION/GETTY IMAGES.*

suffering. Moody's background was not so dissimilar to that of Hargis. Moody was born in Dallas, raised strictly and religiously, and preached at family gatherings by age five. As an adult, he too was a family man, with a wife and children to whom he was devoted. But the positions that he took—favoring women's rights, legal access to abortion, care for prostitutes, and equality for gay, lesbian, and bisexual people—were in thoroughgoing opposition to the fundamentalists in whose world he had been raised.[5]

Frances Kissling's background differed starkly from Moody's. A Polish-American working-class Catholic from Queens and a former postulant in a Long Island convent, Kissling became a nationally recognized leader in the abortion rights movement and, beginning in 1982, served as the president of Catholics for a Free Choice. Like Moody, Kissling was an active participant in the wars over abortion in New York between the late 1960s and the Supreme Court's 1973 verdict in *Roe v. Wade*; indeed, she would remain active long afterward. And like Moody and others before them, what drove her was the plight of women whom she saw seeking abortions: many of them had been sexually exploited or abandoned, and virtually all were frightened as they struggled to address a major life-altering burden they had not asked or planned for. To her mind, a religious worldview that genuinely valued women as highly as it valued men would look compassionately on those reeling from unplanned and unwanted pregnancies and do everything possible to help them.

For both Moody and Kissling, the opposition of conservative religious leaders to abortion was part and parcel of a larger patriarchal worldview that rested on men's authority over women. The Catholic Church and the conservative Protestant groups that most staunchly fought abortion were akin in regarding male leadership as a sacred given, a stance that preserved the privileged status of clerical leaders to make and enforce all the rules. Those male leaders tended to be especially concerned about sex and gender, Moody and Kissling both avowed, because religious rules pertaining to gender hierarchy and sexual morality prevented women from infiltrating the closed and exclusive culture of the clergy. Churchly prohibitions on sexual expression were thus fundamentally about power, and more specifically about the power to restrict the behavior and control the status of women. Moody and Kissling each maintained, in their lives and work, that the true message of Christianity was love for others and liberation from the tyranny of unjust rulers, whether reigning over church or state. These leaders were joined by swaths of Protestant and Catholic pro-choice supporters who had faith in the moral case favoring access to abortion, in opposition to the resistance of their conservative rivals.

BEFORE THE LATE NINETEENTH CENTURY, the practice of intentionally terminating a human pregnancy was quite common and almost wholly unregulated across the United States. No state or federal laws clearly forbade abortion at the beginning of the nineteenth century; as in the tradition of English common law, the prevailing view held that an abortion prior to "quickening"—the stage of pregnancy when the mother first feels the fetus moving—was a misdemeanor at most. Abortions undertaken in the first trimester and somewhere into the second were rarely prosecuted. Abortifacient patent medications were advertised not only in mainstream newspapers but in religious papers as well. During the 1800s, courts in Massachusetts, New Jersey, Maine, Iowa, Alabama, and Kentucky all upheld the position that abortion prior to quickening was not a punishable offense.[6]

It was not until the second half of the nineteenth century that abortion became increasingly outlawed, at the initiative of physicians working to professionalize the practice of medicine. The American Medical Association estimated in 1871 that 20 percent of pregnancies ended via intentional abortions (as opposed to "spontaneous abortion," or miscarriage), while other medical studies claimed even higher rates. As the press began publicizing stories of women dying from botched abortions, physicians spread the message that abortion was medically hazardous and perhaps morally wrong as well.[7] By 1900, laws prohibiting the intentional procurement of an abortion had passed in every state in the country, although all but six states did allow for "therapeutic" abortions under the gravest circumstances, meaning the mother's life was at risk such that continuing the pregnancy would likely kill her. Public attitudes regarding the ethics of abortion shifted from widespread indifference to strong disapproval. A woman distraught over a problem pregnancy could proceed with it and hope for the best; find a doctor willing to attest that an abortion was needed to save her life; attempt to self-induce an abortion, at very great risk; or seek out an illegal, likely painful, and potentially injurious if not lethal abortion.

Throughout the early decades of the twentieth century, there was little public controversy or outcry over abortion and its general inaccessibility. Physicians themselves were often nebulous about the circumstances that would permit a therapeutic abortion; naturally, some obstetricians were more willing to perform abortions than others, and views differed as to whether a fertilized egg was sacred from the moment of conception or not—as well as, if it was sacred, whose life should take precedence if the mother's was at risk. But whatever professionals' personal views about therapeutic abortion, many were quite concerned about criminal abortions—that is, those performed by unlicensed practitioners, countless numbers resulting in injury, others in infertility, and some in death. Birth control advocates, in fact, regularly argued their cause on the grounds that contraception could greatly reduce the incidence of criminal abortion. But the persistent obstacles to obtaining birth control or finding a doctor willing to perform the abortion and deem it "therapeutic" meant that illegal abortions continued to be common. Still, abortion was a taboo topic. Hollywood's Motion Picture Production Code censored mention of abortion, only allowing it to be referenced if it were overtly condemned, and it was not considered a matter of polite conversation. As one writer puts it, by the 1950s abortion was "invisible, unspeakable, yet ubiquitous."[8]

Trying to reduce both its invisibility and its ubiquity, a growing number of professionals sought to bring discussion of abortion into the open. Particularly significant was the 1955 conference organized by Mary Calderone under the auspices of the Planned Parenthood Federation of America. Forty-three men and women from the fields of psychiatry, obstetrics, biology, forensic medicine, law, political science, demography, and public health convened to discuss ways to reduce abortion rates and systematize the rules under which to permit the procedure. In a collective statement issued at the end of the conference, the group maintained, "Present laws and mores have not served to control the practice of illegal abortion." Illegal abortion was so common a practice, in fact, that the group called it a "disease" of American society, one with broad implications for the health of women and the family. Indeed, by the mid-1950s, Chicago's Cook County Hospital alone was annually treating three thousand women for complications from illegal abortions, triple the number it had seen twenty years earlier, while Los Angeles County Hospital was seeing over two thousand such cases a year.[9] While the group's overarching goal was to reduce illegal abortions as much as possible, that reduction could not occur within existing parameters of the law and social attitudes. The conferees called on professionals in medicine, education, religion, and the law to collaborate and strategize ways to alleviate this problem and make abortion law reform a priority. After this conference, Planned Parenthood began openly to advocate the reform of the nation's abortion laws, a focus it would retain for years to come.[10]

Religious support for abortion law liberalization grew over time, largely out of the existing collaborations between clergy and birth control advocates. Protestant clergy in New York, for instance, had continued working for birth control access ever since their early alliance with Margaret Sanger. Clergy working with Sanger in the 1940s had created a National Clergymen's Advisory Council, the first of several demonstrations of clergy encouragement, assistance, and promotion of Planned Parenthood. The council's charge was to be the "spokesman" for "the moral and religious values of planned parenthood," namely, the preservation of the health and happiness of children and the conservation of the family as a whole.[11] The group's first proclamation urging continued religious support to "the principles of responsible parenthood and family planning" garnered 480 Protestant and Jewish clergy signatories from forty-three states, including bishops, deans, seminary presidents, and many other leading lights. Elected members of the first national board included the Reverend Adam Clayton Powell Jr. of Harlem's Abyssinian Baptist Church (later a congressman); Dr. Sidney Goldstein, a prominent rabbi at the Stephen Wise Free Synagogue in New York; and the Reverend Arthur Powell Davies, the minister of All Souls Church, Unitarian, in Washington, DC. By the time of the council's next proclamation a few years later, it received 3,200 signatures from Protestant and Jewish clergy nationwide.[12] The clergy were so supportive of Planned Parenthood, and Planned Parenthood so pleased by this collaboration with influential religious leaders, that the dinner celebrating the twenty-fifth anniversary of Planned Parenthood at the Waldorf-Astoria in 1946 drew its chief sponsorship from the clergy.[13]

Catholic religious spokesmen and Catholic physicians viewed abortion very differently and had grave concerns about attempts at liberalization. Believing abortion under any circumstance to be murder, Catholics worked to persuade others of this view, attempting, for instance, to translate their own language of natural law into the language of international human rights that drew much support from liberals in the wake of

World War II. When the United Nations responded to Nazi atrocities by working to establish a full range of human rights that nations should agree to uphold, Catholic leaders advocated for the "right to life and bodily integrity from the moment of conception," a formulation publicly presented to the UN by the National Catholic Welfare Conference in 1947. While the UN did not adopt their language, Catholic organizers hardly gave up. The next year, the Jesuit medical ethicist Gerald Kelly published a set of directives for Catholic hospital personnel that marked abortion as a human rights issue, insisting, "Every unborn child must be considered a human person, with all the rights of a human person, from the moment of conception." In 1951, Pope Pius XII affirmatively declared, "Every human being, even a child in the mother's womb, has a right to life directly from God." Those who encouraged abortion, including therapeutic abortion, as merely terminating "life without value" were guilty of the same fallacy that prompted the Nazis to exterminate persons with "some physical or mental defect."[14]

This comparison between abortion and Nazi genocide framed the issue in a new way that resonated widely among Catholics. Indeed, it was apparently repeated so much in the Catholic press that one expert notes "it would be hard to find a right-to-life advocate who did not make it." While this framing successfully galvanized the Catholic opposition to abortion, it also stoked fury among supporters of abortion law reform who resented the implication that they did not respect human life. To those outside the Catholic Church (and likely to some within it), the Nazi comparison seemed absurd and felt downright offensive, quite personally so to Jews whose people had been so brutally slaughtered by Hitler's regime.[15] Many non-Catholics questioned the principle by which Catholic authorities equated a newly fertilized egg with a fully formed human, and abortion with murder. The liberalizers' resentment at being compared to Nazis in no way weakened their resolve; if anything, it fueled their determination to fight Catholic intransigence on abortion.

Throughout the 1950s and 1960s, Protestant and Jewish clergy continued to support Planned Parenthood both locally and nationally, often in skirmishes with local hospitals and health departments under pressure from Catholic leaders not to distribute birth control. Indeed, even as American Catholic clergy grappled both theologically and pastorally with birth control—not always in sync with the higher leadership—the non-Catholic clergy played an enormously significant role in working to change both public health policies and social attitudes to look more favorably on contraception of married couples and, at times, even unmarried persons.

This work included conflicts over abortion. When, for instance, the New Hampshire Medical Society in 1961 proposed an amendment to the state constitution that would allow an abortion to save the mother's life—the "live free or die" state was one of the few that had resisted this exception—the New Hampshire Council of Churches and the Manchester Ministerial Association joined the physicians to support the effort, even as the Roman Catholic bishop of Manchester vigorously opposed it. In fact, as one observer noted, the "sharp cleavage of religious opinion on abortion" strikingly revealed itself when legislators voted on the bill in early March: in the state's House of Representatives, virtually every oppositional vote was cast by a Catholic, while in the Senate, "all affirmative votes were either Protestant or non-sectarian; only two Protestants voted in opposition." The measure passed both chambers, and twenty-one clergy leaders—including the state's Episcopal and Methodist bishops and congregational leaders from Baptist, Congregational, Unitarian, and Jewish organizations—issued a joint statement that placed "religious conscience" squarely on the side of abortion access. Wesley Powell, the conservative Republican governor, vetoed it anyway. The Catholic periodical *America* censured the Protestant supporters, lamenting the "permissive attitudes" toward abortion that were growing and the "shallow psychiatric reasons" that were being used to justify therapeutic abortion. "If the churches do not guard morality in a democratic state," warned the writer, "the determination of morality tends to go by default to the majority vote and the popular will."[16]

The gravest threat to morality, in this view, was feminism. The movement was indeed gaining force in the mid-1960s, which witnessed the formation of numerous women's organizations focused on women's equality. The National Organization for Women was formed in 1966, with an initial focus on putting an end to sex discrimination in the workplace, education, and the media. Groups of younger women devoted to what was being termed "women's liberation" flourished in many urban areas and began to argue that "the personal is political," that is, issues such as intimate relationships, housework, and sexuality had profound collective consequences. As they discussed topics relating to sexual exploitation and assault, they contended that women had the right to find joy and pleasure in their sexuality and their relations with sexual partners. And they crafted what one observer has called "a new analysis of legal, available abortion as fundamental to female freedom": "The prohibition of abortion, they argued, forced women to bear children; the state's enforcement of motherhood exemplified the oppression of women."[17] Abortion access, in this view, exemplified women's full sexual liberation, and it needed to be decriminalized.

By the time feminists began gaining momentum in the articulation of this message and their demand for reform and repeal of the old nineteenth-century laws outlawing abortion, clergy collaboration with Planned Parenthood was long established. That collaboration was enormously significant, as was apparent well before the Planned Parenthood Federation of America in 1969 officially came out in support of repealing much traditional anti-abortion legislation. By then, Protestant and Jewish clergy had already established a burgeoning network of religious leaders who assisted women with problem pregnancies to procure safe abortions, without shame or sanction. That group, the Clergy Consultation Service, largely owed its existence to the leadership of a Baptist minister, the Reverend Howard Moody.[18]

SHORTLY AFTER HE STARTED WORK in the senior ministerial position at New York's Judson Memorial Church in the fall of 1956, Howard Moody received a woman who sought his counseling. She was a middle-aged mother, estranged from her husband and pregnant, possibly from an affair. She was desperate and wanted an abortion. Moody sympathized with her plight and traveled with her to find someone who would safely perform an illegal abortion. After several false leads proved fruitless, he managed to help the woman secure the termination for $600 in a secret complex on the Upper West Side. With his associate and collaborator, Arlene Carmen, a church administrator at Judson who worked closely with Moody for many years, he later wrote that he "never forgot this first glimpse of that dark, ugly labyrinthian underground into which women were sent alone and afraid."[19] A few years later, he would be at the forefront of a major movement of Christian and Jewish clergy seeking to help women find safe abortion providers and, ultimately, to overturn the laws banning abortion across the land.

Moody was born in 1921, the same year that Margaret Sanger was seized and arrested in Manhattan's Town Hall raid. New York would eventually become his city too, but he began life in Dallas, Texas, as a conservative Southern Baptist steeped in the Bible and the very tradition that had nurtured the likes of Theodore Bilbo. By Moody's own recollection, he started preaching at the age of five and was teaching Sunday School by the time he was fourteen; at fifteen, he was licensed to preach by his church. Intending to pursue a ministerial career, he attended Baylor University, the Southern Baptist institution in Waco, but left to join the marines. By then, he said, "I realized that Southern Baptism wasn't the only branch of Christianity."[20] He spent four and a half years in the Marine Corps, serving as an aerial photographer in the South Pacific during World War II, but his experience served to make him into an "ardent pacifist" for some time afterward. After finishing college at the Santa Barbara campus of the University of California, he enrolled in seminary, eventually landing at Yale Divinity School. With Liston Pope as dean and notables such as H. Richard Niebuhr and Kenneth Underwood on the faculty at the time, Yale Divinity School was a vital training ground for a robust social gospel, and Moody flourished in his ministerial education during those heady times. While there, he became involved in Judson Memorial Church, which in the fall of 1950, during his final year of seminary, ordained him to the ministry as part of the Northern Baptist Convention (in that year renamed the American Baptist Convention), a more progressive counterpart to the Southern Baptist church of his childhood.[21]

After graduating from Yale in 1951, Moody served as Ohio State University's chaplain for five years. He began serving as Judson's pastor at that time and remained at the church until his retirement in 1992. During the early years of his pastorate in Greenwich Village, Moody's congregation opened the Village Aid and Service Center, the first drug treatment center in the country.[22] As part of Moody's own commitment to the arts and to making the church a part of the community it served, Judson Church also hosted an art gallery that showed abstract paintings, along with supporting any number of theatrical productions. Besides serving as senior pastor, Moody was president of the Village Independent Democrats, a left-leaning challenger to the official Democratic Party operatives in New York, and he later served as chair of the Citizens Emergency Committee, another progressive group that fought what they saw as the New York City Police Department's repressive control over performers in city nightclubs. He wrote frequently for the *Village Voice* and was actively involved in the civil rights movement. He wanted to guide a church that would be wholly inclusive, "broadening the membership and including everyone who wanted to call Judson their community and become part of us . . . including believers, skeptics, agnostics and even atheists in its midst."[23]

Already well-known locally, Moody would gain national prominence with his work on abortion in the mid-1960s. In 1965 and 1966, a progressive member of the New York State Assembly, Al Blumenthal, was working on legislation to loosen the state's restrictions on abortion, but his fellow legislators repeatedly prevented open discussion of the issue. In the meantime, a group of about a dozen Protestant and Jewish clergy began to meet monthly at one of Judson's neighboring churches, Washington Square Methodist Church, to discuss abortion in all of its ethical and theological dimensions. Among this group was Moody, who perceived profound moral implications in the fact that only women, and not men, suffered the consequences of unintended pregnancy. As these clergymen worked to educate themselves about abortion, a physician who was a member of Moody's church had the group meet with a number of his patients who had undergone illegal abortions. The women spoke about their experiences, some quite harrowing, and offered their perspectives about what could have helped them in their time of fear and need. This was "the most important discussion we held," Moody later wrote:

the group learned that the women would never have turned to the clergy or their family doctors during their pregnancy crisis, for they believed both would moralize and try to talk them into carrying the pregnancy to term or even tell their families about the situation. In Moody's understated words, "We sensed that we were up against some long-standing historical biases which would make our job at best rather difficult."[24]

The clergy group gathered encouragement from a number of sources in New York, among them Lawrence Lader, a writer and influential abortion rights activist in New York. Called "the father of abortion rights" by feminist leader Betty Friedan, Lader came to the abortion issue while writing a biography of Margaret Sanger, who, though she never advocated abortion, had thoroughly convinced him of the profound importance of reproductive freedom for women's full equality. As he studied abortion, he came to see it as a fundamental right. He believed that the US Supreme Court's 1965 *Griswold* decision, which established a constitutional right to privacy, was a crucial victory in the fight for abortion reform: If contraception fell under this right to privacy, why not abortion? The line between preventing pregnancy and terminating a very early pregnancy seemed thin, after all; some products sold as birth control could actually work as abortifacients.[25]

Lader was also convinced that there was a need for an unapologetically moral argument favoring abortion rights, lest it appear that morality was solely on the side of the opposition. In his 1966 book *Abortion*, he wrote, "Nothing is stronger than the moral power of an idea once it has come of age." Women, especially, needed to stand up and make the moral case against the powerful forces that had long treated women and their sexuality as iniquitous. Lader noted that more than a million American women sought out secret abortions every year, and yet "almost none has protested publicly against the laws that defiled her." Lader angrily denounced the sustained misogyny that, he intimated, was the product of bad religion, insisting that "the moral power of legalized abortion will surely prevail when women have directed their anger against the superstitions of centuries, and cried out for the final freedom of procreative choice."[26] As he continued his advocacy, Lader became a one-man referral service, helping women find providers whom he believed offered safe abortions. To Lader's mind, he was humanely rescuing countless women from the danger and humiliation of underworld illegal abortions; he was providing a service that appealed, as one observer later put it, to "a higher morality than the law."[27]

On September 6, 1966—the day, coincidentally, that Margaret Sanger died—Lader met with Moody and two other Protestant ministers supportive of abortion law reform: John Krumm, an Episcopal priest in New York (later the bishop of southern Ohio), and Lester Kinsolving, an Episcopal priest in San Francisco (later a conservative talk radio host and White House correspondent for the right-wing WorldNetDaily). This was to be the first of several planning meetings with larger groups of clergy, and Lader's encouragement was instrumental. He challenged the clergy to do more than talk: "Start with the women," he urged, and consider what they lacked.[28] What was needed, he said, was a clergy referral service for women needing safe abortions, not unlike the service he himself was offering but on a larger scale and from a trusted group of leaders. The larger group of twenty to twenty-five clergy soon determined that if Blumenthal's efforts in the legislature did not work, they would take up the matter themselves. Sure enough, Blumenthal's bill failed to get out of the Health Committee in the winter of 1966, and Catholic leaders actively opposed it. A pastoral letter signed by bishops in all eight of New York's dioceses was read at Masses in most of the state's seventeen hundred churches in February 1967, maintaining that laws allowing abortion "violate the unborn child's God-given right" and urging the Catholic populace to do all that they could "to prevent direct attacks upon the lives of unborn children."[29] Moody's clergy group met with additional doctors and also with lawyers from the New York chapter of the American Civil Liberties Union (ACLU) to get an understanding of the legal risks they faced for referrals and procuring abortions: up to a year in jail and a $1,000 fine.

By the spring of 1967, Moody and his clergy circle had established the Clergy Consultation Service on Abortion (CCS), choosing with this name to take that taboo last word "out of the closet and enable the public to hear the word and deal with it."[30] As Lader had urged, the CCS was a counseling and abortion referral service for women in need of safe abortions. Later recalling the conditions under which the group was formed,

Moody and his able coworker, Arlene Carmen, recalled that few professionals could admit that there were many reasons unwanted pregnancies occurred, having to do with "a whole complex of problems related to unsatisfactory sex education, inadequate birth control measures, the heavy moral burden placed on single women if they performed sexually out of marriage, and most importantly related to a way in which men looked at women and put them in their place." Remembering all that women had had to go through in those days in order to secure a risky, painful, and illegal abortion, "one can only conclude that abortion was directly calculated, whether consciously or not, to be an excessive, cruel, and unnecessary punishment, physically and psychologically, of women."[31] It seemed to Moody and his allies that anti-abortion forces were the same people most strongly attached to traditional sexual morality, particularly female chastity. Abortion opponents, Carmen and Moody believed, thus saw an unintended pregnancy as fitting retribution for a wayward woman's sin. To abort was to get off unpunished, scot-free.

The twenty-one clergy who were initially willing to sign on publicly with the CCS included two rabbis and nineteen Protestant ministers from six denominations, and they shared a concern for the impact of current abortion laws on women and the poor. All but one, a "woman Methodist minister" who apparently kept a particularly memorable, anatomically oriented meeting "from deteriorating into a stag party atmosphere," were men.[32] They put together a "Clergy Statement on Abortion Law Reform and Consultation Service on Abortion." It began by noting that current laws led to over a million women annually seeking illegal abortions, "which often cause severe mental anguish, physical suffering, and unnecessary death of women." Prohibitions on abortion also compelled "the birth of unwanted, unloved, and often deformed children" and branded as criminals the "wives and mothers who are often driven as helpless victims to desperate acts." The statement noted that the greatest percentage of abortion deaths throughout the country occurred in middle-aged women who already had five or six children. In New York, the law was especially oppressive to the poor and minority groups, the statement noted, citing a 1965 report showing that "Negroes and Puerto Ricans" accounted for 94 percent of abortion deaths in New York City.[33]

Expressing distress at the resistance to alterations in the New York anti-abortion laws that would allow for exceptions in the cases of rape, incest, and fetal deformity, the clergy decried the emotional tactic of claiming that all abortion is "murder" and directly rebutted the Catholic position: "We affirm that there is a period during gestation when, although there may be *embryo* life in the fetus, there is no living *child* upon whom the crime of murder can be committed." The CCS clergy were insisting on an ethical distinction between "embryo" and "child" and contending that it was a moral act to expand women's access to medical termination of embryonic life.

These religious leaders wanted, as much as anyone, to reduce the abortion rate, and they believed the path to that lay in reducing its root causes—among them, poverty, lack of contraceptive access, and sexual violence. The religious values of this approach lay in an ardent commitment to living people who suffered; the clergy saw this work as an imitation of Jesus's work among the poor and needy. Though it had been the Quaker Mary Calderone who had published the first major book on abortion in 1958, it was the Baptist Moody and his clerical collaborators who successfully brought religious leaders to the forefront of the movement for reproductive rights.

The CCS signers pledged themselves to educating the public and to working toward the liberalization of abortion law in New York and the United States more generally. They might have ended there and patted themselves on the back for taking such a stand. But if current anti-abortion law was immoral, as these clergy vehemently argued, then church leaders could not in good conscience comply with it. Likewise, they were grateful to those physicians, "motivated by compassion and concern for the patient, and not simply for monetary gain," who attempted to help women by performing therapeutic abortions in cases of need. "Therefore," the statement concluded, "believing as clergymen that there are higher laws and moral obligations transcending legal codes, we believe that it is our pastoral responsibility and religious duty to give aid and assistance to all women with problem pregnancies."[34]

On May 22, the religion editor at the *New York Times* introduced the CCS with a front-page news article, "Clergymen Offer Abortion

Advice." It featured Moody as the leader and spokesman for the group, and listed the names and congregations of the other twenty clergy. The piece quoted frequently from the CCS statement and gave a thorough account of the group's plans. It also printed the phone number that women could call to speak with a cleric about a problem pregnancy.[35] Two days later, the *Times* followed up with a report that the CCS had received more than thirty-five calls in its first day of service. Rabbi Lewis Bogage reported the calls came from "the very wealthy, some very fine people and the very poor," including "four or five Catholic women."[36] And two days after that, the newspaper followed up with a report that Moody's group was hearing from clergy all over the country asking how to set up CCS chapters in their own communities.[37] Hopes for loosening strict abortion laws were widespread, gaining steam in June, when the American Medical Association voted for the first time in its history to condone abortion under the following conditions: to protect the health or life of the mother, to preclude bringing a child with a physical or mental defect into the world, or to terminate a pregnancy resulting from rape or incest. This "unequivocal stand," wrote the *Times* reporter covering the AMA's vote, would surely "speed a slowly developing trend toward the liberalization of state laws."[38] And so would the clergy.

The Clergy Consultation Service quickly spread out from New York to become a national network, with clergy in many states participating in the work of providing legal and medical assistance for women seeking abortions. Their work received significant coverage in the local and regional press. The CCS would eventually include somewhere around two thousand clergy across the country, including college chaplains and ministers from many different denominations. The head chaplain at Southern Methodist University launched the CCS in the state of Texas, and the University of Chicago's dean of the chapel established the Illinois branch. Clergy who had supported Planned Parenthood for years were especially ready for this work (although Planned Parenthood itself remained focused on contraception, not abortion), but others had been first mobilized to be activists through the civil rights movement and came to this work as a way to fight sexism in addition to their work against racism.[39] Two clergymen were arrested along the way, inciting outrage against the stringent anti-abortion laws and the law enforcement officers who had targeted clergy. According to Moody, the wives and daughters of police officers used the consulting service for their own abortions with the keen consent of the men, including a captain in the New York City Police Department.[40]

The CCS played a significant role in legitimizing abortion access as a moral crusade and provided crucial support in the heated battle for decriminalization.[41] A 1969 profile of Moody's activism and the CCS by the feminist writer Susan Brownmiller noted that he "considers the [abortion] law to be at the root, man's vengeance on woman, the self-righteous punishment inflicted on women by men who hold to a double standard on sexual relations." And it was farcical to distinguish between legal and illegal abortions as the current laws did: "Legality is determined by the whim of the doctor, expediencey, the looseness of the particular hospital, etc. It's whom you know and how much money you have that makes the difference between a legal and an illegal abortion." Abortion was plainly *not* murder, moreover, since embryonic life could in no way be equated with the life of a viable infant or young child. The moral problem for Moody was not determining what circumstances did or didn't justify terminating a pregnancy, an undertaking he felt smacked of patriarchal condescension; rather, it was how to support the young girl or woman who asserted her own need for an abortion, without imposing upon her "the judging attitude that she has come to expect" from clergy.[42] When New York legislators voted to liberalize the state's abortion laws in 1970, Moody, Carmen, and the CCS established the first legal, nonprofit abortion clinic in the state, soon known as the Center for Reproductive and Sexual Health.

The abortion rights movement had powerful religious support, and the message of compassionate care that he and CCS supporters around the country articulated was critical for helping many Americans understand the diversity of moral and religious views on abortion no less than on the sexuality questions of which it was part. Catholics who opposed abortion held fast to their convictions, but the mood for decriminalizing abortion in other religious settings was strong. Perhaps the most potent statistic publicized by the CCS showed, in different parts of the country, that Catholic women were seeking abortion counseling and referrals in proportion to their population numbers. That is, in a region where 20 percent of the citizens were Catholic, so too were 20 percent of the women being counseled by the local Clergy Consultation Service. Lawrence Lader's *Abortion* had made the same point in 1966, citing four studies that showed, "Catholics comprise over 20 percent of all abortion patients, almost equal to the Catholic ratio of about 25 percent in the total U.S. population."[43] "Naturally," then, as one observer noted, "the ministers involved concluded that religious belief was not a factor in determining which women sought referral services."[44] As with birth control, Catholic leaders might oppose abortion, but people in their parishes seemed to hold a wider range of views and certainly a more varied set of life experiences.

Although a warm and gentle man by accounts of those who knew him, and usually courteous to his foes no less than to his allies, Moody did not refrain from vocal criticism of Catholic anti-abortion activism. In the spring of 1972, fighting a battle against New York's Catholic leaders, who were attempting to repeal the liberal New York abortion laws, Moody spoke out with vehemence at a press conference called by the National Association for the Repeal of Abortion Laws (NARAL):

> I deplore the vicious and scathing attacks on our mothers, sisters and wives being castigated as guilty of *murder* and the most unspeakable of crimes against humanity made by leaders of the Roman Catholic Church and their "right to life" followers. Coming from an institution whose history is replete with the killing of innocent people in the name of God, I find little grace and no charity in their wanton attack upon people who view "life" and "death" differently than they do. The Cardinal, the bishops, and the pastors of the church are sowing the seeds of sectarian hatred that can only lead to religious divisiveness and warfare in this nation. It is a sign of acute desperation that the Church has seen fit to turn an issue on which honest persons disagree into a religious battle ground where righteous protectors of life and God are battering the demonic forces of murder and mayhem.[45]

In the same year, Moody grounded the pro-choice side in the cherished national ideal of religious freedom, again lashing out at Catholic leaders:

> The principle of religious liberty that grants all persons the freedom to follow the practice of one's own religion or conscience in matters of faith and morals touches the abortion issue precisely at the point of a woman's freedom to follow her conviction that abortion is morally permissible even thought for her co-religionist it may be a sin. The Roman Catholic Church and whatever religious allies it has in the attempts to destroy the law are forsaking the basic tenets of our living together in an open, pluralistic society. The issue is *not* when does life *begin* in the womb but rather where does freedom of choice and conscience *end* in society? A more important question than whether feticide is homicide may be whether any one group may impose its moral and religious beliefs by legal sanction upon all society.[46]

Less than a year later, the US Supreme Court issued its decision in *Roe v. Wade*, finding that states could not criminalize abortion in the first trimester and could curb it only within strict bounds beyond that. Moody's side had apparently won against the Catholic hierarchy, but he noted that abortion plainly was "a battleground that would take its toll on human civility and religious tolerance for years to come."[47]

In fact, *Roe* had an intriguingly close link to CCS. Sarah Weddington, the young Texas lawyer who successfully argued the case before the Supreme Court, was the daughter of a United Methodist pastor and described herself as "the traditional preacher's daughter: I sang in the church choir, played the church organ and piano, gave Sunday devotionals and was a youth leader in the church community."[48] She attended McMurry College, a small Methodist school in Abilene, before heading to law school at the University of Texas. After graduating in 1968, she became active in feminist activities in Austin that included an abortion referral project. Project workers collaborated closely with the network of ministers and rabbis who made up the Texas chapters of the Clergy Consultation Service, including one Methodist pastor who was a friend of her father. Like these clergymen, Weddington felt a responsibility to help others that she believed came out of the "gospel of 'Christian social concern'" in which she was raised—the very sense of responsibility that led her to challenge the Texas anti-abortion law all the way to the Supreme Court.[49]

When the *Roe* decision eliminated barriers to safe and legal abortion across the nation, the practical work of the CCS essentially ended. Women seeking to end a pregnancy could turn to reputable doctors and clinics, and if many continued to seek pastoral care in making this decision, they did not need clergy referrals. CCS clergy could and did focus on other issues. Over his career, Moody took bold stands on a number of large social questions, all of which were, to him, chiefly moral in nature. He worked in the civil rights movement, opposed the Vietnam War, advocated the decriminalization of marijuana, served as a member of New York's Democratic Reform movement, initiated an AIDS task force at Judson Memorial Church, and championed the reform of drug laws. He would become a vocal advocate for queer men and women, after living among and working with so many in the LGBT community in Greenwich Village.

In the immediate aftermath of the CCS, Moody and his parishioners, along with Carmen, established the Judson Church Prostitution Project, which reached out to the "working women" of Manhattan who performed sex for pay at massage parlors and on the street. Moody's approach to this work closely resembled his approach to women seeking abortions and again reflected his strong view that women were victims of the Christian tradition's long history of harshly judging female sexuality. He and his coworkers sought out local prostitutes to offer much needed health services, help with child care and housing, and above all be present in a way that would "let the women know that a congregation of people who made no judgment about their profession cared about them as human beings." They worked on the street and on a bus, from which they served hot food, kept a bulletin board on which women proudly posted photos of their children, and offered space for conversation. They learned of the economic deprivations, sexual abuse, and desperation that had led some of these women into prostitution, and they were determined to help them find dignity and happiness. Moody baptized several of the women's children, held baby showers and weddings for some women, and performed memorial services for several prostitutes who were murdered. He and his associates also came weekly to witness arraignments of prostitutes at Manhattan Criminal Court, convinced that simply "being there" for the women was "an important component of our ministry." Judson Church even published a newspaper for working prostitutes, called *The Hooker's Hookup: A Professional Journal*; among other things, it printed the women's own written thoughts on their profession as well as their poetry and creative prose.[50]

Moody's ultimate goal in this work, like his work on behalf of pregnant women seeking abortions, was to eradicate the laws that made prostitutes into criminals and that worked ultimately to endanger the women's lives and complicate the lives of their children. In the interim, it was critical to see and treat each prostitute as a unique human being and to establish connection so as to understand more about her life. The prostitute was hated by many "square" women (including both feminists and those on the religious right), wrote Carmen and Moody, because she represented sexual freedom and the fantasy of full control over her own body. But this hatred did horrific psychological damage to women who worked in the sex trade, analogous to that done to women who sought abortions or to people engaging in same-sex relations during the time when all of these activities were viewed as criminal and immoral. Consistent with his broader moral stance on sex and human personhood, in short, Moody refused to consider prostitutes as sexual deviants, dirty sinners, or lawbreakers, regarding them instead as dignified human beings who perhaps needed help but nonetheless merited thoroughgoing respect. Moody was adamant in believing that the immorality in question was not sex for pay but the double standard—"which grew, let us remember, out of the theology of the church"—and brutality sanctioned by the law.[51]

Yet what may have horrified church authorities most, Moody believed, was the fact of "serendipitous sex"—based on the attitude, exemplified in the prostitute-client relationship (among others) that sex could be "as casual as a friendly handshake." In the prostitute's work world, sex appeared not as the "holy, set-apart activity appropriate only in the most restrictive context" idealized by Jewish and Christian ethics; instead, it was "desacralized" and "deromanticized." Prostitutes laughed about sex, telling stories that were alternately sad and hilarious about their patrons' sexual dysfunctions, hang-ups, and kinky desires. There was nothing holy, mysterious, or unique about any sexual encounter performed for pay; it was not "some momentous, secret act with which we are going to consummate our humanity." This "offhand view of sex" was, Moody believed, what most frightened the religious and political conservatives who were committed to the status quo and who deeply opposed all sexual activity outside of heterosexual marriage; for if sex was a mundane rather than sacred activity, neither "dehumanizing" nor miraculous but simply ordinary and not immutably tethered to any special set of emotions, then there was no longer any urgency to keep it under such strict control. The prostitute, like any unrepentantly promiscuous man or—especially—woman, served as "a living, walking threat to every traditional moral and religious belief that asserts romantic love, or monogamous marriage or relationships to be the exclusive fitting forms for any sexual activity." It was for this reason that prostitutes, much like women seeking abortions, were so ostracized by conservative church leaders, who rightly saw them as "a genuine threat to the church's major teachings about sex" as well as to broader American attitudes toward human sexuality that had been so thoroughly shaped by Christianity.[52]

In the aftermath of *Roe*, it was quickly apparent that opponents of abortion were galvanizing to create what would become a powerful crusade that they would call the right-to-life or pro-life movement, which aimed to overturn the ruling and to recriminalize abortion. Catholic leaders were at the forefront of this effort from the very start, some repeatedly warning that any Catholic who had or helped another person procure an abortion would be punished with excommunication. Anti-abortion activism did not, of course, start with *Roe*.[53] Organizations such as the Catholic-founded Human Life Center and the Society for a Christian Commonwealth had been working on abortion starting in the late 1960s, often as part of a broader agenda that included birth control, traditional marriage, and other issues. But *Roe* catalyzed a new phase of activity, inspiring repeated attempts to gather local and state-level organizations into a massive force that would successfully protect the life of the unborn.

The National Council of Catholic Bishops' Family Life Bureau had created the National Right to Life Committee in 1968, and while it was no longer under the church's control by 1973, it was still dominated by Catholics. The group met in Washington, DC, less than a week after *Roe* to determine its next steps. It took only eight days from the Supreme Court's ruling for a member of the US House of Representatives, a divorced Catholic from Maryland, to introduce a constitutional amendment declaring the fetus a "person" from the moment of conception, a move that would presumably render abortion illegal regardless of context. In August, Catholic leaders protested an episode of the CBS sitcom *Maude*, when the title character's abortion was the focal subject, and in November, the National Council of Catholic Bishops voted to establish a National Committee for a Human Life Amendment (NCHLA), affirming that the passage of a pro-life amendment to the US Constitution was "a priority of the highest order."[54] The first national March for Life took place in January 1974 in Washington, DC, and two months later, four Catholic cardinals—John Cody, John Krol, Timothy Manning, and Humberto Medeiros—testified before a Senate subcommittee to argue for a constitutional amendment banning abortion under all circumstances. As Cardinal Manning put it in his testimony, "The stark fact is that the unborn are being destroyed in our country at an unprecedented rate, and the destruction goes on because there is no adequate protection in the law. No one who cherishes this nation's historic commitment to human rights can contemplate this situation with complacency."[55]

In November 1975, the National Conference of Catholic Bishops voted to approve a "pastoral plan for pro-life activities" that called for the creation of pro-life groups in every congressional district in the United States to persuade congressional representatives to vote for a constitutional amendment banning abortion. These groups would collaborate with diocesan pro-life groups that already existed, but whereas the purpose of the diocesan groups was "pedagogic and motivational," the congressional

Pro-life women protest the increased access to abortion that followed the Supreme Court's *Roe v. Wade* decision, 1973. *KEYSTONE-FRANCE/GAMMA-KEYSTONE VIA GETTY IMAGES.*

groups were organizational. Each unit "can be described as a public interest group or a citizens' lobby," wrote the bishops. "No matter what it is called, its task is essentially political." They urged Catholics to work with non-Catholics on this plan, as this was not merely a Catholic issue. New York's Terence Cardinal Cooke, the chair of the committee that drafted the plan, called the Supreme Court's ruling a "disaster," telling an audience at a news conference, "We have been subjected to a brain-washing by people pushing abortion."[56] The church's anti-abortion campaign was its biggest ever in the United States, and it greatly accelerated and strengthened the grassroots political movement against abortion.

In 1976, a Catholic US senator from Illinois, Henry Hyde, sponsored a piece of congressional legislation that banned the use of federal funds to pay for abortion. Introducing the legislation in June 1976, Hyde emphasized that American taxpayers should not be forced to pay for "the killing of innocent preborn human life." Since this provision would primarily affect those receiving health care through Medicaid who could not afford the cost of an abortion, congressional opponents accused Hyde of targeting the poor, to which he responded, "I would certainly like to prevent, if I could legally, anybody from having an abortion, a rich woman, a middle class woman, or a poor woman."[57] Congress passed what came to be called the Hyde Amendment that year, tinkering with it periodically afterward and much later adding exceptions for abortions needed to save the woman's life or for pregnancies resulting from rape or incest. In the years to come, it would be a focal point for activists on all sides.

In the same year the Equal Rights Amendment failed to get ratified to become part of the US Constitution, 1979, the anti-abortion movement got a major public boost. Leaders in the burgeoning Christian right were organizing themselves into something like an actual movement to stand against abortion and other forces of feminism that they believed threatened the traditional family and American values. In June, the fundamentalist Jerry Falwell founded the Moral Majority, a conservative religious group resolved to combat the atheistic secular humanism seen as plaguing the land. The organization played a critical role in strengthening a social agenda within the Republican Party that actively opposed not only abortion and feminism but also homosexuality and pornography. Epitomizing what one historian calls a "union of deep religious commitment with legal consciousness," Beverly LaHaye that same year founded Concerned Women for America for much the same purpose and expressly to counter through lobbying and legal action abortion as well as sex education, pornography, and what she called the "blatantly pro-lesbian tactics of radical feminists."[58]

For all of these resolutely conservative Christians and their innumerable allies and followers, feminism and abortion were twin evils, two sides of the same dirty coin. By the 1980s, the politics of abortion reverberated in federal and state elections across the country. Ronald Reagan, who campaigned openly in support of the Christian right and advocated for a constitutional amendment against abortion, badly beat the incumbent Democratic president, Jimmy Carter, in 1980. And abortion only intensified as a wedge issue in that decade, fueled by religious and political players on all sides.

Pro-choice religious activism also continued, in organizations such as the Religious Coalition for Abortion Rights, a successor to CCS that had been founded in December 1973. But it wasn't only pro-choice Protestants and Jews who spoke out; pro-choice Catholics who dissented from the Catholic hierarchy's teaching on this issue did too. In fact, a few Catholics created one of the most important religious pro-choice groups in the post-*Roe* years. In 1973, three Catholic lay women—Joan Harriman, Patricia Fogarty McQuillan, and Meta Mulcahy—established Catholics for a Free Choice (CFFC). The organization came out of New York-based Catholics for the Elimination of All Restrictive Abortion & Contraceptive Laws, a pro-choice lobby group formed at the height of the New York legislative abortion battles in 1970.

These pro-choice Catholics wanted other Catholics to remember that their church had not always equated all abortion with homicide; they insistently explained that centuries of church leaders—including such greats as Augustine and Aquinas—had promoted the view that abortion prior to "ensoulment" was a minor offense, one more akin to using birth control than to murder. Those church leaders had taken this view from pre-Christian thinkers: Aristotle, for instance, argued that in the early days of gestation, a human embryo does not yet have a living soul but rather an inanimate "vegetable soul." A fetus would only be animated with a living soul some weeks after conception; this process of "ensoulment" occurred, Aristotle believed, forty days after conception for males and ninety days after conception for females. Later Christians offered different views on this concept of ensoulment, some agreeing with Aristotle's timeline and others arguing that ensoulment occurred as early as during conception or as late as the time of quickening. Christian thinkers routinely condemned abortion after ensoulment as sin, but there was wide variance, for centuries, as to when this occurred, and hence many accepted early abortions.

Catholic pro-life leaders had an easy answer to this argument: church leaders of past centuries did not have the scientific knowledge of how conception actually worked and hence held mistaken views of when ensoulment took place and life began. Pro-choice critics scoffed at the hubris they detected in such a position. But whatever history said, CFFC founders believed the US bishops did not represent the views of most American Catholics. Like many others in the pro-choice movement, these pro-choice Catholics were convinced that Catholic pro-life leaders were motivated more by misogyny and fear of women's freedom than by any consistent adherence to church dogma. To make the point as explicitly as possible, in 1974 McQuillan crowned herself "pope" in a public display at the entrance to New York's historic St. Patrick's Cathedral. The seeming ridiculousness of a woman in papal garb highlighted the entrenchment of male authority in Roman Catholic leadership. So long as female leaders were unthinkable, church leaders would inevitably uphold gender inequality and discrimination against women.

The most prominent leader of CFFC was Frances Kissling, who headed the organization for a quarter century, from 1982 to 2007. Kissling's early life hardly portended such a career. Kissling was born Frances Romanski in New York City in 1943 to Polish American parents. After her parents divorced when she was six, she was adopted by her stepfather, Charles Kissling, and raised in a working-class family in Queens. The stepfather left some years later, refusing to support his wife and four children. Kissling went to an all-girls parochial grammar school and two all-girls Catholic high schools and continued her Catholic education into the early years of college, at which point she entered the Sisters of St. Joseph convent in Brentwood, Long Island.

She had dreamed of becoming a nun since admiring the sisters who taught her in school, and she spent about nine months as a postulant at the Long Island convent. When she initially decided to enter the convent, she discovered that she had been conceived out of wedlock (the convent required her parents' wedding license along with her own birth certificate; her parents wed in February 1943, and she was born in June). The community initially balked at accepting Kissling for this very reason but eventually agreed to take her. As she later recalled, "They decided to make an exception, although it was very clear that they were forced to make the exception. And when I sort of decided to leave—with a little push—they were very glad I was going." The mother superior told her, as she exited, "You know, we never wanted you."[59] This was a formative moment in Kissling's understanding of the church's rigid views on female sexuality and the corrupt sinfulness of women. Because Kissling could not believe in the Catholic Church's strict views on marriage, divorce, and remarriage, she left the convent and entertained no further thoughts of becoming a nun.

After leaving, Kissling finished college at the New School in New York, where she became involved in Students for a Democratic Society. There, she would later note, "my politics changed dramatically, or I got politics that were mine." Then in the fall of 1970, just after the legalization of abortion in New York, Kissling got a job running an abortion clinic, the Pelham Medical Group in Westchester. There she found herself in a world of "feminist women who wanted to see that women got well cared for." Working in the clinic and seeing the care for the women who entered, she remembered, "that was the moment in which I became an active feminist." Kissling would remain active in the abortion movement for the remainder of her career, working periodically for other clinics and then organizations such as International Projects Assistance Services (IPAS) that helped to establish clinics in other parts of the world. Like Moody, Kissling's interest in this issue never had to do with population control; her interest was in the rights of women, and most notably the poor. "I'm on the side of the poor," she reflected. "That probably historically has to do with A, the fact that I'm a working-class person who has been through a broken family with a mother who could just about put shoes on the feet of her children, so this is who I am. . . . And also as a Catholic due by the social mission of the Church and the notion that the poor should be our first priority."[60]

By 1978, Kissling was invited to serve on the board of CFFC, then headed by Patricia McMahon. McMahon's invitation to the board, Kissling later noted, was "the defining moment of my life," the moment where she began at last to think about her Catholicism and her commitment to women and to pro-choice activism together. The deep appeal of CFFC was that it served as "a space where the moral dimensions of the issues could be explored"—moral dimensions that Kissling believed were being avoided by secular women's rights groups such as NARAL, and were therefore conceded to the religious opponents of abortion. The women who sought abortions were always asking themselves the moral questions, wanting to know if their action was right or wrong, sinful or justified. "So in that context, both in terms of my Catholic background, in terms of my experience in the abortion clinic, it always seemed to me that the inability of the movement to deal with the moral questions was problematic for me first and foremost," she later remembered. "And I also believed then, but even believe more strongly now, that the inability to deal with the question [of abortion] as a moral question undercuts the long term success of the pro-choice movement."[61]

Through her work with CFFC, Kissling came to think much more deeply not only about ethics and morals concerning notions such as "life" and "choice" but also about what it meant to be a Catholic, eventually concluding that there are multiples ways to be Catholic and not simply one. Considering both historic and contemporary Catholic figures, she asked, "Was Joan of Arc a Catholic? I mean, she was a heretic one day and now she's a saint. Is Hans Küng, who publicly rejects infallibility? . . . Are they Catholics? Is Pat Buchanan, who rejects the entire social justice teaching of the Church, a Catholic?" Only the "ultra orthodox" believed that the "identifying mark of who you are as a Catholic . . . is loyalty to the Pope." Ultra-orthodox Catholics, she noted, had asked the pope repeatedly to excommunicate those they call "pro-abortionists" such as Kissling, but the Vatican authorities never did so. "And so, in the eyes of the Church, I am a Catholic. I may be a bad Catholic, I may be a good Catholic, I may be a misguided Catholic, but I am a Catholic. I choose to be a Catholic. . . . I don't want to be anything else."[62]

Around the time that Kissling became president of CFFC in 1982, she asked Geraldine Ferraro, a New York Democrat and member of the US House of Representatives, to hold a congressional briefing aimed at Catholic congressional leaders holding pro-choice views or a mixed voting record relating to abortion. A pro-choice Catholic herself, Ferraro did so, issuing a statement noting that "the Catholic position on abortion is not monolithic" and that there could be "a range of personal and political responses to the issue." Ferraro's own stance was that while she was personally opposed to abortion, she believed that the constitutional guarantee of religious liberty and the respect for other religious views necessary in a diverse civil society meant that a woman should have access to abortion and the freedom to have one if she so chose. Her public airing of that view would shortly reap trouble from Catholic leaders.[63]

Two years later, Democratic presidential candidate Walter Mondale named Ferraro his vice presidential running mate in the 1984 election. This move opened up the Democratic ticket to public excoriation, as Ferraro was roundly criticized by high-profile Catholic leaders such as John Cardinal O'Connor, the archbishop of New York, for what he deemed a willful perversion of the church's position on abortion. O'Connor ignited a firestorm after he stated in a televised news conference that he could not fathom how a Catholic "in good conscience" could "vote for an individual explicitly expressing himself or herself as favoring abortion."[64] O'Connor rebuked Ferraro repeatedly in public for misrepresenting the church's teaching on abortion, and church leaders in Philadelphia and Scranton, Pennsylvania, condemned her when she made campaign appearances in their regions. The eighteen Catholic bishops who served the church in New England declared abortion "the critical issue of the moment" to make clear their preference for the Republican candidate, who had long identified himself as a staunch opponent of abortion. Bishops in other regions likewise made sure local parishioners knew their preference, even if they were careful not to officially endorse him. Critics protested that the church was "aggressively involved" in American politics to an inordinate degree; as one Democratic columnist complained, the church hierarchy was "acting like an arm of the Reagan re-election committee."[65]

CFFC was determined to stand behind Ferraro and return fire. The group's leaders pulled out a statement they had drafted some months earlier called "A Catholic Statement on Pluralism and Abortion" that stressed the fact that "a diversity of opinions regarding abortion exists among committed Catholics," and now they decided to make it public. Circulating the statement—whose cowriters included the Catholic ethicist and theologian Daniel Maguire, a professor at the Jesuit-run Marquette University, and the Catholic attorney and theologian Marjorie Maguire, his wife at the time—organizers obtained numerous signatories from liberal Catholics, including nuns, priests, theologians, and Catholic academics of various sorts. With the presidential race heating up in the fall, CFFC advocates made plans to publish a full-page advertisement in the *New York Times* on Sunday, October 7, just a month before the election that pitted Walter Mondale and Ferraro against the popular incumbent Ronald Reagan and his running mate, George H. W. Bush. By the time the ad appeared, it had ninety-seven signatories, including twenty-six women serving as sisters in fourteen canonical communities, two priests, two lay brothers, and sixty-seven additional Catholic sign-ers.[66] CFFC claimed that scores of other priests, theologians, and other Catholic leaders had expressed support but had not publicly signed out of concern for losing their jobs.

The ad frankly and directly conveyed the reality that devout Catholics held many opinions about abortion and that even canonical teachings had not spoken with one voice throughout church history, as illuminated by shifting church doctrines on ensoulment over time. "A large number of Catholic theologians hold that even direct abortion, though tragic, can sometimes be a moral choice," it stated, most particularly because of principles of moral theology such as religious liberty and conscience. The ad also cited poll data from the National Opinion Research Center showing that a mere 11 percent of Catholics disapproved of abortion regardless of the circumstance. Catholics ought to be able to discuss and publicly debate their views without fear of punishment from church authorities, and youth and families ought to be made fully aware of the "complexity of the issues of responsible sexuality and human reproduction." Moreover, the ad argued, Catholics should not seek legislation that limited any citizen's religious freedom and exercise of conscience or laws that discriminated against the poor. Above all, the signatories affirmed the belief "that responsible moral decisions can only be made in an atmosphere of freedom from fear or coercion."[67]

The ad reaped tremendous publicity and a sharp reaction from the Roman Catholic hierarchy well beyond the United States. The Vatican weighed in, calling on canonical signatories—priests and other serving in official church roles—to retract their adherence to the document, with an "explicit threat of dismissal from the community" if they refused retraction. The priests acceded almost immediately: all four of the male signatories who were priests or members of canonical communities retracted within weeks. The sisters and their superiors in most canonical communities instead resisted, debating with Vatican officials the principles of freedom of conscience and subsidiarity versus obedience. As Kissling later wrote about the Vatican's push for retraction, "Rome's quest was not for doctrinal purity"; rather, church leaders sought "to solidify obedience within a clearly delineated hierarchical chain of command."[68] In the meantime, Ferraro continued to reap ferocious attacks from church leaders for her stance.

In November, Ronald Reagan won the election by a landslide, beating the Mondale-Ferraro ticket in forty-nine of fifty states. A solid majority of Catholic voters—estimates ranging between 54 and 61 percent—went for Reagan, who received a higher percentage of the American Catholic vote in 1984 than any Republican candidate in the nation's history to that point. It was a demoralizing loss for Democrats and alarming to see so many people from one of their longtime constituencies—Catholics—abandon them. Pundits nicknamed that group the Catholic "Reagan Democrats," and there was little question what social issues had mattered to them in this decisive election. When the Democratic National Committee commissioned an independent study to understand why their party had fared so poorly in that year's presidential race, they got word that those who had abandoned the party viewed it as controlled by "liberal extremists and special interest groups with values and an agenda foreign to middle-class America," a clear reference to issues that included abortion. "Gays and feminists" threatened American families, those polled declared, and their moral decadence represented what the Democratic Party had become. It was a stark report, and Democratic officials, not wanting to upset groups of people who remained their core supporters, did not release but instead destroyed and buried it.[69]

CFFC leaders wanted their politically pro-choice message to be part of the Catholic mainstream, so they aimed always to spread their moral argumentation to as broad a Catholic audience as possible, especially what Kissling called the "ambivalent . . . middle ground" of Catholics who held positions on abortion somewhere between the extremes of pro-life and pro-choice—that is, between those who opposed abortion in all circumstances and those who supported virtually no restrictions on it. Kissling herself believed in taking seriously the status of the fetus and the question of when life begins, but she was convinced that Catholics should not stop there, since "the whole spectrum of sexual and reproductive issues" needed to be addressed. But her faith in the possibilities of engaging Catholic lay people did not extend to the hierarchy, whose very authority was at stake in the abortion debate. With church leaders appearing to have entirely given up fighting against contraception in the public policy realm, they were not going to budge on abortion, she thought, because "abortion is the most visible sign that a person or a couple, a woman or a couple, does not accept the teachings of the Church relative to sexuality." Abortion, in short, represented a woman who did not accept that every sexual act must be open to conception and who thus bucked the church hierarchy's fundamental teaching on sexuality. She who chose to abort was dirty, just as an unmarried pregnant woman was dirty. And for Catholics such as those in CFFC, the fundamental moral point here concerned "the historic prejudice against women and against sex" that was, ultimately, about *power.* Hence, these Catholics were disdainful of what some nicknamed "Catholic pelvic theology." Dissenters believed that since the Catholic Church upholds a celibate hierarchy— that is, one in which "people who do not have sex are better qualified to hold power"—the effect is that "the prohibition on sexuality enables the maintenance of an elite core of leaders." Any move to liberalize that prohibition, and the rules against sex more generally, would erode the notion "that not having sex makes you a better person qualified to have power."[70]

Needless to say, the Catholic leadership did not hold CFFC and its pro-choice activism in high esteem. More broadly, the authority structure of the church led to a very different reaction among clerical leaders than the Clergy Consultation Service had received from considerable numbers of Protestant leaders. Many of the signers of the *New York Times* ad who stood by their position suffered repercussions for it, both personally and professionally. Daniel Maguire had speaking invitations rescinded from several Catholic universities. Other "disinvitations" greeted several more signers, and some were refused jobs, promotions, and academic tenure in ways that they and CFFC supporters believed were related to their unwillingness to retract their support for the ad. According to Kissling, an executive director of Planned Parenthood was excommunicated because of her work related to abortion, while a twelve-year-old girl was expelled from her Catholic elementary school because she held pro-choice views: "Such are examples of Vatican overkill."[71]

The Conference of Catholic Bishops consistently maintained that CFFC did not represent authentic Catholicism, and eventually, the bishops would condemn CFFC's criticisms of church policy as another in the line of "episodes of anti-Catholic bigotry that the Catholic Church has endured in the past."[72] Catholic feminists and other allies continued to praise CFFC for what they saw as the organization's courageous work both in and far beyond the United States, in partnerships in such places as Bolivia, Brazil, Mexico, Columbia, Chile, and Argentina. But the organization and its leadership repeatedly took fire from church leaders and members passionately committed to upholding the church's strict ban on abortion as the law of the land. That opposition was mostly civil, even if pointed, but not always. As one outraged critic said of Kissling, suggesting both the fury and the misogyny brewing underground, "This woman is a smug, curt, character-assassinating cunt."[73] Not everyone would put it so offensively, to say the least, but those most loyal to the male church hierarchy and its equation of a day-old embryo with a fully formed human being were not about to budge a hair on abortion.

THE CHIEF IMPETUS FOR MOODY, Kissling, and so many others on the religious pro-choice side was the idea that sex was good, in and of itself, and that it ought to be separated from mere procreation. God intended sex to be a source of joy, not a source of fear and shame, they believed. Sexuality was a dynamic, multiplicitous, uncontainable mystery, they repeatedly argued, and the moralizers attempting to restrict it for heterosexual, monogamous, eternal marriage were inflicting misery and terror on far too many people. If most Christian leaders—Protestant but especially Catholic—continued to resist the decoupling of sexuality from reproduction and to refuse to entertain any notion that sex outside of marriage, under appropriate circumstances, could be good, then members of their flocks would simply ignore them, just as Catholics had long ignored the church's ban on birth control. What Daniel Maguire later cheekily called "the long shadow of Augustine's penis"—the church's history of making sex dirty that owed so much to the early Christian bishop's efforts to restrain and eradicate his own sexual desires—may not have been the only factor influencing people's views on abortion, but it was unquestionably an important one. Still, many if not most pro-life Christians were surely sincere in seeing this as an issue of life versus death.[74]

The pre-*Roe* Clergy Consultation Service and post-*Roe* Catholics for a Free Choice (which would later change its name to Catholics for Choice) had different missions, strategies, and constituencies, but both aimed at a common goal: destigmatizing abortion and undermining religious arguments that deemed it an immoral and evil act. Many Protestants and Catholics agreed with some or all that these pro-choice groups stood for, far more than would ever actually be affiliated with either organization, but countless numbers of other Christians in both camps stood in opposition to abortion long after *Roe*. No issue roiled American politics in the 1980s more than abortion, and large sectors of the voting population increasingly saw it as a litmus test for candidates: the staunchest pro-choice feminists vigorously opposed political candidates from their own party if they were lukewarm on reproductive choice, while resolute pro-life conservatives had an equally hard time supporting Republicans who deemed restricting abortion a low priority. At the edges of the abortion debate, anti-abortion activists calling for violence began to emerge, such as the Army of God, an underground group formed in 1982 and viewed by the US government as a terrorist organization for tactics such as kidnapping and murdering doctors who performed abortions. Almost no ordinary citizen opposed to abortion would have advocated the murder of providers, but that extreme element showed how profoundly consequential people on all sides believed this issue to be.

A hallmark of 1980s activism was the growth of overt political outspokenness by religious leaders on questions like that of abortion. The politicization of abortion, however, had mixed effects. During that decade, pollsters noted increasing polarization concerning attitudes toward abortion: whereas the majority of Americans continued to say that they favored the legality of abortion in some but not all circumstances—consistently the most widespread opinion expressed by citizens across the political spectrum—attitudes were gradually shifting toward a more visible pro-choice consensus. Pro-life activism by conservative Protestant and Catholic leaders aimed to stem that tide, and surely stirred up much anti-abortion sentiment in their ranks, but pro-life activists also sufficiently angered enough moderates who had been more or less indifferent to abortion to shift certain voting blocs toward supporting pro-choice candidates, or at least favoring abortion's legality. White evangelical opposition to abortion would eventually exceed that of American Catholics, a slim majority of whom told pollsters abortion should be legal in all or most cases.[75]

Abortion would remain a brutally divisive religious and political issue after the 1980s, of course. But it was during that decade that vast numbers of Americans with passionately held moral viewpoints—feminist and progressive on one side, traditional and conservative on the other—came to fear that there was no political middle ground. The old Christian consensus on gender roles was further splintering, and an ever more divided religious and political culture seemed to be the result. Emotions remained raw into the early 1990s, when another explosive issue burst into the national consciousness and got the whole country talking about yet another topic relating to gender and sex: harassment in the workplace.

CHAPTER 7

SEXUAL HARASSMENT
AT CENTURY'S END

I N THE FALL OF 1991, the nation was transfixed by the confirmation hearings of the conservative African American jurist Clarence Thomas,
whom President George H. W. Bush had nominated as associate justice
of the US Supreme Court. Nearing the end of what had already been a
lengthy review by the Senate Judiciary Committee, a written statement
sent confidentially to staffers for the committee chair, Senator Joe Biden
(D-DE), was leaked to the public. According to the statement's writer, a
law professor named Anita Hill who had worked for Thomas some years
earlier, the nominee had a taste for hard-core pornography and a pen-
chant for discussing it and other sexual matters with subordinates in the
workplace, or at least with her; working under these conditions had made
her extremely uncomfortable. These allegations of sexual harassment
threatened to derail Thomas's nomination and ruin his personal and professional reputation. Hill—who is also African American—was subpoe-
naed and appeared before the committee on October 11, sandwiched in
between appearances by Thomas denying the charges and defending his
record. Millions of Americans tuned in, weighed in, and fiercely debated
which party was telling the truth.

Two and a half years later, sexual harassment allegations again
rocked American politics. This time, they involved the new president of
the United States, William Jefferson Clinton. Paula Jones, a onetime employee of the state of Arkansas, filed a lawsuit in May 1994 alleging that
Clinton, while governor of Arkansas in 1991, had commanded Jones to be

Law professor Anita Hill is sworn in at the Senate Judiciary hearing,
where she elaborated her allegations of sexual harassment against
Clarence Thomas. *BETTMANN VIA GETTY IMAGES.*

brought to his hotel room during a state-sponsored conference. There,
according to her, he behaved abominably and attempted to persuade her
to perform sexual acts before she escaped, shocked and shaken. Once
again, Americans were treated to explicit details of alleged sexual intimidation and a bitter he said/she said exchange over the truth. And once
again, Americans expressed strikingly divergent views toward a woman
asserting actionable mistreatment by a prominent government official.

The scandals surrounding Thomas and Clinton produced competing, utterly polarized, and often sensationalized story lines about
each protagonist. Many of these drew on old stereotypes about wanton
women and black hyper-sexuality, others on victimization plotlines sympathizers were eager to believe. Anita Hill was a courageous heroine to
women everywhere, or she was a shrew whose unrequited sexual obsession for her boss had prompted her to seek revenge. Clarence Thomas
was a successful lawyer who had overcome racial barriers only to be persecuted by a hoax because he was a conservative and a Christian, or he
was a bullying boss with some twisted erotic tastes. Paula Jones was a

Paula Jones, a former Arkansas
state employee, speaks to a reporter
about her sexual harassment lawsuit
against President Bill Clinton.
*CYNTHIA JOHNSON/THE LIFE IMAGES
COLLECTION/GETTY IMAGES.*

brave ingénue defending her dignity, or she was slutty trailer park trash
out for fame and money. Bill Clinton was a brilliant politician with desperate enemies, or he was a mendacious playboy whose slick affability
masked a gross sense of sexual entitlement. Whatever the facts in either
case—and none of the charges were definitively proven in either—both
expanded the nation's interest in sexual harassment and fostered discussion of women's rights, workplace boundaries, and the reach of the law.
Far from unifying Americans in a shared commitment to dignity for female workers, however, these events tore further asunder norms of civility between political rivals, resulting in an intensely partisan discussion
riven by divergent aims.

Many other divisive developments around gender and sexuality were
occurring in this same period, as an organized religious right continued

to rise and mobilize conservatives against a wide range of feminist and progressive causes. Sex education controversies persisted in school districts across the country. Conflicts over abortion remained potent, and mass marches organized by both sides attracted large crowds to Washington, DC: the 1989 and 1992 pro-choice March for Women's Lives and the 1990 pro-life Rally for Life each attracted hundreds of thousands of people. The AIDS crisis brought with it a backlash against gays, lesbians, and bisexuals, and a growing LGBT rights movement was rising. All of these issues generated tumultuous hostility in the 1990s. But among all the battles that resulted from that hostility, nothing better revealed the hardening—and increasingly politicized—divisions among American Christians over matters of sexual morality than did the linked sexual harassment scandals ensnaring Thomas and Clinton. For while Christian conservatives rallied solidly to Thomas's side against Hill in 1991, they doggedly supported Jones against Clinton, raising a new, religiously inflected outcry against sexual harassment at the very time that it served their own political ends.

The harassment debates of the 1990s revealed a coming of age in the sexual politics of the Christian right, as conservative Christian leaders found a way to shift from a purely "anti" politics—anti–sex education, anti-abortion, etc.—to a politics that blended a defense of public propriety with a selective, politically expedient quasi-feminism. That position sprang out of a selective concern regarding sexual harassment, a concern that was surely earnest to a degree but that also served broader goals of electing candidates sympathetic to the moral vision of the Christian right. In navigating the sexual harassment debate, conservative Christians both appropriated and distanced themselves from contemporary feminist commitments and ideas. In so doing, they flipped from merely opposing "sexual harassment" as an idea cooked up by lefty feminists to deploying it selectively in defense of Christian virtue. That shift helps explain why, by the end of the Clinton presidency, Americans had lost any consensus that might have been forged regarding sexual harassment or the definition of modern feminism: these had been turned into political weapons used on both sides of the aisle.

Anita Faye Hill was born into a family of African American farmers in Okmulgee County, Oklahoma, the youngest of thirteen children. She grew up in modest surroundings and was encouraged to work hard at everything she did. With the rest of her family, she was active in the local Baptist church and identified as a devout Christian. Shy and bookish by nature, Hill performed at a very high level in school—"one of the two smartest kids I've taught in the last thirty years," stated one teacher to journalists Jane Mayer and Jill Abramson in the aftermath of the Thomas hearings—and graduated as the valedictorian from her predominantly white high school in 1973.[1] She earned an undergraduate degree in psychology from Oklahoma State University in 1977 and a JD from the School of Law at Yale University in 1980. After a year working at a law firm in Washington, DC, she met Clarence Thomas through a mutual friend. He had just been appointed assistant secretary of education for civil rights and offered her a job in his office; she accepted and began working for him in the summer of 1981.

Both Hill and Thomas later agreed that their professional relationship at the beginning of this period was very cordial and productive. From there, their stories dramatically diverged: according to Hill, Thomas persistently asked her out and used work situations to talk about sex acts, sexual organs, and scenes he'd watched in pornographic films, as well as "his own sexual prowess"; her efforts to change the subject were "rarely successful."[2] The following year, after what she described to the Senate Judiciary Committee as a temporary end to Thomas's "offensive" behavior, she accepted his offer to move with him to the Equal Employment Opportunity Commission (EEOC). There, Hill said, his sexual overtures and vulgar banter resumed and worsened until she began to look for other work. (Thomas denied all of these allegations.) In 1983, Hill joined the law faculty at Oral Roberts University in Tulsa, a good fit for her own Christian faith even if a big step down professionally.[3]

Hill taught for three years at Oral Roberts before the university sold the law school in 1986 to Pat Robertson's Christian Broadcasting Network University in Virginia (later Regent University). She then accepted a faculty position at the University of Oklahoma, where she earned tenure in 1990. At both law schools, Hill was a well-regarded member of the faculty. The University of Oklahoma awarded her a prestigious post as a faculty administrative fellow in the Office of the Provost. Until President Bush nominated Thomas to the Supreme Court, there were no indications that she ever planned to tell her account of working with him to any but a few very close friends. As she later recounted in her autobiography, she felt she had "successfully overcome my experience with Thomas to the point of disregarding it," rising above the harassment for the sake of her own happiness.[4]

Then, on July 1, 1991, President Bush announced Thomas as his choice to succeed Justice Thurgood Marshall, who had announced his retirement after nearly twenty-four years on the nation's highest court as its first black justice. Although Thomas's name had been in wide circulation as a potential nominee, he lacked judicial experience, having served on the DC Circuit Court of Appeals for less than two years. He was extremely conservative in his politics and seemed, if confirmed, almost certain to move the court to the right. It was widely believed that Bush had specifically aimed to replace a black liberal justice with a black conservative, a point that angered many American liberals. African Americans were particularly divided over Thomas: supporters such as writer Maya Angelou worried that if his appointment were scuttled, "another conservative possibly more harmful, and one who has neither our history nor culture in common with us" would get the seat instead; opponents concerned about his anti–affirmative action record, such as civil rights leader Julian Bond, countered that there was no way Thomas's race would "overcome his hostility toward civil rights remedies" or equal opportunity, making his appointment a true disaster for black Americans.[5]

As news of the nomination began to sink in, Hill later recalled, a friend urged her to disclose her experience with Thomas, but Hill replied that she was not certain what she should or would do. Days before the Senate Judiciary Committee confirmation hearings were to start on September 10, according to Hill, staffers who worked for members of that committee contacted her and asked about allegations of harassment against Thomas and rumors that he had sexually harassed Hill herself. Worried about the consequences of proceeding, she waited a few days before saying that she would disclose the information as long as it remained confidential and out of the press. To avoid the appearance of looking partisan, the matter was passed to the FBI for investigation. Hill wrote a four-page statement of her experience working with Thomas; she faxed it to a staffer on September 23, the same day two FBI agents came to interview her at her house.[6]

On Friday, September 27, when the Senate Judiciary Committee voted on whether to recommend Thomas's candidacy to the full Senate, the vote was deadlocked at 7–7. The committee then voted 13–1 to present Thomas's candidacy to the full Senate, with no favorable recommendation attached. Determined reporters—notably, Nina Totenberg of National Public Radio and Timothy Phelps of *Newsday*—began investigating why the vote was so close. Over the following week, as word of Hill's statement began to leak, both Totenberg and Phelps contacted Hill, who agreed to speak with Totenberg only when the reporter appeared to have already received her written statement from other sources. On the evening of October 5, Phelps's story hit the news wires; Totenberg's radio broadcast, which included excerpts from a taped interview with Hill, came the next morning. The impact was stunning and, for Thomas, devastating. He later told the Senate Judiciary Committee that when he learned this story was going to be in the press, "I died. The person you knew, whether you voted for me or against me, died."[7]

Thomas's Senate supporters were also mortified and appalled by the charges. These included political moderates, like those who initially championed him for his independent intellect, sense of fairness, and overall integrity. Prominent supporters who had worked closely with him over the years were certain that Thomas could not be guilty of the vile conduct alleged by Hill and were outraged that such dirty tricks were in play to derail his nomination. A decent man's reputation was being sullied by charges forged out of fantasy or revenge, and his very career was at stake.

The allegations against Thomas, now public, occasioned a second round of Judiciary Committee hearings later that week. The hearings were a national spectacle and unquestionably a source of humiliation for Thomas and Hill alike. With millions of Americans glued to their

TV screens, senators prodded both Thomas and Hill with repetitious questions about highly personal and embarrassing sexual matters. Senators seeking to discredit Hill, who was questioned for nearly nine hours, impugned her motivations, one asking in quick succession, "Are you a scorned woman? . . . Are you a zealoting civil rights believer that progress will be turned back, if Clarence Thomas goes on the Court? . . . Do you have a militant attitude relative to the area of civil rights? . . . Do you have a martyr complex?" Thomas, returning to the stand after Hill's testimony, denounced the day's event as a "travesty" and a "national disgrace," a "disgusting" display of "sleaze," "dirt," "gossip," and "lies" that had been orchestrated by committee staffers, leaked to the media, and then "validated" through this prime time display over national television. His opening statement concluded powerfully that the proceedings represented "a high-tech lynching for uppity blacks who in any way deign to think for themselves, to do for themselves, to have different ideas, and it is a message that unless you kowtow to an older order, this is what will happen to you. You will be lynched, destroyed, caricatured by a committee of the U.S. Senate rather than hung from a tree."[8] Whoever was telling the truth, this had been a soul-destroying day for both parties.

The politics of race were central to this inquiry, and no community was more divided in their views of it than African Americans. Across the country, black men typically (but not always) rallied to Thomas's side. Black women were more divided: many passionately favored Hill, but large numbers backed Thomas instead. The legal scholar Kimberlé Williams Crenshaw later remembered a group of African American Christians, mostly women, who at the Capitol surrounded her and two other African American lawyers working to defend Hill against Thomas's denials, their "hands linked in song and praise, seeking God's help to vanquish this latest threat to Thomas's elevation to the Supreme Court." Black feminists who were frustrated by that attitude would eventually write a manifesto, signed by nearly sixteen hundred women and published in the *New York Times* as well as other papers across the country, that denounced "the racist and sexist treatment of Professor Anita Hill."[9]

In the end, Thomas's nomination withstood Hill's testimony, and the Senate voted 52–48 to confirm him to the Supreme Court.

"Whoop-dee-damn-doo," he later recalled responding when his wife, Virginia, told him about the vote; the ordeal had just been too brutal for him to feel triumphant.[10] Both Hill and Thomas later disclosed private moments of hopeless despair in the wake of the hearings. Nonetheless, he took the oath of office into government service on October 18, 1991, exactly one week after Hill's testimony.

The rival behind-the-scenes campaigns to discredit both figures abated little after the hearings, and the relentless mockery of everyone involved had to be tough to take.[11] Popular TV shows repeatedly skewered the congressional proceedings for mortifying everyone involved while failing to get anywhere close to determining the truth.[12] Thomas later recalled that God had helped him to rise "phoenixlike from the ashes of self-pity and despair" after his confirmation, yet his "wounds were still raw" and would only heal "in time."[13] He felt he had received sickening treatment from "my enemies," a phrase that appeared ten times in Thomas's memoir; all but one referred to his opponents during the hearings, and the last came from Psalm 30: "*I will praise you, LORD, for you have rescued me. You refused to let my enemies triumph over me.*"[14] Thomas had many supporters who bore him up, but moving on from his own lynching, as he continued to feel it, was no simple task.

Neither was it for Hill, whose world had likewise been forever transformed by her televised testimony. Messages poured in, by phone and mail, from people who praised or excoriated her. Many letters came from people outraged by what they deemed the unfair treatment of her by Senate interrogators, from people who had experienced sexual harassment themselves, and from people who were simply indignant at the apparent ineptitude of their representatives in Congress. Some offered her their "support and prayers."[15] Others, though fewer, sent "threatening, vulgar, and just plain cruel messages," she later recalled. But she took strength in the letters of support, which "were crucial to my endurance and ultimately to my recovery," as were the comforts of daily prayer, friends, and family.[16] The solace Hill took in correspondence from harassment victims highlighted what she perceived to be the cosmic gap in understanding between those who had experienced harassment and those insulated from it. Hill felt the sympathizers understood her; she shared a "common experience" with those who believed her, whatever the detractors might say.[17]

The hearings left the nation raw as well, on the right no less than the left. For some conservatives, the hearings provided an important lesson in the dangers of feminism run amok, blind to justice and truth as it sought women's empowerment at any cost. The Harvard sociologist Orlando Patterson may have spoken for many when he acknowledged the believability of Hill's account while deriding as "unfair and disingenuous" her choice, as he saw it, to raise this issue ten years after the fact. The alleged infraction didn't matter anyway, argued Patterson, since it was simply talk that "neo-Puritan America" could not abide. Thomas's words, if spoken, caused no harm and were certainly no basis for losing a seat on the nation's highest court. Even if Thomas had said these things, wrote Patterson, he was right to deny them because the "grossly unfair punishment"—losing the chance to be a Supreme Court justice—was disproportionately severe. Women, Patterson noted, needed to "escape the trap of neo-Puritan feminism with its reactionary sacralization of women's bodies" and learn better ways of getting along with men in the workplace. Fortunately, justice had prevailed, and the nation was newly aware of "the progress in racial and gender relations already achieved by this country," despite the "superficial liberal stereotypes" of kneejerk feminism, the chief subject of Patterson's ire.[18]

Many conservative Christians also saw feminists as the real troublemakers in the Hill-Thomas debacle, and their analysis aligned precisely with the critiques that had been emerging from Christian right leaders for decades. Writing in the conservative Protestant periodical *Christianity Today* a month after Thomas's confirmation, the evangelical Christian leader Chuck Colson blamed the lies promoted by Hill's supporters on the "militant feminism" that came from a "diabolical source" opposed to God, calling feminism a force that undermined "the very notion of what it means to be a man, what it means to be a woman." Colson drew connections to many of the sexual controversies of the past: "Think back to the sexual revolution of the 1960s, propelled largely by feminists who insisted that women could be just as sexually free (read promiscuous) as men and just as explicit in their language (read obscene). The birth-control pill and, eventually, legalized abortion meant that women could be as free as men from the burden of childbearing, and more able to compete in the workplace."[19] Right-wing radio host Rush Limbaugh, who famously scorned Hill's supporters and other feminists as "femi-Nazis," echoed Colson's critique that the hearings revealed "the extent to which feminists and their political allies are willing to go to advance their proabortion, militant leftist, antimale agenda." Hill lied—of that Limbaugh was certain—but liberals were either too dumb to see that or too ideological to care, holding a hypocritical "double standard" that looked away from the egregiously harassing behavior of liberal men such as Ted Kennedy to push their own interests.[20]

Thomas had already been a rising star in conservative political circles—indeed, they had played a large role in propelling his nominations both to the DC Circuit and the highest court—and the hearings deepened admiration for him among a broad range of social conservatives, including many who were leaders in the Christian right. Besides Colson and Limbaugh, his influential conservative Christian supporters included Paul Weyrich, an architect of the new Christian right who famously came up with the name "Moral Majority" for Jerry Falwell's political organization and who founded several influential groups such as the Free Congress Foundation; Pat Robertson and Ralph Reed, whose Christian Coalition promoted Thomas's candidacy through a $1 million ad campaign; and Gary Bauer of the Family Research Council, who chaired the Citizens Committee to Confirm Clarence Thomas. Other prominent conservatives who supported Thomas included lawyer and commentator Laura Ingraham, who clerked for Thomas during his second year on the Supreme Court, and media personality Limbaugh—who became a close personal friend and whose third wedding Thomas hosted and officiated less than three years after his confirmation.[21] Rosalie ("Ricky") Silberman, who had served with Thomas at the EEOC, ardently supported him during the confirmation hearings and called Hill's supporters "extreminists." Afterward, she worked with others to turn an informal network of women calling itself Women for Judge Thomas into the Independent Women's Forum, a nonprofit political organization focused on policy issues pertaining to women—what the group called a "conservative alternative to feminist tenets."[22]

Indeed, Thomas Jipping of Weyrich's Christian think tank later wrote of Thomas, "the *entire* conservative movement not only supports him, but *believes* in him."²³ Weyrich's group, the Free Congress Foundation, worked hard for Thomas's nomination, drafting countless press releases and other reports shopped to the media and circulated in the Senate. A year after Thomas's confirmation, Jipping and Phyllis Berry-Myers—who worked together with Hill and Thomas at the EEOC and who testified in Thomas's favor during the hearings—wrote for the Free Congress Foundation to explain the deceitfulness they spied behind Hill's testimony: "Left-wing interest groups, intent on derailing Clarence Thomas's nomination to the Supreme Court, knew they had to manufacture a bombshell relative to Thomas's character because they would not defeat him on the merits. Like aggressive public-interest lawyers, they picked their plaintiffs and developed their facts."²⁴ The Christian groups were certainly no less aggressive in fighting what they believed was a holy war: as one journalist later wrote, "most important" to this confirmation battle "was Paul Weyrich's network of antiabortion, antipornography, pro-school prayer activists stretching across the country" and the "war room" Weyrich set up in DC to rebut each charge against Thomas.²⁵

To these Christian conservatives, despite her own claims to Christian faith, Hill was a liar pure and simple—a shill to the special interest groups who invented her tall tale—and sexual harassment was a laughable charge. Gary Bauer's Citizens' Committee ran ads on television that showed mud being splattered on Thomas's face; other ads likewise paid for by conservative religious and political groups similarly claimed Hill's charges were the invention of abortion-rights-forever feminists out to smear Thomas's good character. Most agreed with the outburst of one senator during the confirmation hearings who, while saying he took the issue seriously, called Hill's charges "this sexual harassment crap."²⁶

The Christian Coalition, an enormously successful and influential conservative political advocacy group—the brainchild of religious broadcaster Pat Robertson that was led by executive director Ralph Reed—also worked hard for Thomas's confirmation and outright dismissed any chance that Hill could be telling the truth. Coalition members reportedly bombarded the Senate with a hundred thousand petitions, letters, and phone calls promoting him.[27] Later recalling Thomas's successful confirmation as "one of our biggest victories," Reed wrote that Christian Coalition national and state leaders all agreed that "Thomas' confirmation was a major priority," as his was believed to be a reliable pro-family voice on the court. It was hoped that he would be the fifth vote in a much anticipated effort to overturn *Roe v. Wade*, the 1973 opinion that removed restrictions on abortion.[28] The conservative Christian pro-family movement for Thomas's confirmation was about abortion and family values; it was not an attack on sexual harassment law per se. The real damage done was by "the feminists and the pro-abortion lobby," wrote Reed, though it ultimately came to good ends: "I have always felt that the vicious treatment of Thomas (and Robert Bork) by the radical left helped to inspire our movement to encourage people of faith to make a difference and become an influential force on Capitol Hill."[29]

In fact, Reed started writing a novel about Thomas's battle in 1991, at the very time that he headed the Christian Coalition and was mobilizing support for Thomas's nomination. Published later, the novel, titled *The Confirmation*, featured characters and events bearing more than a passing resemblance to those in the hearings. Interestingly, the figure representing Anita Hill—Maria Solis (homophonous with "soulless"), the Latina ex-girlfriend of Supreme Court nominee Marco Diaz—is a troubled person who means no real harm and winds up dead before she can testify; the real evildoer is the white feminist Christy Love, a ferocious "lobbyist-cum-grassroots agitator" who is "borderline irrational" and described as "that witch at Pro-Choice PAC" who would "back over her own mother to stop Diaz from getting on the Court."[30] (Reed was not going for literary nuance.) The villainous Love is blamed for Solis's death, while the curse of another feminist kills the unborn child in Diaz's wife's womb ("I think she must be a witch or something"). The treachery all comes down to feminism, but in the end Diaz is confirmed, simply and completely "because of the power of prayer."[31] The point of the book, as Reed said, was to show that the hearings were not just a political battle but a spiritual battle between good and evil, and that all the attacks in the world could not compare to godly people working to build God's kingdom. The moral of the story: the "good guys"—men much like Reed and his allies saw themselves, men of faith and prayer, conservative men opposed to feminists and witches and other agents of evil—*win*.[32]

This was a pretty standard view of feminism among conservative Christians during the Thomas hearings: sexual harassment claims could still seem laughable and exaggerated, or the fault of feminist political correctness. Influential spokesmen for the right seemed to waver in discussing sexual harassment, vacillating between claims that (a) sexual harassment as a national problem deserving attention is vastly overblown and (b) sexual harassment is liberals' fault. Limbaugh made both arguments. An example of argument (a) appeared in his 1992 book, *The Way Things Ought to Be*, in which he wrote, "The vast majority of American women, 63 percent according to the polls, didn't believe Anita Hill and don't think sexual harassment is the most important issue of our time. Plus, they also think they can handle the situation themselves."[33] Argument (b) made a stronger appearance in his 1993 book, *See, I Told You So*, which contains several passages such as this one:

> Isn't it also ironic that the same crowd that supports handing out condoms to students is shocked that there is a rise in sexual harassment in the schools? What do you expect when you teach kids moral relativism and that premarital, and perverted, sex is to be encouraged? When the Ten Commandments are off limits, and it's against the law to teach abstinence, what kinds of messages are we sending these children? We give kids condoms, we tell them how to use them, and, when they do, we're shocked.

These arguments coexisted easily: in the second book, Limbaugh insisted that feminists were hypersensitive enough to insist that merely "looking at someone is sexual harassment," that "all men are rapists," and that "all sex is rape."[34] To the extent that sexual harassment was a problem—mostly for children forced to grow up in a sex-obsessed culture—liberals were to blame; for real grownups, though, it was no problem at all.

Limbaugh's speech sometimes veered into the margins of far-right conspiratorialism; here, however, his words sounded representative of a fairly commonplace aversion to feminism. While his usual put-down—"Feminism was established so that unattractive women could have easier access to the mainstream of society"—was fairly toothless, his real message was more dire. Even without feminism, women were fearsome, potentially terrifying creatures: "The fact of the matter is that women have far more power than most of them realize. It's a biological fact that males are the aggressors. We all know this is true. That means that the ultimate power—the power to say yes or no—lies with women." Unfortunately, "some militant feminists apparently harbor such animosity for the opposite sex that they want to criminalize the process of courtship—the old-fashioned 'chase.'" This was a real problem, that "seduction is being confused with harassment." As a result, men were being persecuted unfairly, solely because of a "political agenda . . . called breaking down barriers" that was really about stoking hatred between the sexes and dividing people. That "elite corps of abortion-on-demand zealots I call femi-Nazis" were playing a "victimization game" that would ultimately destroy men. It would furthermore spread homosexuality, "moral relativism," and other "sick and weird behavior." In the end, the femi-Nazis' political agenda would "consume our culture" until the nation was destroyed.[35] Limbaugh offered a vivid illustration of the powerful connections between fear of women's freedom, self-determination, and resistance to gender hierarchies; fear of "the other" (in this case, LGBT people); and fear of a declining, degraded American nation, irreparably damaged by the sexual activities of an inside enemy.

Just as the hearings cemented the support of conservative Christians for Thomas, the hearings made Hill an overnight celebrity among liberals, particularly liberal women. They pledged to make the Beltway culture of Washington more hospitable to women and vowed to put sexual harassment at the forefront of policyholders' minds and to work for stronger enforcement of harassment laws in the workplace. Progressive Christians, and especially progressive Christian women, redoubled their own commitment to fighting sexual harassment and other modes of sexual misconduct within the church. As one writer put it, "The name 'Anita Hill' has become a metaphor for women's issues."[36]

Democrats invited Hill to speak at the 1992 Democratic National Convention, where Bill Clinton was nominated as the party's candidate against President Bush. Hill declined that invitation, feeling that most Democrats "had done little to show any real concern about the issue of sexual harassment" or sexual assault. But she wept when she watched the convention and heard Senator Barbara Mikulski (D-MD) declare that no woman who came forward with her story would again be treated the way Hill was at the hearings. "As Senator Mikulski spoke and introduced the female candidates for the Senate, for the first time in months I believed that change was possible—that no other woman would have to face the public spectacle I underwent."[37]

Indeed, the 1992 election saw a record number of women run for office in both major parties, leading the news media to call it "The Year of the Woman." One hundred and fifty women (ninety-four of them Democrats, fifty-four Republicans, and two independents) filed early for seats in the US House of Representatives; twenty-one African American women were among these. Twenty-nine women filed for the US Senate, and seven ran for governor. In November, four women were elected to the Senate—Barbara Boxer (D-CA), Dianne Feinstein (D-CA), Carol Moseley Braun (D-IL), and Patty Murray (D-WA)—joining the two already serving, Nancy Kassebaum (R-KS) and Mikulski. (After a special election the next year, they were joined by Kay Bailey Hutchison [R-TX].) Forty-seven women won election or reelection to the House, a gain of nineteen seats; thirty-five were Democrats and twelve Republicans. African Americans gained numbers as well: Moseley Braun was the first African American woman in the Senate, while the election increased black representation in the House from twenty-five to thirty-eight. The Senate's treatment of Hill was widely believed to have spurred more women to run for office and to have motivated female voters to support them.[38]

Beyond the political realm, countless numbers of women who had been harassed sexually at work felt newly empowered to act on their experience. In the year that followed Hill's testimony, harassment complaints filed with the EEOC rose by more than 50 percent over the previous year.[39] The Tailhook scandal—in which eighty-three women and seven men alleged that they were sexually assaulted and/or harassed by US Navy and Marine officers at the annual Tailhook Association Symposium in Las Vegas in the same fall of 1991—incited further outrage about men's apparent sense of sexual entitlement. Women were tired of simply swallowing gross forms of harassment as if it were their due, and many determined they weren't going to take it anymore.

The events of 1991 prompted a new focus on the problem of sexual harassment and a new determination to end it. The landscape of sexual harassment—including both the attitudes that had fostered and tolerated it and the regulations building to dismantle it—began rapidly changing across the nation. But this focus and determination were largely the province of feminists and liberals. As the conservatives who rallied around Thomas and against Hill suggested, sexual harassment would be an intensely contested issue. Indeed, at the 1992 Republican convention, delegates stalked Nina Totenberg—whom they blamed for breaking the Hill story during Thomas's hearings—and to her face repeatedly called her a "whore," a sexually harassing word if there ever was one.[40]

Understanding the problem of sexual harassment as it burst into national consciousness in the wake of the Thomas-Hill hearings requires understanding the longer, entwined history of working women and forced sexual intimacy by those wielding economic power over them. Sexual coercion of women by masters and overseers was endemic to the American slave system. But "free" women also experienced sexual pressure, and sometimes outright assault, in the households, manufacturing plants, and clerical offices where they worked. In 1887, Helen Campbell's book about women wage-workers, *Prisoners of Poverty*, pointedly noted that "household service has become synonymous with the worst degradation that comes to woman. . . . Domestic service is the cover for more licentiousness than can be found in any other trade in which women are at work."[41] And in his 1905 muckraking novel *The Jungle*, Upton Sinclair wrote of women's harsh work lives in the meat-packing industry:

> Here was a population, low-class and mostly foreign, hanging always
> on the verge of starvation, and dependent for its opportunities of
> life upon the whim of men every bit as brutal and unscrupulous as
> the old-time slave drivers; under such circumstances immorality was

exactly as inevitable, and as prevalent, as it was under the system of chattel slavery. Things that were quite unspeakable went on there in the packing houses all the time, and were taken for granted by everybody; only they did not show, as in the old slavery times, because there was no difference in color between the master and slave.[42]

Even bracketing cases of physical violence and rape, the situation for working women was often dire. As Gloria Steinem put it, the behaviors that would come to be called sexual harassment were for years "just called 'life'" for working women, who were expected to deal uncomplainingly with whatever lewd teasing and advances their male supervisors cared to press upon them.[43]

Well into the twentieth century, the law made it very difficult for women to sustain complaints of unwanted sexual advances against employers.[44] Old notions that the public sphere was for men and that women should only occupy the private, domestic sphere were shored up by a legal apparatus that restricted women's ability to participate in the public sphere and refused to adjudicate claims of harm brought by women in the private sphere. Women who entered the public workforce basically did so at their own risk, as courts excluded them from protective labor laws while also deeming sexual coercion a private sphere matter. Reformers worked to address this issue, but it was not until the civil rights movement and second-wave feminism arose that opposition to men's aggressive and degrading sexual behavior in the workplace coalesced into a wider cause.

Eventually, the concept of sexual harassment crystallized in the spring of 1975 on the campus of Cornell University, where the first public "speak-out" on sexual harassment took place. A group of feminist activists and lawyers had rallied around the case of Carmita Wood, a Cornell employee who had quit her job after several instances of unwanted sexual groping by a distinguished professor but who was unable to receive unemployment benefits. Nearly three hundred women showed up to talk publicly about the workplace harassment they had endured, often without telling anyone and always without knowing how to make it stop without losing their jobs. As Susan Brownmiller later wrote, "The inappropriate male behavior in the workplace revealed at the speak-out ran the gamut: crude propositions to barter sex for employment, physical overtures and masturbatory displays, verbal abuse and hostile threats that appeared patently designed to intimidate a woman and drive her out of her job."[45] When a survey of the group was taken, 70 percent of the respondents claimed to have been sexually harassed at work, and 92 percent considered sexual harassment a serious problem.

A *New York Times* story on the event, headlined "Women Begin to Speak Out Against Sexual Harassment at Work," was syndicated nationally and, as one organizer later said, "put sexual harassment on the map." The *Wall Street Journal* followed a few months later with a front-page story on harassment, and other nationally circulated publications ran pieces over the next year.[46] In 1979, feminist lawyer Catharine MacKinnon published the landmark book *Sexual Harassment of Working Women*, which forcefully argued that such harassment was a form of sex discrimination based on both the sexual and the economic inequality of women, a theory that had a major impact on legal debates about sexual harassment law. As MacKinnon put it, "Economic power is to sexual harassment as physical force is to rape."[47] By the time the Hollywood comedy *Nine to Five* came out in 1980—starring Jane Fonda, Lily Tomlin, and an unforgettable Dolly Parton doing her best to stave off the advances of her male boss (and taking sweet revenge)—sexual harassment as a pervasive form of sex-based discrimination had seeped into the nation's consciousness.[48]

It also had begun to become part of its laws. By 1977, appellate decisions in three important court cases had affirmed the right of a woman to sue corporate employers for sexual harassment under Title VII of the 1964 Civil Rights Act. The EEOC, led by Eleanor Holmes Norton, took an active role in investigating sexual harassment claims, and businesses began doing more to monitor the behavior of supervisors in a position to harass subordinates. Under Norton, who had been appointed to the EEOC post by President Jimmy Carter, the EEOC in 1980 issued guidelines affirming sexual harassment to be a violation of section 703 of Title VII. The 1980 guidelines defined harassment on the basis of sex in the workplace as unwelcome sexual behavior that created a hostile working

environment or otherwise clearly affected the recipient's ability to perform on the job.[49]

The administration of President Ronald Reagan, who took office
shortly after the 1980 guidelines on sexual harassment were adopted,
initially opposed this approach to sexual harassment, if not the concept
itself, and sought to loosen the regulations. In the spring of 1981, the anti-
feminist activist Phyllis Schlafly, a Reagan ally, testified before a Senate committee reviewing new federal guidelines and suggested that men
only harassed women who were asking for it: "Sexual harassment is not
a problem for virtuous women, except in the rarest of case," she stated.
"Men hardly ever ask sexual favors of women from whom the certain answer is no. Virtuous women are seldom accosted." According to Schlafly, "some women have abandoned the commandments against adultery
and fornication": if harassed, that is, they got what they richly deserved.[50]
Clarence Thomas, while serving on Reagan's transition team to advise
him on civil rights, joined in a report arguing that in seeking to eliminate
"personal slights and sexual advances which contribute to an 'intimidat-
ing, hostile or offensive working environment,'" the guidelines aimed at
"a goal impossible to reach" and were certain to lead to "a barrage of triv-
ial complaints against employers around the nation." The report urged,
"Expenditure of the EEOC's limited resources in pursuit of this goal is
unwise."[51]

Six years later, the US Supreme Court ruled in the plaintiff's favor
in *Meritor Savings Bank v. Vinson*, a sexual harassment case brought
by Mechelle Vinson and the first ever such case heard by the nation's
highest court. By then, Thomas's office had shifted course, and Thomas
had pressed the US solicitor general to defend the EEOC guidelines in
a friend-of-the-court brief, landing Thomas on the winning side of the
court's ruling. The court's opinion, written and delivered by Justice William H. Rehnquist, cited the EEOC guidelines and agreed with the commission that sexual harassment is a violation of women's rights: "Without
question, when a supervisor sexually harasses a subordinate because of
the subordinate's sex, that supervisor 'discriminate[s]' on the basis of
sex," thereby violating Title VII; moreover, and against the petitioner's
argument that any damage to the plaintiff was more "psychological" in

nature and therefore not subject to this law, "the EEOC Guidelines fully support the view that harassment leading to noneconomic injury can violate Title VII." A "hostile or abusive work environment" based on sexual discrimination was enough to establish violation of the law.[52] Justices ruled 9–0 in favor of Vinson, a landmark decision that permanently enshrined protections against sexual harassment in the nation's legal code.

Five years later, the nation got its crash course in sexual harassment from the Thomas hearings. Some observers noted a grim irony: if any part of Hill's testimony was truthful, Thomas had been harassing her in the very same period that, as chair of the EEOC after succeeding Norton, he was the top federal government official charged with enforcing the laws against sexual harassment. That he had seemed lukewarm about those laws when he entered the office was not forgotten. But despite the Reagan-era EEOC's hesitation about sexual harassment litigation, during his 1991 confirmation hearings Thomas and his supporters wanted Americans to know that he—and they—strongly opposed sexual harassment and supported women's rights. The fact that, in this case, they trusted Thomas over Hill could not be taken as a policy position. Indeed, one Republican ally of Thomas's was at the very time of the hearings the chief sponsor of a civil rights bill (enacted later that year) that, among other things, extended protections against sexual harassment to new sectors of federal government employees and, more generally, expanded the options for litigating sexual harassment.[53]

In any event, the confirmation hearings were the jumping-off point not only for evolutions in sexual harassment law but also for renewed public interest in stories about victims. Hill's account had struck a deep chord in working women across the country, many if not most of whom could conjure memories of harassment on the job. Popular periodicals seized the moment: *People* magazine ran a profile of Hill in late October and, not to take sides, two weeks later did a feature on Clarence Thomas's wife, Virginia, that depicted her as a similar kind of victim. The short article on Hill was followed by several more pages of narratives and photos from half a dozen other women who spoke of their own experiences of sexual harassment. *People* also included interview segments with Catharine MacKinnon and linguist Deborah Tannen on harassment's definition and differing perceptions by men and women. The spread on Virginia Thomas shared the first article's theme of defeating the silence inflicted by shame and thus rising triumphantly over those who sought to hurt you—Hill's piece was titled "She Could Not Keep Silent," Thomas's "Breaking Silence"—and sought sympathy from the magazine's mostly female readers for all that she and her husband had endured during his ordeal. Thomas also told of being the victim of sexual harassment in the workplace. In this moment, to claim harassment and present oneself as a survivor of it was a badge of pride.[54]

Whether true or false, Anita Hill's testimony had an immediate impact. By many measures, women outraged by her treatment at the hands of the Senate Judiciary Committee provided the margin of victory in the 1992 election that swept Bill Clinton into the presidency alongside the new women legislators. In the same month as the election, claims of sexual assault and abuse were leveled by ten women against Senator Bob Packwood of Oregon, a situation that led to his resignation three years later. The number of sexual harassment claims filed with the EEOC and its state counterparts more than doubled between 1991 and 1998, going from 6,883 to 15,618. Hill, who never brought formal charges against her supervisor and, by her account, never intended to go public, wound up being a national symbol of the sexual harassment cause, albeit a deeply divisive one. Ironically, if her testimony helped get Bill Clinton into the White House, it also facilitated the conditions of his 1998 impeachment.

THAT IMPEACHMENT BEGAN, IN MANY ways, with Paula Corbin Jones, who grew up in tiny Lonoke, Arkansas, as the youngest daughter of a Nazarene preacher who forbade television, makeup, short dresses, and most other "outside world" influences. Jones barely graduated from high school and dropped out of a junior college in Little Rock before working several low-paying clerical and sales jobs. In the spring of 1991, she took a position at the Arkansas Industrial Development Commission (a state government organization) that paid her an annual salary of $10,270. Three years later, in May 1994, Jones filed a sexual harassment lawsuit against President William Jefferson Clinton that asked for $700,000 in damages. While she was alone with him in a Little Rock hotel room, she alleged, Clinton had fondled and attempted to kiss her before dropping his pants and requesting oral sex. Her accusations against him included unwanted touching, penile exposure, and threats against her if she did not acquiesce. Clinton's sexual escapades had made news since long before he won the presidency, but this brutish behavior was shocking stuff. Almost immediately, Jones became a household name across the nation.[55]

Jones's sexual harassment allegations against Clinton captured the energetic attention of conservative pundits, politicians, and religious leaders and inexorably shifted the public discourse around harassment claims. Conservatives plainly believed that Jones's case against Clinton was credible in a way that Hill's allegations against Thomas were not. There may have been evidence-based reasons for this assessment, but it was hardly clear that evidence was the driving engine of this shift. The conservative change of heart concerning sexual harassment seemed to reveal more than the progression in recognizing the seriousness of that crime. When "sexual harassment" was seen as a feminist—and therefore liberal—issue, few conservatives engaged sympathetically with the idea. Few, after all, had delved deeply into questioning whether Anita Hill might be telling the truth, and what should be done if she were. It was Paula Jones's case against Bill Clinton that opened the door for conservatives to express indignation on behalf of women against a man who would sexually harass them—especially if that harasser were a Democratic president of the United States. Clinton opponents seized on the image of the president as a sexual predator and wielded it for political advantage.

The Clinton sex scandals changed the way conservatives talked about sexual harassment and women's equality in the workplace. They had been no fans of feminism before, but now they were expressing outrage at the sexual mistreatment of a woman by a man with power over her job. Even some conservative women, who decried the hypocrisy of feminists who were turning cartwheels in their attempts to defend Clinton, rolled their eyes at the "double standards" of "the conservatives who discovered sexual harassment when they discovered Paula Jones." These latecomers were not very convincing in their sincerity, noted one contrarian female writer, who complained that such "posturing sends the message that harassment charges are easily used as a political weapon" while also making conservatives answerable for "the Blob-like spread of the sexual harassment concept," which had reached some bizarre and even "Orwellian" extremes.[56]

Conservative Christian legal organizations came out in support of Jones and pointed out the politics on the other side, criticizing the deafening silence of many feminist groups and leaders—a stark contrast to their earlier support of Anita Hill. In May 1994, shortly after Jones filed suit, the Christian Defense Coalition (not part of Reed's Christian Coalition) announced the creation of the Paula Jones Legal Defense Fund. Katie Mahoney, heading the Washington, DC, press conference that announced the new organization, adopted feminist rhetoric while taking on feminists directly:

> What women want is a chance to come forward and speak their piece without political bias or preconceived ideas because of someone's ideological view or support of the accused. We want to be afforded the opportunity to expose the pressure placed upon us behind closed doors, when no one else is looking, and expect to be taken seriously, not laughed at, not prejudged according to how we appear, and certainly not dismissed as ludicrous because someone in a position of power is being protected. . . . Where are the so-called feminist groups now?

Mahoney went on, "I find it very interesting now that the quote 'women's groups' are the ones who are hurting women, and I feel this very strongly." Feminist groups, by not standing up to defend Jones, were exposed as hypocrites and opportunists, Mahoney argued. Rita Schulte, who followed Mahoney on the stage, went further: "I'm a director of this fund because I believe Paula Jones deserves the same respect that was afforded to Anita Hill. This is not a liberal or conservative issue but one of fairness and justice to treat all women equally."[57] This was an intriguing shift: from a Schlafly-type argument that women brought harassment on themselves, religious conservatives were now appropriating feminist arguments about women's equality.

The Reverend Patrick Mahoney, national media director of the combative anti-abortion group Operation Rescue and the Christian Defense Coalition's executive director, spoke at the same press conference to call women's groups "shameful" in their refusal to entertain Jones's charges. Just as it was "a disgrace to all women" to call Hill "a pawn of the Left," so too it was to suggest Jones was "a pawn of the Right." Defending himself to a room of acerbic Beltway reporters, Mahoney fumed, "You know what my comment to the conservatives is? If you vilified Anita Hill, then you have no right to speak about Paula Jones—it's that simple! . . . But if you supported Anita Hill, then stand for Paula Jones!" One reporter asked Mahoney about his recent comment that President Clinton's policies were the most un-Christian of this century and possibly ever, a comment Mahoney defended and repeated ("from abortion to Haiti to Bosnia"). The righteous indignation was palpable, and Mahoney was adamant. However, reporters did not ask, nor did the speakers articulate, what was specifically Christian about Paula Jones's legal case above any other, enough to make her the special beneficiary of a Christian legal defense fund.[58] Arguably, the very framing of this group as a "Christian Defense" concern suggested that Jones might be a pawn. In other words, the Right responded to the Left's apparent hypocrisy by creating new Christian organizations that, directly or indirectly, had the aim of attacking a liberal president.

Other Christian groups varied in their responses to sexual harassment charges against Clinton. Robertson's Christian Broadcasting Network aired a television interview with Jones; the network's news director defended this decision to a reporter who expressed surprise, noting without apology that sometimes "news is tawdry."[59] Gilbert Davis, one of two Virginia lawyers who took over Jones's case from her first Arkansas attorney, worked with the Christian Action Network, a public advocacy and education group focused on protecting "America's religious and moral heritage" (based on "biblical principles, values, traditions and American ideals").[60] But the Christian Coalition's Reed claimed to take the high road and declined to get involved in the Jones case, writing, "I have always deliberately confined my criticism of Clinton to public policy issues, not his character or moral shortcomings."[61]

After three years of public legal wrangling and Jones's team upping the financial ante, in August 1997 Clinton's lawyers offered a settlement of $700,000; Jones rejected it because it did not include an apology from Clinton, who continued to deny that the incident Jones alleged had occurred. The lawyers who had been working for Jones, disagreeing with her decision not to settle, abruptly quit her case. At that point John W. Whitehead, head of the Rutherford Institute (TRI), a Christian legal association, stepped into the gap and took up Jones's suit.[62] His office offered to bankroll the case, and he phoned a lawyer friend in Dallas, Donovan Campbell, a TRI board member who had previously defended Texas's anti-sodomy law at the Supreme Court. Campbell agreed to represent Jones, and his firm hired a husband-and-wife private investigation team, Rick and Beverly Lambert, self-described "Christian conservatives" who came to see the case "not only as a job but also as a cause."[63] The cause, for all these Christian players, seemed to be that of toppling Clinton's presidency, viewed as ungodly and rotten to the core—not eradicating sexual harassment per se. This all may have been too tasteless for some Christian conservatives: when TRI took up Jones's case, one of the country's largest Christian broadcasting networks, Moody Broadcasting Network, canceled a program sponsored by the institute, allegedly because of its involvement.[64]

Whitehead was a graduate of the University of Arkansas Law School who, as a young radical, had once published an interview in the student newspaper with a young Professor Bill Clinton, who taught law there in the mid-1970s. Whitehead had converted to a particularly politicized version of Christianity under the tutelage of antimodernist thinkers including R. J. Rushdoony (who influentially argued that biblical law should replace civil law) and Francis Schaeffer. In 1982, Whitehead founded the Rutherford Institute as a nonprofit organization primarily dedicated to taking on cases for religious freedom. Having defended the religious activities of public school students, the right of employees to wear Christian symbols, the teaching of creation science, and the rights of abortion clinic protesters, he was already well-known in the Christian legal world before taking on the Jones case against President Clinton.[65] If there was a religious freedom claim to be made in this case, Whitehead would make it.

As Whitehead wrote, what Clinton allegedly did to Jones seemed "like a clear assault on Christ's view of how men and women should relate to each other in the workplace." He took the case on, he said, because, "I thought it would be a great opportunity for Christians to say, 'We really do care about sexual harassment in the workplace.' In my opinion, we were long overdue for the first foray of Christians into a significant sexual harassment case."[66] While critics accused him of being politically motivated, Whitehead responded, "The Jones case was not about politics. It was about a woman's fundamental human and constitutional right to be free from sexual harassment in the workplace." Lest anyone mistake the relevance of this issue to his own faith, Whitehead cited not only Jesus's respectful treatment of women—a topic he'd examined in his earlier book, *Women's Rights and the Law*—but also the fact that "all rights hang together." That is, "if one freedom can be violated, they all can be, including religious freedom."[67]

Fourteen years earlier, in fact, Whitehead had spent a semester teaching at the law school of Oral Roberts University, where he and his wife had developed a friendship with none other than Anita Hill. "We had several conversations about being a Christian in the legal profession," he recalled later, "and I found her to be a genuinely nice person." Hill was one of the few faculty members who engaged with his five children instead of ignoring them, and she treated them, he said, "with genuine affection." When she testified during the Thomas confirmation hearings, wrote Whitehead, "it was difficult for me to believe that Anita made up the charges she leveled at Thomas, and I believed her testimony." It was the more disappointing to him, then, that Hill remained publicly silent about the case of Paula Jones.[68]

Whitehead was lambasted from both the secular left and the Christian right for taking on Jones. Whatever his motivations for representing her, he was hardly the only conservative to take interest or to refocus attention on President Clinton's sexual misbehavior and possible sexual harassment. The Independent Women's Forum (IWF) spoke out frequently against what it called the "war of intimidation against Paula Jones in the courtroom of public opinion." Citing the promise by Clinton's attorney, Robert Bennett, to make Jones's sexual history an issue, for instance, IWF leaders condemned these "sexist and misogynistic tactics" and denounced feminists—or "the popular new women's sports event, the Feminist Flip-Flop"—for standing silently by their man instead of living up to their professed principles.[69] Ann Coulter, the lawyer and commentator, advised Paula Jones's first set of lawyers in their legal battle against Clinton and may have helped secure the Rutherford Institute's involvement. She made an even bigger name for herself with her first book, *High Crimes and Misdemeanors: The Case Against Bill Clinton*, which meticulously detailed the president's sexual misconduct as well as his cover-up lies and argued for his impeachment.[70] As Coulter angrily told a journalist, "We're shrugging about this guy using this woman like a dog. . . . He's behaving like some sort of sultan or tin-pot dictator."[71] The outrage expressed by conservative women and men toward Clinton could not have been stronger.

Conservative Christian fury toward Clinton's alleged harassment included disgust toward previously disclosed affairs and other sexual misdeeds. In the midst of the Jones scandal, explosive revelations of Clinton's affair with a White House intern, Monica Lewinsky, came to light and once more roiled the nation. Now the rage at Clinton focused not only on his exploitative behavior toward women but on the disgrace his behavior brought to the office of the presidency. Clinton had offended norms of public propriety with his undignified behavior—having an affair, conducting it in the White House, and lying about it as a sitting president. An Indiana-based conservative Christian talk show host and blogger named Mike Pence—a future state governor and US vice president—invoked this point in several pieces published during the Clinton years. In one, "Why Clinton Must Resign or Be Impeached," Pence quoted Herbert Hoover on the presidency representing "more than executive responsibility" and serving as "the inspiring supreme symbol of all that is highest in our American ideals."[72] In another, he argued that Jones's civil suit should have been deferred until he was out of the White House, which would have saved the nation from "the obscene, anti-marriage media circus" the case unleashed.[73]

In November 1998, Clinton and Jones reached an out-of-court agreement: Clinton would pay $850,000 but would neither apologize nor acknowledge wrongdoing. Both sides claimed victory.[74] Meanwhile, a recently released report that detailed a wide-ranging investigation of Clinton by independent counsel Kenneth Starr was about to exert a blockbuster impact on the sitting president's impeachment.

THE ACTS THAT PAULA JONES attributed to Clinton were far worse, ethically and legally, than anything Thomas allegedly said or did to Anita Hill. So if the same groups that avidly promoted Clarence Thomas's Supreme Court nomination—and worked to demolish Hill's standing as a means to that end—later worked as aggressively to defend Paula Jones against President Clinton, perhaps they simply saw clearer truth and greater injustice in the second case. Possibly their minds had been opened to the brutal realities often faced by working women on the job, exposed to crudeness of the most disgusting kind. Maybe they were just finally fed up with sexual harassment and the vulgar loutishness of entitled male bosses who thought they owned the world and every body in it.

Or maybe that's just religion, sex, and politics. On December 19, 1998, the US House of Representatives voted to impeach President Clinton on two charges: perjury and obstruction of justice. The winding path that led to this historic vote was plowed by Starr and included a multitude of alleged abuses by the president—including the failed land deal known as Whitewater, the firing of travel agents in the White House, alleged misappropriation of FBI files, and, above all, the sexual harassment case of Jones, which ended one month prior to the impeachment vote. It was through Starr's wide-ranging investigation that Lewinsky's office affair with Clinton came to light, thanks to the phone conversations Linda Tripp taped between her and Lewinsky and submitted to Starr; and it was Clinton's denial of that affair that paved the way to impeachment. Starr was the Texas-born son of a Church of Christ minister and, at this time, an active member of the independent evangelical McLean Bible Church. (He would go on to serve as the dean of Pepperdine University's law school and the president of the Southern Baptist Convention's Baylor University.) He oversaw the eponymous report that turned "the once clear line between public and private behavior" into "a big sloppy lipstick

President Bill Clinton addresses a 1998 White House prayer breakfast shortly after admitting to an "improper physical relationship" with Monica Lewinsky, in what became known as his "I Have Sinned" speech. *DAVID HUME KENNERLY/GETTY IMAGES.*

smear," in one journalist's words, by detailing the Clinton-Lewinsky affair "down to the kinkiest details."[75] The Far Right had succeeded in what had come to seem an obsession: presidential destruction and absolute humiliation.

The report and impeachment vote were salvos in the ongoing culture war over sex, and conservatives on the Far Right reveled in it. Richard John Neuhaus, the Catholic priest and editor of the conservative journal *First Things*, had advocated impeachment for the purification of the nation, calling for an "enormous emetic" that "would purge us." Robert Bork, the judge whose own nomination to the US Supreme Court had been destroyed by liberal and feminist groups, said an impeachment would be a good thing to "kill off the lax moral spirit of the sixties." The *National Review* wanted Clinton's impeachment as a cure to what editors decried as the "womanly 'sogginess' that pervades our culture and 'undermines masculine intractability that serves as a bulwark for republicanism.'" And Lamar Smith, a Republican congressman from Texas, advocated impeachment to "set an example for our children and grandchildren."[76] Or, as the *Wall Street Journal* editorial board mused, praising Starr for his persistence in going after Clinton despite the invective thrown his way for it, "Who better to bring Bill Clinton to justice than a hymn-singing son of a fundamentalist minister?"[77] In the end, Clinton survived to the end of his presidential term, as his 1999 Senate trial failed to garner the necessary two-thirds majority to convict and remove him from office. It had been a sordid spectacle, and the muted outcome stirred little emotion, mostly relief that all this was now history.

What remained of Clinton's sex scandals was less an increased awareness of sexual harassment than increased polarization among Americans who held conflicting views of the significance of his sexual behavior, depending on their political commitments. By the end of the 1990s, Americans were well aware that they were divided by two warring understandings of sexual morality that were profoundly politicized. The nation lacked a common understanding of sexual ethics and seemingly possessed virtually no shared language for discussing values. The one side had staked its claim on public propriety and traditional virtue, wedded to a desire to oppose a president who supported abortion rights and LGBT rights, at least moderately more than his conservative counterparts. The other side, averse to moral crusading on sexual matters, valued sexual freedom and a dividing line between private consensual behavior and public concern, wedded to support for a president and his feminist spouse who favored liberal causes. These were not consistently pure philosophies—there were hypocrisies, contradictions, and blind spots on both sides—but they offered genuine differences in overall priorities and worldviews. The broader war over Clinton, including but by no means limited to sexual harassment, revealed and continued to shape that divergence of worldviews extending to a whole range of gendered issues as they impinged on the political realm.

In the end, the Christian right successfully utilized the Clinton scandals to expand and solidify its power, leading up to the 2000 presidential election of George W. Bush, the first self-described evangelical Christian elected with the full backing of a mature religious right. But the election was extremely close: Bush actually lost the popular vote by a slim margin to his Democratic rival, Al Gore, and errors and irregularities in voting procedures in the state of Florida left the results in doubt for over a month before a Supreme Court decision determined the outcome. Liberals and progressives were incensed, but the Right had won, thanks in no small part to the mobilization of Christian conservatives spurred by sex.

CHAPTER 8

SAME-SEX MARRIAGE AND LGBT RIGHTS IN THE NEW MILLENNIUM

THE CLINTON IMPEACHMENT LAID BARE the diverging worldviews that divided American Christians, and more generally split the nation, at the end of the twentieth century. As the post-Clinton era dawned, the two camps remained political enemies on other issues as well— inevitably feminism, and notably abortion, which seemed the perennial focus of those religious conservatives who believed that abortion was murder and that outlawing it was of critical import to the country's moral health. A different issue fraught with its own conflict-laden history also loomed large both in the churches and in the wider culture during this period: the fight over homosexuality was reaching a crisis point and would soon crack apart still more of the adhesive feelings of trust and goodwill that had bound many together despite their differences.

Attitudes toward same-sex love and marriage underwent an interpretive sea change in the early years of the new century. Long habits of treating lesbian, gay, bisexual, and transgender (LGBT) people with scorn, contempt, and pity had been melting for some years prior to that, but the pace of change picked up rapidly during the Bush presidency. Television and movie depictions of LGBT characters expanded and grew popular with wide ranges of viewers. Parents and relatives of LGBT children progressively sloughed off the old shame and silence to stand up for their loved ones with pride. Anti-discrimination laws went from unthinkable impossibilities in the outlook of most citizens to justifiable if not indispensable and fundamental rights. Eventually, marriage between two people of the same sex became officially authorized, first state by state and, in 2015, for the entire nation.[1]

Growing numbers of Americans, including religious liberals and progressives, rejoiced at these changes in the legal, social, and cultural status of sexual minorities and adjusted their vocabularies to use the terminology preferred by queer people themselves. Many others, if not quite rejoicing, dutifully tolerated the social, political, and legal shifts around them and gradually came around to new contemporary realities and embodied identities. But outrage and resistance remained potent in certain quarters, most notably among vocal subsets of fundamentalists and some other conservative Christians—belying yet again any hope of genuine national unity or even modest rapprochement. Nowhere were national divisions over homosexuality deeper than in the church.

Those deep religious divisions faced a number of challenges, epitomized by the events surrounding a historic milestone in the Episcopal Church. In the spring of 2003, Episcopalians in the diocese of New Hampshire were facing the election of a new bishop. Four candidates were on the ballot, two women and two men. All were worthy; all had lengthy, impressive histories of serving the Episcopal Church. But unlike most ordinary diocesan elections, this was not a discreet affair watched mostly by lay and clerical insiders. As election day grew closer, throngs of reporters from the national press flocked to Concord, where the vote was to take place at St. Paul's Church. On June 7, the clergy and laity together speedily elected Gene Robinson, a Kentucky-born fifty-six-year-old divorced father of two grown daughters who had served thirty years as a priest. He was also the first openly gay and partnered man ever to win diocesan election to the office of bishop in the Episcopal Church.

Reactions to Robinson's election came fast and furious. Messages flooded diocesan offices, split between those who passionately applauded the election of Bishop Robinson and those who just as passionately denounced it. "There were those who felt that it was the worst *possible* thing that could happen to the church and those who saw it as *salvation*, the most redeeming thing the church could have done," said the election and

Bishop V. Gene Robinson speaks at a ceremonial
event that was part of the inaugural celebration
for President Barack Obama, 2009. *KEVIN MAZUR/
WIREIMAGE VIA GETTY IMAGES.*

transition chair some time later.[2] Virtually overnight, Robinson went from being a priest little-known beyond his own circles to the most famous Episcopal leader in the country and possibly the world. As he later put it, "On June 6 I was just Gene Robinson, on June 7 I'm elected, and on June 8 I'm heading to New York to be on Anderson Cooper and *The Today Show* with Matt Lauer."[3]

The next step toward the formalization of Robinson's appointment was to take place two months later, at the denomination's triennial General Convention, representing the leadership of the Episcopal Church across the nation. The country's lay and clergy representatives to the General Convention would be voting on whether this bishop-elect were "of such sufficiency in learning, of such soundness in the Faith, and of such godly character as to be able to exercise the Office of a Bishop to the honor of God and the edifying of the Church, and to be a wholesome example to the flock of Christ."[*] Since the church leadership and laity were divided in their views about the moral status of same-sex relationships, the result was in no way a foregone conclusion. The convention, held in Minneapolis over the course of nearly a week, was filled with public discussion both for and against Robinson's election. On August 5, the House of Bishops voted 62–43 (with two abstentions) in favor of his election, and he was consecrated to the office in early November.

Coming in the wake of widespread political, social, and religious conflict over homosexuality that had characterized recent decades, Robinson's election was momentous. That the Protestant denomination most closely associated with the nation's traditional small-c conservative elite would elect a gay man bishop was remarkable, most especially because it risked ecclesiastical rupture on a broad scale. Indeed, that rupture came swiftly: several ultra-conservative bishops, priests, and parishes renounced the US denomination to form a new ecclesiastical body—the Anglican Church in North America—and affiliate with the Global Anglican Future Conference, an international body that broke away from the worldwide Anglican Communion in 2008; a smaller number of departing Episcopalians joined the Roman Catholic Church, whose stance against same-sex relationships was unwavering. This entire falling-out reflected other acute rifts across American Christianity, as various Protestant organizations and denominations faced internal divisions and departures over homosexuality. Opposing sides coalesced their respective forces. And as the LGBT rights movement progressively won victory after victory, its staunchest foes—representatives of the Christian right—stoked fear about the future of America in a bid to stem the tide.

By the time the *Obergefell v. Hodges* decision legalized same-sex marriage across the land, American Christianity seemed to have split into two oppositional, mutually hostile faiths. Christianity had never been a unified tradition within the United States, of course—one could make the case for ten or fifty or five hundred different versions of Christian affiliation, depending on different criteria of belief and belonging. But this split inside the nation's largest religious tradition felt monumental precisely because the two sides fought against each other's worldview so bitterly, reading wholly different values and commitments in the tradition itself. The Christian right was far larger than its progressive counterpart, but the progressives were in good company with a whole host of other groups, including many Jews and the majority of secularists. However one parsed it, sex had torn American Christianity asunder into enemy faiths.

VICKY GENE ROBINSON GREW UP in rural Kentucky, the child of to-bacco sharecroppers. The family home had no running water or indoor plumbing. He was a faithful member of Bethany Christian Church (Disciples of Christ), and his upbringing was "steeped in and nourished by a constant study of Scripture." By his own telling, that nourishment went deep: "My greatest desire was to lead a Christ-centered life."[5]

From an early age and continuing into adolescence, young Gene felt inwardly troubled, as he faced "a growing self-understanding that I was different—and not in a positive way." As a teen, he realized that he was not aroused by things such as naked photos of women in *Playboy* magazine, and he also recognized that it would be very uncomfortable, possibly even dangerous, to admit what he was feeling instead. In the 1950s, he felt there was only one option, and he took it: "I pretended to be someone I was not." Having learned from his religious upbringing that homosexuality was "repugnant to God" and the homosexual person an "abomination," this deeply religious boy found the possibility that he fit such a category to be "an almost unbearable possibility." He desperately prayed that he was not truly *one of those homosexuals*, as he thought anxiously of such people, and he prayed too that if he actually were that kind of man, God would change him.[6]

Robinson attended the University of the South, an Episcopal college in Sewanee, Tennessee, on a four-year full scholarship. While there, he was confirmed in the Episcopal Church and began to feel a call to ordination in the priesthood. By 1969, the year he graduated from college and headed to General Theological Seminary in New York, he knew beyond all doubt that he was attracted to men, and he despised himself for it. He attempted to get "cured" from this ostensible affliction and hoped that he would be able successfully to marry a woman and have a family. He did meet a woman for whom he developed loving feelings, and as their relationship deepened, he confessed to her his past relationships with men and his ardent hope that he had changed.[7]

They went through with the marriage in 1972, and after Robinson left his first parish ministerial position, they worked closely together for some years, running a Christian conference and retreat center in New Hampshire and having two daughters before finding the marriage untenable. While he loved his wife and the family they had created, Robinson's longing for men and for a male partner intensified; through extensive therapy and open communication with his wife, he came to know that "'gay' was who I was, not just what I was drawn to do."[8] The book that "turned the key" for him and gave him the courage to come out was *Embracing the Exile: Healing Journeys for Gay Christians*, a book that told of one man's journey toward knowing that his sexual orientation made him no less worthy to God than any straight person. It felt to Robinson that the book was written directly for him: "For the first time, not only did I think that my sexuality and my faith could exist together but that they *must*, that I simply could not go on [living a lie]."[9] He decided he needed to end his marriage but worried that his religious vocation might also be over, believing that while he would still be able to attend church worship services as a congregant, the church's moral disapproval of homosexuality meant "I could certainly not function as a priest." This anticipated loss was frightening, yet he felt he had no choice but to be truthful and live "a life of authenticity," as his sermons regularly exhorted congregants to do. Keeping his sexuality secret had become indefensible.[10]

In 1986 Robinson and his wife divorced amicably. They brought a priest to the judge's quarters for the divorce decree and then, still with the priest, held a religious service together to mourn the ending of their marriage, to pray for and forgive one another, and to commit their cooperative dedication to their daughters, whom they would jointly raise. "Somehow," he later wrote, "we had managed to end our marriage in a loving way and not just slink away from God under cloak of night."[11] Robinson's former wife remarried, and Robinson met and fell in love with a man, Mark Andrew, who would become his partner of more than twenty-five years. Raised by two sets of parents who cooperated well with each other, the daughters remained close to both.

Contrary to his expectations, coming out as gay did not mean the end of Robinson's ministry. Instead, he began to work half-time for the bishop and the rest of the time as a ministry coordinator for the seven Episcopal dioceses in New England. Within two years, he had a full-time job as canon to the ordinary, the chief assistant to the New Hampshire bishop. He "never, from that point on, never made a secret of my being gay," he later recalled. Over the next few years, most everyone with whom he worked or who was connected to the Episcopal Church in that region came to know about his sexuality, and while some talked to him about the problem they had with it, his work as a priest never faltered.[12] It was a mark of real openness in the church that Robinson was able to stay on working within it despite his open sexuality.

Major changes were sweeping the nation as he moved into this new life stage, and Robinson, who was keen to see same-sex relationships normalized in American society and the law as well as the church, traveled the path of ferocious conflict that characterized the nation's struggle with homosexuality in these years. America's clash over LGBT rights and legal same-sex marriage was the larger context for what was occurring in churches, where the divisions were deepest. The Episcopal Church was one of many religious bodies that struggled over homosexuality for years, as more conservative priests and congregations broke their ties with leaders who looked to be liberalizing Christian tradition. These splits exemplified the gulf that had come to separate two oppositional forces within American Christianity, and the politics that went with them.

SAME-SEX LOVE, SEX, AND INTIMATE relationships did not, of course, suddenly appear out of nowhere in the twentieth century, however much some detractors may have reckoned that the case. In America, laws against same-sex eroticism guided the norms of the English Puritan settlers, whatever breaches occurred, and same-sex unions were rendered unthinkable to many if not most Anglo-Protestants in that period. Well before that, however, early European settlers and missionaries traveling to America wrote of witnessing both male and female same-sex couples among indigenous people. Among Anglo-Americans there were examples of "female husbands," cross-dressing women who lived in marriage-like relationships; numerous published accounts of such stories included repeated comments that neighbors, relatives, and others did not recoil at the relationship under scrutiny but rather accepted it as, one relative put it, a bond "no less sacred to them than the tie of marriage."[13] Up through World War I, passionate romantic friendships between women were common and mostly considered innocent and nonthreatening by others; these emotional bonds continued even after women married men, and though they often included some measure of physical affection, so long as they did not test the hierarchical order of marriage, they were within acceptable limits.

Views toward male same-sex partnerships were less positive, as these uncomfortably suggested practices of sodomy. The leader whom many later wished to claim as the nation's first gay US president—James Buchanan, a lifelong bachelor who served in that office from 1857 to 1861—was so close to his live-in male companion, Alabama senator William Rufus King, that political rivals openly mocked the pair, calling King "Mrs. Buchanan," "Buchanan's wife," "Miss Nancy," and more. Ridicule aside, police raids on spaces where men congregated with one another for companionship frequently uncovered male relationships described in marital terms.[14]

The language of marriage, and the staging of both male and female same-sex weddings, increased in the twentieth century, as queer subcultures flourished and spread across the United States. Partnerships between two women—nicknamed the Boston marriage—were not uncommon in affluent, educated circles, even if actual state-sanctioned marriages remained impossible. Sailors in the US Navy and commercial sailors alike were part of a maritime culture that gave limited accommodation to same-sex companions, including shipboard wedding ceremonies that mirrored those of heterosexual unions. As some sea personnel wryly quipped, "nothing's queer once you've left the pier." Army weddings during World War II—womanless weddings, that is—were part of a larger military domain that also celebrated drag shows, as did men's colleges and other all-male spaces. White and African American lesbian couples also partook of weddings, which were popular in Harlem in the 1920s and 1930s. And while most religious leaders of that era may have balked at this specter suggestive of homosexuality, there were occasional exceptions. For instance, Mabel Hampton, a lesbian entertainer in New York, later described to an interviewer a black gay minister who would marry male and female same-sex couples in services "just like the regular," down to the traditional vows.[15]

The relationship between efforts to improve the lot of LGBT people, on the one hand, and to advocate for something as radical-sounding as same-sex marriage, on the other, was contested within the community itself. When in 1953 the nation's first openly published and widely circulated gay periodical—ONE Magazine, the young brainchild of an influential "homophile" organization called the Mattachine Society—displayed the title "Homosexual Marriage?," it reaped consternation not only among the Los Angeles postal authorities, which seized the issue briefly before releasing it, but among readers critical of the feature essay arguing that the emergent movement should concern itself more intently with the legalization of "homosexual marriage." The author's chief rationale pertained to equality and respectability, as he noted that the push for marriage would enhance public relations for this scorned class, assuring critics that gays "are sincere in wanting respect and dignity!"[16] Reader responses in the next issue were critical: one writer complained of the effort to constrain gay people with more rules and restrictions, while another resisted respectability another way, calling himself "an abnormal whose subnormality seems permanent" and who sought not acceptance for purported normalcy but rather "simple justice as what I am."[17] Another issue published ten years later with a lead essay titled "Let's Push Homophile Marriage," which also criticized promiscuous bar cruising, reaped similar reactions by readers who wrote that the piece "just stinks!" and excoriated ONE's staff for printing a piece by a "humdrum" and narrow-minded writer who drearily aspired "to copy heterosexual life."[18]

Despite marriage's appeal to some gays, lesbians, and bisexuals, there was little large-scale effort to prioritize its legalization. To many, marriage felt conservative, unadventurous, and unappealing. Like many straight men and women who were living by much loosened sexual rules, men and women in the queer community wanted more freedom, not more constraint. Some would doubtless chuckle knowingly at the pointed question Howard Moody used in counseling premarital couples: "Why do you want to get married and spoil a beautiful friendship?"[19]

More importantly, the religious consensus regarding homosexuality's sinfulness remained powerful in the wider culture and the nation's social and legal institutions, so that openly gay people still faced abundant discrimination in the 1960s, even criminalization. Illinois in 1961 had been the first state in the union to repeal its anti-sodomy law, and such laws stayed on the books in most states for years. The American Psychiatric Association deemed homosexuality a mental disorder until 1973. At risk for consensual sex acts performed in the privacy of their own homes, and deemed by society to be mentally disturbed, those identifying as homosexual reasonably did not see marriage as an urgent matter. After a police raid set off the Stonewall riots in 1969, catalyzing and rapidly expanding the modern LGBT rights movement, the fight for equality and justice for sexual minorities emphasized pride and in-your-face revolutionary politics. A lot of people in these circles were not merely indifferent to marriage; they detested it. As activists in the Gay Liberation Front put it shortly after Stonewall, the institution was "one of the most insidious and basic sustainers of the system" and the family "the microcosm of oppression." Same-sex marriage was still marriage, so it could only be "classed as reactionary."[20] Radical lesbians favored the elimination of marriage altogether, while other sex radicals called for an expansion of marriage beyond monogamy, to include all manner of polyamorous relationships. In its 1972 list of reform demands, the National Coalition of Gay Organizations included the repeal of all marriage laws that constrained the sex or number of individuals who could enter into an official marriage. The group also called for the expansion of the legal benefits accorded to married persons to all persons who cohabit, apart from the sex or numbers of people involved.

But for those who did prioritize marriage rights for same-sex couples, this priority was often closely linked to religious faith. Some didn't care if was called "marriage" or not. For example, New York's Church of the Beloved Disciple was a predominantly gay congregation whose priest was openly performing religious ceremonies of "holy union" for same-sex couples. As Father Clement stated to one interviewer, "We don't use the term marriage because that implies a legal concept and a marriage certificate through the Bureau of Vital Statistics, and we are interested in a church concept which is spiritual: people pledging their love together in the eyes of God and asking the blessing of God."[21] This was a religious rite that had nothing to do with the state; government officials, allies believed, had no right to interfere. The right to solemnize partnerships outside the reach of the state mattered, and in 1971 the Gay Activists Alliance staged a protest inside the New York Marriage License Bureau, along with an engagement party for same-sex couples; this was to protest the threat by the city clerk to take legal action against the Church of the Beloved Disciple for its ceremonies.

The state-sanctioned institution of marriage meant a great deal more to some others who tried to enter into it, and changes to support that effort were clearly underway in some progressive precincts of Christianity. In 1970, Richard John Baker and James Michael McConnell asked the Catholic priest in charge of the University of Minnesota's Newman Center if he believed Jesus would approve of a loving union between two people of the same sex; the priest said yes. Overjoyed, the two men acquired wedding rings, planned a religious wedding ceremony, and applied for a marriage license. County officials denied their request precisely because they were both men. They filed suit, arguing that to limit marriage to different-sex couples violated several constitutional rights; the trial court dismissed these claims. The following year, their appeal went to the Minnesota Supreme Court, whose justices treated them coldly at best—one contemptuously swiveled his chair around to turn his back on their lawyer—and affirmed the trial court's dismissal, declaring, "The institution of marriage as a union of man and woman, uniquely involving the procreation and rearing of children, is as old as the book of Genesis."[22] The couple's appeal to the US Supreme Court was no more successful:

in 1972, the high court dismissed it in a single sentence, noting the case's lack of an actual federal question. In effect, this dismissal set a governing precedent on marriage—explicitly, that states should develop their own marriage laws—that would last for years.[23]

While this case wound through the courts, Baker and McConnell obtained a license in another county, and a Methodist minister officiated at their wedding in 1971. To many thereafter, that event was the first legal same-sex marriage in the United States, and a long-lived one: forty-four years later, the couple was still together. Few accepted its legality at the time, although the two men did receive national fame, appearing as "The Homosexual Couple" in a *Look* magazine issue devoted to "The American Family" as well as on television talk shows hosted by Phil Donahue and David Susskind. Their union failed to generate much of a pro-same-sex-marriage movement, however, and changed very few heterosexual minds about the purportedly commonsense view of the matrimonial norm (one man and one woman).[24]

Intermittent attempts at securing marriage rights prompted the beginnings of legislative restriction. In 1970, Tracy Knight and Marjorie Jones's request for a marriage license in Kentucky earned an irate response from the district attorney, who said such a union represented "the pure pursuit of hedonistic and sexual pleasure." In more apocalyptic terms, the county clerk testified that a marriage between two women would "lead to a breakdown in the sanctity of government," endanger the morality of the whole nation, and potentially "spread all over the world." This couple, too, sued and lost, the Kentucky Supreme Court in 1973 holding that "marriage has always been considered as the union of a man and a woman" and that the case gave no basis for changing that.[25] That same year, Maryland legislators took matters into their own hands and enacted a law banning same-sex marriage. Virginia followed suit two years later, and more states followed.

In 1975, the county clerk in Boulder, Colorado, supplied marriage licenses to several same-sex couples—subjecting herself to vicious hate mail and death threats—until the state's attorney general stopped her, releasing a legal opinion that voided any marriages performed under those licenses. One couple married during that time was Richard

A gay couple appears to celebrate their union in 1976, decades before same-sex marriage became legal. *JACK MITCHELL/GETTY IMAGES.*

Adams, a US citizen, and his Australian partner, Tony Sullivan. After the ceremony, Adams immediately sought a green card to validate the immigration rights accorded to spouses of American citizens; the US Department of Justice's Immigration and Naturalization Service denied the request, writing to Adams, "You have failed to establish that a bona fide marital relationship can exist between two faggots." Adams sued the US government and lost on familiar grounds, a federal judge noting in the court's 1982 decision that civil law took its conceptions of sex from ecclesiastical law, and the "vehement condemnations in the scriptures" of "all homosexual relationships" meant that the law could not sanction any such marriage.[26] Minnesota, Kentucky, Colorado, and more: this string of negative decisions effectively closed the early push to legalize same-sex civil marriage.

Marriage still had meaning to people of faith such as John Fortunato and Wayne Schwandt, whose interest in the institution was more
spiritual than legal. When they decided to celebrate their loving commitment in 1976, they were dedicated parishioners of an Episcopal church
in Washington, DC, St. Stephen and the Incarnation. Fortunato was a
former Carmelite brother who had once been a candidate for the Roman
Catholic priesthood, while Schwandt was a graduate of Wesley Theological Seminary who hoped to be ordained to the Episcopal priesthood; both, in other words, were devoted to their faith and the Christian
church, as well as to each other. They felt theirs to be a sacred love, "a
gift—from God," as Fortunato later wrote, and they wanted a liturgical
ceremony of public blessing to establish it as a "holy union." The rector,
who months earlier had been reprimanded by an ecclesiastical court for
sanctioning a woman to celebrate communion in the church, wholeheart-
edly agreed. The bishop coadjutor of Washington, however, issued his
strong disapproval of the ceremony and threatened to cut off all diocesan
funds to the church for the next fiscal year. The ceremony was moved
from St. Stephen to a Congregational church, and, with Schwandt's
young son at their side and their rector officiating, took place on November 21.[27] Six years later, Fortunato would write the book for gay Christians that would redirect and transform Gene Robinson's life, *Embracing
the Exile*. And in this same era, New York's ever progressive Judson Memorial Church, with Howard Moody still presiding, adopted a committee report calling for "a new rite of passage . . . or a new rite of sustenance"
to celebrate same-sex couples who wanted such a wedding-like ceremony,
a sign of the church's blessing of same-sex committed relationships and
an effort to "redeem the church's history of anti-homosexual bias."[28]

All of these accounts suggest that, while marriage meant something
profound and even sacred for many couples in the 1970s, there was not
sufficient support either in the gay activist world or the broader US populace to pursue its legalization. Some advocates grew frustrated with
such apathy. Baker and McConnell, for instance, took heat from gay activist leaders for being "crazies" who would not make political compro-
mises; disillusioned, at the end of the decade they withdrew from public
life and lived quietly in Minneapolis.[29] But portents of the future could be

seen in the detailed pro-same-sex-marriage thesis written by a Harvard Law School student named Evan Wolfson, "Samesex Marriage and Morality: The Human Rights Vision of the Constitution." Wolfson would spend his career focused on LGBT rights and marriage, founding the National Freedom to Marry Coalition and becoming a chief architect of the movement that ultimately overcame all legal barriers to same-sex marriage across the nation.[30]

Tragically, what would come to be known as the AIDS epidemic was imperceptibly gestating in the mid to late 1970s; as it erupted into view, shocking the LGBT community and the wider world in the early 1980s, political activists turned their attention to the disease and those afflicted, demanding a more effective political and medical response than what President Ronald Reagan's administration was offering. With gay and bisexual men experiencing dire health problems, suffering unbearable pain, and dying in grievous numbers, it could seem ludicrous to think about fighting for such a bourgeois luxury as same-sex marriage.

Many whose lives were touched by AIDS were faced with a more prosaic problem: the lack of inheritance and death benefits for surviving partners of the dead. Over and over, men who nursed and cared for their ailing lovers through this gruesome illness to certain death found themselves legally unentitled to any property, pensions, or life insurance their partners would have wished for them to have. Parents, siblings, and other family members who may have shunned a gay relative in life could take all of his possessions in death; so said the law. Legal changes were necessary to correct this wrong—the question was what changes would best serve their beneficiaries and give them legal standing.

By the end of the 1980s, the debate over same-sex marriage received new life. Its reemergence was aided by several city and state law changes that gave some benefits to unmarried partners, as well as by European examples—above all, Denmark's passage of a law allowing same-sex couples to unite in "registered partnerships" and receive many rights enjoyed by married couples. In July 1989, the New York Court of Appeals ruled that, regardless of gender, a couple who had lived together ten years could be defined as a "family" under the rent-control regulations there. The following month, the prominent writer Andrew Sullivan published a widely read essay in the *New Republic* that made a conservative case for same-sex marriage as superior to the concept of "domestic partnerships" on several grounds. Like different-sex marriage, same-sex marriage would bestow societal approval upon committed couples and promote "social cohesion, emotional security, and economic prudence" and could also "help nurture children."[31] Shortly thereafter, attendees at the State Bar Association of California's annual convention passed a resolution advocating the recognition of marriage between same-sex partners, with all the "very substantial benefits" that heterosexual married couples had. Paula Ettelbrick, the legal director of the Lambda Legal Defense and Education Fund and a vocal critic of institutional marriage, somewhat hyperbolically (and perhaps sullenly) attributed the revival of the debate over marriage to "well meaning straight people" more than members of the LGBT community. Nevertheless, it is true that growing numbers of straight allies were taking part in the LGBT rights movement, including marriage.[32]

As the wider movement for LGBT rights gathered steam in the post-Stonewall years, and as LGBT people came to be more visible to those outside those communities, many prominent conservative religious leaders began speaking more directly about homosexuality and its potential to destroy the United States. To them, it seemed clear that the movement was one more arm of the secular humanist campaign to destabilize the nuclear family, weaken male authority, and de-Christianize the nation. Its impact urgently needed to be contained.

In 1975, the Sacred Congregation for the Doctrine of the Faith—the body of the Roman Catholic Church charged with transmitting and preserving Catholic doctrine—issued *Persona Humana*, a declaration of the church's teachings on sexuality and sexual ethics. Describing the current era as one in which "the corruption of morals has increased" and where there was an "unbridled exaltation of sex," the document condemned all manner of "licentious hedonism" infecting the contemporary world. Reminding Catholics that the true meaning of the sexual function was to be found only in "true marriage" and that sexual acts must "preserve the full sense of mutual self-giving and human procreation" within that marriage, the text affirmed the church's unyielding stance against premarital sex, homosexual relations, and masturbation. The latter two categories were "intrinsically disordered," while homosexual sex was a "serious depravity" whether same-sex orientation was a matter of a "pathological constitution" or a state that was "transitory or at least not incurable." None of this was new teaching, as the document emphasized; it was simply a reiteration and a moral warning to Catholics to remain sexually pure within an increasingly corrupt world.[33]

Conservative Protestant leaders and spokespersons likewise sought to shore up the rules on sexuality, and often in much more aggressive and colorful terms. The 12.7-million-member Southern Baptist Convention, in the throes of a bitter struggle between fundamentalists and the more liberal moderates, declared at its 1976 annual convention that "homosexuality is a sin" and asserted the importance of keeping gay people out of the clergy—indeed, out of church employment more generally. The winning resolution, this denomination's first official statement on homosexuality, also urged local congregations not to "afford the practice of homosexuality any degree of approval." While some clergy and messengers attempted to include a final paragraph exhorting "Christian compassion" for all people "whatever their lifestyle," that passage was removed.[34]

In the same year, Tim and Beverly LaHaye's best-selling *The Act of Marriage*—the first evangelical sex manual—proclaimed from the start that sexual intercourse was a "sacred experience" that was "shared uniquely by a husband and wife in the privacy of their love." Masturbation, though not technically sinful (their view differed from the Catholic position on this issue), was problematic and a "psychologically damaging habit." Premarital sex was unquestionably sinful but, with repentance, could be forgiven. Homosexuality was another thing altogether, an "abnormal, deviant practice" that was "increasingly rampant in the world." That proliferation was intentional, the LaHayes taught: "Every homosexual is potentially an evangelist of homosexuality, capable of perverting many young people to his sinful way of life." It was "propaganda" from atheistic humanists and liberal institutions such as higher education and the entertainment industry that was pushing social acceptance of gay people—and winning. The passage of laws in several states that were "overturning centuries of opposition to homosexuality" was an important factor in allowing gay people "to multiply tragically." Christians needed to stop being passive and "encourage lawmakers to enact laws against this trend."[35] As they made the battle against gay rights the very center of their politics, the LaHayes' message presaged the coming surge of Christian literature and other materials that called Christians to mobilize politically by identifying the LGBT rights movement as a threat to the nation.[36] That opposition to homosexuality and support for a traditionalist gender hierarchy went together was clear: in another best-selling book published around the same time, Beverly LaHaye admonished her female readers to remember the divine order in which a Christian woman must "die to oneself" and submit to her husband's authority.[37]

In 1977, the popular entertainer Anita Bryant further activated Christian opponents of gay rights with her campaign to repeal an ordinance in her home seat of Dade County, Florida, that outlawed discrimination on the basis of sexual orientation in the arenas of housing, employment, and public accommodation. Heading an alliance comprised predominantly of conservative Protestants and Catholics called Save Our Children, Bryant was tireless in describing "militant homosexuals" as sick deviants bent on recruiting children and teens into their immoral and disgusting lifestyle. Occasional insinuations of even more wicked behavior were dramatic: the fundamentalist leader Jerry Falwell, a staunch opponent of gay rights, appeared at a rally shortly before the referendum took place and told the crowd gathered that "so-called gay folks would just as soon kill you as look at you."[38] On the date of the June vote, the community voted overwhelmingly by a 2–1 ratio to repeal the ordinance. Save Our Children campaigns developed in other locales.[39] Delegates to the Southern Baptist Convention annual meeting, meanwhile, voted to adopt a resolution commending Bryant for her "courageous stand against the evils inherent in homosexuality."[40]

For traditionalist Christians like these, the prospect of socially approved homosexuality was outrageous and alarming because it cast the entire nation in danger. One of their chief concerns was plainly the authority of the Bible and of the one true God who ruled over the world: if the Bible, as God's Word, spoke clearly against homosexuality and the

Christian singer and anti-gay activist Anita
Bryant condemns a local gay rights ordinance
on behalf of her group Save Our Children, 1977.
ASSOCIATED PRESS.

practice of sodomy, as these believers felt certain it did, then to resist
this clear teaching was, ipso facto, nothing less than a spurning of God
and a wholesale rejection of God's plan for humanity. This was not a justice issue, or an equal rights issue, or a compassion issue; the matter was
far deeper, and far greater, than those human inventions. The issue was
obedience to core teachings that had been passed down for thousands of
years—humble compliance with the will of God, whatever one's personal
preference.

All this time, city councils and state legislatures were battling over
nondiscrimination laws like the one in Miami. When San Francisco
passed a civil rights bill outlawing sexual orientation discrimination, a
state senator sponsored Proposition 6, a measure to fire any teacher or
public school employee who openly supported gay rights; California voters rejected the measure by over a million votes. Weeks later, California's

best known gay rights activist—Harvey Milk, the sponsor of the San Francisco anti-discrimination bill—was assassinated, angering and invigorating activists in the gay rights movement and mobilizing others to confront the prejudice and vicious hate facing gay Americans. The following year, the National March on Washington for Lesbian and Gay Rights attracted an estimated seventy-five thousand supporters, the largest political gathering ever organized in support of gay rights. Successes by Christian right leaders had served to galvanize the gay rights movement, leading to gradual expansion of the legal rights accorded to gays, lesbians, and bisexuals.

The more these rights expanded, the more some ultra-conservative Christian constituencies raged. Tim LaHaye's 1978 book, *The Unhappy Gays: What Everyone Should Know About Homosexuality*, expressed the views of many in that constituency: homosexuals were "self-indulgent, self-centered, undisciplined" people, the secular opposites of Christians—they caused heartache to good people around them, deceived others, despised women, lived only for sex, and skillfully recruited others into the fold. Homosexuality was such a "blight on humanity" and homosexuals themselves such immoral people that, LaHaye wrote, many parents "would prefer the death of their child to his adopting the unhappy wretchedness of homosexuality."[41] Certainly both LaHayes understood the links between equal rights for women and equal rights for gay people that would include marriage; as Beverly wrote, "lesbians, homosexual men, and feminists" were in cahoots to nullify the traditional definition of a family in order to secure "the legal right to live their perverted lifestyle protected by the laws of the land."[42]

As AIDS burst into public view in the early 1980s, some Christian leaders saw the epidemic as God's righteous judgment. In the epidemic's early, harrowing years, little was known about the cause or treatment of this mysterious virus, only that it was mostly hitting gay and bisexual men, who were dying in droves. It looked as if sexual promiscuity, routinely condemned in Christian circles, had finally wreaked its long predicted catastrophe on American civilization. Or as Falwell put it, "AIDS is not just God's punishment for homosexuals. It is God's punishment for the society that tolerates homosexuals."[43] In the panic surrounding the disease, some hospitals refused to treat infected patients, funeral home directors were afraid of embalming their bodies, and many dentists would not see gay men even for a routine teeth cleaning. The epidemic itself fired up further hatred of the LGBT community, and gay rights organizations reported increased homophobia, discrimination, and attacks on gay people. Ryan White, a teenage hemophiliac who contracted HIV from a blood transfusion, was banned from his Indiana middle school and mercilessly shunned by local citizens, people on the street reportedly shouting, "We know you're queer," at him on a regular basis. The toleration of gay people, with their supposed lifestyle of disorderly and unrestrained sex, seemed to have brought America under siege, and these swaths of conservative Christians were determined to shift course.[44] Repeated talk that the United States was under siege generated widespread fear and anger that had material effects: in the mid-1980s, LGBT rights and AIDS organizations testified before Congress about rising anti-gay violence at local, state, and national levels.

In 1986, the fundamentalist leader David Noebel coauthored one of the most infamous anti-gay manifestos published in the United States, *Special Report: AIDS*, which was revised and expanded in 1987. Summit Ministries distributed both versions of the book, each filled with so-called research compiled by Paul Cameron of the Family Research Institute and listing as a third coauthor the white supremacist Wayne C. Lutton.[45] Patrick Buchanan, then the White House director of communications in the Reagan administration, praised the book in a back-cover blurb, affirming, "In a healthy society, [homosexuality] will be contained, segregated, controlled and stigmatized." The book opened by telling readers that AIDS "has the potential of destroying our society" and condemned the "lobbying by homosexual medical activists" who sought greater help for the diseased while protecting licentious behavior. Deriding liberals for efforts to shield gay people and present "a positive view of homosexuality," the authors' position was this: "Homosexuals should cease homosexual conduct, become celibate or change to heterosexuality; the homosexual subculture should be suppressed by being declared illegal under state sodomy laws." The situation was so dire, in fact, that for the sake of public health and America's very survival, gay people should be detained in holding camps similar to those used for Japanese Americans during World War II.[46]

The book's organization into fifty-two "Recommendations" urged a return to the Bible and the godly model of gender complementarity in which women submit to male authority; a heightened suspicion of the "pro-homosexual news media" and entertainment industries; rejection of the civil rights claims of gay people in such arenas as housing, health insurance, classroom hiring, and adoption; the enforcement and expansion of state laws criminalizing sodomy; denial of US citizenship to "all alien homosexuals and sexual deviates" and deportation of any aliens found to have AIDS; and the testing of all homosexuals for AIDS every thirty days, with AIDS-positive persons quarantined from the public and forced to disclose their AIDS status in health-care cards and driver's licenses. As recommendation forty-two more or less summarized, "Homosexuals are advised to return quietly and hastily to their closets and cease all homosexual activity." But even these recommendations might not be enough, the authors reflected. Hence, "we may have to think of forcefully exiling all AIDS-carriers and sexually active homosexuals who feel they must continue to practice 'the gay life.'" Detention, quarantine, and deportation: rapid and final action was essential.[47]

These forms of anti-gay messaging and the activism that went with them continued into the 1990s and beyond, as the Christian right continued to battle the loosening of anti-gay laws and cultural attitudes. After the Hawaii Supreme Court issued a 1993 ruling that the state marriage law did not limit marriage to male-female couples, the legislature changed the marriage law to institute such a limit. Supporters of traditional marriage around the country got the drift. The Christian right called for marriage protection laws, and in 1996 President Clinton signed the Defense of Marriage Act (DOMA), which stipulated that no state rejecting same-sex marriage was required to recognize same-sex marriages performed in other states and defined marriage at the federal level as restricted to a union between one man and one woman, thus denying federal benefits to partners in a same-sex marriage. Given the pressure already exerted on Clinton by Christian right leaders—the Paula Jones lawsuit had been filed two years earlier and was a heavy weight on his presidency at this time—it was significant that Clinton, who had been elected as a supporter of gay rights, felt the need to sign DOMA and thus stem the fury stirred up by the Hawaii case. Once again, the predominant religious voices carrying political heft appeared to be conservative, anti-gay ones.

Meanwhile, these Christian right leaders also saw a growing threat to their cause in popular culture, as more LGBT people were becoming visible. Southern Baptists called for a boycott of the Walt Disney Company in June 1997, asserting that Disney opposed Christian values by offering benefits to employees' same-sex partners and hosting "Gay Days" convened by LGBT groups. They and others complained when Ellen Degeneres, whose highly rated television sitcom *Ellen* aired on ABC from 1994 to 1998, came out as a lesbian on Oprah Winfrey's show in February 1997; her character on the show came out soon afterward. And leaders protested when the sitcom *Will and Grace*, which featured two gay male lead characters and started airing on NBC in 1998, aired an episode that mocked a show's character who was the ex-gay leader of a gay reparative ministry. These conservative Christians knew they faced a tidal wave of liberalizing sentiment on homosexuality, and they were determined to resist.

For those mobilized by this message, opposition to homosexuality and opposition to feminism were still hand in glove, and Falwell remained one of the most visible exemplars of this union. He made an especially memorable and revealing statement two days after the September 11, 2001, terrorist attacks on the United States, saying to Christian broadcaster Pat Robertson: "I really believe that the pagans, and the abortionists, and the feminists, and the gays and the lesbians who are actively trying to make that an alternative lifestyle, the ACLU, People For the American Way, all of them who have tried to secularize America—I point the finger in their face and say 'you helped this happen.'"[48] Falwell stepped back on this statement after receiving heavy criticism and a public rebuke from President George W. Bush, but the uninhibited listing of those he considered enemies of God and the nation revealingly placed feminists and queer people together at its secularizing core: left unchecked, these venal, anti-religious anti-citizens would destroy America.

The animus toward homosexuality in Christian right circles grew with time. As the progressive religious case came into its own with the

Clergy speak at a press conference to advocate for same-sex marriage, 2004. *GREG WAHL-STEVENS, COURTESY OF ASSOCIATED PRESS.*

issue of same-sex marriage, this oppositional contingent remained steadfast in its conviction that homosexuality was the sin of sins, the grossest insult to God's gendered order. Liberal and progressive Christians had a major fight ahead.

LIBERAL AND PROGRESSIVE CHRISTIANS IN the pews had been growing increasingly open on matters pertaining to homosexuality and LGBT rights. In fact, progressive Christians had been part of the gay rights movement from the outset, at least since the 1964 founding of the Council on Religion and the Homosexual, which incorporated Christians across Protestant denominations joining together with gay activists. Years later, many were still working for changes in their congregations and denominational organizations as well as the broader society.[49]

Noting that Jesus had said nothing about homosexuality (at least nothing that biblical writers reported) but an awful lot about caring for the poor, the vulnerable, and the outcast in society, Christian progressives had long prioritized such issues as poverty and homelessness over sexual morality. If homosexuality were so terrible, they said now, surely Jesus would have emphasized it, but in fact he spurned the moral authorities of his day as judgmental hypocrites while ministering to the oppressed and afflicted, and he called on his followers to do likewise. Not all religious liberals were yet ready to welcome gay clergy or to celebrate same-sex unions; it would take more time for some to feel comfortable around LGBT people at all. But they were uninterested in, indeed disdainful of, the conservative Christian discourse railing at homosexuality (and feminism) for destroying the nation. Liberal and progressive Catholics, often dismayed at how much emphasis church leaders put on sexual activities, were far less worried about homosexuality (if at all) than their conservative counterparts, and many increasingly supported LGBT rights, including marriage equality.

A year and a half or so after his divorce, Robinson entered into his relationship with Mark Andrew. After some time dating, they made a decision to commit to one another as a couple and as a family, since Andrew would help Robinson raise his two daughters. Robinson very much felt this relationship to be a holy union. He later wrote of his early experience of that partnership: "In a way I had never before experienced, I understood what the prayer book means when it describes marriage as a union 'in heart, body, and mind.' I experienced a wholeness and integration between body and spirit I had only dreamed about. I remember thinking, 'So *this* is what all the fuss is about! No wonder people like—and hallow—this!'"[50] As his own right to marry began to weigh on him, starting in the early 1990s Robinson was among a group of gay Episcopal Church activists who would come to call themselves Claiming the Blessing and contended that the church ought to offer a blessing for same-sex unions. With marriage such a contentious issue, Claiming the Blessing did not even talk about the institution itself but focused on developing a liturgical celebration of same-sex love.[51]

The Episcopal Church had long talked about gays, lesbians, and bisexuals in a more welcoming way than did fundamentalists like Falwell, Bryant, Noebel, and the LaHayes. As early as 1976, amid the early surge of the conservative Christian anti-gay campaigns, the General Convention of the Episcopal Church proclaimed that "homosexual persons are children of God who have a full and equal claim with all other persons upon the love, acceptance, and pastoral concern and care of the Church."[52]

That was also the year, not incidentally, that Episcopal Church leaders approved women's ordination, after some years of in-fighting. But just as church members and leaders held a wide spectrum of views on women in the priesthood, so too did homosexuality and issues touching it remain divisive. Integrity, an LGBT group within the church that was founded in 1974 and would play an important role in the coming years, had voiced support for same-sex marriage the year before but had upset some church leaders and so curbed public discussion of it for a few years. When, in 1977, the second openly gay person was ordained a priest, there was an outcry at all levels of the church by those who believed that unrepentant homosexual behavior was sin and must never receive church sanction. But when church leaders and delegates at the 1979 General Convention passed a resolution against ordaining a "practicing homosexual, or any person who is engaged in heterosexual relations outside of marriage," twenty-one bishops signed a "statement of conscience" that opposed this declaration and stated that they could not conform to it because such "would involve a repudiation of our ordination vows as bishops."[53] Arguments over the moral status of homosexuality and its place in the church would continue for years.

As the church was drawn more and more into caring for people with AIDS, attitudes toward LGBT people shifted in a positive direction. In the same year that the National Episcopal AIDS Coalition spawned the provocative "Our Church has AIDS" slogan, the 1988 General Convention featured a display of the famous AIDS quilt in the convention center. Robinson, just two years past his coming out, was there and remembered later that "all but the most hateful visited that [quilt], and of course it's an incredibly powerful experience." Bishops, priests, and parishioners all over the country began pressing their congregations to work and minister among people with AIDS living in shelters and those in household or hospice care. Robinson served as the editor of a four-part AIDS curriculum, *Youth Ministry in the Age of AIDS*, which the church released in 1989, sending copies to every Episcopal congregation. Progressive groups like the Unitarians and Quakers were already laboring intently in this area. But Episcopalians were at the forefront among mainline denominations in committing themselves to people with

AIDS—and, by extension, to the broader LGBT community whom the crisis had united.[54]

So things went for the church during the 1990s and into the early years of the twenty-first century: more discussions, debates, and controversies, with nothing close to consensus on any question pertaining to homosexuality in the church. Many other denominations were also making changes, as were Jewish groups. Most of them had long contained denominational factions devoted to pro-gay advocacy on relevant church policy, and by the mid-1990s institutional resolutions were coming rapidly across a spectrum of responses. In 1996, the Unitarian Universalist Association officially called for full marriage equality, while United Methodist Church leaders voted for a ban on church ceremonies celebrating same-sex unions—Methodists, in fact, were deeply divided on sexual questions for years. In 1997, the General Assembly of the Union of American Hebrew Congregations—then the name of the congregational branch of Reform Judaism—voted to support secular efforts advancing legislation for same-sex civil marriage, as well as religious efforts to develop an appropriate Jewish ceremony for committed same-sex couples. That same year, the Religious Coalition for the Freedom to Marry emerged as a group of more than seven hundred liberal and progressive clergy, congregations, and organizations from twenty-three faith traditions across Massachusetts (mostly Protestant and Reform Jewish). The coalition engaged at a number of levels in support of civil rights for LGBT people. Among other efforts, it submitted an influential brief in a case that would result in state legalization of same-sex marriage: the brief distinguished sharply between the function and meaning of civil marriage versus religious marriage, a distinction that would be cited in the court's final opinion. Other religious organizations and denominations continued to debate same-sex marriage during this period and landed all over the place on this issue, deliberating as well over questions of whether to support openly LGBT clergy.

Back in the Episcopal Church a blow struck pro-gay forces in 1998, when bishops at the international Lambeth Conference passed a resolution that declared homosexuality to be "incompatible with Scripture." Claiming the Blessing, with Robinson a founding member, convened with resolve and focus for the purpose of obtaining authorization of a liturgical rite to bless monogamous same-sex couples, authorization the group would seek at the next General Convention in 2003. Leaders made clear that they did not wish to compel any priest to perform such same-sex blessings; they did, however, challenge critics "to stop scapegoating lesbian and gay Christians for every contemporary ill in the church, particularly for our current state of disunity or the potential for the unraveling of the Anglican Communion." The group met success: delegates to the 2003 General Convention passed a resolution recognizing the differing views within the church about how best to care for LGBT people and maintaining: "local faith communities are operating within the bounds of our common life as they explore and experience liturgies celebrating and blessing same-sex unions."[55] The following year, a commission from the Anglican Church headquarters issued the *Windsor Report*, which rebuked the Episcopal Church for this statement, seeing it as contrary to "the interests of the wider [Anglican] Communion."[56]

The utmost challenge to the Episcopal Church's ability to stay united despite the divisions on sexuality questions had been quietly percolating for a few years: Robinson had felt God calling him to become a bishop, and despite the storm that surrounded his nomination, he felt this to be his true vocation. The election and consecration of a gay bishop constituted a momentous event in the global Anglican Communion and also in American Christianity writ large. It carved a rift so deep in the Episcopal Church that many of those adamantly convinced that the election constituted a breach of gospel truth left for ultra-conservative Anglican organizations. These groups embraced literalist positions on women no less than gay people—moving closer to official Roman Catholic teachings and ever further to the right on gender issues more generally. They held a dim view of Robinson's election, one worlds apart from the view of his supporters.

To those who departed, Robinson's election proved that the church had lost its biblical foundations and succumbed to the cultural drift leftward they believed had been brewing since the 1960s sex revolution; teachings on sexuality and Christian marriage, to their minds, were too fundamental for human beings to amend. Whatever the source, for those who equated homosexuality with an attack on Christianity itself, the very idea of a noncelibate gay man rising so high in the Episcopal hierarchy—a permanent member of what the church considers an unbroken succession of bishops stretching back historically to Jesus's apostles—was a sickening sign of social and ecclesiastical decline. That the leader of the global Anglican Communion, the archbishop of Canterbury, refused to invite Robinson to the triennial Lambeth Conference in which bishops worldwide participate, showed the contentiousness of the international response to his election.[57]

Perhaps it did not matter that gospel truth on marriage had changed before: Doug Theuner, Robinson's predecessor as the eighth diocesan bishop of New Hampshire, pointed out the irony of one prominent lay leader who left the church after Robinson's election, exclaiming incredulously about the departed, "He's divorced!" While no biblical passage depicts Jesus condemning homosexuality, he did denounce divorce; yet "the church has come to accept divorce. The church has *changed its mind about divorce*." In Theuner's eyes, animus toward homosexuality was not about faith or biblical devotion; rather, this attitude reflected a cultural prejudice that those holding it "use the tools of faith to justify."[58]

To those who cheered Robinson's election and remained within the church—and to those watching approvingly from other religious denominations—the successful election of a gay bishop augured for the church a new day of loving inclusion for all genders and all sexual minorities. The church could now embrace all of these human beings, not condescendingly as sick or suffering persons on account of their unfortunate orientation but joyously as fully equal, fully healthy, and fully valued members of the church—and of humanity. For LGBT people and their allies, Robinson acquired something of the status of a saint, the very embodiment of grace in the face of prejudice, and of prejudice overcome. His outspoken feminism further endeared him to feminists as well, for he linked hatred of women to these other prejudices, repeatedly maintaining, "At their root, heterosexism and homophobia are expressions of misogyny." He considered much of the current social and ecclesiastical turmoil a sign of (and reaction to) "the early stage of the end of male dominance, male superiority, and male privilege." The "link between homophobia and misogyny" meant that "this battle over homosexuality is as much about the end of patriarchy as anything else."[59] His enthusiasts admired his outlook as much as his enemies despised it; for people on both sides, there was a crucial lesson to be learned in the outcome of, and the fallout from, New Hampshire Episcopalians' choice of a gay bishop.

Christians thus remained profoundly divided on homosexuality, and denominational divides were often stark. Differences in views on the morality of homosexuality and same-sex marriage varied according to whether one were a biblical literalist or a flexible interpreter of Scripture, and they also tended to follow patterns pertaining to one's overall view of the nature of gender and equality. These two worldviews both played significant roles in the political conflicts of the coming years.

NINETEEN DAYS AFTER ROBINSON'S DIOCESAN election, on June 26, 2003, the Supreme Court issued a 6–3 ruling in *Lawrence v. Texas* that struck down Texas's anti-sodomy law and the thirteen others that still remained. According to the justices' reading of the Constitution, LGBT people deserved privacy and dignity no less than heterosexuals. While Justice Kennedy's majority opinion and a concurring opinion by Justice O'Connor both noted that this decision did not indicate that same-sex marriage was warranted, Justice Scalia's dissent warned that state laws prohibiting "bigamy, same-sex marriage, adult incest, prostitution, masturbation, adultery, fornication, bestiality, and obscenity" were all potentially destabilized by this decision's invalidation of laws grounded in moral choices.[60]

Conservatives saw it more as Scalia did: lawmakers like Pennsylvania senator Rick Santorum, already on record for supporting anti-sodomy laws, denounced the *Lawrence* decision and the push for same-sex marriage, arguing again that marriage was "the union of a man and a woman."[61] Shortly after the *Lawrence* decision, two officials at the Alliance Defense Fund (later the Alliance Defending Freedom), a conservative Christian legal advocacy organization, coauthored *The Homosexual Agenda: Exposing the Principal Threat to Religious Freedom Today*, which argued that same-sex marriage "tramples religious freedom and leaves a trail of broken bodies in the dust." Gay people did not want marriage so that they could gain equal benefits; rather, "they want marriage so they can take a wrecking ball to the institution itself." In their hands, "marriage will be no better than anonymous sodomy in a bathhouse."[62] Indeed, with the anti-sodomy statutes removed, the push for same-sex marriage could move forward.

Just a few months after that ruling, the Supreme Judicial Court in Massachusetts declared a right to marriage for same-sex couples in that state, in its ruling on *Goodridge v. Department of Public Health*. The Massachusetts court stated clearly that the state constitution "affirms the dignity and equality of all individuals" and "forbids the creation of second-class citizens." Importantly, the court followed one line of argument that had been presented in an amicus brief submitted by the Religious Coalition for the Freedom to Marry, along with a number of liberal religious groups: "The injection of religion—indeed any religious view—into civil marriage by the Trial Court is particularly inappropriate in light of the great diversity of opinion among voices of faith with regard to marriage," the brief stated. The court concurred, noting that there were "religious, moral, and ethical" arguments on both sides of the debate, but none was relevant to a decision about civil marriage. Quoting *Lawrence*, the court noted, "Our obligation is to define the liberty of all, not to mandate our moral code." The court rejected the arguments put forward in another amicus brief by the Catholic Action League of Massachusetts, including one that asserted the unnaturalness of same-sex sexual relations and concluded, "How can conduct subject to criminal penalties throughout history demonstrate the pedigree of a fundamental right?" The court also denied the claim that this decision would damage the institution of marriage itself; in fact, extending civil marriage bolstered its importance: "That same-sex couples are willing to embrace marriage's solemn obligations of exclusivity, mutual support and commitment to one another is a testament to the enduring place of marriage in our laws and in the human spirit."[63]

Back and forth went the states, and the nation. In 2004, the year after the Massachusetts court decision, President George W. Bush called for a constitutional amendment to define marriage as a union between one man and one woman; three states had already amended their constitutions for this purpose. Religious leaders assisted this effort, as when Bishop Eddie Long, a prominent African American pastor of an Atlanta megachurch then numbering twenty-five thousand members, led a massive march in opposition to same-sex marriage. Long persistently called on black churches to become stronger voices in this fight, as it was not a top priority for most African American religious leaders. Some congressional leaders tried but could not pass a federal marriage amendment in this period, but voters in thirteen states that same year passed constitutional amendments enacting such a definition. Ten more states passed such amendments in the following two years.

In 2008 California's Supreme Court struck down a state law against same-sex marriage, and same-sex couples began marrying in June. Legislatures and state voters continued to battle out amendments, and judges sometimes assessed those passed as unconstitutional. Barack Obama, running for president, went on the record as deeming marriage the union between a man and a woman and said he favored same-sex civil unions but did not support same-sex marriage. Months later, when LGBT rights advocates protested President Obama's selection of the Reverend Rick Warren—a California-based opponent of same-sex marriage—to deliver the invocation at his inauguration, he compensated by adding to another inaugural event an invocation by the married Bishop Robinson.

The debate continued: Connecticut's Supreme Court and Iowa's Supreme Court sanctioned same-sex marriage in 2008 and 2009, respectively, while other states battled it out. Many went the opposite way of Connecticut and Iowa: all told, by 2012, thirty-one states had moved to block legal recognition of same-sex marriage. The legal machinery erected in the first decade of the twenty-first century alone was vast, and its hodgepodge makeup was a glaring indicator of how profoundly split US citizens were on this question.

However, the tide began to turn when, in 2010, a US district court judge struck down a section of DOMA that had authorized the federal government to withhold benefits from same-sex couples whose marriages were recognized under state law. Months later, the Obama administration said it would no longer defend DOMA. Two years after that, President Obama announced in a nationally televised interview that his views on same-sex marriage had evolved to the point that he could affirm his view that same-sex couples deserved the right to get married.

Months later, Gene Robinson published his second book, *God Believes in Love: Straight Talk About Gay Marriage*, with an endorsement from the president. The book argued, among other things, that Jesus himself, that champion of the outcast, would have condemned any system set up to favor heterosexuals over homosexuals; it was hard, if not impossible, to imagine "Jesus joining in the wholesale discrimination against LGBT people." Jesus would have offered love instead of hate, sympathy instead of stigma, justice instead of bigotry. Everything we know about Jesus, Robinson maintained, suggested that he would see the enduring, loving relationship enshrined in marriage between two men or two women as "life-giving and holy."[64] The book may not have persuaded the most conservative opponents—a review in one conservative Christian periodical castigated the book's "undercurrent of self-centeredness" and "speculative" religious arguments—but it received a warm reception elsewhere and extensive media coverage in outlets like the National Public Radio program *Fresh Air*.[65]

The next year, 2013, Supreme Court rulings in two cases—*US v. Windsor* and *Hollingsworth v. Perry*—struck down more barriers to same-sex marriage and strengthened hopes that full and final legalization was forthcoming. But the court was divided, just as the nation remained. Many agreed with the skepticism Supreme Court justice Samuel Alito showed when, during oral arguments for *Hollingsworth* (the challenge to California's Proposition 8 that had rendered same-sex marriage illegal), he asserted that same-sex marriage is an "institution which is newer than cellphones or the Internet."[66] Others jeered at the religiously narrow-minded homophobia they believed the Catholic justice betrayed in that remark. There was virtually no middle ground left.

In January 2015, the Supreme Court agreed to hear four cases on appeal from the Sixth Circuit Court of Appeals, whose ruling had upheld bans on same-sex marriage in Kentucky, Michigan, Ohio, and Tennessee. These would be consolidated into one, called *Obergefell v. Hodges*, and the decision promised to finally bring order to the nation's marriage laws. Briefs were filed for and against same-sex marriage by religious groups. One came from a broad coalition of progressive religious organizations, groups, and leaders (including nearly two thousand individual clergy) who supported same-sex civil marriage. Among others, the brief was signed by numerous Episcopal Church officials, the United Church of Christ, the Union for Reform Judaism, the Unitarian Universalist Association, and the United Synagogue of Conservative Judaism, as well as LGBT supporters within the United Methodist Church, the Presbyterian Church (U.S.A.), the Lutheran Communion, the Society of Friends, and many more. Many "anti" briefs were also filed by religious organizations and leaders whose Christian commitments took them to a different stance from the progressives'. It could seem yet again that these were two Christianities, two religions that were born of the same roots but had very little in common—not mere strangers, they were enemies to one another.

Oral arguments in *Obergefell* took place in April. Among the hundreds of people who gathered outside the court on that day was Gene Robinson, now retired from the episcopate and a senior fellow at the liberal Center for American Progress in Washington, DC. He had announced his divorce from his husband a year before, so the court's decision would not have an impact on his own marital state, but personal impact hardly mattered—this had been a struggle for an entire people, of whom he was merely one. Euphoric and seemingly optimistic, he happily told a reporter that he could not have dreamed that same-sex marriage had a chance of being legalized nationwide so quickly. "To stand here today and to have all this happen in one lifetime is just astounding to me."[67]

On June 26, 2015, the Supreme Court ruled in a 5–4 decision that bans on same-sex marriage were unconstitutional. The court's majority opinion, stating that "no union is more profound than marriage," maintained that it was wrong to imagine that gay and bisexual men and women "disrespect the idea of marriage"; to the contrary, they "respect it so deeply that they seek to find its fulfillment for themselves." The "equal dignity in the eyes of the law" sought by same-sex couples was granted to them by the Constitution—for them too, marriage was a fundamental right.[68] While the scathing dissents issued by the four justices opposed to this ruling offered some comfort to the religious opponents of same-sex marriage, the full and equal right to marriage for same-sex couples was now the law of the entire land. President Obama lauded the decision, saying, "Today we can say, in no uncertain terms, that we have made our union a little more perfect."[69]

The Episcopal Church's General Convention was in session on the day the Supreme Court released its ruling, and one topic on the docket was whether to offer church blessings to same-sex marriages. Gene Robinson, still an active church leader, spoke for the majority of bishops in asserting that it was time for the church to open marriage to same-sex couples, who were "living out their lives in holy ways." Opening up a path for them to marry "allows us to recognize this" and to "declare how far we have come." The majority of delegates at the convention agreed, and, in a historic move, they voted to approve canonical and liturgical changes that granted marriage equality within the church. New marriage rites would alter the ceremonial language for weddings to be inclusive of same-sex couples, with no further definition of marriage as solely between a man and a woman. Clergy could refuse to officiate such a ceremony, just as they could refuse to officiate any wedding, and individual bishops had the ability to forbid clergy in their own dioceses from performing such rites between persons of the same gender. Still, the church's official position now recognized the validity of same-sex marriage.[70]

Although the votes were overwhelmingly in favor of these changes, there were dissenters: one bishop stood at the convention to oppose opening marriage to same-sex couples, avowing that the church's message to these couples should instead be, "Do you love your partner enough not to engage in sexual intimacy?" After the affirmative vote, twenty bishops signed a minority report dissenting from these changes and reaffirming the traditional definition of marriage.

More opposition came, in its usual forms. Ultra-conservative evangelical spokesman Franklin Graham, lamenting that the Supreme Court was "endorsing sin," channeled Falwell in warning that "God could bring judgment upon America" for the ruling.[71] Focus on the Family's Jim Daly insisted that no court could ultimately change the "eternal truth" that "marriage is, and has always been, between a man and a woman."[72] Robert George, the Catholic past chairman of the National Organization for Marriage, repeatedly condemned *Obergefell* as an anti-constitutional seizure of power that rightly belonged to the people. The president of the US Conference of Catholic Bishops, pronouncing the *Obergefell* decision a "tragic error," called it "profoundly immoral and unjust for the government to declare that two people of the same sex can constitute a marriage."[73] When, a year after *Obergefell*, Vice President Joe Biden, a devout Catholic, solemnized the wedding of two men who were White House staffers, prominent US bishops denounced the act as "a counter-witness" to sound Catholic doctrine.[74]

Even as wider societal attitudes toward homosexuality and LGBT people seemed to be shifting from general tolerance toward acceptance of full citizenship rights, resistance remained among those Christians still committed to what they saw as traditional values but what their opponents saw as the patriarchal, hierarchical model of the church. These conservatives, in both Catholic and Protestant camps, were completely at odds with other members of their own faith traditions who celebrated the ruling as a victory for justice, seeing it as a triumph for those hungering and thirsting for righteousness, a fulfillment of Jesus's call to love one another above all. The fight over same-sex marriage might be in the books, but reactions to it bespoke profoundly deepening divisions within American Christianity and across the nation writ large.

"IN THE FIRST FIFTY-SIX YEARS of my life," Gene Robinson once mused during his time as bishop of New Hampshire, "I think I was known as a passionate preacher and communicator of the Gospel, lived out in my ministry as a parish priest, retreat center founder/director, program coordinator for the seven dioceses of New England, and assistant to the Bishop of New Hampshire." Since his election, however, "you'd surmise from press reports that the only thing I care about is the inclusion of gay, lesbian, bisexual, and transgendered Christians in the church."[75] Many other people identifying as queer could make a comparable point: living rich and varied lives, caring about diverse issues of local and global import, embracing countless pursuits and commitments, reaching for any number of aims and aspirations, they have often been characterized by critics as unidimensional egotists narrowly fixated on sex and their own pleasure, whatever the expense to the nation.

Deplored as a faction of the broader liberal and secular humanist agenda, LGBT people continued to be targets of hate well into the twenty-first century; even when not targeted with vicious words or violence, they faced discrimination and treatment as second-class citizens. A year after *Obergefell*, there were still twenty-nine states where a person could legally be fired from a job, turned out of a hotel, and thrown out of an apartment simply for being gay, lesbian, or bisexual—thirty-one states for being transgender—and there was no recourse in the courts. Robinson expressed profound concern about this situation in 2016, noting that the LGBT rights movement to date had largely been funded by "white, upper middle-class gay men living on one of the two coasts." With marriage won, those men's lives were "pretty perfect," and many were no longer donating to rights organizations focused on job protections. "It turns out that the more common face of a gay couple is not those two white, upper middle-class men arguing over where to have brunch on Sunday, but two African American lesbians raising two or more children at or below the poverty level in Mississippi," Robinson declared. And to most LGBT men and women, job protections were more important than marriage: "They can live together and have a relationship without benefit of marriage easier than they can live without a job."[76] Robinson was right about the law: in August 2016, for instance, a federal judge ruled in favor of a Detroit funeral home owner who fired his transgender director on the grounds that gender transition violated the conservative Christian owner's "sincerely held religious beliefs."[77] Other cases were pending, and most cases of this kind did not even make it to federal court. This issue had nothing to do directly with his own church, but it was a justice issue as well as a pastoral issue, and Robinson was ready for the fight.

Whether job protections were the next frontier of LGBT rights activism was unclear, but there seemed little doubt that those Christian traditionalists long invested in defending a norm in which the only appropriate outlet for sexual activity was heterosexual, monogamous, potentially procreative marriage, and in which men would reign dominant over women in religious, domestic, and societal realms alike, would keep fighting too—in the legal and political realms where possible, in religious and social realms where not. The stakes simply remained too high to surrender. At the heart of this dispute over same-sex marriage and related sexual norms, as Robinson and his opponents alike knew, lay a deeply entrenched struggle over power and freedom, authority and coercion, and the very core of the Christian message. The battle over marriage was a battle in which "freedom" to one cohort meant submission to clerical authority and its power to define morality, even reality itself, without state interference; while to another, it meant the legally and religiously sanctioned freedom to love and behave ethically without fixating on gender roles and conventional sexual rules. To both, and indeed to all invested parties within and beyond the church, the nation's future was at stake.

EPILOGUE

T HE OBERGEFELL DECISION MARKED THE end of one phase of the battle over same-sex marriage, but it hardly quieted the political and religious controversies over sexuality. If anything, the court's decision flamed the fires of resistance. As same-sex couples across American made plans to wed, some cake bakers, florists, and photographers morally opposed to same-sex marriage refused to accommodate them. They and their outraged supporters insisted that it was not simply conscience that was at stake but the constitutional rights of Christians—particularly their right to religious freedom that should exempt them from following laws that infringed on their beliefs. Skeptics doubted such claims, noting that these wedding vendors rarely if ever had refused to serve straight couples whose histories included, for instance, adultery or divorce. But the appeal to religious freedom was a powerful one. In several speeches delivered during his tour of the United States weeks after the *Obergefell* announcement, Pope Francis himself praised the "fundamental right" of religious freedom and later made international headlines when he denounced the "global war" against marriage driven by the secular "theory of gender," a theory he said went against God's creation of man and woman and that threatened the church with "ideological colonization."[1] Same-sex marriage, so went the argument, was a threat to the liberty of the church itself. The appeal to religious freedom increasingly appeared to be a strategy embraced by conservative Christians in the wake of losing the legal battle over marriage, adopted for a world in which the old Christian consensus on sex had completely fractured.

Even as the fight over same-sex marriage pivoted in new directions, another chapter in America's long conflict over religion, sex, and politics was beginning in June 2015. Ten days before the release of *Obergefell*, a New York billionaire—best known for his bombastic showmanship, real estate empire, and philandering through three marriages, the last to a woman twenty-four years his junior—announced his candidacy for president of the United States. Many scoffed at the idea that Donald Trump could be a serious candidate, since he had no political experience, regularly insulted vast sectors of the population and the globe—Mexicans, African Americans, Muslims, and more—and routinely did things— bend the truth, reveal his ignorance, traffic in conspiracy theories— that had disqualified candidates in the past. He seemed a particularly unlikely standard-bearer for the contemporary Republican Party, given that, although he had grown up Presbyterian and as an adult had worshiped sporadically at New York's Marble Collegiate Church, by this time he had no regular religious affiliation and held no discernible faith. Although he prevailed in the primaries and became the party's official nominee a year later, many still doubted that Trump could win the general election against Hillary Clinton, a former US senator and secretary of state. But after a rancorous and drama-filled campaign, and against the predictions of most pundits and national political experts, on November 8, 2016, Trump was elected the forty-fifth president of the United States.

Following the election, shocked liberals and progressives sought frantically to understand how this swaggering braggart with a seemingly insatiable appetite for attention and adulation but scant interest in policy could have possibly won. Many explanations were debated: economically distressed voters blamed their woes on globalization, immigrants, free trade deals, and neoliberal elites who ignored their plight, personified in Clinton and her husband, former president Bill Clinton. Or: Trump voters were driven by racism and hatred of the prior president, Barack Obama, and believed that Trump's promise to "Make America Great Again" would restore white supremacy. Or: Trump voters were poorly educated dupes swayed by right-wing radio shows, conspiracy websites, and the Fox News Channel, where audiences had learned nothing of Trump's failings while consuming vicious lies about his opponent. Whatever the case, Trump voters believed that the man was on their side.

Many of the specific flashpoints of America's past century of moral combat were again debated in the course of the 2016 election, a reminder of the deep and persisting political divide that followed the country's ruptured consensus regarding sex and sexual morality. At issue were debates over contraceptive access that recalled the birth control controversy, arguments over abortion rights, disputes over the significance of sexual harassment, and continued wrangling over same-sex marriage, to name but a few. Trump pledged to cut government funding for Planned Parenthood and stated that "there should be some kind of punishment" for women who had abortions; Clinton stood up for reproductive rights. Trump threatened to sue or censor women who feuded with him or who had accused him of sexual assault; Clinton presented herself as a tireless fighter for all women. White nationalists who condemned interracial marriage, like the radio host James Edwards, were among Trump's staunchest supporters; Clinton condemned them.[2] In an attempt to turn the tables, Trump brought Paula Jones and other accusers and adulterous lovers from Bill Clinton's past to the second presidential debate, hoping their visible presence would rattle his wife on stage. That didn't work, but the stunt became a major news story that caught fire among Trump supporters who found political merit in the idea that Clinton's husband was a predatory sleazebag.[3]

But aside from the specific sexual issues raised, the election revealed the depth of the national divide in a still more fundamental way. Trump's opponent was a woman, the first female presidential candidate of a major political party in all of American history and a liberal feminist who supported gender equality, abortion access, and LGBT rights. Since her husband's first presidential run in 1992, it had been clear that Clinton wanted to have a professional identity of her own, separate from his and concurrent with her own role as a mother. That year, she had told a reporter asking about her career, "I suppose I could have stayed home, baked cookies and had teas, but what I decided to do was to fulfill my profession, which I entered before my husband was in public life." The statement infuriated voters who felt Clinton was sneering at traditional stay-at-home women, and her active political role in her husband's administration—she was the first presidential wife to have an office in the West Wing, where she worked on domestic policy issues—had only intensified conservatives' disgust toward her. Her work on health care and, especially, abortion alienated them still further: as one evangelically bred writer later remembered, Clinton was the first woman she ever heard being called a "feminazi," and she was roundly booed and called a "bitch" in the writer's traditionalist Christian circles.[4]

None of that aversion to Clinton had faded when she became the Democratic nominee for president. For her to run at all seemed overly ambitious—"She wants it [the presidency] too much," many said, as if desire for the job were itself disqualifying. For an independent-minded, nontraditional woman like Clinton, perhaps it was.

In view of the fact that Clinton was a committed Christian with Methodist bona fides going back to her childhood, she could have expected to win over Christian voters. Since serving as first lady, she had spoken periodically about the need for "a new politics of meaning," saying things like, "We have to summon up what we believe is morally and ethically and spiritually correct and do the best we can with God's guidance." And her campaign rhetoric was for more explicitly indebted to Christian precepts than Trump's. Several times during her campaign, she cited a saying from her Methodist faith as her "creed": "Do all the good you can, in all the ways you can, in all the places you can, at all the times you can, to all the people you can, as long as ever you can."[5] She frequently referenced the Bible, as in, "Scripture tells us to incline our ears to wisdom and apply our hearts to understanding," and, quoting Galatians, "'Let us not grow weary in doing good, for in due season we shall reap if we do not lose heart.'"[6]

Progressive Christians roundly supported Clinton in the general election and outspokenly condemned Trump's xenophobic, sexist, and bigoted words as the very antithesis of Christian faith. They were certainly not the only constituency to do so. Her coalition also included less frequent churchgoers, nonbelievers, non-Christians, women, nonwhites, and other people supportive of issues that could be seen through a Christian lens *or* a secular justice lens: gender equality and sexual freedom, racial and economic justice, and humane policies for immigrants, among others. Ultra-conservative Christians, however, were not won over and certainly did not see her professed faith as an asset. Many claimed throughout her campaign that she was a liar and a crook, pointing to apparent scandals that they believed made their case and joining in at rallies with other Trump supporters to shout, "Lock her up!" Most evangelical Christian voters did not like Clinton's feminism, and her support for abortion rights kept away many who saw that issue as an urgent one and the appointment of anti-abortion Supreme Court justices the most important factor in the election. Trump had once held pro-choice views but had recanted, pledging to cut government funding for Planned Parenthood and appointing a staunchly pro-life, self-proclaimed "evangelical Catholic" as his running mate.[7] The splintering of American Christianity into two distinct and divergent moral systems, long in the making, was nowhere better personified than in the clash between the campaigns and constituencies of Trump versus Clinton.

As it turned out, conservative Christians were among Trump's most dedicated voters. Exit polls showed that the majority of white evangelicals, white Catholics, and Mormons voted for Trump. Eighty-one percent of voters who described themselves as evangelical or born-again voted for Trump, 3 percent more than had voted for the Republican candidate Mitt Romney four years before. Sixty percent of white Catholics voted for Trump. Sixty-one percent of Mormon voters voted for Trump. When interviewed, many conservative Christian voters said that Trump would protect their religious freedom better than his opponent and would appoint Supreme Court justices who strongly opposed abortion. Even though several high-profile religious figures had condemned his behavior or openly opposed him—including Michael Gerson, a widely read *Washington Post* columnist and former George W. Bush speechwriter; Eric Teetsel, the president of the Family Policy Alliance of Kansas; Beth Moore and Jen Hatmaker, Christian writers and frequent public speakers; and Russell Moore, president of the Ethics & Religious Liberty Commission, the public-policy arm of the Southern Baptist Convention—those leaders with the widest influence supported him, including James Dobson, Jerry Falwell Jr., Franklin Graham, and many more. Ultimately, a solid majority of white religious conservatives found reason to vote for him and came out in droves to do so.

Suddenly, it seemed, the very Christians who had long guarded against sexual immorality had shucked that principle for the sake of gender hierarchy, or at least of putting this one particular woman in her place so as to elect a macho man. The T-shirts and campaign paraphernalia popular at Trump's rallies spoke volumes about this sexualized divide, loaded with vulgar slogans praising Trump for having "balls" while jeering Clinton's outward appearance and calling her "bitch," "tramp," "cunt," and more. Any differences between Trump's Christian and non-Christian supporters were difficult to discern in this resort to crudeness, but if it's true, as one Christian witness said, that "Christians aren't allowed to say 'bitch,' but they make an exception for Hillary," then it's not hard to imagine some of the faithful participating in such ribaldry.[8] While advocates of gender equality were infuriated by this boorish treatment, Clinton supporters were ultimately outmatched by a campaign whose most fervent advocates reveled in pro-Trump mantras drenched in choleric, often sexually explicit misogyny. Even if Trump had been incoherent on issues such as abortion and marriage equality, the election seemed to be about the candidates' very identities, embodying the culture war over sexuality in the most literal way.[9]

Many observers were shocked that Trump's misogyny did not doom his campaign. Trump won despite a long history of insulting women with names like "dog," "slob," "bimbo," and much else. He won despite well publicized demeaning comments about female media personalities from Rosie O'Donnell to Megyn Kelly, numerous allegations of sexual harassment and sexual assault, and revelations that his first wife had leveled rape accusations in a deposition during their divorce. He won despite the release of lewd audiotapes in which he was heard bragging about his aggressive sexual approach to women and how he could, as a celebrity, simply "grab 'em by the pussy." He won despite his slut-shaming of former Miss Universe Alicia Machado and sexually inappropriate comments made about young girls and his own daughter Ivanka. And he won despite insulting Clinton with a series of sexist comments and innuendos—"If Hillary Clinton can't satisfy her husband what makes her think she can satisfy America?" he repeated on Twitter, a nod to the Monica

A Donald Trump supporter wears a crude campaign T-shirt praising the candidate's male anatomical parts at a rally in Virginia, 2016. *ANDREW HARRER/BLOOMBERG VIA GETTY IMAGES.*

Lewinsky scandal—that culminated in his declaring her "such a nasty woman" in a debate weeks before the election.[10] Those sporting misogynistic slogans at his rallies were following his lead, and the #NeverTrump conservatives, however horrified by him, hardly rallied to Clinton's defense.

Feminist Clinton supporters were most disheartened to learn that while 54 percent of female voters overall voted for her, the majority of white women voted for Trump, including over 60 percent of white women without college degrees. That number showed a sharp contrast with black women voters, 94 percent of whom voted for Clinton (she also won among Hispanic and other women of color). And it also differentiated working-class white women from white women with college degrees, 51 percent of whom voted for Clinton and 45 percent for Trump. Analyzing what these disparities said about race and class, one observer noted that when speaking to women, Clinton and her supporters spent too much time talking about shattering the glass ceiling to get the first woman elected president: "If Clinton had really focused on sexual harassment, which is a very common experience for women in low wage jobs and middle class jobs, instead of focusing on the glass ceiling, I think that she could have had more white working class votes," especially white working class *women's* votes. Clinton's feminism, according to this argument, looked privileged and elitist, and it did not move vast numbers of white women.[11]

History suggests how Trump may well have won not in spite of his attitude toward women but because of it. Polls persistently showed that most Republicans felt that Trump "tells it like it is" rather than stooping to the so-called political correctness of people committed to gender and racial equality. Huge numbers of his supporters apparently saw his open sexism as refreshing. At least among Trump's most loyal base, men and women alike cheered his putdowns of Clinton and the virile potency they believed his words and actions embodied. For many, Trump, the avatar of a patriarchal and largely white Christian right, was distinctly preferable to Clinton, the so-called elitist pseudo-Christian feminist who could appear to be, as one evangelical periodical made explicitly clear two months before the election, the Grim Reaper, à la her pro-choice stance on abortion.

Nearly a full century after American women gained the right to vote and fought successfully for the right to speak publicly about contraception without threat of arrest, the nation's colossal clash over gender and sexuality was nowhere near over. In fact, sexism and outright misogyny seemed to be undergoing a resurgence amid Trump's campaign. The more that feminists, liberals, and progressives publicly condemned the latest chauvinistic statement by Trump, the stronger his support seemed to grow. One might have expected his manifestly immoral personal behavior or his past support of abortion rights and same-sex marriage to have undermined this support (as indeed it did early in the primaries). But because he shared, in the coarsest fashion, a worldview shaped by fear of women's empowerment and a determined opposition to gender equality, the majority of conservative Christians trusted him to defend their moral outlook in the political realm. In other words, it was because the election showcased such a clash of worldviews that Trump got the same sort of conservative Christian support that had traditionally been bestowed upon much more conventional Christian candidates.

A cover image on a fall 2016 issue of the biweekly evangelical magazine *World* shows Hillary Clinton and her pro-choice supporters to be agents of death. After the audiotapes surfaced the following month, *World* editors denounced Trump also, on grounds of "character" that included extramarital sex. *FRONT COVER OF WORLD, SEPTEMBER 17, 2016. USED WITH PERMISSION.*

PERHAPS NOTHING BETTER INDICATED THE extent to which the election had been at bottom a battle in America's culture war over sexuality than the fact that the first major resistance to Trump after his presidential inauguration occurred under the umbrella of a Women's March. Trump's opponents found much to protest about his new administration, including his attitudes toward nonwhite Americans and immigrants, but sexual politics were the glue that held the broad anti-Trump coalition together at the outset. At the Women's March on Washington, DC, on January

21, 2017—the day before the forty-fourth anniversary of the *Roe v. Wade* decision—feminist liberals and progressives condemned Trump's treatment of women in the starkest terms: pink "pussy hats," posters of female genitalia, and "nasty woman" T-shirts abounded alongside signs mocking Trump's masculinity. Clergy and religious progressives from many traditions were visibly present and made their faith known: many priests wore their priestly collars, many Muslim women wore hijabs, a number of Jewish men wore skullcaps, and signs abounded with religious messages. "I'm a WITNESS for JUSTICE!" read signs held aloft by members of the United Church of Christ, the progressive denomination's logo proudly stamped on both sides, along with its motto, "That They May All Be One."

The DC event, with sister marches in cities all over the United States and the world, was not a Christian march or a religious gathering of any kind, but its goal very much aligned with that UCC assurance—"I see you!," marchers reassured one another, over and over—and its call to oneness in diversity. Beneath the focal emphasis on women, the march honed in on what marchers perceived to be the immorality of many of the policies promoted by the new administration and was broadly inclusive of a wide range of groups and individuals across countless affiliations. Muslims, Jews, and Christians marched side by side with secular humanists and atheists, people of all genders, countless children amid teens and adults. All joined in a call for women's rights that seemed more at risk than ever, and for human rights more expansively. Intersectionality was a pervasive motif, a reminder that feminism was no longer the movement of white elites that it once seemed to be but a sprawling, richly colorful coalition of people whose identities and concerns complexly reflected the crossing points of race, class, and gender: people fighting for the rights of immigrants and refugees, African Americans, Muslims, Native Americans, trans and queer persons, and more. For those who attended, it was an unforgettably exhilarating—for some, even sacred—event.

The march did not aim to heal the broader ruptures in the nation, as indeed it could not. A century after American women attained suffrage, the stage was set for the next conflagration in the long battle over religion, sex, and politics. That Christians would be part of that battle was certain, and just as certain was the fact that different groups of Christians would fight one another from opposite sides. Each side would insist that the other was attempting to force its worldview on the other and impose it by law. A protracted moral combat seemed nowhere near a truce.

It would be naïve to imagine that Americans in this standoff can return to any consensus regarding sex and gender and impossible to imagine what such a consensus could possibly look like. Widespread agreement seems hopeless, and common ground difficult to find. Recognizing and acknowledging the fears animating citizens across a broad ideological spectrum is no quick-fix for our politics, but it is a necessary start. A kind of glue that once held Americans together—problematically, to be sure—has been dissolving for a century. Finding a way to live together despite our deep differences over sex (and many other issues besides) demands participation in a larger project of reckoning, engaging, and willfully empathizing with others in our common humanity, so as to rouse a fractured nation to build a bearable peace. Maybe we will get there one day, but not without first committing to a full and thorough reckoning of precisely how and why our divisions got so deep.

ACKNOWLEDGMENTS

THIS BOOK WAS BORN OUT of a decades-long interest in a puzzle: of all the moral subjects and ethical rules elaborated deeply throughout the Bible and the history of Christianity, why have so many American Christians seemed disproportionately obsessed with *sex*? My growing-up years coincided with the rise of the new Christian right, a wave in which it seemed people of faith were directing much greater energy toward erecting fortresses against sexual activity outside of marriage than participating regularly in activities Jesus emphasized more: feeding the hungry, welcoming the stranger, clothing the needy, tending the sick, and visiting the prisoner. The Baptists of my childhood stressed that the core of the Christian message was caring for "the least of these," but most of the nation's most visible Christian leaders targeted sexual sin far more than any sin of neglecting the neighbor. My quest in this project was to analyze both the reasons for and the effects of this sexual preoccupation.

The manuscript underwent several stages of revision, if not revolution, and I have many to thank from different stages of its progress. Early encouragement came from Lara Heimert and Alane Salierno Mason. Archivists and library staff at the following institutions facilitated the research in crucial ways: the Library of Congress, the New York Public Library, the American Catholic Research Center and University Archives at Catholic University of America, the Kinsey Institute at Indiana University, Vassar College, the Schlesinger Library and Andover Library at Harvard University, Princeton Theological Seminary, the Divinity School Library at Yale University, the Paulist Archives in Washington, DC,

St. Mark's Library at General Theological Seminary, Occidental College, the University of Virginia, the University of Minnesota Library, Firestone Library at Princeton University, Olin Library at Washington University in St. Louis, and Southwest Harbor Public Library on the coast of Maine.

A number of influential people consented to interviews with me, and while not all appear in the final book, each was illuminating and contributed to my understanding of the stories told here. Those interviewed include Ellen Chesler, Harvey Cox, the late Elizabeth Genné (with thanks to her children for facilitating that), Debra Haffner, Joseph Hough, Frances Kissling, the late John J. McNeill, Gene Robinson, Paul Simmons, the late Ruth Proskauer Smith, and Susie Wilson. Karen Myers transcribed these and other interviews for me with speed and skill.

I've taught at three universities during the course of writing this book—Princeton University, Harvard University, and Washington University in St. Louis—and I'm grateful to colleagues and students who engaged my work in classrooms, colloquia, and hallways. Special thanks for research assistance and related support go to Lynne Gerber, Rachel Gross, Ryan Harper, Elizabeth Jemison, Emily Johnson, Rachel Lindsey, John Lomperis, Max Mueller, Anthony Petro, the late Melissa Proctor, Amy Sitar, Heather White, and Leslie Wingard. Audiences at numerous other educational institutions have also engaged different pieces of this research over time: Amherst College, Brown University, Clemson University, Columbia University, Eden Theological Seminary, Lehigh University, the University of Michigan, the University of Notre Dame, the University of Pennsylvania, Rice University, Samford University, the University of Tennessee at Chattanooga, the University of Virginia, and Yale University. Four anonymous readers for the *Journal of American History*—three of whom later outed themselves as Amy DeRogatis, Donna Drucker, and Susan Henking—offered excellent suggestions for my article on Alfred Kinsey, as did the journal's then editor, Edward Linenthal.

I am particularly indebted to the following close readers and conversation partners who gave valuable feedback on specific pieces of the project at different points: Scott Appleby, Wallace Best, Fannie Bialek, Anne Blankenship, Kathleen Cummings, Rebecca Davis, Darren Dochuk, Tanya Erzen, Marla Frederick, Andrea Friedman, Stephanie Gaskill, Healan Gaston, Eddie Glaude, Sarah Barringer Gordon, David Hollinger, John

Inazu, Mark Jordan, Maryam Kashani, Moshe Kornfeld, Scott Libson, Kathryn Lofton, Dana Logan, Lerone Martin, Elizabeth McCloskey, Robert Orsi, Leigh Schmidt, Ronit Stahl, Leslie Woodcock Tentler, Lauren Turek, Mark Valeri, Judith Weisenfeld, Lauren Winner, Stephanie Wolfe, and Gene Zubovich. Three colleagues read earlier versions of the manuscript and provided exceptional feedback: Laurie Maffly-Kipp, Melani McAlister, and Jana Riess. And then there are the comrades who offered crucial conversation and loving sustenance over years of intellectual and personal friendship, especially Jennifer Gess, Courtney Lamberth, Martha Easton, Anthea Butler, Charles Marsh, Ted Trost, and Jonathan Walton.

It has been an honor to serve as the first permanent director of the John C. Danforth Center on Religion and Politics and to engage regularly with Jack Danforth. Our shared belief in the importance of building bridges across differences—including our own—with respect and warmth has made working with him a great experience, and I admire him very much. The Center also has a dream team of outstanding coworkers; in addition to the faculty, I extend deep thanks to Debra Kennard, Tiffany Stanley, Sheri Peña, and Leslie Davis for all that they do.

My agent, Geri Thoma, saw the project through many stages with tireless enthusiasm and superb guidance that have been vital to its completion. Sarah Flynn provided outstanding editorial work during a crucial period and helped jump-start the final stage of revision. Creighton Coleman provided excellent fact-checking and corrections in the final stages. Brian Distelberg improved the book immeasurably with his incisive editorial suggestions, Collin Tracy and Beth Wright did superb work in editing and production, and I could not be happier to be part of Lara Heimert's team at Basic Books.

Finally, my immediate family has supported and made sacrifices for this book more than anyone else. My parents and my in-laws have encouraged me throughout the process. Leigh, my spouse, remains a ballast in life as well as in work, and his contributions to this book's completion as well as to my sanity are immeasurable. Zachary, Ella, and Jasper are everything to me, and none can remember a time when my office shelves weren't lined with books about religion and sex—a fact that has both amused and bemused each in turn. With my hope that they will live in and contribute to a more equitable world, the book is for them.

NOTES

INTRODUCTION

1. John Stonestreet, "Breakpoint Commentaries: Christian Leaders Respond to Obergefell vs. Hodges: A Symposium," *Breakpoint*, June 26, 2015, http://www .breakpoint.org/bpcommentaries/entry/12/27686.

2. "Falwell and Robertson on the 700 Club after 9/11," YouTube video, 1:22, from an episode of *The 700 Club* televised by the Fox Family Channel (now Freeform) on September 13, 2001, posted by "Veracifier," November 7, 2007, https://www.youtube.com/watch?v=H-CAcdta_8I.

3. Mike Huckabee, "Huckabee: 'We Have a Sin Problem,'" *Fox News*, July 23, 2012.

4. Jillian Rayfield, "James Dobson Blames Gays, Abortion for Shootings," *Salon*, December 17, 2012, http://www.salon.com/2012/12/17/james_dobson _blames_gays_abortion_for_shootings/.

5. Michael F. Haverluck, "Anne Graham Lotz Warns US in Last Judgment Stage," *One News Now*, May 28, 2016, http://www.onenewsnow.com/church /2016/05/28/anne-graham-lotz-warns-us-in-last-judgment-stage.

6. The literature on religion and sexuality in US history has burgeoned over the past decade, especially work on evangelical attitudes toward sex. A comprehensive list would be too long here, but see especially Rebecca L. Davis, *More Perfect Unions: The American Search for Marital Bliss* (Cambridge, MA: Harvard University Press, 2010); Leigh Eric Schmidt, *Heaven's Bride: The Unprintable Life of Ida C. Craddock, American Mystic, Scholar, Sexologist, Martyr, and Madwoman* (New York: Basic Books, 2010); Lynne Gerber, *Seeking the Straight and Narrow: Weight Loss and Sexual Reorientation in Evangelical America* (Chicago: University of Chicago Press, 2011); Mark R. Jordan, *Recruiting Young Love: How Christians Talk About Homosexuality* (Chicago: University of Chicago Press, 2011); Amy DeRogatis, *Saving Sex: Sexuality and Salvation in American*

Evangelicalism (New York: Oxford University Press, 2015); Sara Moslener, *Virgin Nation: Sexual Purity and American Adolescence* (New York: Oxford University Press, 2015); Anthony M. Petro, *After the Wrath of God: AIDS, Sexuality, and American Religion* (New York: Oxford University Press, 2015); and Heather R. White, *Reforming Sodom: Protestants and the Rise of Gay Rights* (Chapel Hill: University of North Carolina Press, 2015).

7. Scholarly interest in the nation's religious, cultural, and political divisions that have markedly deepened during recent decades is long-standing, and many books have been written about the culture wars and the religious and political realignments that have occurred in these years. Many have used the 1960s as a general starting point for understanding that trajectory, a timeline that has allowed for breadth of coverage across many subjects, figures, and events that this book, attending to a longer timeline while focusing on particular stories, does not cover; others focus more particularly on the history of American evangelicalism and its impact on the nation's politics. Like any historian studying these deep conflicts, I am indebted to this robust literature. Of particular note are the following: James Davison Hunter, *Culture Wars: The Struggle to Define America* (New York: Basic Books, 1991); William C. Martin, *With God on Our Side: The Rise of the Religious Right in America* (New York: Broadway Books, 1996); Lisa McGirr, *Suburban Warriors: The Origins of the New American Right* (Princeton, NJ: Princeton University Press, 2001); Randall Balmer, *Thy Kingdom Come: How the Religious Right Distorts the Faith and Threatens America* (New York: Basic Books, 2006); Daniel K. Williams, *God's Own Party: The Making of the Christian Right* (New York: Oxford University Press, 2010); Darren Dochuk, *From Bible Belt to Sun Belt: Plain-Folk Religion, Grassroots Politics, and the Rise of Evangelical Conservatism* (New York: W. W. Norton, 2011); Robert O. Self, *All in the Family: The Realignment of American Democracy Since the 1960s* (New York: Hill and Wang, 2012); Robert Wuthnow, *Red State Religion: Faith and Politics in America's Heartland* (Princeton, NJ: Princeton University Press, 2012); Molly Worthen, *Apostles of Reason: The Crisis of Authority in American Evangelicalism* (New York: Oxford University Press, 2014); Andrew Hartman, *A War for the Soul of America: A History of the Culture Wars* (Chicago: University of Chicago Press, 2015); Neil J. Young, *We Gather Together: The Religious Right and the Problem of Interfaith Politics* (New York: Oxford University Press, 2016); Kevin M. Kruse, *One Nation Under God: How Corporate America Invented Christian America* (New York: Basic Books, 2015); and Stephen Prothero, *Why Liberals Win (Even When They Lose Elections)* (New York: HarperCollins, 2016).

8. As Virginia Woolf drolly remarked, "The history of men's opposition to women's emancipation is more interesting perhaps than the story of that emancipation itself." Virginia Woolf, *A Room of One's Own*, annotated and with an introduction by Susan Gubar (1929; reprint, New York: Harcourt, 2001), 55.

9. Grover Cleveland, "Would Woman Suffrage Be Unwise?" *Ladies' Home Journal* 22, no. 11 (October 1905): 7, 8.

10. *The Woman Patriot* 1, no. 1 (April 1918): 1.

CHAPTER 1

1. The literature on Comstock and this spate of vice societies is extensive; useful interpretations include Nicola Beisel, *Imperiled Innocents: Anthony Comstock and Family Reproduction in Victorian America* (Princeton, NJ: Princeton University Press, 1997); Paul Boyer, *Purity in Print: Book Censorship in America from the Gilded Age to the Computer Age*, 2nd ed. (Madison: University of Wisconsin Press, 2002); Donna Dennis, *Licentious Gotham: Erotic Publishing and Its Prosecution in Nineteenth-Century New York* (Cambridge, MA: Harvard University Press, 2009); Gaines M. Foster, *Moral Reconstruction: Christian Lobbyists and the Federal Legislation of Morality, 1865-1920* (Chapel Hill: University of North Carolina Press, 2002); Andrea Friedman, *Prurient Interests: Gender, Democracy, and Obscenity in New York City, 1909-1945* (New York: Columbia University Press, 2000); and Helen Lefkowitz Horowitz, *Rereading Sex: Battles over Sexual Knowledge and Suppression in Nineteenth-Century America* (New York: Vintage Books, 2002).

2. US Congress, "Comstock Law," in "United States Statutes at Large, 42nd Cong. Sess. III, Chp. 258," in *A Century of Lawmaking for a New Nation: U.S. Congressional Documents and Debates, 1774–1875*, 598–600, Library of Congress, http://memory.loc.gov/cgi-bin/ampage?collId=llsl&fileName=017/llsl017.db&recNum=639.

3. Janet Farrell Brodie, *Contraception and Abortion in 19th-Century America* (Ithaca, NY: Cornell University Press, 1994), 257.

4. According to biographer Ellen Chesler, Sanger's baptism at the age of thirteen is recorded in the registry of St. Mary's Catholic Church in Corning, New York. See Ellen Chesler, *Woman of Valor: Margaret Sanger and the Birth Control Movement in America* (New York: Simon & Schuster, 2007), 29. See also Madeline Gray, *Margaret Sanger: A Biography of the Champion of Birth Control* (New York: R. Marek, 1979), 17. Sanger never wrote of her baptism or confirmation in her autobiographical accounts.

5. Margaret Sanger, *My Fight for Birth Control* (New York: Farrar & Rinehart, 1931), 6, 8.

6. Ibid., 49.

7. Ibid.

8. "Anthony Comstock Dies in His Crusade," *New York Times*, September 22, 1915, 1.

9. Chesler, *Woman of Valor*, 66; Margaret Sanger, *Woman and the New Race* (New York: Truth Publishing, 1920), 189, 191, 193.

10. On Sanger's goad to Ryan and other Catholic reformers in the 1910s, see Leslie Woodcock Tentler, *Catholics and Contraception: An American History* (Ithaca, NY: Cornell University Press, 2004), 40–41. John A. Ryan, "Family Limitation," *Ecclesiastical Review* 54, no. 6 (June 1916): 684–696. Ryan is treated at length in many scholarly histories of American Catholicism; a good, short introduction to his writings on birth control in the broader context of his social views is Clement Anthony Mulloy, "John A. Ryan and the Issue of Family Limitation," *Catholic Social Science Review* 18 (2013): 91–104. See also Sharon M. Leon, *An Image of God: The Catholic Struggle with Eugenics* (Chicago: University of Chicago Press, 2013), 30–33 and passim.

11. M. P. Dowling, "Race-Suicide," in *Race-Suicide—Birth-Control* (New York: America Press, n.d. [1915?]), 9.

12. Tentler, *Catholics and Contraception*, 31.

13. For more details in the overall narrative of Sanger's story, see Chesler, *Woman of Valor*; Jean H. Baker, *Margaret Sanger: A Life of Passion* (New York: Hill and Wang, 2011); and Gray, *Margaret Sanger*. An earlier biography of Sanger that presents her in unflattering and, to later readers, sexist psychological terms—an overly emotional woman afraid of what she believed to be "an aggressive, threatening, masculine sexual instinct"—yet is strong on historical detail is David M. Kennedy, *Birth Control in America: The Career of Margaret Sanger* (New Haven, CT: Yale University Press, 1970), 3. The most detailed and influential histories of the long birth control movement in the United States are Linda Gordon, *The Moral Property of Women: A History of Birth Control Politics in America* (1974; reprint, Urbana: University of Illinois Press, 2002); and James Reed, *The Birth Control Movement and American Society: From Private Vice to Public Virtue* (Princeton, NJ: Princeton University Press, 1978).

14. Sanger, *Woman and the New Race*, 167, 178.

15. Margaret Sanger to Juliet Barrett Rublee, August 25, 1921, reprinted in *The Selected Papers of Margaret Sanger*, ed. Esther Katz, vol. 1, *The Woman Rebel, 1900-1928* (Urbana: University of Illinois Press, 2003), 310.

16. Conference Committee members are listed in *Birth Control: What It Is, How It Works, What It Will Do* [The Proceedings of the First American Birth Control Conference] (New York: The Birth Control Review, n.d. [1921]), 1–3; hereinafter referred to as *Birth Control: Proceedings*.

17. "Dr. Reiland Dead; Was Rector Here," *New York Times*, September 13, 1964, 86.

18. Dr. Karl Reiland, quoted in Dorothy Dunbar Bromley, "This Question of Birth Control," *Harper's Monthly* 160 (December 1929): 42.

19. Edith Houghton Hooker, "Opening Address," in *Birth Control: Proceedings*, 12.

20. Ibid., 14. Molly Ladd-Taylor has marked a similar connection between the discourse of eugenics and the practice of marriage counseling, as witnessed in the prominent figure of Paul Popenoe. See Ladd-Taylor, "Eugenics, Sterilisation and Modern Marriage in the USA: The Strange Career of Paul Popenoe," *Gender & History* 13, no. 2 (August 2001): 298–327.

21. On the history of eugenics, see Daniel J. Kevles, *In the Name of Eugenics: Genetics and the Uses of Human Heredity* (New York: Knopf, 1985); and Edwin Black, *War Against the Weak: Eugenics and America's Campaign to Create a Master Race*, expanded ed. (Washington, DC: Dialog, 2012). The role of American religious leaders in the eugenics movement is well told in Christine Rosen, *Preaching Eugenics: Religious Leaders and the American Eugenics Movement* (New York: Oxford University Press, 2004). For a detailed analysis of the relation between the eugenics movement and the birth control movement, see Gordon, *Moral Property of Women*. More on Sanger's engagement with eugenics can be found in Baker, *Margaret Sanger*, 159–164 (Baker notes that Sanger was "never an orthodox eugenicist" and was rejected by the American Eugenics Society [164]); and Chesler, *Woman of Valor*, 195–196 and 216–217.

22. Margaret Sanger, untitled address at First Session, in *Birth Control: Proceedings*, 14–18; quotes on 15, 15–16.

23. This phrase comes from the letter Sanger had sent out to potential program participants earlier in 1921, with four questions to address. The first was, "Is not over-population a menace to the peace of the world?" Ibid., 4.

24. Ibid., 158, 173, 185. Additional invocations of "choice" appear, for instance on 77, 144, and 176.

25. Ibid., 60, 62, 65; Deaconess Virginia C. Young, "The Delinquent Girl— One of Our Liabilities," *Medical Times* 49, no. 12 (December 1921): 289.

26. "Police Veto Halts Birth Control Talk; Town Hall in Tumult," *New York Times*, November 14, 1921, 1.

27. Catholic interference was never proven, but historians have long agreed that Archbishop Hayes was very likely or at least "plausibly" involved. See John T. McGreevy, *Catholicism and American Freedom* (New York: W. W. Norton, 2003), 159.

28. "Birth Control Raid Made by Police on Archbishop's Order," *New York Times*, November 15, 1921, 1.

29. "Asks Police Aid for Birth Control Talk," *New York Times*, November 16, 1921, 17.

30. "Police Denounced for Stopping Meeting," *New York Times*, November 17, 1921, 5.

31. "Cornerstone Laid for Public Forum," *New York Times*, January 25, 1920, 10.

32. "Birth Control Talk Guarded by Police," *New York Times*, November 19, 1921, 1.

33. Ibid., 1, 5.

34. Margaret Sanger, untitled address, *Birth Control: Proceedings*, 171.

35. Ibid., 172.

36. Ibid., 171.

37. Ibid., 172, 173, 174.

38. "Birth Control Talk Guarded by Police," 1, 5.

39. On Chase and his shifting alliances with female reformers, see Leigh Ann Wheeler, "Rescuing Sex from Prudery and Prurience: American Women's Use of Sex Education as an Antidote to Obscenity, 1925–1932," *Journal of Women's History* 12, no. 3 (Autumn 2000): 173–195.

40. Sanger, "First American Birth Control Conference: Closing Remarks," November 18, 1921, reprinted in *Selected Papers of Margaret Sanger* 1:328. (The discussion among birth control opponents that occurred after Sanger's lecture and her final comments were not reprinted in *Birth Control: Proceedings*.)

41. Ibid., 1:328–329.

42. "Birth Control and Free Speech," *The Outlook*, November 30, 1921, 507. For a different perspective on the press reaction to Sanger, see Kathleen A. Tobin, *The American Religious Debate Over Birth Control, 1907-1937* (Jefferson, NC: McFarland & Company, 2001), 78–85.

43. "Birth Control and Taboo," *New Republic*, November 30, 1921, 9.

44. Margaret Sanger, *The Pivot of Civilization* (New York: Brentano's, 1922), 30, 195, 196, 198.

45. Chesler, *Woman of Valor*, 198.

46. Margaret Sanger, "The War Against Birth Control," *American Mercury* (June 1924): 233.

47. "Mrs. Sanger Replies to Archbishop Hayes," *New York Times*, December 20, 1921, 24.

48. Sanger, *Woman and the New Race*, 66, 72, 73.

49. Patrick W. Carey, *Catholics in America: A History* (Westport, CT: Praeger, 2004), 57.

50. Timothy A. Byrnes, *Catholic Bishops in American Politics* (Princeton, NJ: Princeton University Press, 1991), 27.

51. John A. Ryan, "Birth-Control: An Open Letter," in *Race-Suicide—Birth-Control*, 25; also published online: http://transporter.com/Apologia/Life/Birth_Control.htm.

52. "Hayes Denounces Birth Control Aim," *New York Times*, November 21, 1921, 1.

53. Ibid.

54. Sanger, *Woman and the New Race*, 167.

55. J. Elliot Ross, "A Study in Numbers," *Catholic World* 117, no. 699 (June 1923): 313, 318–319.

56. "Catholics in Cleveland," *Time*, September 30, 1935.

57. "Text of Sermon by Cardinal Hayes Denouncing Birth Control Advocates," *New York Times*, December 9, 1935, 5.

58. See Tentler, *Catholics and Contraception*, 57.

59. McGreevy, *Catholicism and American Freedom*, 223.

60. Quoted in McGreevy, *Catholicism and American Freedom*, 223.

61. Patrick J. Ward, "Memorandum to Father [John] Burke," February 20, 1926, Box 117, Folder 4, Records of the Office of the General Secretary, United States Conference of Catholic Bishops Office of the General Secretary, American Catholic History Research Center and University Archives (hereafter ACUA), Catholic University of America, Washington, DC. This incident is also cited and analyzed in Tentler, *Catholics and Contraception*, 46.

62. Ward, "Memorandum to Father [John] Burke," ACUA (emphasis in original).

63. Ibid.

64. Sanger, untitled address, in *Birth Control: Proceedings*, 172.

65. The renowned philosopher George Santayana had used the "solvent" language as early as 1916, predicting happily "that American freedoms would act as a 'solvent' upon Catholic distinctiveness"; cited in McGreevy, *Catholicism and American Freedom*, 165.

66. William R. Inge, "Catholic Church and Anglo-Saxon Mind," *Atlantic Monthly* 131 (April 1923): 442, 443, 444, 445, 446, 448.

67. "Ask Churches' Aid for a Better Race," *New York Times*, March 31, 1925, 7.

68. Harry Emerson Fosdick, "Shall the Fundamentalists Win?," *Christian Work* 102 (June 10, 1922): 716–722. The sermon was preached on May 21 of that year and has been reprinted numerous times.

69. "Dr. Fosdick Urges Birth Rate Control," *New York Times*, December 5, 1927, 30. Fosdick continued to speak in favor of birth control; see, e.g., "Fosdick for Candor on Birth Control," *New York Times*, November 20, 1929, 25. For more details on Fosdick's support of birth control, see Robert Moats Miller, *Harry Emerson Fosdick: Preacher, Pastor, Prophet* (New York: Oxford University Press, 1985), 429–432.

70. Harry Emerson Fosdick, *Religion and Birth Control* (New York: Committee on Federal Legislation for Birth Control, 1929); reprinted from the June 19, 1929, issue of the *Outlook and Independent*.

71. Tentler, *Catholics and Contraception*, 21.

72. John Haynes Holmes to Sanger, April 19, 1929, Box 69, reel 45, "Community Church of New York" file, Margaret Sanger Papers, Manuscript Division, Library of Congress, Washington, DC.

73. Sanger to Holmes, May 6, 1929; Holmes to Mrs. Walter Timme, September 29, 1930; Holmes to Sanger, June 1, 1931; Sanger to Holmes, June 9, 1931;

Mortimer Haarstick to Sanger, February 10, 1932; Sanger to Haarstick, February 18, 1932, Box 69, reel 45, "Community Church of New York" file, Margaret Sanger Papers. Holmes to Timme, February 9, 1931; American Civil Liberties Union letter signed by Holmes et al., February 10, 1931, Box 69, reel 46, "Congressional campaign 71st Congress 1928-1932" file, folder 2, Margaret Sanger Papers.

74. "Birth Control," *Afro-American*, February 9, 1923, 9; William N. Jones, "Day By Day: The Progress of Birth Control," *Afro-American* April 18, 1925, 11; "Nannie Burroughs 'Crazy,' Dr. Clayton Powell Tells National Training School," *Afro-American* June 18, 1932, 8.

75. "Birth Control Advocate Speaks to Large Audience at Public Library," *New York Amsterdam News*, March 7, 1923, 1; "Mrs. Margaret Sanger's Move Assures Birth Control Clinic for Harlemites," *New York Amsterdam News*, October 16, 1929, 3; "Research Bureau Has 'Open House,'" *New York Amsterdam News*, November 26, 1930, 11; "The Feminist Viewpoint," *New York Amsterdam News*, June 15, 1932, 5.

76. "The Birth Control Thunder-Bolt Strikes the Church," *Atlanta Daily World*, October 27, 1934, 2.

77. "Questionnaire by Sidney L. Lasell Jr.," February 13, 1934, in *Selected Papers of Margaret Sanger* 2:278.

78. Earl Conrad, "American Viewpoint: On U.S. Birth and Bias Control," *Chicago Defender*, September 22, 1945, 11; Martin Luther King Jr., "Family Planning—A Special and Urgent Concern," speech upon accepting the Planned Parenthood Federation of America Margaret Sanger Award, May 5, 1966, reprinted by Planned Parenthood Federation of America, 2004. On the rebranding of birth control as "family planning" in the early 1940s, see Chesler, *Woman of Valor*, 393.

79. The Lambeth Conference Resolutions Archive from 1930 (Anglican Consultative Council, 2016): http://www.anglicancommunion.org/resources/document-library/lambeth-conference/1930/resolution-15-the-life-and-witness-of-the-christian-community-marriage?author=Lambeth+Conference&year=1930.

80. T. S. Eliot, *Thoughts After Lambeth* (London: Faber and Faber, 1931), 17.

81. J. Conway Davies, "Lambeth, Sex, and Romanticism," *Church Quarterly Review* 114 (1932): 60, 64, and 66.

82. Ibid., 78 and 79.

83. See also Chesler, *Woman of Valor*, 318–320.

84. "Birth Control: Protestant View (Full Text of Federal Council Report)," *Current History* 34, no.1 (April 1931): 97–100; quotes on 97, 100, 99, 100. While the full text of the Federal Council Committee Report notes that all but three committee members signed the document, an informal listing elsewhere suggests that an additional three committee members offered "no judgment,"

presumably meaning they were not signatories after all. Those three are listed as the Rev. Charles K. Gilbert, suffragan bishop of the Protestant Episcopal Diocese of New York; the Rev. Dr. Ben R. Lacy, president of Union Theological Seminary in Richmond, Virginia; and Mrs. W. A. Newell of Greensboro, North Carolina, the chair of the Bureau of Service of the Women's Missionary Council of the Methodist Episcopal Church, South. "Vote of Com. On Marriage & The Home of the Federal Council of Churches of Christ in America," Box 110, reel 72, "FCCC" file, Margaret Sanger Papers.

85. "Birth Control: Protestant View," 98, 99, 100.

86. Russell J. Clinchy, "Birth Control: An Exposition of the Federal Council Report," *Congregationalist and Herald of Gospel Liberty*, May 28, 1931, 714, 721.

87. Dietrich Bonhoeffer, "The Report of the Federal Council of Churches on Birth Control," Dietrich Bonhoeffer Works vol. 10, *Barcelona, Berlin, New York: 1928-1931*, trans. Douglas W. Stott, ed. Clifford J. Green (Minneapolis: Fortress, 2008), 437.

88. Kennedy, *Birth Control in America*, 164, 170.

89. Worth M. Tippy to Sanger, April 14, 1931; Sanger to Tippy, April 18, 1931, Box 11, reel 8, "Federal Council of the Churches of Christ in America, 1930-1940" file (folder 1, Oct. 1930–Dec. 1934), Margaret Sanger Papers.

90. Sanger to George Blumenthal, July 7, 1933; Sanger to Tippy, August 8, 1933, "Federal Council of the Churches of Christ in America, 1930-1940" file (folder 1), Margaret Sanger Papers.

91. Committee on Marriage and the Home, *A Bibliography on Young People's Relationships, Marriage and Family Life* (New York: Commission on the Church and Social Service, Federal Council of the Churches of Christ in America, 1932), 3.

92. "The Federal Council's 'Tainted Contacts,'" *Sunday School Times*, August 13, 1932, 422, 426.

93. Cited in Reed, *Birth Control Movement*, 240.

94. "State-Aided Birth Control Clinic Opened, First Subsidized Project in New York," *New York Times*, January 24, 1940, 22.

95. For helpful correctives to over-readings of Sanger as a thoroughgoing eugenicist, see Baker, *Margaret Sanger*, 3–5 and passim; and Chesler, *Woman of Valor*, 195–196 and 214–217.

CHAPTER 2

1. Examples of immediate news coverage include "Two Found Guilty, Sentenced in Sale of 'Obscene' Books," *Atlanta Constitution*, November 26, 1929, 5; and "Notables Testify for Booksellers," *New York Times*, December 20, 1929, 32. See also "Introduction: D. H. Lawrence and the 'Censor Morons,'" in D. H. Lawrence, *Sex, Literature, and Censorship: Essays*, ed. Harry T. Moore (New York: Twayne, 1953), 25.

2. DeLacey quoted in "Notables Testify for Booksellers"; Bushnell quoted in "Cambridge Bookseller Gets a Month in Jail and $500 Fine for Sale of 'Obscene' Volume," *New York Times*, December 21, 1929, 1.

3. "Cambridge Bookseller Gets a Month in Jail"; Bushnell quoted in "Judge Revokes 'Obscene' Book Case Sentence," *Chicago Daily Tribune*, June 6, 1930, 4. See also "Boston Bookseller Freed of Jail Term," *New York Times*, June 6, 1930, 16. "Watch, Ward Society to Investigate Self," *Atlanta Constitution*, January 14, 1930, 2. For a fuller account of these events and the larger context of the Watch and Ward Society, see Neil Miller, *Banned in Boston: The Watch and Ward Society's Crusade Against Books, Burlesque, and the Social Evil* (Boston: Beacon, 2010).

4. The story of Watch and Ward's invitation to the cardinal is told in Miller, *Banned in Boston*, 129.

5. All quoted in Paul S. Boyer, *Purity in Print: Book Censorship in America from the Gilded Age to the Computer Age*, 2nd ed. (Madison: University of Wisconsin Press, 2002), 200, 202, 206.

6. John Worthen, *D. H. Lawrence: The Life of an Outsider* (New York: Counterpoint, 2005), 13.

7. Brenda Maddox, *The Married Man: A Life of D. H. Lawrence* (London: Sinclair-Stevenson, 1994), 101.

8. Recounted in ibid., 220.

9. Detailed in ibid., 292–293.

10. D. H. Lawrence, *Women in Love* (1920; reprint, New York: Dover, 2002), iii.

11. D. H. Lawrence, "Making Pictures," in *Phoenix II: Uncollected, Unpublished, and Other Prose Works by D. H. Lawrence*, ed. Warren Roberts and Harry T. Moore (New York: Viking, 1968), 606; D. H. Lawrence, *Letters* V 648, quoted in *D. H. Lawrence's Paintings*, with introduction by Keith Sagar (London: Chaucer, 2003), 43; Lawrence, *Letters* VI 406, cited in *Paintings*, 47; Michael Squires and Lynn K. Talbot, *Living at the Edge: A Biography of D. H. Lawrence and Frieda von Richthofen* (Madison: University of Wisconsin Press, 2002), 357.

12. "D. H. Lawrence as Painter," *Daily Express* (London), June 17, 1929, 11; "Police Seize 12 Paintings," *Daily Mirror* (London), July 6, 1929, 3; "D. H. Lawrence's Art Seized in Police Raid," *New York Times*, July 6, 1929, 4; "Exhibition Ban on Pictures: Court Sequel to a Raid on a London Gallery," *Daily Mirror*, August 9, 1929, 18; "Magistrate Orders Prints of D. H. Lawrence Paintings to Be Destroyed," *Daily Express*, August 9, 1929, 9; "Frees Lawrence Pictures: London Court Orders Seized Work of Novelist Returned," *New York Times*, August 9, 1929, 6. Worthen, *D. H. Lawrence*, 399, 400. Lawrence quoted in Edward de Grazia, *Girls Lean Back Everywhere: The Law of Obscenity and the Assault on Genius* (New York: Vintage, 1992), 88.

13. His frequent use of "grey Puritan" appears, for example, in D. H. Lawrence, "Pornography and Obscenity," in *Sex, Literature and Censorship*, 69–88. "D. H. Lawrence Dies; Noted Novelist," *New York Times*, March 4, 1930, 23.

14. Sir Chartres Biron quoted in Diana Souhami, *The Trials of Radclyffe Hall* (New York: Doubleday, 1999), 221. A lively take on modern literary censorship trials and the books that provoked them is Elisabeth Ladenson, *Dirt for Art's Sake: Books on Trial from "Madame Bovary" to "Lolita"* (Ithaca, NY: Cornell University Press, 2007).

15. William Bradford, *Of Plymouth Plantation*, quoted in Boyer, *Purity in Print*, 167.

16. Anthony Comstock, *Frauds Exposed; Or, How the People Are Deceived and Robbed, and Youth Corrupted* (New York: J. Howard Brown, 1880), 416, 417.

17. On the Jurgen case, see Boyer, *Purity in Print*, 75–78. Theodore Dreiser quoted in Helen Richardson to William Shaw, January 23, 1940, folder "William Shaw to Theodore Dreiser," Box 5, MSS 6220, University of Virginia Special Collections.

18. For an excellent, thoroughgoing analysis of the link between ideas of sexual purity and fear of national ruin since the nineteenth century, see Sara Moslener, *Virgin Nation: Sexual Purity and American Adolescence* (New York: Oxford University Press, 2015).

19. Morris Ernst, "Foreword," *Ulysses* (New York: The Modern Library, 1934, 1961), v.

20. Alison M. Parker, "Mothering the Movies: Women Reformers and Popular Culture," in *Movie Censorship and American Culture*, ed. Francis G. Couvares (Washington, DC: Smithsonian Institution Press, 1996), 73–96; quotes on 74, 86.

21. James M. Skinner, *The Cross and the Cinema: The Legion of Decency and the National Catholic Office for Motion Pictures, 1933-1970* (Westport, CT: Praeger, 1993), 15.

22. Quoted in Ruth A. Inglis, *Freedom of the Movies: A Report on Self-Regulation from The Commission on Freedom of the Press* (Chicago: University of Chicago Press, 1947), 133–134.

23. Quoted in Skinner, *Cross and the Cinema*, 19.

24. "The Traffic in Smut," *Christian Century* 48 (December 9, 1931): 1552–1553.

25. Una M. Cadegan, *All Good Books Are Catholic Books* (Ithaca, NY: Cornell University Press, 2013), 129–134.

26. See Aljean Harmetz, *The Making of Casablanca: Bogart, Berman, and World War II* (New York: Hyperion, 2002); and Skinner, *Cross and the Cinema*.

27. Pius XI, "Vigilanti Cura: Encyclical Letter of Pope Pius XI on the Motion Picture," *Libreria Editrice Vaticana*, June 29, 1936, http://w2.vatican.va/content/pius-xi/en/encyclicals/documents/hf_p-xi_enc_29061936_vigilanti-cura.html.

28. The story of NODL is recounted in Thomas F. O'Connor, "The National Organization for Decent Literature: A Phase in American Catholic Censorship," *Library Quarterly* 65, no. 4 (1995): 386–414; and Una M. Cadegan, "Guardians of Democracy or Cultural Storm Troopers? American Catholics and the Control of Popular Media, 1934-1966," *Catholic Historical Review* 87, no. 2 (April 2001): 252–282.

29. "Vatican Over Hollywood," *Nation* 143 (July 11, 1936), 33.

30. Drew Pearson, "Effective Censorship," *Washington Post*, March 25, 1943, 12; "Vigilante Censorship Is Spreading," *Christian Century* 70 (April 8, 1943), 404; Charles Clayton Morrison, *Can Protestantism Win America?* (New York: Harper, 1948), 64. All are cited in Cadegan, "Guardians of Democracy or Cultural Storm Troopers?," the first two references on 252, the latter on 267n46. Edmund Wilson to Allen Tate, January 4, 1951, in Edmund Wilson, *Letters on Literature and Politics, 1912-1972*, ed. Elena Wilson (New York: Farrar, Straus and Giroux, 1977), 495.

31. Cadegan, "Guardians of Democracy or Cultural Storm Troopers?," 266.

32. R. L. Duffus, "Things That Make Boston What She Is," *New York Times*, February 16, 1930, 85. See also Boyer, *Purity in Print*, 167–206.

33. "D. H. Lawrence to Edward Garnett (22 April 1914)," in *The Letters of D. H. Lawrence*, Vol. 2, June 1913-October 1916, ed. George J. Zytaruk and James T. Boulton (Cambridge: Cambridge University Press, 2000), 165.

34. D. H. Lawrence, "Apocalypse, Fragment 2" and "Apocalypse, Fragment 1," in *Apocalypse and the Writings on Revelation*, ed. Mara Kalnins (1931; reprint, London: Penguin, 1995), 190, 155.

35. George A. Panichas, *Adventure in Consciousness: The Meaning of D. H. Lawrence's Religious Quest* (The Hague: Mouton, 1964), 17.

36. D. H. Lawrence, "Hymns in a Man's Life," in *Pheonix II: More Uncollected Writings by D. H. Lawrence*, ed. Warren Roberts and Harry T. Moore (New York: Viking, 1968), 597, 598, 599. This essay was first published in German as "Kirchenlieder im Leben Eines Mannes," in *Buch des Dankes für Hans Carossa* (Berlin: Insel Verlag, 1928) and shortly thereafter, in the English version in *Evening News* (London), October 13, 1928.

37. Anne E. Fernald, "'Out of It': Alienation and Coercion in D. H. Lawrence," *Modern Fiction Studies* 49, no. 2 (Summer 2003): 192.

38. D. H. Lawrence, "A Propos of Lady Chatterley's Lover," in *Sex, Literature, and Censorship*, 102–103.

39. D. H. Lawrence, "Making Love to Music," in *Sex, Literature, and Censorship*, 41.

40. D. H. Lawrence, "The State of Funk," in *Sex, Literature, and Censorship*, 67, 68.

41. D. H. Lawrence, *Lady Chatterley's Lover*, ed. Michael Squires (1928; reprint, New York: Penguin, 1994), 6, 46, 47, 48, 49, 54, 55. I am following the novel's usage of first names for the Chatterleys and surname for the gamekeeper.

42. Ibid., 66, 117, 134, 136, 137.

43. Ibid., 246, 247.

44. Lawrence, "A Propos of Lady Chatterley's Lover," 115, 116; Lawrence, *Lady Chatterley's Lover*, 206, 277, 302.

45. D. H. Lawrence, "The State of Pornography and Obscenity," in *Sex, Literature, and Censorship*, 74, 75.

46. Lawrence, "A Propos of Lady Chatterley's Lover," 92.

47. Ibid., 116, 118.

48. John Middleton Murry, *Son of Woman: The Story of D. H. Lawrence* (London: Jonathan Cape, 1931), 21, 54.

49. Thomas Stearns Eliot, "Preface," in Eliot, *For Lancelot Andrewes: Essays on Style and Order* (London: Faber & Gwyer, 1928), ix.

50. *Egoist* 4, no. 10 (November 1917): 151, cited in C. E. Baron, "Lawrence's Influence on Eliot," *Cambridge Quarterly* 5, no. 3 (Spring 1971): 238.

51. T. S. Eliot, "Les Lettres Anglaises," *La Nouvelle Revue Française* 28 (1927): 671, 672; Eliot's original English text appears in "T. S. Eliot, from 'The Contemporary Novel,' in *D. H. Lawrence: The Critical Heritage*, ed. R. P. Draper (New York: Barnes & Noble, 1970), 275–277.

52. See Baron, "Lawrence's Influence on Eliot," 236.

53. Lawrence, *Lady Chatterley's Lover*, 16.

54. T. S. Eliot, review of *Son of Woman: The Story of D. H. Lawrence*, by John Middleton Murry, *Criterion: A Quarterly Review* (July 1931): 769, 772, 771, 773. See also F. R. Leavis, "D. H. Lawrence and Professor Irving Babbitt," *Scrutiny* 1, no. 3 (Dec. 1932): 277, 278.

55. T. S. Eliot, *After Strange Gods: A Primer of Modern Heresy* (New York: Harcourt, Brace, 1934), 63, 64, 65, 66, 39.

56. Ruth Frisbie Moore, "Spades and D. H. Lawrence," *The Bookman: A Review of Books and Life* 72, no. 2 (October 1930): 118, 119, 122; Harold C. Gardiner, *Norms for the Novel*, rev. ed. (New York: Hanover House, 1960), 58, 60.

57. George Every, S.S.M., review of *After Strange Gods* by T. S. Eliot, in *Theology* 29 (July 1934): 57; Every, "D.H. Lawrence," in *The New Spirit*, ed., E. W. Martin (Dennis Dobson LTD, 1946), 63.

58. Thomas Merton, "D.H. Lawrence Who Saw Himself as a Messiah," *New York Times Book Review*, January 14, 1940, BR3. See William York Tindall, *D.H. Lawrence and Susan His Cow* (New York: Columbia University Press, 1939).

59. George Every, "D. H. Lawrence," in *The New Spirit*, ed. E. W. Martin (London: Dobson, 1946), 65.

60. William Tiverton [Martin Jarrett-Kerr], *D. H. Lawrence and Human Existence* (London: Rockliff, 1951), xi.

61. Nathan A. Scott Jr., *Rehearsals of Discomposure: Alienation and Reconciliation in Modern Literature: Franz Kafka, Ignazio Silone, D. H. Lawrence, T. S. Eliot* (New York: King's Crown, 1952), 132.

62. H. W. Reimann, review of *Love Ethic of D. H. Lawrence* by Mark Spilka, *Concordia Theological Monthly* 28, no. 10 (October 1957): 782; Mark Spilka, *The Love Ethic of D. H. Lawrence* (Bloomington: Indiana University Press, 1955), 217; see also A. Whigham Price, "D. H. Lawrence and Congregationalism," *Congregational Quarterly* 34 (July 1956): 242–252.

63. Horton Davies, "The God of Light and the Dark Deities: A Revaluation of D. H. Lawrence," *Religion in Life* 38, no. 2 (Summer 1969): 231. Reprinted as "D. H. Lawrence: A Revaluation" in Horton Davies, *Catching the Conscience: Essays in Religion and Literature* (Cambridge, MA: Cowley, 1984), 25–39.

64. For a firsthand account of the *Lady Chatterley's Lover* trial and other obscenity cases, see Charles Rembar, *The End of Obscenity* (New York: Random House, 1968). For a range of contemporary media coverage covering the Catholic Brennan and his majority opinions, see *Catholic Standard and Times*, July 3, 1964; *Operation Yorkville*, September–October 1964; *Tablet*, September 3, 1964; *New York Times*, June 23, 1964.

CHAPTER 3

1. Martha Hodes, *White Women, Black Men: Illicit Sex in the Nineteenth-Century South* (New Haven, CT: Yale University Press, 1997), 1.

2. Peggy Pascoe, *What Comes Naturally: Miscegenation Law and the Making of Race in America* (New York: Oxford University Press, 2009), 1.

3. John D'Emilio and Estelle E. Freedman, *Intimate Matters: A History of Sexuality in America*, 3rd ed. (1988; reprint, Chicago: University of Chicago Press, 2012), 35.

4. Catherine Clinton, "Breaking the Silence: Sexual Hypocrisies from Thomas Jefferson to Strom Thurmond," in *Beyond Slavery: Overcoming Its Religious and Sexual Legacies*, ed. Bernadette J. Brooten (New York: Palgrave Macmillan, 2010), 215.

5. "Elijah Fletcher's Account of a Visit to Monticello, [8 May 1811]," in *The Papers of Thomas Jefferson*, Retirement Series, vol. 3, *12 August 1810 to 17 June 1811*, ed. J. Jefferson Looney (Princeton, NJ: Princeton University Press, 2006), 610–611, available online: http://founders.archives.gov/documents /Jefferson/03-03-02-0483.

6. See Paul Harvey, *Freedom's Coming: Religious Culture and the Shaping of the South from the Civil War Through the Civil Rights Era* (Chapel Hill: University of North Carolina Press, 2005), 229.

7. Samuel A. Cartwright, "Unity of the Human Race Disproved by the Hebrew Bible," *De Bow's Review* 29 (August 1860), cited in George M. Fredrickson, *The Black Image in the White Mind: The Debate on Afro-American Character and Destiny, 1817-1914* (1971; reprint, Middletown, CT: Wesleyan University Press, 1987), 87.

8. Ariel [Buckner H. Payne], *The Negro: What Is His Ethnological Status?* (1867), cited in Jane Dailey, "Sex, Segregation, and the Sacred After *Brown*," *Journal of American History* (June 2004): 123.

9. Cartwright, cited in Fredrickson, *Black Image in the White Mind*, 88. For more on white Christian readings of racial amalgamation as the "root of all evil," see Charles Marsh, *God's Long Summer: Stories of Faith and Civil Rights* (Princeton, NJ: Princeton University Press, 1997), 93 and surrounding.

10. Southern Baptist Convention *Proceedings*, 1863, 54; North Carolina Baptist State Convention *Minutes*, 1861, 22; and Baptist General Association of Virginia *Minutes*, 1861, 15–16, all quoted in Paul Harvey, *Redeeming the South: Religious Cultures and Racial Identities Among Southern Baptists, 1865-1925* (Chapel Hill: University of North Carolina Press, 1997), 18.

11. Paul Harvey, "God and Negroes and Jesus and Sin and Salvation: Racism, Racial Interchange, and Interracialism in Southern Religious History," in *Religion in the American South: Protestants and Others in History and Culture*, ed. Beth Barton Schweiger and Donald G. Mathews (Chapel Hill: University of North Carolina Press, 2004), 284, 286.

12. Fay Botham, *Almighty God Created the Races: Christianity, Interracial Marriage, and American Law* (Chapel Hill: University of North Carolina Press, 2009), 145, 156; see also Michael Kent Curtis, "A Unique Religious Exemption from Antidiscrimination Laws in the Case of Gays? Putting the Call for Exemptions for Those Who Discriminate Against Married or Marrying Gays in Context," in *The Rule of Law and the Rule of God*, ed. Simeon O. Ilesanmi, Win-Chiat Lee, and J. Wilson Parker (New York: Palgrave Macmillan, 2014), 91–96.

13. "Caucasian" [William Campbell], *Anthropology for the People: A Refutation of the Theory of the Adamic Origin of All Races* (Richmond, VA: Everett Wadly, 1891), 29–30, cited in Harvey, *Freedom's Coming*, 43.

14. H. Paul Douglass, *Christian Reconstruction in the South* (Boston, 1909), 114, cited in Dailey, "Sex, Segregation, and the Sacred," 124.

15. Charles Carroll, *The Negro A Beast . . . Or . . . In the Image of God* (St. Louis: American Book and Bible House, 1900), 164.

16. Crystal N. Feimster, *Southern Horrors: Women and the Politics of Rape and Lynching* (Cambridge, MA: Harvard University Press, 2009), 51.

17. Henry McNeal Turner, "On the Anniversary of the Emancipation," *Colored American*, January 13, 1866, in *Moral Evil and Redemptive Suffering: A History of Theodicy in African-American Religious Thought*, ed. Anthony B. Pinn (Gainesville: University Press of Florida, 2002), 102–110.

18. Dr. J. A. Rice, quoted in Ray Stannard Baker, *Following the Color Line: An Account of Negro Citizenship in the American Democracy* (New York: Doubleday, 1908), 165.

19. W. E. B. Du Bois, "Intermarriage," *Crisis* 5, no. 4 (February 1913): 181.

20. Equal Justice Initiative (EJI), *Lynching in America: Confronting the Legacy of Racial Terror* (Montgomery, AL: Equal Justice Initiative, 2015), 31, 33. EJI documented 3,959 racial terror lynchings across twelve Southern states; other sources claim well over 4,000 such lynchings in that era.

21. J. T. Winston, "Lynching Defended," *Nation* (June 22, 1916), 671.

22. EJI, *Lynching in America*, 31.

23. Leon F. Litwack, *Trouble in Mind: Black Southerners in the Age of Jim Crow* (New York: Knopf, 1998), 297.

24. Grace Elizabeth Hale, *Making Whiteness: The Culture of Segregation in the South, 1890-1940* (New York: Vintage, 1998), 212, 213. This is part of Hale's longer, astute analysis of "spectacle lynching."

25. 62 Cong. Rec. 548 (December 19, 1921) (statement of Representative Garrett); 62 Cong. Rec. 1426 (January 19, 1922) (statement of Representative Rankin).

26. Bethune's pledge for the National Council of Negro Women: http://66.132.241.16/about/bethune.htm. "Marian Anderson 1939 Lincoln Memorial Speech and Song," YouTube video, 5:31, posted by "Thomas David Franklin," December 7, 2008, https://www.youtube.com/watch?v=AkPIoVKM4Fk.

27. Kristina DuRocher, *Raising Racists: The Socialization of White Children in the Jim Crow South* (Lexington: University Press of Kentucky, 2011), 157.

28. 83 Cong. Rec. 873 (January 21, 1938) (statement of Senator Bilbo). Biographical studies of Bilbo include A. Wigfall Green, *The Man Bilbo* (Baton Rouge: Louisiana State University Press, 1963), and Chester M. Morgan, *Redneck Liberal: Theodore G. Bilbo and the New Deal* (Baton Rouge: Louisiana State University Press, 1985).

29. "Race Relations and Home Missions," *Home Missions* 14 (April 1943): 3; *Annual*, Florida, 1943, 74, quoted in Mark Newman, *Getting Right with God: Southern Baptists and Desegregation, 1945-1995* (Tuscaloosa: University of Alabama Press, 2001), 18.

30. Olive Schreiner, *Woman and Labour*, 8th ed., 258, 19, quoted in Margaret M. Caffrey, *Ruth Benedict: Stranger in This Land* (Austin: University of Texas Press, 1989), 71.

31. Benedict's paper receives discussion in Lois W. Banner, *Intertwined Lives: Margaret Mead, Ruth Benedict, and Their Circle* (New York: Knopf, 2003), 148. [Undated], in Margaret Mead, *An Anthropologist at Work: Writings of Ruth Benedict* (Boston: Houghton Mifflin, 1959), 147.

32. Caffrey, *Ruth Benedict*, 135.

33. Ruth Benedict, *Patterns of Culture*, 7th ed. (Boston: Houghton Mifflin, 1934), 36–37.

34. Ruth Benedict to Margaret Mead, February 14, 1936, Library of Congress, Margaret Mead Papers, S-5, quoted in Banner, *Intertwined Lives*, 211.

35. Benedict, *Patterns of Culture*, 126.

36. Caffrey, *Ruth Benedict*, 214. Caffrey analyzes *Patterns of Culture* and its popular impact, 206–214.

37. *Can You Name Them?* (New York: American Committee for Democracy and Intellectual Freedom, 1939), 8, quoted in Zoë Burkholder, *Color in the Classroom: How American Schools Taught Race, 1900-1954* (Oxford: Oxford University Press, 2011), 58.

38. *Can You Name Them?* quoted in Burkholder, *Color in the Classroom*, 59. The story of Boas and Benedict's involvement in anti-racism work for the public education system receives much attention in this book. I've relied on Burkholder's research and analysis for important contextual information in this section of the chapter.

39. Burkholder, *Color in the Classroom*, 46.

40. Ruth Benedict and Mildred Ellis, *Race and Cultural Relations: America's Answer to the Myth of a Master Race*, Problems in American Life: Unit No. 5 (Washington, DC: National Education Association, 1942), 7.

41. Ruth Benedict and Gene Weltfish, *The Races of Mankind*, Public Affairs Pamphlet No. 85 (New York: Public Affairs Committee, 1943), 3, 5. The pamphlet was reprinted in Ruth Benedict, *Race: Science and Politics*, rev. ed. (New York: Viking, 1959), quotes on 171, 172.

42. Benedict and Weltfish, *Races of Mankind*, 14.

43. Maxwell S. Stewart, *20th Century Pamphleteering: The History of the Public Affairs Committee* (New York: Public Affairs Committee, 1976), 12.

44. Burkholder, *Color in the Classroom*, 79.

45. Quoted in Stewart, *20th Century Pamphleteering*, 12–13.

46. James Edmund Boyack, "USO Bans Pamphlets Dealing with Races," *Pittsburgh Courier*, January 22, 1944, 4; "Army Orders Booklets to Curb Race Ignorance," *Atlanta Daily World*, February 4, 1944, 6. Likewise, an editorial in the *New York Amsterdam News* opined, "If the USO is willing to bar any scientific truth because it is concerned about the way it will be accepted by Southerners or Northerners, then the USO is certainly not serving its purpose. On the other hand, it is serving to perpetuate ignorance and prejudice" (January 29, 1944, 6A). The CIO decision was widely reported; see "CIO to Send Soldiers Banned Race Pamphlet," *Chicago Defender*, February 19, 1944, 19.

47. Recounted in Stewart, *20th Century Pamphleteering*, 13.

48. Cited in Stetson Kennedy, *Southern Exposure* (Garden City, NY: Doubleday, 1946), 86.

49. "Hits 'Races of Mankind,'" *New York Times* April 28, 1944, 7; "Racial Book Used by Army Hit in House," *Washington Post*, April 28, 1944, 3. See also Lt. Col. Arthur Farlow, "Supplementary Notes on Hearing of Special Committee, House Military Affairs Committee," March 8, 1944, File SPMS 352.11, Box 310, Entry (NM3) 285 Classified Decimal Correspondence File, 1942–1948, Records of the Troop Information and Education Division, Records of the Army Staff, Record Group 319, National Archives, College Park, MD. In the memo, marked "Confidential" and only declassified later, Farlow wrote of the special committee members grilling him with "'wife-beater' questions" about the pamphlet; working to persuade his questioners that its use was meant to counteract Nazi and Japanese racial propaganda, Farlow wrote that he was repeatedly asked "whether I did not think that the fact that the pamphlet might not have one or another specific reaction within the South, and repeatedly was asked questions concerning my knowledge of an interest in the problem of the American Negro" (1, 2).

50. Benedict and Weltfish, *The Races of Mankind*, reprinted in Benedict, *Race*, 179.

51. 90 Cong. Rec. 2396, 2397 (March 8, 1944) (statement of Representative Bryson). Pascoe, *What Comes Naturally*, 124.

52. George Lewis, *The White South and the Red Menace: Segregationists, Anticommunism, and Massive Resistance, 1945-1965* (Gainesville: University Press of Florida, 2004), 16.

53. David H. Price, *Threatening Anthropology: McCarthyism and the FBI's Surveillance of Activist Anthropologists* (Durham, NC: Duke University Press, 2004), 115.

54. 90 Cong. Rec. 4408, 4413 (May 12, 1944) (statements of Senators McClellan and Bilbo). For earlier anti–poll tax references to raping the Constitution, see, e.g., 88 Cong. Rec. 8836, 8844 (November 13 and 14, 1942). Bilbo himself publicly disclosed his Klan membership on the Mutual Broadcasting System's radio program *Meet the Press* in 1946. See "Senator Bilbo States He Is a Klan Member," *New York Times*, August 10, 1946, 15.

55. 90 Cong. Rec. 5028 (May 26, 1944) (statement of Representative Tarver).

56. 90 Cong. Rec. 6251 (June 20, 1944) (statement of Senator Bilbo); Franz Boas, "The Real Race Problem," *Crisis* 1, no.2 (December 1910), 25; 90 Cong. Rec. A1798, A1801 (April 1944) (address of Hon. Theodore G. Bilbo, placed in the Record by himself). Allen Drury, then a Senate reporter for the United Press, wrote in his diary that the June 20 oration was "a vicious, dirty speech

by Bilbo, who was hissed from the galleries and deserved it"; a month earlier, he called Bilbo "evil and ruthless" (Drury, *A Senate Journal, 1943-1945* [New York: McGraw-Hill, 1963], 200, 168). The role of race in this opposition to the FEPC is discussed (with additional sources) in Nancy Beck Young, *Why We Fight: Congress and the Politics of World War II* (Lawrence: University Press of Kansas, 2013), 123–126.

57. Harvey, *Freedom's Coming*, 238; Archibald Coody IV, *The Race Question* (Vicksburg, MS: Mississippi Printing Company, 1944), 86, 87, 99, 97.

58. On Coody and his connection to Bilbo, see Randy J. Sparks, *Religion in Mississippi* (Jackson: University Press of Mississippi, 2001), 231–234; Harvey, *Freedom's Coming*, 238; and Dennis J. Mitchell, *A New History of Mississippi* (University Press of Mississippi, 2014), 419–420.

59. White's speech was entered into the congressional record for both the House of Representatives and the Senate; see 90 Cong. Rec. A2926-A2927 (June 9, 1944) (address of Walter White, placed in the Record by Hon. Martin J. Kennedy of New York); and 90 Cong. Rec. A3264-A3265 (June 22, 1944) (address of Walter White, placed in the Record by Hon. Arthur Capper of Kansas).

60. 91 Cong. Rec. 6807, 6806, 6816, 6807 (June 27, 1945) (statement of Senator Bilbo).

61. Ira Calvin, *The Lost White Race* (Brookline, MA: Countway-White, 1945), 115–116, 10, 78, 24, 108, 21. The same quotes appear in Ira Calvin White, *Only Blondes Are Angels* (Brookline, MA: Countway-White, 1945), 61, 57, 31, 18, 55, 16.

62. Theodore G. Bilbo, *Take Your Choice: Separation or Mongrelization* (Poplarville, MS: Dream House, 1947), 166, 79, 108, 164, 162, 183, 182, 183. This publisher seems not to have published any other books. Eric J. Sundquist writes that Dream House was Bilbo's own mansion (Sundquist, *Faulkner: The House Divided* [Baltimore: Johns Hopkins University Press, 1983], 146). See G. A. Borgese, "A Bedroom Approach to Racism," *Negro Digest*, December 1944, 31, cited in S. W. Garlington, "Newsettes," *New York Amsterdam News*, December 23, 1944, 15; and "Bedroom Seen Place to Solve Race Problem," *Chicago Defender*, December 23, 1944, 18.

63. Strom Thurmond quoted in Joseph Crespino, *Strom Thurmond's America* (New York: Hill and Wang, 2012), 68, 71. This clip from the audio recording of Thurmond's speech can be heard on *The Daily Show*: Jon Stewart, "Racists Have Birthdays Too!" *The Daily Show with Jon Stewart*, 4:45, December 11, 2002, www.cc.com/video-clips/ot856d/the-daily-show-with-jon-stewart-racists-have -birthdays-too-. Essie Mae Washington-Williams, *Dear Senator: A Memoir by the Daughter of Strom Thurmond* (New York: HarperCollins, 2005). See also Clinton, "Breaking the Silence."

64. This event is detailed in Price, *Threatening Anthropology*, 126–131.

65. Rev. G. T. Gillespie, *A Christian View on Segregation* (Greenwood, MS: Citizens' Councils, 1954), 2, 3, 2, 8, 11; also cited in Marsh, *God's Long Summer*, 232n124.

66. Jerry Falwell, "Segregation or Integration—Which?," sermon preached at Thomas Road Baptist Church and reprinted in *Word of Life*, October 1958; quoted in Daniel K. Williams, *God's Own Party: The Making of the Christian Right* (New York: Oxford University Press, 2010), 46.

67. Paul S. Boyer, *Purity in Print: Book Censorship in America from the Gilded Age to the Computer Age*, 2nd ed. (Madison: University of Wisconsin Press, 2002), 286, 282; Williams quoted in Douglas Martin, "Emily W. Reed, 89, Librarian in '59 Alabama Racial Dispute," *New York Times*, May 29, 2000.

68. John R. Rice, *Negro and White* (Wheaton, IL: Sword of the Lord, 1956), 3, quoted in Bill J. Leonard, "A Theology for Racism: Southern Fundamentalists and the Civil Rights Movement," in *Southern Landscapes*, ed. Tony Badger, Walter Edgar, and Jon Nordby Gretlund (Tübingen: Stauffenburg, 1996), 169–170.

69. "An Address by Dr. W. A. Criswell, Pastor, First Baptist Church, Dallas, Texas, to the Joint Assembly, State of South Carolina, Wednesday, February 22, 1956, 12:30 PM" (n.p., n.d.); T. C. Hardman to the *Christian Index*, July 22, 1954; both quoted in Newman, *Getting Right with God*, 60.

70. Montague Cook, "Racial Intergration [*sic*] Opposes the Purpose of God," in *Racial Segregation Is Christian: Two Sermons on Racial Segregation* (n.p., n.d.), quoted in Newman, *Getting Right with God*, 61.

71. James F. Burke, "Integration or Segregation," *Religious Herald*, May 3, 1956, quoted in Newman, *Getting Right with God*, 56.

72. Noel Smith, "The 'Insight' King Brought McCall," *Baptist Bible Times*, May 26, 1961, 4, quoted in Williams, *God's Own Party*, 48.

73. Loving v. Virginia, 388 US. 1, 3 (1967).

CHAPTER 4

1. An earlier version of this chapter appeared as R. Marie Griffith, "The Religious Encounters of Alfred C. Kinsey," *Journal of American History* 95, no. 2 (September 2008): 349–377.

2. Alfred C. Kinsey, Wardell B. Pomeroy, and Clyde E. Martin, *Sexual Behavior in the Human Male* (Philadelphia: Saunders, 1948); Alfred C. Kinsey, Wardell B. Pomeroy, Clyde E. Martin, and Paul H. Gebhard, *Sexual Behavior in the Human Female* (Philadelphia: Saunders, 1953); Donald Porter Geddes and Enid Curie, ed., *About the Kinsey Report: Observations by 11 Experts on "Sexual Behavior in the Human Male"* (New York: New American Library, 1948), 17; *Washington Post*, November 14, 1948, M19.

3. Alfred C. Kinsey to Leonard Anderson, September 26, 1944, November 3, 1945; Kinsey to Fay Campbell, January 1, 1945; Campbell to Kinsey, January

5, 1945, Kinsey Personal Correspondence files, Kinsey Institute, Bloomington, Indiana.

4. "Pandering to Prurience," *America*, January 3, 1948, 371–72.

5. Kinsey, Pomeroy, and Martin, *Sexual Behavior in the Human Male*, 465–468 [pages interrupted by chart], 487.

6. "News Release on the Kinsey Report," issued by Loyola University, Chicago, January 15, 1948.

7. George Gallup, "Kinsey Survey of Sex Habits Is Widely Approved by Public," *Washington Post*, February 21, 1948, 11.

8. Charles G. Wilber, "Religious Aspects—A Catholic Viewpoint," in *Sex Habits of American Men: A Symposium on the Kinsey Report*, ed. Albert Deutsch (New York: Prentice-Hall, 1948), 187, 191.

9. Louis I. Newman, "Religious Aspects—A Jewish Viewpoint," in Deutsch, ed., *Sex Habits of American Men*, 199, 200.

10. Seward Hiltner, "Religious Aspects—A Protestant Viewpoint," in Deutsch, ed., *Sex Habits of American Men*, 181.

11. Bruce Bliven, "Appraising 'The Kinsey Report,'" *New York Times*, May 16, 1948, BR4. See also Sterling North, "Two 'Footnotes' Illuminate Kinsey Report," *Washington Post*, May 16, 1949, B7.

12. Reinhold Niebuhr, "Sex Standards in America," *Christianity and Crisis*, May 24, 1948, 65, 66. A month later, Union Theological Seminary president Henry Van Dusen would concur in the same magazine: "The Moratorium on Moral Revulsion," *Christianity and Crisis*, June 21, 1948, 81 and surrounding.

13. "Sex and the Church," *Time*, June 7, 1948, 76.

14. Wesley J. Buck's letter to Kinsey is not in the files of the Kinsey Institute, but Kinsey's response makes clear Buck's request. Kinsey to Wesley J. Buck, August 7, 1948, Kinsey Personal Correspondence files.

15. Rev. Ward Avery to Kinsey, July 11, 1948, Kinsey to Avery, August 12, 1948, Avery to Kinsey, August 20, 1955, Kinsey Personal Correspondence files.

16. Samuel M. Carter to Kinsey, September 10, 1948, Kinsey Personal Correspondence files.

17. "Kinsey Report Hit in Catholic Group," *New York Times*, September 15, 1948, 20.

18. Roy A. Burkhart, "The Church Can Answer the Kinsey Report," *Christian Century*, September 15, 1948, 942, 943. Burkhart's work, including his controversial marriage clinics and "seminars on sex adjustment problems" had been profiled by *Time* magazine a year earlier ("Beloved Fellowship," *Time*, August 11, 1947).

19. Leslie Woodcock Tentler, *Catholics and Contraception: An American History* (Ithaca, NY: Cornell University Press, 2004); John T. McGreevy, *Catholicism and American Freedom* (New York: W. W. Norton, 2003), esp. 221–249.

20. Otis R. Rice, "Educational Considerations from the Church Point of View," in *Problems of Sexual Behavior; Research, Education, Community Action* (New York: ASHA, 1948), 130–136, esp. 136. This volume compiled the proceedings of a symposium held by the American Social Hygiene Association in New York, March 30–April 1, 1948, to consider the first Kinsey report and "its relation to the social hygiene program" (title page). "Effects Weighed of Kinsey Report," *New York Times*, April 1, 1948, 50.

21. Kinsey to Otis R. Rice, October 18, 1948, Kinsey Personal Correspondence files.

22. Kinsey to Rice, November 7, 1948, Kinsey Personal Correspondence files.

23. Joseph Barth, "Religion and the Kinsey Report," typescript sermon, November 21, 1948, 1, 2, 4, Binder 72, p. 62, Media Responses to Kinsey collection, Kinsey Institute.

24. *Washington Post*, November 14, 1948, M19.

25. See, for instance, Kinsey to J. Carlton Babbs, January 8, 1949, Kinsey Personal Correspondence files.

26. Kinsey to Bishop Karl Morgan Block, June 13, 1951, July 10, 1951; Block to Kinsey, April 10, 1952, Kinsey to Block, April 15, 1952, Kinsey Personal Correspondence files.

27. John Chapple to Kinsey, telegram, August 21, 1953, Binder 72, p. 102, Media Responses to Kinsey collection.

28. National Council of Catholic Women to Herman Wells, August 24, 1953, Wells to Mrs. Harold D. Brady of the National Council of Catholic Women, September 2, 1953, Binder 72, p. 80, Media Responses to Kinsey collection. Wells also reprinted these letters in his memoir; see Herman B. Wells, *Being Lucky: Reminiscences and Reflections* (Bloomington: Indiana University Press, 1980), 182–185.

29. Kinsey et al., *Sexual Behavior in the Human Female*, 324, 345. On rates of premarital sex, see 282–345.

30. Ibid., 320, 368.

31. Ibid., 233, 231, 264, 154.

32. Ibid., 316, 285, 14, 269, 282.

33. Ibid., viii.

34. William D. Wyatt, "The Kinsey Report," typescript sermon, August 30, 1953, Binder 72, p. 93, Media Responses to Kinsey collection.

35. John S. Wimbish, "The Kinsey Report in the Light of the Bible," sermon, 1, 9, Binder 72, p. 91, Media Responses to Kinsey collection. Reprinted as "Kinsey in the Light of the Bible," in *I Accuse Kinsey! Startling Exposé of Kinsey's Sex Reports*, ed. E. J. Daniels (Orlando: Christ for the World Publishers, 1954), 113–126.

36. Torrey M. Johnson, "The Kinsey Report and the Bible," typescript sermon, October 11, 1953, 5, 6, Binder 72, p. 86, Media Responses to Kinsey collection. Jean S. Milner, minister of the Second Presbyterian Church in Indianapolis, also equated the Kinsey report with Communism; see Milner, "The Celestial Fire," sermon, October 18, 1953, esp. 10–12, Binder 72, p. 89, Media Responses to Kinsey collection.

37. For Billy Graham's sermon, "The Bible and Dr. Kinsey," delivered on *The Hour of Decision* radio program on September 13, 1953, see Daniels, *I Accuse Kinsey!*, 103–112, esp. 103, 104; and Billy Graham, "The Bible and Dr. Kinsey," *Moody Monthly* (November 1953): 13, 44.

38. Johnson, "The Kinsey Report and the Bible," 2.

39. Lawrence K. Whitfield, "Dr. Kinsey Goes to Church," sermon, December 27, 1953, p.2, 5, Binder 72, p. 90, Media Responses to Kinsey collection.

40. Wells, *Being Lucky*, 181–182.

41. Reinhold Niebuhr, "Sex and Religion in the Kinsey Report," *Christianity and Crisis*, November 2, 1953, 140, 141; Seward Hiltner, "Niebuhr on Kinsey," *Christianity and Crisis*, January 11, 1954, 181–82; Niebuhr, "More on Kinsey," *Christianity and Crisis*, January 11, 1954, 182; see also Ursula M. Niebuhr, review of *Sex Ethics and the Kinsey Reports* by Seward Hiltner, *Religion in Life* 23 (Summer 1954): 472–474. The historian Paul Robinson, arguing that Kinsey's works ultimately demonstrated loyalty to heterosexual marriage, took Niebuhr to task for his repeated critique, citing him explicitly in noting that "Kinsey was unquestionably wronged when he was made the prophet of 'anarchism in the field of sex'" (Paul Robinson, *The Modernization of Sex: Havelock Ellis, Alfred Kinsey, William Masters, and Virginia Johnson* [New York: Harper & Row, 1976], 80).

42. Kinsey to Block, November 25, 1953; Block to Kinsey, November 30, 1953; Kinsey to Block, December 4, 1953, January 9, 1954; Kinsey Personal Correspondence files.

43. Daniels, *I Accuse Kinsey!*; Kinsey to E. J. Daniels, January 8, 1954, E. J. Daniels File, Kinsey Correspondence Collection.

44. Daniels, *I Accuse Kinsey!*; Kinsey to E. J. Daniels, January 8, 1954. Seward Hiltner to Kinsey, January 8, 1954; Kinsey to Hiltner, January 18, 1954, Kinsey Personal Correspondence files.

45. Sexson Humphreys, "Kinsey Says Churches Are His Backers Now," *Indianapolis, IND News*, February 5, 1954; Rice to Kinsey, February 5, 1954; Kinsey to Rice, February 8, 1954, Kinsey Personal Correspondence files.

46. Derrick Sherwin Bailey to Kinsey, October 18, 1954; Kinsey to Bailey, November 10, 1954; Kinsey to Bailey, June 25, 1956; Bailey to Kinsey, August 8, 1956; Bailey to Eleanor Roehr, September 10, 1956 [final letter in the Bailey correspondence file], Kinsey Personal Correspondence files.

47. Jonathan Gathorne-Hardy, *Sex the Measure of All Things: A Life of Alfred C. Kinsey* (Bloomington; Indiana University Press, 2000), 412.

48. Derrick Sherwin Bailey, *The Mystery of Love and Marriage: A Study on the Theology of Sexual Relation* (New York: Harper & Bros., 1952); Derrick Sherwin Bailey, *Homosexuality and the Western Christian Tradition* (London: Longmans, 1955); Derrick Sherwin Bailey, *Sexual Relation in Christian Thought* (New York: Harper & Bros., 1959). Robert M. Grant, review of *Sexual Relation in Christian Thought, Journal of Religion* 40 (July 1960): 212–213. Examples of how Bailey is still cited in scholarly sources include William A. Percy's review of *The Invention of Sodomy in Christian Theology* by Mark D. Jordan, *American Historical Review* 103 (April 1998): 496; "Bailey, Derrick Sherwin," in *Encyclopedia of Homosexuality*, ed. Wayne R. Dynes (New York: Garland, 1990), 103–104. A more intriguing source is a 2004 article by Dr. Gordon Hugenberger, senior minister of the landmark evangelical Park Street Church in Boston, titled "Questions and Answers on Issues Related to Homosexuality and Same-Sex Marriage." Hugenberger criticizes Bailey's "speculative views" that aimed to show that the Bible did not oppose homosexuality as strenuously as conservatives insist. Gordon Hugenberger, "Questions and Answers on Issues Related to Homosexuality and Same-Sex Marriage," June 15, 2004, http://www.gracecovenantpca.org /devotionals/2007/120907.html.

49. Seward Hiltner, "A Descriptive Appraisal, 1935-1980," *Theology Today* 37 (July 1980): 211. An unpublished paper on "Homosexuality and the Churches," written in 1975, also referred to *Sex Ethics and the Kinsey Reports* and lamented that church leaders had apparently "ignored it completely." Hiltner, "Homosexuality and the Churches," unpublished paper, Princeton Theological Seminary, Princeton, NJ, January 1975, Kinsey Institute.

50. Elizabeth Steel Genné and William Henry Genné, eds., "Call to the Conference," in *Foundations for Christian Family Policy: The Proceedings of the North American Conference on Church and Family, April 3-May 5, 1961* (New York: Department of Family Life, National Council of the Churches of Christ in the U.S.A., 1961), 23.

51. Elizabeth Genné and William Genné, *Christians and the Crisis in Sex Morality* (New York: Association Press, 1962), 16–17, 77.

52. Wardell B. Pomeroy, *Dr. Kinsey and the Institute for Sex Research* (New York: Harper & Row, 1972), 453.

53. Genné and Genné, *Christians and the Crisis in Sex Morality*, 119, 120,

54. Harvey Cox and Robert E. Fitch, "The New Protestant Debate over Sex," *Redbook* (October 1964): 104, 56, 104, 105.

55. W. Norman Pittenger, *The Christian View of Sexual Behavior: A Reaction to the Kinsey Report* (Greenwich, CT: Seabury, 1954) [originally a series of articles in *Episcopal Churchnews*, revised for publication as a book], 5.

56. Norman Pittenger, *Time for Consent: A Christian's Approach to Homosexuality* (London: SCM, 1967); Norman Pittenger, *Making Sexuality Human* (Philadelphia: Pilgrim, 1970); Norman Pittenger, *Love and Control in Sexuality* (Philadelphia: Pilgrim, 1974); Norman Pittenger, *Gay Lifestyles: A Christian Interpretation of Homosexuality and the Homosexual* (Los Angeles: Universal Fellowship Press, 1977). The quote is from *Making Sexuality Human*, 10. Pittenger's views grew increasingly liberal over time, and he acknowledged his own homosexuality beginning in the mid to late 1960s.

57. Pittenger, *Making Sexuality Human*, 62–63.

58. Richard A. Norris Jr., "Memorial Eucharist for W. Norman Pittenger, Chapel of the Good Shepherd, The General Theological Seminary, The Feast of Lancelot Andrewes, 1997," *Anglican Theological Review* 80 (Winter 1998): 6, 7.

59. One useful source from the period is John H. Phillips, "Sex Education in Major Protestant Denominations," National Council of the Churches of Christ in the U.S.A. (1968).

CHAPTER 5

1. On Brown, see Jennifer Scanlon, *Bad Girls Go Everywhere: The Life of Helen Gurley Brown* (New York: Oxford University Press, 2009). Friedan's life and impact are chronicled in Susan Oliver, *Betty Friedan: The Personal Is Political* (New York; Parson Longman, 2008).

2. Cited in Jeffrey P. Moran, *Teaching Sex: The Shaping of Adolescence in the Twentieth Century* (Cambridge, MA: Harvard University Press, 2000), 160.

3. Emily Hartshorne Mudd, cited in Rebecca L. Davis, *More Perfect Unions: The American Search for Marital Bliss* (Cambridge, MA: Harvard University Press, 2010), 44.

4. Kristin Luker, *When Sex Goes to School: Warring Views on Sex—and Sex Education—Since the Sixties* (New York: W. W. Norton, 2006), 61.

5. Former student cited in Moran, *Teaching Sex*, 140.

6. Quoted in Moran, *Teaching Sex*, 133.

7. Moran, *Teaching Sex*, 150.

8. Clara recounted her childhood, including her Southern roots and regular participation in camp meetings, in a remarkable unpublished manuscript, where she recorded family legends, her slaveholding grandfather, her Southern pride and practice of "rebel yells," and the experience of going to camp meetings; see Clara Smith Steichen, "An Ozark Childhood," n.d., State Historical Society of Missouri, Collection 3819, folder 1. The life of Edward Steichen (as well as more details about Clara gleaned from oral interviews) is recounted in Penelope Niven, *Steichen: A Biography* (Fort Washington, PA: Eastern National, 1997).

9. Record of Calderone is located in "James E. Hazard Index: The Records of New York Yearly Meeting of the Religious Society of Friends," Swarthmore

College, accessed August 12, 2014, http://www.swarthmore.edu/library /friends/hazard/index.html.

10. Mary Calderone, *Friends and Womankind* (Philadelphia: Friends General Conference, 1970), 7.

11. Calderone gave this account of the conference's genesis in an oral history interview: James Reed, "Interview with Mary Steichen Calderone, M.D." (hereafter "Interview with MSC"), August 7, 1974, 15, Schlesinger-Rockefeller Oral History Project, Schlesinger Library on the History of Women in America, Radcliffe Institute for Advanced Study, Harvard University. The criminal nature of abortion at the time was summarized by the anthropologist M. F. Ashley Montagu in his "Introduction" to Mary Steichen Calderone, ed., *Abortion in the United States: Report of a Conference Sponsored by the Planned Parenthood Federation of America* (New York: Harper & Brothers, 1958), 3–5.

12. Calderone, ed., *Abortion in the United States*, 180, 68, 4.

13. Mary Steichen Calderone, "Illegal Abortion as a Public Health Problem," *American Journal of Public Health and the Nation's Health* 50, no. 7 (July 1960): 948–954; Calderone, "'I'm Only Half Here,'" *American Journal of Public Health and the Nation's Health* 50, no. 9 (September 1960): 1368–1369.

14. Statement no. 12 in "Birth Control in Comprehensive Health Care," *Journal of the American Medical Association* 196 (June 20, 1966): 1084.

15. Reed, "Interview with MSC," 24.

16. "Family Planning and Christian Ethics: Complete Text of Address by Dr. Mary Steichen Calderone, Medical Director, Planned Parenthood Federation of America, Inc., Before Plenary Session—North American Conference on Church & Family of the Canadian Council of Churches and the National Council of Churches of Christ in the U.S.A., Green Lake, Wisconsin," May 4, 1961, 179, M-125, Box 6, folder 85, Mary Steichen Calderone Papers, 1904–1971, Schlesinger Library on the History of Women in America, Radcliffe Institute for Advanced Study, Harvard University.

17. Calderone to William Genné, May 11, 1961; Calderone to Dr. Evelyn Millis Duvall, May 12, 1961, M-125, Box 6, folder 85, Mary Steichen Calderone Papers, 1904–1971.

18. Reed, "Interview with MSC," 28, 29.

19. Ibid., 29.

20. "The SIECUS Purpose," *SIECUS Newsletter* 1, no. 1 (February 1965): 2. This purpose statement was frequently restated; see, for instance, SIECUS, *Sexuality and Man* (New York: Charles Scribner's Sons, 1970), vii.

21. SIECUS, *Sexuality and Man*, 122.

22. Mary Steichen Calderone, ed., *Manual of Contraceptive Practice* (Baltimore: Williams & Wilkins, 1964), xii; Calderone cited in Ruth Brecher and

Edward Brecher, "Every Sixth Teen-Age Girl in Connecticut," *New York Times*, May 29, 1966, SM4 (photo caption); Mary Breasted, *Oh! Sex Education!* (New York: Praeger, 1970), 256; Nat Lehrman, "*Playboy* Interview: Dr. Mary Calderone," *Playboy* 18 (April 1970): 74–76.

23. Reed, "Interview with MSC," 44–45, 47. See also Nadine Brozan, "For Decades, a Voice of Reason on Sex," *New York Times*, June 28, 1974, 39. Brozan wrote that Calderone "refuses to pontificate or moralize, despite the fact she decries sexual anarchy and sexual exploitation and is a proponent of marriage and fidelity."

24. Calderone, *Friends and Womankind*, 4; Mary Calderone, "Sex, Religion, and Mental Health," *Journal of Religion and Health* 6, no. 3 (July 1967): 196; Mary Calderone, "Sex Education and the American Democratic Process," *Journal of Religion and Health* 9, no. 1 (January 1970): 18, 19. See also Calderone's Rufus Jones Lecture to the Friends General Conference: Calderone, *Human Sexuality and the Quaker Conscience* (Philadelphia: Friends General Conference, 1973).

25. Griswold v. Connecticut, 381 U.S. 479 (1965); "Let's Talk Sex," *Washington University Magazine* 36, no. 2 (Winter 1966): 43, 45, Bernard Becker Medical Library Archives, Washington University School of Medicine, Saint Louis, Missouri, digitalcommons.wustl.edu/ad_wumag/22.

26. Calderone, cited in Moran, *Teaching Sex*, 169.

27. See Moran, *Teaching Sex*, 171.

28. Information on Hargis's earlier career can be found in a number of sources. Richard V. Pierard, "*Christian Crusade*, 1948-1969," in *The Conservative Press in Twentieth-Century America*, ed. Ronald Lora and William Henry Longton (Westport, CT: Greenwood, 1999), 471–478; Fernando Penabaz, "*Crusading Preacher from the West*": *The Story of Billy James Hargis* (Tulsa, OK: Christian Crusade, 1965); John H. Redekop, *The American Far Right: A Case Study of Billy James Hargis and Christian Crusade* (Grand Rapids, MI: Eerdmans, 1968). A few recent scholars have written briefly about Hargis; see, e.g., Tanya Erzen, *Straight to Jesus: Sexual and Christian Conversions in the Ex-Gay Movement* (Berkeley: University of California Press, 2006), 190–193. The Federal Bureau of Investigation kept extensive files on Hargis and the Christian Crusade; these are now publicly available in print and electronic form from the FBI: file 97-3475 (Hargis) and file 100-424820 (Christian Crusade).

29. Thomas H. Uzzell, "Billy James Hargis: A Pitch for God and Country," *Nation*, February 17, 1962, 140–142; quotes on 142.

30. Penabaz, *Crusading Preacher*, 63, 64.

31. On Hargis's brief stint at Ozark Bible College, see Penabaz, *Crusading Preacher*, 48–49. Arnold Forster and Benjamin R. Epstein, *Danger on the Right: The Attitudes, Personnel and Influence of the Radical Right and Extreme Conservatives* (New York: Random House, 1964), 86; Pierard, "*Christian Crusade*,

1948-1969," 474. Carl McIntire has received significantly more scholarly attention than Hargis; see, most recently, Markku Ruotsila, *Fighting Fundamentalist: Carl McIntire and the Politicization of American Fundamentalism* (New York: Oxford University Press, 2016).

32. For a contemporary assessment of his influence, see Forster and Epstein, *Danger on the Right*, 68–86.

33. "What to Do About Pornography," *Christian Crusade* 16, no. 2 (February–March 1964): 4–5.

34. See the profile on Gordon Drake, titled "Open New Front in Battle Against Communism," *Christian Crusade* 20, no. 3 (March 1968): 22–24.

35. Gordon V. Drake, *Blackboard Power: NEA Threat to America* (Tulsa, OK: Christian Crusade, 1968), 182, 134, 137, 137–138, 135. Drake's story, including his relation to Hargis and the impact of his writings on the Anaheim sex education controversy of 1968, has been recounted in Breasted, *Oh! Sex Education!*; and Moran, *Teaching Sex*, 179–184.

36. Gordon V. Drake, "NEA and Sex Education," *Christian Crusade* 20, no. 7 (July 1968): 7–8, quote on 8.

37. See Gordon V. Drake, "Touch and Tell: A New Kind of Religious Service," *Christian Crusade* 21, no. 6 (June 1969): 13; and Gordon V. Drake, "Sneak Attack on American Morals," *Christian Crusade* 21, no. 7 (July 1969): 14–15; Gordon V. Drake, "Sexual Revolution in America," *Christian Crusade* 21, nos. 8–9 (August–September 1969): 28.

38. Gordon V. Drake, *Is the School House the Proper Place to Teach Raw Sex?* (Tulsa, OK: Christian Crusade Publications, 1968), 2, 3, 4. For contemporary critical discussions of Drake's book and the larger context of this debate, see Luther G. Baker Jr., "The Rising Furor over Sex Education," *Family Coordinator* 18, no. 3 (July 1969), 210–217; and Breasted, *Oh! Sex Education!*

39. Moran, *Teaching Sex*, 181; Drake, *Raw Sex*, 15, 17–18, 17, 20.

40. Drake, *Raw Sex*, p. 31; Breasted, *Oh! Sex Education!*, p. 242.

41. Drake, *Raw Sex*, 31, 33.

42. "Statewide Family, Schools and Morality Seminars," *Christian Crusade* 21, no. 1, 2 (January–February 1969): 22.

43. "David Noebel's March Speaking Tour," "Drake in Eastern States," *Christian Crusade* 21, no. 3 (March 1969): 6D. For the national press reaction see, for instance, John Leo, "Fight on Sex Education Is Widening," *New York Times*, May 20, 1969, 49; Fred M. Hechinger, "Storm Over the Teaching of Sex," *New York Times*, September 7, 1969, E11; and Douglas Robinson, "Sex Education Battles Splitting Many Communities Across U.S.," *New York Times*, September 14, 1969, 1.

44. Breasted, *Oh! Sex Education!*, 23.

45. Quoted in ibid., 47. The Anaheim sex education controversy has received much attention, and Breasted's account is the most thorough; other accounts appear in Moran, *Teaching Sex*; Janice M. Irvine, *Talk About Sex: The Battles over Sex Education in the United States* (Berkeley: University of California Press, 2004); and Luker, *When Sex Goes to School*.

46. Breasted, *Oh! Sex Education!*, 89.

47. Ibid., 125.

48. Moran, *Teaching Sex*, 184–185.

49. Breasted, *Oh! Sex Education!*, 85, 86.

50. Recounted in ibid., 219. Hargis, leery of alienating local supporters who might hold a range of views on this issue, urged Drake to drop the suit, but to no avail. Drake would ultimately leave the Christian Crusade over this conflict.

51. [Drake,] *SIECUS—Corrupter of Youth* (Tulsa, OK: Christian Crusade, 1969), 16.

52. Breasted, *Oh! Sex Education!*, 234, 235.

53. Letter to Mary Steichen Calderone, May 13, 1983, 83-M184, Container 1, folder 12, Mary Steichen Calderone Papers, 1904–1971.

54. Letter to Mary Steichen Calderone, postmarked August 1, 1969; letter to Calderone, December 1968, 73-150-81-M35, T50, Box 1, folder 11, Mary Steichen Calderone Papers, 1904–1971.

55. Gary Allen, "Sex Study: Problems, Propaganda, and Pornography," *American Opinion* (March 1969): 1–20; quotes on 5, 7.

56. Ibid., 19, 20.

57. *It's Time to Save Our Schools*, distributed by the United Klans of America, Inc., Knights of the Ku Klux Klan, Greenwood Indiana. In Federal Bureau of Investigation files on Christian Crusade, 1969(?).

58. Hargis, *Sex Revolution in the United States*, 29.

59. The first SIECUS Officers and Board of Directors are listed in the *SIECUS Newsletter* 1, no. 1 (February 1965): n.p. (last page); see the shifts and additions that had already been made by the fall of that year in *SIECUS Newsletter* 1, no. 3 (Fall 1965): 8.

60. Interfaith Commission on Marriage and Family Life, "Interfaith Statement on Sex Education," by the National Council of Churches, Synagogue Council of America, and United States Catholic Conference, approved for release June 8, 1968. Calderone cited this document to counter her conservative Christian critics; see, for instance, a display ad published in the *New York Times* in 1969 that quoted the statement at some length (*New York Times*, October 16, 1969, 37).

61. Lehrman, "*Playboy* Interview," 70, 237.

62. SIECUS, *Sexuality and Man*, 160–161, 161, 162.

63. Calderone, *Human Sexuality and the Quaker Conscience*, 18, 17; Mary S. Calderone, ed., *Sexuality and Human Values: The Personal Dimension of Sexual Experience* (New York: Association Press, 1974), 10.

64. Lehrman, "*Playboy* Interview," 70; Calderone to Father John C. Knott, April 19, 1962, MC179/M–125, Box 12, folder 203, Mary Steichen Calderone Papers, 1904–1971.

65. Calderone to Sister Mary Nora, June 26, 1956, MC179/M-125, Box 12, Folder 203, Mary Steichen Calderone Papers, 1904–1971.

66. Calderone to Jack Heber, June 3, 1958, MC179/M-125, Box 12, Folder 203, Mary Steichen Calderone Papers, 1904–1971.

67. Ibid.

68. Mary Calderone, Phyllis Goldman, and Robert P. Goldman, *Release from Sexual Tensions: Toward an Understanding of Their Causes and Effects in Marriage* (New York: Random House, 1960), 3 (and 236), 238, 102, 220, 38, 93. For an interesting analysis of George Kelly's use of fear (along with that of other American Catholic priests writing about marriage in the twentieth century), see Timothy Kelly and Joseph Kelly, "American Catholics and the Discourse of Fear," in *An Emotional History of the United States*, ed. Peter N. Stearns and Jan Lewis (New York: New York University Press, 1998), 259–279.

69. Calderone, "Family Planning and Christian Ethics," 2.

70. Earl Ubell, "New Council Reflects Rising Sex Concern," *Los Angeles Times*, January 24, 1965, 19.

71. Ibid.

72. Reed, "Interview with MSC," 31.

73. Leslie Woodcock Tentler, *Catholics and Contraception: An American History* (Ithaca, NY: Cornell University Press, 2004), 178; Peter McDonough, *Men Astutely Trained: A History of the Jesuits in the American Century* (New York: Free Press, 1992), 433, 435.

74. Father John L. Thomas, S.J., Ph.D., "Sexuality and the Total Personality," *SIECUS Newsletter* 1, no. 3 (Fall 1965): 1.

75. John L. Thomas, "The Role of Woman," *Commonweal*, May 18, 1956, 171, 174, 172; "Some Moral Guidelines in Sex Education: An interview with Father John L. Thomas, S.J.," *Catholic School Journal* (March 1968): 26; McDonough, *Men Astutely Trained*, 438.

76. John L. Thomas, S.J., *The American Catholic Family* (Englewood, NJ: Prentice-Hall, 1956), 8, 33, 44; Thomas, "The Role of Woman," 173; John L. Thomas, S.J., "The Catholic Position on Population Control," *Daedalus* 88 (Summer 1959): 444–453, quote on 445. On "headship," see Thomas, *American Catholic Family*, 303–304, where he defines the husband's headship as "functional," a status that "flows from and is limited by his role as protector and provider of the reproductive unit" (304).

77. John L. Thomas, "The Catholic Position on Population Control," 445; Thomas, "A Sociologist Looks at the Future of the American Catholic Community," *Social Justice Review* 140 (September–October 1982): 142, 159, 143, 142–143.

78. George Hagmaier, C.S.P., and Robert W. Gleason, S.J., *Counselling the Catholic: Modern Techniques and Emotional Conflicts* (New York: Sheed & Ward, 1959), 9.

79. Hagmaier and Gleason, *Counselling the Catholic*, 9, 10.

80. Father George Hagmaier to the Superior General, the General Council, and the Director, Paulist Institute for Religious Research, February 4, 1969, Paulist Archives, Paulist Fathers General Office, New York.

81. Paul Robichaud, C.S.P., ed., "George Glein Hagmaier," *Paulist Archives Newsletter* 1, no. 2 (September 1990): 3.

82. Mary S. Calderone, "Report on: Colloquium on the Sexuality of Woman," typescript manuscript, 3, John T. McGinn, C.S.P. papers, Paulist Archives.

83. Ibid., 5, 6.

84. On the impact of *Humanae Vitae*'s forceful linkages among contraception, abortion, and sexuality, see Robert N. Karrer, "The National Right to Life Committee: Its Founding, Its History, and the Emergence of the Pro-Life Movement Prior to Roe v. Wade," *Catholic Historical Review* 9, no. 3 (July 2011): 535.

85. Tentler, *Catholics and Contraception*, 266. For an excellent analysis of official Catholic documents such as *Humanae Vitae* that focus on the regulation of sexuality, marriage, gender relationships, and reproduction, see Aline H. Kalbian, *Sexing the Church: Gender, Power, and Ethics in Contemporary Catholicism* (Bloomington: Indiana University Press, 2005).

86. Reed, "Interview with MSC," 28 (emphasis in original).

87. "ND Counsels Wedding Game Preparation," *Observer*, March 1, 1968, 2; Pat Gafney, "Sex Is Sex Is Sex," *Observer*, March 15, 1968, 2, http://www .archives.nd.edu/Observer/v02/1968-03-15_v02_053.pdf. See also the program brochure: "1968 Notre Dame Marriage Institute," University of Notre Dame Department of Information Services Records (hereafter cited as UDIS) 44/39, Folder: Marriage Institute 1955–1979, University of Notre Dame Archives (hereafter cited as UNDA).

88. Barbara Abel, "Angry Critics Don't Bother Sex Educator," *Milwaukee Journal*, December 14, 1969, 2.

89. Mary S. Calderone, "Human Sexuality—Battleground or Peaceground?" in *Progress in Sexology: Selected Papers from the Proceedings of the 1976 International Congress of Sexology*, ed. by Robert Gemmé and Connie Christian Wheeler (New York: Plenum, 1977), 587–593, quotes on 589, 591, 592, 593.

90. Mary Calderone, "Sex Education for the Society: The Real Stumbling Block," *Pastoral Psychology* 21, no. 9 (November 1970): 51, 52.

91. Ibid., 52.

92. Ibid., 52, 4.

93. Reed, "Interview with MSC," 34–35. For a contemporary sociological analysis of the turn-of-the-twenty-first-century conflicts over abstinence-only education versus the comprehensive sexuality programs favored by SIECUS, see Irvine, *Talk About Sex*, 187–199.

94. Billy James Hargis, with Cliff Dudley, *My Great Mistake* (Green Forest, AR: New Leaf, 1985), 89, 93, 108–109.

CHAPTER 6

1. George Gallup, "Abortion Seen Up to Woman, Doctor," *Washington Post, Times Herald*, August 25, 1972, A2. See also Robert O. Self, *All in the Family: The Realignment of American Democracy Since the 1960s* (New York: Hill and Wang, 2012), 156. The literature on abortion politics is voluminous; Self provides a thorough analysis with admirable brevity, 134–160.

2. Laurence H. Tribe, *Abortion: The Clash of Absolutes* (New York: W. W. Norton, 1992), 145; Catherine Whitney, *Whose Life? A Balanced, Comprehensive View of Abortion From Its Historical Context to the Current Debate* (New York: William Morrow, 1991), 78.

3. Southern Baptist Convention, "Resolution on Abortion," 1971, http:// www.sbc.net/resolutions/13/resolution-on-abortion; W. A. Criswell, quoted in Daniel K. Williams, *God's Own Party: The Making of the Christian Right* (New York: Oxford University Press, 2010), 117.

4. David Noebel was one conservative Protestant who strongly opposed abortion at the time of Roe; see David A. Noebel, *The Slaughter of the Innocent* (Tulsa: American Christian College Press, 1973). For a look into Hargis's Americans Against Abortion organization, see Dan Lyons and Billy James Hargis, *Thou Shall Not Kill . . . My Babies* (Tulsa: Christian Crusade, 1977).

5. Early profiles of Moody include "Folk-Singing Pastor: Howard Russell Moody," *New York Times*, May 8, 1961, 41; and Lyn Tornabene, "Way-Out Minister of Washington Square," *New York Times*, June 6, 1965, SM116.

6. Kristin Luker, *Abortion and the Politics of Motherhood* (Berkeley: University of California Press, 1984), 15, 265n11.

7. Ibid., 21.

8. Tom Davis, *Sacred Work: Planned Parenthood and Its Clergy Alliances* (New Brunswick, NJ: Rutgers University Press, 2005), 122.

9. Leslie J. Reagan, *When Abortion Was a Crime: Women, Medicine, and Law in the United States, 1867–1973* (Berkeley: University of California Press, 1997), 209–210.

10. Mary Steichen Calderone, ed., *Abortion in the United States: Report of a Conference Sponsored by the Planned Parenthood Federation of America* (New York: Harper & Brothers, 1958), 181, 182.

11. "Proposed Functions and Powers of the National Clergymen's Advisory Council . . . as Defined by the Executive Committee of the Planned Parenthood Federation of America," June 6, 1944, quoted in Davis, *Sacred Work*, 55.

12. Unsigned letter, quoted in Davis, *Sacred Work*, 56.

13. PPFA *News Exchange*, February 1946, 2, quoted in Davis, *Sacred Work*, 60.

14. "Catholics Draft Human-Rights Aim," *New York Times*, February 2, 1947; John T. McGreevy, *Catholicism and American Freedom* (New York: W. W. Norton, 2003), 258; Pius XII, "Marriage and the Moral Law," Address to the Italian Association of Catholic Midwives, Rome, November 26, 1951; all quoted in Daniel K. Williams, *Defenders of the Unborn: The Pro-Life Movement Before "Roe v. Wade"* (New York: Oxford University Press, 2016), 37–38.

15. Williams, *Defenders of the Unborn*, 38.

16. Lawrence Lader, *Abortion* (Indianapolis: Bobbs-Merrill, 1966), 114, 115; "Abortion and the Law," *America*, March 25, 1961, 811. See also Davis, *Sacred Work*, 123.

17. Reagan, *When Abortion Was a Crime*, 229.

18. On the Clergy Consultation Service on Abortion, see Arlene Carmen and Howard Moody, *Abortion Counseling and Social Change: From Illegal Act to Medical Practice* (Valley Forge, PA: Judson, 1973); Davis, *Sacred Work*, esp. 126–135; and Joshua D. Wolff, "Ministers of a Higher Law: The Story of the Clergy Consultation Service on Abortion" (BA thesis, Amherst College, 1998). Gillian Frank is working on a new history of the Clergy Consultation Service across the United States, tentatively titled "Making Choice Sacred: Liberal Religion and Reproductive Politics in the United States Before *Roe v. Wade*"; for a preview, see Gillian Frank, "The Surprising Role of Clergy in the Abortion Fight Before *Roe v. Wade*," *Time*, May 2, 2017, and Frank's web page about the project, https://gillianafrank.wordpress.com /the-clergy-consultation-service.

19. Carmen and Moody, *Abortion Counseling and Social Change*, 23. In *A Voice in the Village: A Journey of a Pastor and a People* (Xlibris, 2009), Howard Moody wrote that this incident took place in 1957 (312), but if it truly was immediately after he began his ministry, then the 1956 date reported by Carmen and Moody's much earlier book is correct.

20. Ed Gold, "Profile: Rev. Howard Moody Reflects on 50 Years of Activism," *Villager*, December 24–30, 2003, http://www.thevillager.com/villager_34 /reverendhoward.html. Other biographical details can be gleaned from Moody, *Voice in the Village*.

21. "Folk-Singing Pastor," 41. Interview with Harvey Cox, Cambridge, MA, August 14, 2008.

22. Ellen Chesler, "Interview with Arlene Carmen," January 1976, 8, Schlesinger-Rockefeller Oral History Project, Schlesinger Library on the

History of Women in America, Radcliffe Institute for Advanced Study, Harvard University.

23. Moody, *Voice in the Village*, 50.

24. Ibid., 313.

25. Elizabeth Mehren, "Champion of Choice," *Los Angeles Times*, November 30, 1995; Douglas Martin, "Lawrence Lader, Champion of Abortion Rights, Is Dead at 86," *New York Times*, May 10, 2006, A23.

26. Lader, *Abortion*, 175.

27. Joshua D. Wolff, "Ministers of a Higher Law: The Story of the Clergy Consultation Service on Abortion" (B.A. Thesis, Amherst College, 1998), 42.

28. Lawrence Lader, *Abortion II: Making the Revolution* (Boston: Beacon, 1973), 44.

29. George Dugan, "Bishops Ask Fight on Abortion Bill: Pastoral Letter Read," *New York Times*, February 13, 1967, 1.

30. Moody, *Voice in the Village*, 313.

31. Carmen and Moody, *Abortion Counseling and Social Change*, 18–19, 19.

32. Ibid., 24.

33. The statement is reprinted in ibid, 30–31.

34. Ibid, 31.

35. Edward B. Fiske, "Clergymen Offer Abortion Advice," *New York Times*, May 22, 1967, 1.

36. "35 Call Clergymen for Aid on Abortion," *New York Times*, May 24, 1967, 95.

37. "More Clerics Plan Advice on Abortion," *New York Times*, May 26, 1967, 32.

38. Donald Janson, "A.M.A., in Reversal, Favors Liberalizing of Abortion Laws," *New York Times*, June 22, 1967, 1.

39. Davis, *Sacred Work*, 131.

40. Carmen and Moody, *Abortion Counseling and Social Change*, 36.

41. See Nanette J. Davis, *From Crime to Choice: The Transformation of Abortion in America* (Westport CT: Praeger, 1985), 129.

42. Susan Brownmiller, "Abortion Counseling: Service Beyond Sermons," *New York Magazine*, August 4, 1969, 26, 28, 29.

43. Lader, *Abortion*, 7.

44. Sarah Weddington, *A Question of Choice*, 40th Anniversary Ed., rev. and updated (New York: Feminist Press, 2013), 38.

45. Howard Moody, "Statement by Reverend Howard Moody at NARAL Press Conference," April 25, 1972, CCS Archive, cited in Wolff, "Ministers of a Higher Law," 220 (emphasis in original).

46. Moody, *Voice in the Village*, 329 (emphasis in original).

47. Ibid., 329. For a recent Christian defense of abortion rights from an obstetrician and abortion provider, see Dr. Willie Parker, *Life's Work: A Moral Argument for Choice* (New York: Atria, 2017).

48. Weddington, *Question of Choice*, 20.

49. Ibid., 51.

50. Arlene Carmen and Howard Moody, *Working Women: the Subterranean World of Street Prostitution* (New York: Harper & Row, 1985), 151, 47.

51. Ibid., 164, 165, 166.

52. Ibid., 171, 172, 174, 175.

53. On the pre-*Roe* pro-life movement, see especially Williams, *Defenders of the Unborn*.

54. Quoted in Patricia Miller, *Good Catholics: The Battle over Abortion in the Catholic Church* (Berkeley: University of California Press, 2014), 73.

55. His Eminence Timothy Cardinal Manning, "Testimony Before the Subcommittee on Constitutional Amendments of the Senate Committee on the Judiciary," March 7, 1974, http://www.priestsforlife.org/magisterium/bishops/cardinalmanningtestimony.htm .

56. George Dugan, "Catholic Bishops Approve a Plan to Mobilize Public Support Against Abortions on Request," *New York Times*, November 21, 1975, 19.

57. Henry Hyde, quoted in Mary Ziegler, *After Roe: The Lost History of the Abortion Debate* (Cambridge, MA: Harvard University Press, 2015), 50.

58. Sarah Barringer Gordon, *The Spirit of the Law: Religious Voices and the Constitution in Modern America* (Cambridge, MA: Harvard University Press, 2010), 138; Beverly LaHaye, *Who But a Woman?* (Nashville: Thomas Nelson, 1984), 25. For a richly detailed account of anti-feminism and the rise of this evangelical movement for family values, see Self, *All in the Family*, 309–338 and passim. Self's book does an excellent job of analyzing the nation's religiously inflected political battles over gender roles and the traditional family since the 1960s.

59. Frances Kissling, interview by Rebecca Sharpless, transcript of audio recording, September 13–14, 2002, Population and Reproductive Health Oral History Project, Sophia Smith Collection, 2, 10–11. The length of nine months in the convent is noted on page 3.

60. Ibid., 16, 37, 38, 56–57.

61. Ibid., 58, 59, 71.

62. Ibid., 63, 66, 67.

63. Rick Atkinson, "Ferraro Denies Charge on Abortion Stand," *Washington Post*, September 11, 1984, A9.

64. Joe Klein, "Abortion and the Archbishop," *New York*, October 1, 1984, 38.

65. William B. Prendergast, *The Catholic Vote in American Politics* (Washington, DC: Georgetown University Press, 1999), 189, 187.

66. Mary E. Hunt and Frances Kissling, "The *New York Times* Ad: A Case Study in Religious Feminism," *Journal of Feminist Studies in Religion* 3, no. 1 (Spring 1987): 115–127.

67. "A Diversity of Opinions Regarding Abortion Exists Among Committed Catholics," display ad, *New York Times*, October 7, 1984, E7.

68. Hunt and Kissling, "The *New York Times* Ad," 118, 120. The battle continued until most of the sisters' canonical superiors finally relented and offered "clarifications" of their views that amounted to retractions. Only two nuns, Barbara Ferraro and Patricia Hussey, refused to "clarify" or retract their statement; four years later, feeling a strong sense of betrayal, both left the Sisters of Notre Dame.

69. Prendergast, *Catholic Vote*, 193.

70. Kissling, interview, 105, 108, 110, 111. On his own shift away from "Catholic pelvic theology," see Daniel C. Maguire, *A Merry Memoir of Sex, Death, and Religion* (Thiensville, WI: Caritas Communications, 2013). He uses the term on page 60.

71. Kissling and Hunt, "The *New York Times* Ad," 123.

72. "NCCB/USCC President Issues Statement on Catholics for a Free Choice," May 10, 2000, archived at http://www.usccb.org/news/2000/00-123.cfm.

73. Interview with Frances Kissling, Washington DC, June 3, 2009. Also cited in Frances Kissling, "Blogging for Bottle Caps," Women = Books, September 14, 2009, http://www.wcwonline.org/Women-=-Books-Archive/blogging-for-bottle-caps. Response was to Frances Kissling, "Mel Gibson's Family Values," *Salon*, April 26, 2009, http://www.salon.com/2009/04/26/mel_gibson.

74. Maguire, *A Merry Memoir*, 21 and passim. As pro-life Christian leader and *World* magazine editor Marvin Olasky told me, "Thirty-five years in the pro-life movement have shown me that the abortion issue has such salience among Christians because it is about life and death, not about sex" (Marvin Olasky, email message to author, March 22, 2017).

75. Hannah Fingerhut, "On Abortion, Persistent Divides Between—and Within—the Two Parties, *Factank*, July 7, 2017, http://www.pewresearch.org/fact-tank/2017/07/07/on-abortion-persistent-divides-between-and-within-the-two-parties-2/.

CHAPTER 7

1. Bill Bearden, quoted in Jane Mayer and Jill Abramson, *Strange Justice: The Selling of Clarence Thomas* (Boston: Houghton Mifflin, 1994), 87.

2. *Nomination of Judge Clarence Thomas to Be Associate Justice of the Supreme Court of the United States: Hearings Before the Committee on the Judiciary, United States Senate*, 102nd Cong. 37 (October 11, 1991) (Testimony of Anita F. Hill, Professor of Law, University of Oklahoma, Norman, OK).

3. Ibid., 44. Thomas has written that, rather than his inviting her to come with him, Hill herself "immediately said that she wanted to go with me" and that he had to "think about it." Clarence Thomas, *My Grandfather's Son: A*

Memoir (New York: HarperCollins, 2007), 150. He writes elsewhere in this book about Hill and tells things differently; interested readers should consult his memoir for his own depiction.

4. Anita Hill, *Speaking Truth to Power* (New York: Anchor Books, 1997), 89.

5. Maya Angelou, "I Dare to Hope," *New York Times*, August 25, 1991, E15; Julian Bond, Letter to the Editor, *New York Times*, September 12, 1991, A24.

6. The most comprehensive version of Hill's account is found in her autobiography: Hill, *Speaking Truth to Power*.

7. *Nomination of Clarence Thomas*, 257 (Further Testimony of Hon. Clarence Thomas, of Georgia, to be Associate Justice of the U.S. Supreme Court, afternoon session).

8. *Nomination of Judge Clarence Thomas*, 157 (Further Testimony of Hon. Clarence Thomas, of Georgia, to be Associate Justice of the U.S. Supreme Court).

9. Kimberlé Williams Crenshaw, "Black Women Still in Defense of Ourselves," *Nation*, October 5, 2011; Kimberlé Williams Crenshaw, "African American Women in Defense of Ourselves," *New York Times*, November 17, 1991, 53.

10. Thomas, *My Grandfather's Son*, 280.

11. This campaign is recounted in several places, notably Mayer and Abramson, *Strange Justice*. Thomas's experience is well told in John C. Danforth, *Resurrection: The Confirmation of Clarence Thomas* (Norwalk, CT: Easton, 1994). Senator Danforth later wrote again about the hearings, and their impact on Thomas, in John C. Danforth, *Faith and Politics: How the "Moral Values" Debate Divides America and How to Move Forward Together* (New York: Viking Penguin, 2006), 204–208. Hill's account of her own experience appears in Hill, *Speaking Truth to Power*.

12. See, for instance, "Clarence Thomas Hearings," *Saturday Night Live*, Episode no. 309, , directed by Dave Wilson and written by James Downey, NBC, October 12, 1991; "The Strange Case of Clarence and Anita," *Designing Women*, Episode no. 6.8, directed by David Steinberg and written by Linda Bloodworth-Thomas, CBS, November 4, 1991; "Send in the Clowns," *Murphy Brown*, Episode no. 4.18, directed by Lee Shallat Chemel and written by Diane English and Peter Tolan, CBS, February 24, 1992.

13. Thomas, *My Grandfather's Son*, 282.

14. Ibid., 282 (emphasis added). Other references to "my enemies" appear on 158, 229, 233, 239, 257 ("my liberal enemies"), 260, 266, 274, and 276.

15. Hill, *Speaking Truth to Power*, 199–200.

16. Ibid., 5, 6.

17. Ibid., 200.

18. Orlando Patterson, "Race, Gender and Liberal Fallacies," *New York Times*, October 20, 1991, E15. As far back as 1979, the feminist legal scholar

Catherine MacKinnon had argued, "Objection to sexual harassment is not a neopuritan protest" (Carol Krucoff, "Careers: Sexual Harassment on the Job," *Washington Post*, July 25, 1979, B5). This quote was repeated by reporters the day after Patterson's op-ed appeared, along with a contrasting quote from the critic Camille Paglia more in line with Patterson's view: "This psychodrama is puritanism reborn." Ted Gest and Amy Saltzman, "Harassment: Men on Trial," *US New & World Report*, October 21, 1991, 40.

19. Charles Colson, "The Thomas Hearings and the New Gender Wars," *Christianity Today*, November 25, 1991, 72.

20. Limbaugh's mock advertisement for "Feminazi Trading Cards" began with a woman saying, "I'll give you two Gloria Steinems for one Anita Hill." Rush Limbaugh, *The Way Things Ought to Be* (New York: Pocket Books, 1992), 115, 121; quote in this note from 202.

21. Mayer and Abramson, *Strange Justice*, 356, 357; Jeffrey Toobin, "The Burden of Clarence Thomas," *New Yorker*, September 27, 1993, http://www.newyorker.com/magazine/1993/09/27/the-burden-of-clarence-thomas. The affection and respect between Limbaugh and Thomas is evidenced in Rush Limbaugh, "Rush Interviews Justice Clarence Thomas," *The Rush Limbaugh Show*, October 1, 2007, http://www.rushlimbaugh.com/daily/2007/10/01/rush_interviews_justice_clarence_thomas4.

22. Felicity Barringer, "One Year Later, Anita Hill Interprets Thomas Hearings," *New York Times*, October 17, 1992, 6; Joe Holley, "Rosalie Silberman; Created Independent Women's Forum," *Washington Post*, February 21, 2007, B6.

23. Thomas L. Jipping, "'Judge Thomas Is the First Choice': The Case for Clarence Thomas," *Regent University Law Review* 12 (1999–2000): 400, http://www.regent.edu/acad/schlaw/student_life/studentorgs/lawreview/docs/issues/v12n2/12RegentULRev397.pdf.

24. "Interview of Tom Jipping, March 25, 1992," quoted in David Brock, *The Real Anita Hill: The Untold Story* (New York: Free Press, 1993), 81; Thomas L. Jipping and Phyllis Berry-Myers, "Declaration of Independence: Justice Clarence Thomas, One Year Later," Free Congress Foundation, October 1992, quoted in Brock, *Real Anita Hill*, 26.

25. David Brock, *Blinded by the Right: The Conscience of an Ex-Conservative* (New York: Three Rivers Press, 2002), 99.

26. Ruth Marcus, "Thomas, Allies Step Up Counterattack," *Washington Post*, October 13, 1991, A1.

27. Brock, *Real Anita Hill*, 81.

28. Ralph Reed, *Active Faith: How Christians Are Changing the Soul of American Politics* (New York: Free Press, 1996), 134.

29. Ibid., 135–136.

30. Ralph Reed, *The Confirmation* (Nashville: B&H Publishing, 2010), 21, 24, 330.

31. Ibid., 286, 389.

32. Conversation between Ralph Reed and Pat Robertson, "Ralph Reed: Turning Beliefs into Votes," *The 700 Club*, CBN News, October 21, 2010, http://www.cbn.com/cbnnews/us/2008/June/Ralph-Reed-Turning-Beliefs-into-Votes-/.

33. Limbaugh, *The Way Things Ought to Be*, 115.

34. Rush Limbaugh, *See, I Told You So* (New York: Pocket Books, 1993), 196–197, 202.

35. Ibid., 200, 203, 204, 208, 209, 211, 210, 213. His statement about feminism and "unattractive women" was one of his "Thirty-Five Undeniable Truths of Life," so it was repeated many times elsewhere.

36. Geneva Smitherman, "Introduction," in *African American Women Speak Out on Anita Hill-Clarence Thomas*, ed. Geneva Smitherman (Detroit: Wayne State University Press, 1995), 8–9.

37. Hill, *Speaking Truth to Power*, 312, 313.

38. Adam Clymer, "Democrats Promise Quick Action on a Clinton Plan: The New Congress," *New York Times*, November 5, 1992, B6; Maria Braden, *Women Politicians and the Media* (Lexington: University Press of Kentucky, 1996), 122.

39. Some statistics for sexual harassment charges filed and resolved under Title VII by the EEOC and state and local Fair Employment Practice Agencies (FEPAs) are available online; for cases from 1992 through 1996, see US Equal Employment Opportunity Commission, "Sexual Harassment Charges—EEOC & FEPAs Combined: FY 1992–FY 1996," U.S. Equal Opportunity Employment Commission, https://www.eeoc.gov/eeoc/statistics/enforcement/sexual_harassment-a.cfm; For cases from 1997 through 2011, see: U.S. Equal Employment Opportunity Commission, "Sexual Harassment Charges—EEOC & FEPAs Combined: FY 1997–FY 2011," U.S. Equal Opportunity Employment Commission, https://www.eeoc.gov/eeoc/statistics/enforcement/sexual_harassment.cfm.

40. Ralph Reed sought to correct the perception that those calling her "whore" were members of the Christian Coalition; see Ralph Reed, *Active Faith: How Christians Are Changing the Soul of American Politics* (New York: Free Press, 1996), 141. Others continued to insist they were Christians; see Robert Orsi, "Christian Right Learning Ropes," *Baltimore Sun*, July 14, 1996.

41. Helen Campbell, *Prisoners of Poverty: Women Wage-Workers, Their Trades and Their Lives* (1887; reprint, Boston: Little, Brown, 1900), 234, http://www.gutenberg.org/files/34060/34060-h/34060-h.htm.

42. Upton Sinclair, *The Jungle* (New York: Penguin Classics Deluxe Edition, 2006), 120.

43. Gloria Steinem, interviewed by HBO, "Gloria: In Her Own Words: Interview with Gloria Steinem," *HBO*, 2011, http://www.hbo.com/documentaries /gloria-in-her-own-words/interview/gloria-steinem.html.

44. For a very brief legal history that also cites Helen Campbell and Upton Sinclair, see Reva B. Siegel, "Introduction: A Short History of Sexual Harassment," in *Directions in Sexual Harassment Law*, ed. Catharine A. MacKinnon and Reva B. Siegel (New Haven, CT: Yale University Press, 2004), 1–39.

45. Susan Brownmiller, *In Our Time: Memoir of a Revolution* (New York: Dial, 1999), 282.

46. Recounted in ibid., 283–284 (quote on 284); Enid Nemy, "Women Begin to Speak Out Against Sexual Harassment at Work," *New York Times*, August 19, 1975, 38; Mary Bralove, "A Cold Shoulder: Career Women Decry Sexual Harassment by Bosses and Clients," *Wall Street Journal*, January 29, 1976, 1. This story is recounted in detail in Carrie N. Baker, *The Women's Movement Against Sexual Harassment* (New York: Cambridge University Press, 2008), 27–36.

47. Catharine A. MacKinnon, *Sexual Harassment of Working Women* (New Haven, CT: Yale University Press, 1979), 217–218.

48. The longer story of how the concept of sexual harassment entered the public consciousness during the 1970s and 1980s is told in Baker, *Women's Movement Against Sexual Harassment*. Baker's Acknowledgments begin with her "vivid memories," while a law student at Emory, of watching Anita Hill's televised testimony about Clarence Thomas.

49. EEOC, Guidelines on Discrimination Because of Sex, 29 C.F.R. § 1604.11 (1980); Civil Rights Act of 1964, 42 U.S.C. § 2000–2(a) (1).

50. Schlafly quoted in "Asking for it?" *Time*, May 4, 1981, 37.

51. Paul Taylor, "Thomas's View of Harassment Said to Evolve," *Washington Post*, October 11, 1991, A10.

52. Meritor Savings Bank v. Vinson, 477 U.S. 57 (1986).

53. William J. Eaton, "Senate Oks Compromise Civil Rights Bill in 93-5 Vote," *Los Angeles Times*, October 31, 1991, 1; George Bush, "Statement on Signing the Civil Rights Act of 1991," November 21, 1991, The American Presidency Project, http://www.presidency.ucsb.edu/ws/?pid=20258; Danforth, *Resurrection*.

54. Bill Hewitt, "She Could Not Keep Silent," *People*, October 28, 1991, 40–43; Marilyn Balamaci, Gayle Verner, Gail Wescott, Nina Burleigh, and Linda Marx, "The Price of Saying No," *People*, October 28, 1991, 44–48 (interviews with Catharine A. MacKinnon, Deborah Tannen, and neurosurgeon Dr. Frances Conley follow). Virginia Lamp Thomas, "Breaking Silence," *People*, November 11, 1991, 108–116; "Mail," *People*, November 18, 1991, 13–14; "Mail," *People*, December 2, 1991, 5–6. For another discussion of these contrasting *People* profiles, see Wahneema Lubiano, "Black Ladies, Welfare Queens, and

State Minstrels: Ideological War by Narrative Means," in *Race-ing Justice, Engendering Power: Essays on Anita Hill, Clarence Thomas, and the Construction of Social Reality*, ed. Toni Morrison (New York: Pantheon Books, 1992), 359–361.

55. Details of Jones's early life, including remembrances from family members, are recounted in David Ellis, "The Perils of Paula," *People*, May 23, 1994, 33ff.

56. Cathy Young, "Groping Toward Sanity: Why the Clinton Sex Scandals Are Changing the Way We Talk About Sexual Harassment," *Reason* 30, no. 4 (Aug./Sept. 1998): 24, 26, 27, 30, 27.

57. Katie Mahoney and Patrick Mahoney, "Paula Jones Legal Defense Fund," from a Christian Defense Coalition press conference televised by C-Span on May 12, 1994, https://www.c-span.org/video/?56763-1/paula-jones-legal-defense-fund.

58. Ibid. See also Michael Isikoff, "Christian Coalition Forms Legal Expenses Fund for Clinton Accuser," *Washington Post*, May 13, 1994, A11. (A correction was issued by the *Post* the next day noting that the Christian Defense Coalition "has no connection with the Christian Coalition.")

59. Howard Kurtz, "The Plunge into Paulagate: The Media See Two Sides, Two Spins," *Washington Post*, May 14, 1994, D1.

60. Brock, *Blinded by the Right*, 199; Christian Action Network, "Christian Action Network: About," http://www.christianaction.org/can, accessed August 13, 2015.

61. Reed, *Active Faith*, 261.

62. See Peter Baker, "Paula Jones Lawyers Ask to Quit Case," *Washington Post*, September 9, 1997, A1; Jay Branegan, "In Paula We Trust," *Time*, November 24, 1997, 54; James Bennett, "Pasts Are Prologue as Jones v. Clinton Moves Closer to Trial," *New York Times*, November 9, 1997, 24.

63. Lorraine Adams, "For Paula Jones, a Bolder but Riskier Tack: Her New Lawyers Changed Course of Sex Harassment Suit Against President," *Washington Post*, February 8, 1998, 1.

64. Ceci Connolly, "Radio Show Dropped for Paula Jones Link," *Washington Post* March 15, 1998, A20. Spokespersons for the Rutherford Institute insisted to the reporter that the boycott had rather to do with Whitehead's renunciation of his own earlier anti-gay statements.

65. R. Jonathan Moore, *Suing For America's Soul: John Whitehead, the Rutherford Institute, and Conservative Christians in the Courts* (Grand Rapids, MI: Eerdmans, 2007), 2.

66. John W. Whitehead, *Slaying Dragons: The Truth Behind the Man Who Defended Paula Jones* (Nashville: Thomas Nelson, 1999), 4.

67. Ibid., 9.

68. Ibid., 208, 209.

69. "Independent Women's Forum Condemns Intimidation of Paula Jones," *PR Newswire*, June 3, 1998, http://www.prnewswire.com/news-releases

/independent-womens-forum-condemns-intimidation-of-paula-jones-75777562
.html.

70. "Books in Brief," *New American*, October 26, 1998, 34.

71. Ann Coulter, *High Crimes and Misdemeanors: The Case Against Bill Clinton* (Washington, DC: Regnery, 1998); Howard Kurtz, "The Blonde Flinging Bombshells at Bill Clinton," *Washington Post*, October 16, 1998, D1.

72. Mike Pence, "Why Clinton Must Resign or Be Impeached," republished in Patrick Hogan, "Here Are Some of the Weirdest Columns Mike Pence Wrote in the '90s," http://fusion.kinja.com/here-are-some-of-the-weirdest -columns-mike-pence-wrote-1793860259, July 14, 2016.

73. Andrew Kaczynski, "Mike Pence Railed Against Adultery, Otters, and Paula Jones in Old Blog Posts," *BuzzFeed*, July 18, 2016, https://www.buzzfeed .com/andrewkaczynski/mike-pence-railed-against-adultery-otters-and-paula -jones-in?utm_term=.cmJLoNJX4#.njBYwDAvo .

74. Peter Baker, "Clinton Settles Paula Jones Lawsuit for $850,000," *Washington Post*, November 14, 1998, A1.

75. Joel Achenbach, "On the Hill, They Still Swear It's Not About Sex," *Washington Post*, December 19, 1998, C6. Kenneth Starr's religious background and church affiliations are well chronicled in Bobby Ross Jr., "Kenneth Starr Plans to Join Baptist Church," *Christian Chronicle*, April 2010, http://www .christianchronicle.org/article/kenneth-starr-plans-to-join-baptist-church.

76. Michael Powell, "One Nation, Torn Apart: The '60s Culture Clash Underlies a New Crisis," *Washington Post*, December 19, 1998, C1, C2.

77. "Starr's Hour," *Wall Street Journal*, September 11, 1998, A14.

CHAPTER 8

1. After *Moral Combat* went into initial production at Basic Books, a new and very thorough history of same-sex marriage appeared, one that would have greatly benefited my own work on this chapter if it had come out sooner. The book traces the marriage equality movement from the 1950s through *Obergefell*; see Nathaniel Frank, *Awakening: How Gays and Lesbians Brought Marriage Equality to America* (Cambridge: Harvard University Press, 2017).

2. Judith Esmay, quoted in Elizabeth Adams, *Going to Heaven: The Life and Election of Bishop Gene Robinson* (Brooklyn, NY: Soft Skull, 2006), 101 (emphasis in original).

3. Interview with Gene Robinson, Washington, DC, July 15, 2016.

4. The General Convention of the Episcopal Church, Canon III.16.3, *Constitutions & Canons 2003*, 90, https://www.episcopalchurch.org/files/documents /2003_candc.pdf.

5. Gene Robinson, *God Believes in Love: Straight Talk about Gay Marriage* (New York: Random House, 2012), 4.

6. Ibid., 4, 5.

7. Ibid., 5.

8. Ibid., 7.

9. Interview with Robinson.

10. Ibid.

11. Robinson, *God Believes in Love*, 11.

12. Interview with Robinson.

13. William Cullen Bryant, letter, *New York Evening Post*, July 13, 1843, cited in Rachel Hope Cleves, "'What, Another Female Husband?': The Prehistory of Same-Sex Marriage in America," *Journal of American History* 101, no. 4 (March 2015): 1059.

14. All examples are from Cleves, "'What, Another Female Husband?'" The policing of homosexuality in US history is critical context, of course, as is the pervasive regulation of it by the federal government; see e.g. Margot Canaday, *The Straight State: Sexuality and Citizenship in Twentieth-Century America* (Princeton, NJ: Princeton University Press, 2011).

15. Joan Nestle, "Excerpts from the Oral History of Mabel Hampton," *Signs* 18 (Summer 1993): 934, in Cleves, "'What, Another Female Husband?,'" 1078.

16. E. B. Saunders, "Reformer's Choice: Marriage License or Just License?," *One Magazine* 1, no. 8 (August 1953): 11, 12.

17. R. H. Karcher, letter to the editor, *One Magazine* 1, no. 10 (October 1953): 14.

18. Randy Lloyd, "Let's Push Homophile Marriage," *One Magazine* 11, no. 6 (June 1963): 5; "Letters," *One Magazine* 11, no. 7 (July 1963): 29; "Letters," *One Magazine* 11, no. 8 (August 1963): 29.

19. Howard Moody, *A Voice in the Village: A Journey of a Pastor and a People* (Xlibris, 2009), 111.

20. Gay Liberation Front members quoted in William N. Eskridge Jr. and Darren R. Spedale, *Gay Marriage: For Better or for Worse?—What We've Learned from the Evidence* (New York: Oxford University Press, 2006), 17. The sexual politics of the Gay Liberation Front and radical lesbians during that period are well examined in Robert O. Self, *All in the Family: The Realignment of American Democracy Since the 1960s* (New York: Hill and Wang, 2012), 222–235 and passim.

21. "Gay Marriage Bureau Takeover 1971," YouTube video, 9:59, posted by "Randolfe Wicker," March 15, 2010, https://www.youtube.com/watch?v=Z7NU8B1EGnU, in Garance Franke-Ruta, "The Prehistory of Gay Marriage: Watch a 1971 Protest at NYC's Marriage License Bureau," *Atlantic*, March 26, 2013.

22. Quoted in Eskridge and Spedale, *Gay Marriage*, 22.

23. Sarah Barringer Gordon narrates the religious history of legal battles over same-sex marriage between 1970 and 2007 in her book *The Spirit of the Law: Religious Voices and the Constitution in Modern America* (Cambridge, MA: Harvard University Press, 2010), 169–207.

24. Erik Eckholm, "Same-Sex Marriage? Done That, Back in 1971," *New York Times*, May 17, 2015, A1, A15.

25. *Jones v. Hallahan*, in Eskridge and Spedale, *Gay Marriage*, 22.

26. Robert Barnes, "40 years later, Story of a Same-Sex Marriage in Colo. Remains Remarkable," *Washington Post*, April 18, 2015; court opinion quoted in Eskridge and Spedale, *Gay Marriage*, 23.

27. John E. Fortunato, *Embracing the Exile: Healing Journeys of Gay Christians* (New York: Seabury, 1982), 14. Reporters in DC covered this story; see Marjorie Hyer, "Homosexual Marriage Plans Cause Episcopal Problems," *Washington Post*, November 12, 1976, C2; Marjorie Hyer, "Bishop's Threat Halts Homosexual Union," *Washington Post*, November 15, 1976, B6; Jeannette Smyth, "'To Love, to Share, to Help': Taking the Vows, Making a Statement," *Washington Post*, December 12, 1976, K1.

28. Moody, *Voice in the Village*, 130.

29. Eckholm, "Same-Sex Marriage?," A15.

30. Evan Wolfson, "Samesex Marriage and Morality: The Human Rights Vision of the Constitution" (thesis, Harvard Law School, 1983), 3, 31–32, http://freemarry.3cdn.net/73aab4141a80237ddf_kxm62r3er.pdf.

31. Andrew Sullivan, "Here Comes the Groom: A (Conservative) Case for Gay Marriage," *New Republic*, August 28, 1989.

32. Philip S. Gutis, "Small Steps Toward Acceptance Renew Debate on Gay Marriage," *New York Times*, November 5, 1989, E24.

33. Sacred Congregation for the Doctrine of the Faith, "*Persona Humana*: Declaration on Certain Questions Concerning Sexual Ethics," December 29, 1975, http://www.vatican.va/roman_curia/congregations/cfaith/documents/rc_con_cfaith_doc_19751229_persona-humana_en.html.

34. Kenneth A. Briggs, "Baptists, in Shift, Ask Members to Seek Antiabortion 'Climate,'" *New York Times*, June 18, 1976, A11. On Protestant clergy and the LGBT rights movement, see Heather R. White, *Reforming Sodom: Protestants and the Rise of Gay Rights* (Chapel Hill: University of North Carolina Press, 2015); and Anthony M. Petro, *After the Wrath of God: AIDS, Sexuality, and American Religion* (New York: Oxford University Press, 2015).

35. Tim LaHaye and Beverly LaHaye, *The Act of Marriage* (Grand Rapids, MI: Zondervan, 1976), 11, 182, 279, 278, 279. For an excellent analysis of this and other evangelical marriage manuals, see Amy DeRogatis, *Saving Sex: Sexuality and Salvation in American Evangelicalism* (New York: Oxford University Press, 2015).

36. Didi Herman, *The Antigay Agenda* (Chicago: University of Chicago Press, 1998), 67.

37. Beverly LaHaye, *The Spirit-Controlled Woman* (Irvine, CA: Harvest House, 1976), 73.

38. Falwell quoted in Hans Johnson and William Eskridge, "The Legacy of Falwell's Bully Pulpit," *Washington Post*, May 19, 2007, A17.

39. Jean O'Leary and Bruce Voeller, "Anita Bryant's Crusade," *New York Times*, June 7, 1977, 35.

40. "3,000 in Houston Protest Anita Bryant Appearance," *New York Times*, June 17, 1977, A12.

41. Tim LaHaye, *The Unhappy Gays: What Everyone Should Know About Homosexuality* (Carol Stream, IL: Tyndale House, 1978), 76, 150, 157.

42. Beverly LaHaye, *Who But a Woman?* (Nashville: Thomas Nelson, 1984), 45.

43. Falwell quoted in Johnson and Eskridge, "The Legacy of Falwell's Bully Pulpit," A17.

44. See Anthony Petro, *After the Wrath of God: AIDS, Sexuality, and American Religion* (New York: Oxford University Press, 2015).

45. Sutton went on to be a leader in the Council of Conservative Citizens, a white-supremacist group. Southern Poverty Law Center, "A Dozen Major Groups Help Drive the Religious Right's Anti-Gay Crusade," *Southern Poverty Law Center*, April 28, 2005, https://www.splcenter.org/fighting-hate/intelligence -report/2005/dozen-major-groups-help-drive-religious-right's-anti-gay-crusade. The Southern Poverty Law Center lists the Family Research Institute as an extremist group.

46. David A. Noebel, Wayne C. Lutton, and Paul Cameron, *AIDS: A Special Report*, 2nd rev. ed. (Manitou Springs, CO: Summit Research Institute, 1987), back cover, 3, 5, 6.

47. Ibid., 15, 79, 116, 139.

48. Robertson responded, "Why, I totally concur." "Falwell and Robertson on *The 700 Club* After 9/11," YouTube video, 1:22, from an episode of *The 700 Club* televised by the Fox Family Channel [now Freeform] on September 13, 2001, posted by "Veracifier," November 7, 2007, https://www.youtube.com/watch?v =H-CAcdta_8I.

49. See Heather R. White, *Reforming Sodom: Protestants and the Rise of Gay Rights* (Chapel Hill: University of North Carolina Press, 2015).

50. Robinson, *God Believes in Love*, 12–13.

51. Interview with Robinson.

52. General Convention, *Journal of the General Convention of . . . The Episcopal Church, Minneapolis 1976* (New York: General Convention, 1977), C-109, http://www.episcopalarchives.org/cgi-bin/acts/acts_resolution.pl?resolution =1976-A069.

53. Nathaniel Sheppard Jr., "Episcopal Group Limits Homosexuals' Ordination," *New York Times*, September 19, 1979, A16.

54. Interview with Robinson.

55. Jan Nunley, "Advocates Gather to Claim Blessing Rite for Same-Sex Couples," Episcopal News Service, November 11, 2002, http://arc.episcopalchurch.org/ens/archives/2002-258.html.

56. The Lambeth Commission on Communion, *The Windsor Report 2004* (London: The Anglican Communion Office, 2004), 50, http://news.bbc.co.uk/nol/shared/bsp/hi/pdfs/18_10_04_windsor_report.pdf.

57. The story of Robinson's exclusion from Lambeth, and his decision to come to London anyway to speak to people at the edges, is rivetingly told in a documentary film: Macky Alston and Sandra Itkoff, *Love Free or Die*, directed by Macky Alston (Dallas, TX: Reveal Productions, 2012).

58. Doug Theuner, quoted in Adams, *Going to Heaven*, 276.

59. Gene Robinson, *In the Eye of the Storm: Swept to the Center by God* (New York: Seabury, 2008), 25, 40.

60. Lawrence v. Texas, 539 U.S. 558 (2003).

61. Rick Santorum, "Americans Must Preserve Institution of Marriage," *USA Today*, July 9, 2003.

62. Alan Sears and Craig Osten, *The Homosexual Agenda: Exposing the Principal Threat to Religious Freedom Today* (Nashville: Broadman & Holman Books, 2003), 2–3, 96.

63. "Excerpts From the Massachusetts Ruling," *New York Times*, November 19, 2003, A24.

64. Robinson, *God Believes in Love*, 100, 110.

65. Dennis Di Mauro, "Gene Robinson Makes the Case for Gay Marriage: A Review of *God Believes in Love: Straight Talk About Gay Marriage*," *First Things*, March 11, 2014: https://www.firstthings.com/web-exclusives/2014/03/gene-robinson-makes-the-case-for-gay-marriage; "Retired Bishop Gene Robinson On Being Gay and Loving God," *Fresh Air*, January 10, 2013, http://www.npr.org/2013/01/14/169066917/retired-bishop-gene-robinson-on-being-gay-and-loving-god.

66. Justice Samuel Alito, cited in Amy Davidson, "What Each Justice Said About Gay Marriage," *New Yorker*, March 28, 2013.

67. Amanda Terkel, Christine Conetta, and Elise Foley, "Battle for Marriage Equality Unfolds Outside the Supreme Court," *Huffington Post*, April 28, 2015, http://www.huffingtonpost.com/2015/04/28/supreme-court-marriage_n_7165076.html.

68. Obergefell v. Hodges, 576 U.S. ___ (2015), https://www.supremecourt.gov/opinions/14pdf/14-556_3204.pdf.

69. President Barack Obama quoted in Adam Liptak, "Supreme Court Ruling Makes Same-Sex Marriage a Right Nationwide," *New York Times*, June 26, 2015.

70. George Conger, "The Episcopal Church Approves Religious Weddings for Gay Couples After Controversial Debate," *Washington Post*, July 1, 2015.

71. Todd Starnes, "Franklin Graham: Christians Should Prepare for Persecution," *Christian Examiner*, June 26, 2015, http://www.christianexaminer.com /article/franklin.graham.christians.should.prepare.for.persecution/49166.htm.

72. Daly quoted in John Stonestreet, "Christian Leaders Respond to *Obergefell v. Hodges*: A Symposium," June 26, 2015, http://www.breakpoint.org /bpcommentaries/entry/12/27686.

73. "Supreme Court Decision on Marriage 'A Tragic Error' Says President of Catholic Bishops' Conference," United States Conference of Catholic Bishops, June 26, 2015, http://www.usccb.org/news/2015/15-103.cfm.

74. Catholic News Service, "Biden Called 'Counter-Witness' to Church Teaching for Presiding at Wedding," *Catholic News Service*, August 5, 2016, http://www.catholicnews.com/services/englishnews/2016/biden-called-counter -witness-to-church-teaching-for-presiding-at-wedding.cfm. Biden's home bishop in the diocese of Wilmington, Delaware, concurred with the statement; see "Bishop Malooly's Statement Regarding Biden Officiating at Same-Sex Marriage," *Dialog*, August 8, 2016, http://thedialog.org/bishop-maloolys -statement-regarding-biden-officiating-at-same-sex-marriage/.

75. Robinson, *In the Eye of the Storm*, 3.

76. Interview with Robinson.

77. Equal Employment Opportunity Commission v. R.G. & G.R. Harris Funeral Homes, Inc., Case No. 14-13710 (D.Mich., 2016).

EPILOGUE

1. Inés San Martin, "Pope Calls Gender Theory a 'Global War' Against the Family," *Crux*, October 1, 2016, https://cruxnow.com/global-church/2016/10/01 /pope-calls-gender-theory-global-war-family.

2. Dean Obeidallah, "Behind Trump, the GOP Really Is Becoming the Racist Party," *Daily Beast*, August 31, 2015, http://www.thedailybeast.com/articles /2015/08/31/behind-trump-the-gop-really-is-becoming-the-racist-party.html; and Bill Morlin, "Radio Show Host with Racist, Anti-Semitic Legacy Given Press Credentials for Trump Rally," Southern Poverty Law Center, *Hatewatch*, March 2, 2016, https://www.splcenter.org/hatewatch/2016/03/02/radio-show -host-racist-anti-semitic-legacy-given-press-credentials-trump-rally.

3. See Rush Limbaugh, "They're Worried Silly Over Mrs. Clinton," *The Rush Limbaugh Show*, May 28, 2015, http://www.rushlimbaugh.com/daily/2015/05/28 /they_re_worried_silly_over_mrs_clinton. See Paul Thompson, "EXCLUSIVE: 'Don't Let Bill Back in the White House, He Abused Women and He'll Do It Again.' Paula Jones Warns Against Voting for Hillary—Because She Also Lied

About Sex Case Which Almost Cost Him Presidency," *Daily Mail*, May 28, 2015; Lindsay Kimble, "Bill Clinton Sexual Harassment Accuser Paula Jones Wants to Attend Presidential Debate to Make Hillary 'Nervous,'" *People*, September 26, 2016.

4. Rachel Held Evans, quoted in Sarah Pulliam Bailey, "The Deep Disgust for Hillary Clinton That Drives So Many Evangelicals to Support Trump," *Washington Post*, October 9, 2016. https://www.washingtonpost.com/news /acts-of-faith/wp/2016/10/09/the-deep-disgust-for-hillary-clinton-that-drives -so-many-evangelicals-to-support-trump/?utm_term=.656a191ad7e6.

5. "Hillary Clinton: My Creed Is 'Do All the Good You Can in All the Ways You Can,'" YouTube video, :54, posted by "LoneWolf & The Three Miskadoggies," September 30, 2016, https://www.youtube.com/watch?v=DEE7pCa1PK8.

6. "Clinton Offers Sympathies to Those Affected in Dallas," Hillary Clinton Speeches, July 8, 2016, https://hillaryspeeches.com/2016/07/08/clinton -offers-sympathies-to-those-affect-in-dallas.

7. Max Perry Mueller, "The Christian Worldview of Mike Pence," *Religion & Politics*, October 10, 2016, http://religionandpolitics.org/2016/10/10 /the-christian-worldview-of-mike-pence/.

8. Rachel Held Evans, quoted in Pulliam Bailey, "The Deep Disgust for Hillary Clinton."

9. See Claire Landsbaum, "The Most Misogynistic Gear Spotted at Trump Rallies," *New York*, October 12, 2016; Michelle Goldberg and Chelsea Hassler, "A Children's Treasury of Misogyny at the Republican National Convention," *Slate*, July 20, 2016, http://www.slate.com/blogs/the_slatest/2016/07/20/misogyny _is_alive_and_well_at_the_republican_national_convention.html; and Adele M. Stan, "At Trump Rallies from Rust Belt to Bible Belt, Threats of Violence Combine with Nostalgia for White Man's Glory," *Alternet*, October 25, 2016, http://www.alternet.org/election-2016/trump-rallies-south-and-rust-belt.

10. See Claire Cohen, "Donald Trump Sexism Tracker: Every Offensive Comment in One Place," *Telegraph*, January 20, 2017.

11. Joan C. Williams, interviewed in "What Politicians and Pundits Get Wrong About White Working Class Voters," *1A*, National Public Radio, May 22, 2017, http://www.npr.org/podcasts/510316/1a.

INDEX

RANDALL KAHN

R. MARIE GRIFFITH is the John C. Danforth Distinguished Professor at Washington University in St. Louis, where she directs the Danforth Center on Religion and Politics. She lives in St. Louis, Missouri.